When should I travel to get the best airfare?
Where do I go for answers to my travel questions?
What's the best and easiest way to plan and book my trip?

frommers.travelocity.com

Frommer's, the travel guide leader, has teamed up with **Travelocity.com**, the leader in online travel, to bring you an in-depth, easy-to-use resource designed to help you plan and book your trip online.

At **frommers.travelocity.com**, you'll find free online updates about your destination from the experts at Frommer's plus the outstanding travel planning and purchasing features of Travelocity.com. Travelocity.com provides reservations capabilities for 95 percent of all airline seats sold, more than 47,000 hotels, and over 50 car rental companies. In addition, Travelocity.com offers more than 2,000 exciting vacation and cruise packages. Travelocity.com puts you in complete control of your travel planning with these and other great features:

Expert travel guidance from Frommer's – over 150 writers reporting from around the world!

Best Fare Finder – an interactive calendar tells you when to travel to get the best airfare

Fare Watcher – we'll track airfare changes to your favorite destinations

Dream Maps – a mapping feature that suggests travel opportunities based on your budget

Shop Safe Guarantee – 24 hours a day / 7 days a week live customer service, and more!

Whether traveling on a tight budget, looking for a quick weekend getaway, or planning the trip of a lifetime, Frommer's guides and Travelocity.com will make your travel dreams a reality. You've bought the book, now book the trip!

Travelocity.com
A Sabre Company

Frommer's

A New Star-Rating System & Other Exciting News from Frommer's!

In our continuing effort to publish the savviest, most up-to-date, and most appealing travel guides available, we've added some great new features.

Frommer's guides now include a new **star-rating system**. Every hotel, restaurant, and attraction is rated from 0 to 3 stars to help you set priorities and organize your time.

We've also added **seven brand-new features** that point you to the great deals, in-the-know advice, and unique experiences that separate travelers from tourists. Throughout the guide look for:

Finds	Special finds—those places only insiders know about
Fun Fact	Fun facts—details that make travelers more informed and their trips more fun
Kids	Best bets for kids—advice for the whole family
Moments	Special moments—those experiences that memories are made of
Overrated	Places or experiences not worth your time or money
Tips	Insider tips—some great ways to save time and money
Value	Great values—where to get the best deals

We've also added a **"What's New"** section in every guide—a timely crash course in what's hot and what's not in every destination we cover.

Other Great Guides for Your Trip:

Frommer's Vancouver and Victoria

Frommer's BC & the Rockies

Frommer's Canada

Frommer's Portable Vancouver

Frommer's Irreverent Vancouver

Frommer's Toronto with Kids

Frommer's Ottawa with Kids

Frommer's™

Vancouver with Kids

1st Edition

by Eve Lazarus

Here's what the critics say about Frommer's:

"Amazingly easy to use. Very portable, very complete."
—*Booklist*

"The only mainstream guide to list specific prices. The Walter Cronkite of guidebooks—with all that implies."
—*Travel & Leisure*

"Complete, concise, and filled with useful information."
—*New York Daily News*

"Detailed, accurate and easy-to-read information for all price ranges."
—*Glamour Magazine*

CDG Books Canada
Toronto, ON

About the Author

Originally from Australia, **Eve Lazarus** arrived in Vancouver in 1984 and now lives on Vancouver's North Shore with her husband and three children. She is a former newspaper reporter and has written for a variety of magazines in Canada and the United States. Lazarus is currently the Vancouver Correspondent for Toronto-based *Marketing Magazine* and has won Canadian Business Press gold and silver awards for her work. While she writes mostly about business issues, she really enjoys writing about and for children.

Published by:

CDG Books Canada, Inc.

99 Yorkville Avenue, Suite 400
Toronto, ON M5R 3K5

National Library of Canada Cataloguing in Publication Data

Lazarus, Eve, 1959–

Vancouver

(Frommer's with kids)

Includes index.

ISBN 1-894413-34-2

ISSN: 1499-1616

1. Children—Travel—British Columbia—Vancouver—Guidebooks.
2. Family recreation—British Columbia—Vancouver—Guidebooks.
3. Vancouver (B.C.)—Guidebooks. I. Title. II. Series.

FC3847.18.L39 2001   917.11'33044'083   C2001–901477–5
F1089.5.V22L39 2001

FROMMER'S is a registered trademark of Arthur Frommer. Used under license.

Editorial Director: Joan Whitman
Editor: Jennifer Lambert
Director of Production: Donna Brown
Production Editor: Rebecca Conolly
Copy Editor: Madeline Koch
Cartographer: Mapping Specialists
Map Editor: Allyson Latta
Cover design by Kyle Gell
Cover illustration by Kathryn Adams
Text layout: IBEX Graphic Communications
Special Help: Susan Johnson

Special Sales

This book is available at special discounts for bulk purchases by your group or organization for sales promotions, premiums, fundraising and seminars. For details, contact: CDG Books Canada Inc., 99 Yorkville Avenue, Suite 400, Toronto, ON, M5R 3K5. Tel: 416-963-8830. Toll Free: 1-877-963-8830. Fax: 416-923-4821. Web site: cdgbooks.com.

1 2 3 4 5 TRANS 05 04 03 02 01

Manufactured in Canada

Contents

List of Maps

For Mike, Mark, Megan, and Matthew.

Acknowledgments

One of the reasons I was so keen to write *Frommer's Vancouver with Kids* is that I could really include my three children, then aged 2, 5, and 8, in much of the research for the book. And, I did. We ate out at kid-friendly restaurants, visited dozens of parks and gardens, hiked trails, went to attractions, and uncovered places and things to do that we never knew were here. So, guys, this book is really a joint family effort. Thanks for being so great when I had to disappear to my office for all those weeks at the end.

And, thanks to my editor Jennifer Lambert, for her professionalism and guidance. A special thanks to the librarians at the North Vancouver district library (Lynn Valley branch) and to the city of North Vancouver for being so knowledgeable, fast, and helpful with my queries. I was especially grateful for all the information on why BC is known as Lotus Land.

—Eve Lazarus

An Invitation to the Reader

In researching this book, we discovered many wonderful places—hotels, restaurants, shops. And more. We're sure you'll find others. Please tell us about them, so we can share the information with your fellow travelers in upcoming editions. If you were disappointed with a recommendation, we'd love to know that too. Please write to:

Frommer's Vancouver with Kids, 1st Edition
CDG Books Canada • 99 Yorkville Ave., Suite 400 • Toronto, ON M5R 3K5

An Additional Note

Please be advised that travel information is subject to change at any time—and this is especially true of prices. We therefore suggest that you write or call ahead for confirmation when making your travel plans. The authors, editors, and publishers cannot be held responsible for the experiences of readers while traveling. Your safety is important to us, however, so we encourage you to stay alert and be aware of your surroundings. Keep a close eye on cameras, purses, and wallets, all favorite targets of thieves and pickpockets.

New! Frommer's Star Ratings & Icons

Every hotel, restaurant and attraction listing in this guide has been ranked for quality, value, service, amenities, and special features using a star-rating scale. In country, state, and regional guides, we also rate towns and regions to help you narrow down your choices and budget your time accordingly. Hotels and restaurants in the Very Expensive and Expensive categories are rated one star (highly recommended) to three stars (exceptional). Those in the Moderate and Inexpensive categories rate from zero (recommended) to two stars (very highly recommended). Attractions, towns, and regions are rated according to the following scale: zero stars (recommended), one star (highly recommended), two stars (very highly recommended), and three stars (must-see).

In addition to the rating system, we also use seven icons to highlight insider information, useful tips, special bargains, hidden gems, memorable experiences, kid-friendly venues, places to avoid, and other useful information:

(Finds   (Fun Fact   (Kids   (Moments   (Overrated   (Tips   (Value

The following abbreviations are used for credit cards:

AE	American Express	DISC	Discover	V	Visa
DC	Diners Club	MC	MasterCard		

FROMMERS.COM

Now that you have the guidebook to a great trip, visit our website at **www.frommers.com** for travel information on nearly 2,000 destinations. With features updated regularly, we give you instant access to the most current trip-planning information available. At Frommers.com, you'll also find the best prices on airfares, accommodations, and car rentals—you can even book travel online through our travel booking partners. At Frommers.com you'll find the following:

- Daily Newsletter highlighting the best travel deals
- Hot Spot of the Month/Vacation Sweepstakes & Travel Photo Contest
- More than 200 Travel Message Boards
- Outspoken Newsletters and Feature Articles on travel bargains, vacation ideas, tips & resources, and more!

Introducing Vancouver for Families

Bruce Hutchison, a rather famous local journalist now deceased, coined the term "Lotus Land" to describe British Columbia. He could have taken the term from a Tennyson poem called "The Lotus Eaters," or from classical mythology where Odysseus visits the coastal people of Africa on his journey home from the Trojan War. In this particular myth, the people he visited received the name lotus eaters from a honey-sweet fruit that made all who tasted it lose any desire to return home. The fruit produced a kind of dreamy contentment, languor, and forgetfulness, or so the story goes. I warn you to be careful, it just may be true…

I arrived in Vancouver in 1982 for 2 weeks en route to England. Apart from a 6-month stint back in my native Australia, I've lived here ever since. My three kids were all born here and, frankly, I can't imagine living anywhere else.

Vancouver is a young city, as cities go, with few buildings still standing that date before 1900. Expo 86 marked Vancouver's 100th birthday. It transformed our city. The world fair with the theme *World in Motion, World in Touch* opened on May 2, 1986, and closed 5 months later. It was attended by more than 20 million people and was the largest single-theme exposition ever held. After Expo, Vancouver reinvented itself as a cosmopolitan city—Canada Place and the Vancouver Trade and Convention Centre, major hotels, restaurants, retailers, arts and entertainment all popped up. Our multicultural population flourished.

For the second year in a row, a global consulting firm ranked Vancouver as one of the two best places in the world to live because of our quality of life—things such as political and economic stability, our social fabric, and the environment. It may be unnecessary to add—but I'll do it anyway—that Vancouver is also one of the best places in the world to visit.

When the sun shines, Vancouver is breathtakingly beautiful. Framed by Burrard Inlet and the waters of English Bay, it has a majestic backdrop of soaring, mostly snowcapped mountains. It's impossible to think of Vancouver without Stanley Park, and what other city can boast a thousand-acre rain forest minutes from its downtown core? However, we're not called the "wet coast" for nothing, and in April you'll find us feeling a little giddy after months of rain. In the spring, clouds of pink and white blossoms explode from more than 40,000 cherry trees, and the blooming rhododendrons, azaleas, and magnolia trees add splashes of color to the otherwise green landscape. The snowcapped Lions peaks, which are hidden behind cloud cover for much of the winter, suddenly spring up again. Of course, if you hit a rainy spot, do what the locals do—suit up, grab an umbrella, moan just a little, and ignore it.

We have learned to blend our urban culture with a healthy respect for the wilderness. You will often hear Vancouverites brag about how you can sail in the afternoon and ski at night, or, to quote one tourist brochure: "Here you can ski, golf, and go sailing all on the same day, catch an opera or a Broadway musical by night." It's hard to imagine anyone quite that enthusiastic, and, as one British wag wrote, it's only possible because Vancouver is very small. And so it is. Get in the car and in 20 minutes you can be riding a gondola to the top of a mountain, hiking in an old-growth forest, swimming in a mountain lake, or tubing down a ski hill. Bears in North Shore backyards are common, cougars are reported, coyotes hang out in Vancouver parks, and raccoons and skunks form part of inner city living.

You should also know that we're coffee obsessed. Kids are too, only they are weaned on $1-a-cup hot chocolate, lollipops, and caramels before moving on up to $3 coffees with multiple names. My son's third word was "Starbucks."

This book will help you and your family get to know Vancouver and enjoy all it has to offer. Whether your kids are 2 or 12 (or 2 *and* 12), you will find the things to do, places to eat, and places to stay that will suit your family's needs. Kids can be your key to interacting with the city. You don't just do the Stanley Park Seawall, you investigate it. You don't just take a snap of Hollow Tree, you walk in it and stare up at it, walk around it, and explore it. You don't walk through the forest, you look for what lives inside it. You hunt for giant banana slugs in the woods, watch chipmunks leap about trees, search the sky for soaring eagles, and discover a massive ancient tree in the forest.

You don't take public transit because you have to, you take a SeaBus and a SkyTrain for the adventure. Leave the car at home and take a mini-ferry to Granville Island. You don't just stop for fudge at the public market, you experience it being made. Hang out with your kids at a park and you'll soon strike up a conversation with locals and visitors, and you'll learn still more about the secrets of our city.

With three young kids, I may not see as many plays as I used to, but I know Science World intimately. Ask me the names of all the rides on the Virtual Simulator at the Planetarium or which displays a 5-year-old likes best at the Maritime Museum. We must have visited the Vancouver Aquarium a dozen times in the last year, and I'm happy to go back another dozen times in the next. When you visit with children, their delight is always fresh and everything is new.

And, that's what makes Vancouver fun for a family. It's a place that has no preconceived rules or conventions. It's about being here, not being seen. So read on and discover your own family favorites as you explore the magic of Vancouver.

1 The Best Vancouver Experiences with Kids

Here are some of the best activities to do with your kids in and around Vancouver. Tailor each one to suit the ages and interests of your family. See chapter 6, "What Kids Like to See & Do" for specific age recommendations.

- **Walking, biking, or rollerblading the Stanley Park Seawall:** You could walk it in 2 hours, but why would you want to? There's too much to stop and look at along the way. Savor the Seawall, explore the trails that crisscross it, investigate the human-made wonders, drink in the views and all of the park's natural splendor. See chapters 6 and 7, pp. 103 and 142.

- **Hiking the North Shore:** Twenty minutes after you leave the city, you are in the wilderness. Take the trails in Lynn Canyon Park and cross a suspension bridge, where you dangle 20 stories above the roaring waters of Lynn Creek. Swim in a mountain lake, fish for trout, marvel at a waterfall, or wander through an old-growth rain forest. See chapters 6 and 7, pp. 131 and 148.

- **Riding the mini-ferries to Granville Island:** Two adventures in one. You get to sail along False Creek and arrive at this magical spot in the middle of the city. Eat at the public market, shop at the Kids' Market, visit a train museum, and watch the kids at the water park. See chapter 6, p. 131.

- **Wandering through a virgin rain forest in Lighthouse Park:** Climb the seaside cliffs and take in the views of the Burrard Inlet and the Strait of Georgia. Check out Point Atkinson, one of the last working lighthouses on the coast, and do all this while walking through an old-growth, unlogged forest. See chapter 7, p. 150.

- **Eating in Chinatown:** The kids get to wander through the butcher and fish shops and get a lesson on food production, before they go for dim sum and eat it. Then you get to walk off lunch while you poke around the trading stores, talk to a Chinese herbalist, and wind down at the Dr. Sun Yat-sen Classical Chinese Garden, or the free park next door to it. See chapter 8, p. 160.

- **Dining at Jericho Beach:** Take a hibachi along and have dinner on a warm summer's night by the pond at Jericho's park. Move to the beach, sit on a log, and take in one of Vancouver's killer pink and purple sunsets. See chapter 7, p. 153.

- **Watching the cruise ships from Caulfield Cove:** Sit on the rocks and dip your feet in the ocean, comb the beach for treasures, scamper along the cliffs, and watch the huge white ships glide by on their way to Alaska. See chapter 7, p. 149.

- **Riding the Royal Hudson:** The only steam engine in regular service in North America, the *Royal Hudson* gives you the thrill of the rails, combined with drop-dead scenery and views of Howe Sound, plus you can peek into the backyards of one of Canada's wealthiest neighborhoods. See chapter 6, p. 122.

- **Walking the promenade at Canada Place:** You get to see the magnificent five "sails" up close, listen for the buzzing of the seaplanes and watch them take off and land, get up close to a cruise ship, and take in the views of Stanley Park, Burrard Inlet, and the North Shore mountains without worrying that your kids will fall into the ocean. Best for kids under 10 or for the young at heart. See chapter 8, p. 156.

- **Riding public transit after everyone else has gone to work:** The kids think the bus is cool, but I'll take an inner harbor cruise by the SeaBus from Waterfront Station to Lonsdale Quay, or ride the driverless SkyTrain to New Westminster any day. See chapters 3 and 6, pp. 45 and131.

- **Window shopping on Robson Street:** Teens and tweens will love this strip. You'll find everything from Armani Exchange and Banana Republic, to the Virgin Megastore and Planet Hollywood, and dozens of places to stop for a snack. It's also The Spot to sight a celebrity. See chapter 10, p. 184.

- **Bard on the Beach:** It is almost enough just to know that this Shakespearean Festival takes place every summer at Vanier Park under a big tent, even if you can't ever go. See chapters 2 and 9, pp. 21 and 177.

Vancouver Dateline

Vancouver has a rich history and a fascinating present. As you wander our parks and streets, tell your family what has gone on before you.

Prehistory   Archaeologists estimate the first Coast Salish tribal villages were established on the shores of the Burrard Inlet and Fraser River delta around 3000 bc.

1774   Capt. Juan Perez Hernandez drops anchor off Vancouver Island and trades for furs with natives.

1790   The Songhees Coast Salish people find explorer Manuel Quimper claiming their land as Spanish territory.

1791   Navigator Jose María Narváez sails into the Burrard Inlet, but doesn't explore the inner harbor.

1792   Capt. George Vancouver charts the Burrard Inlet on his search for the Northwest Passage. He claims the land as British territory.

1808   North West Company fur trader Simon Fraser survives the Hell's Gate rapids and lands at the mouth of the Fraser River, only to be chased back upstream by Musqueam warriors.

1827   The Hudson's Bay Company establishes Fort Langley as a fur-trading post.

1831   Trade between Fort Langley and Hawaii begins.

1842   Hudson's Bay Company chief factor James Douglas selects Camosack as the company's new depot site. He builds Fort Victoria there.

1846   The Oregon Treaty sets the 49th parallel as the U.S.–Canadian boundary.

1849   The British crown grants the Hudson's Bay Company rights to Vancouver Island.

1858   Some 30,000 prospectors flood in from the United States to search for gold in the Fraser River valley and on Vancouver Island. The British crown claims British Columbia as a colony.

1861   The first West Coast hockey game is played on the frozen Fraser River.

1862   Three early BC settlers ("The Three Greenhorns") acquire 500 acres of land for $1 per acre to start a brickworks, which fails. They later attempt to develop it for housing, which also fails. This area is now Vancouver's West End. Victoria is incorporated.

1865   The first telegraph line reaches from San Francisco to British Columbia en route to Alaska.

1866   The colonies of British Columbia and Vancouver Island are united.

1868   Victoria becomes the colonial capital.

1869   The town that grew up around Gassy Jack's Globe Saloon is incorporated as the town of Granville.

1871   British Columbia enters Confederation and becomes a Canadian province.

1886 On April 6, the town of Granville is incorporated and becomes the city of Vancouver. On July 13, Vancouver is consumed by fire in less than an hour.

1887 A Canadian Pacific Railway steam train completes its maiden coast-to-coast voyage when it arrives in Vancouver.

1893 The Hudson's Bay Company replaces its fur-trading post with its first department store.

1895 For the first time, Vancouver's population surpasses that of Victoria.

1908 The University of British Columbia is founded.

1912 Vancouver's first reinforced-concrete structure, the fireproof Hotel Europe, opens as a luxury lodging.

1929 The Marine Building, a masterpiece of Art Deco design, opens just in time for the Great Depression. The owners offer to sell it to Vancouver as a new city hall for C$1 million, but the city declines.

1936 Vancouver's permanent City Hall is completed.

1938 The Guinness Brewing Company builds the Lions Gate Bridge, linking its extensive North Shore property holdings to the city of Vancouver.

1939 A decade after construction was suspended during the Great Depression, the Canadian Pacific's Hotel Vancouver opens its doors.

1965 Designed by Arthur Erickson, Simon Fraser University opens its doors.

1967 The first issue of the weekly independent paper the *Georgia Straight* appears.

1969 Hippies hold their first love-in at Stanley Park.

1970 The Vancouver Canucks play their first National Hockey League game.

1977 The SeaBus commuter catamaran ferry service begins regular runs between North Vancouver's Lonsdale Quay and downtown Vancouver.

1986 Vancouver celebrates its centennial by hosting Expo 86.

1990 After Chinese tanks crush demonstrations in Tiananmen Square, many Hong Kong residents begin applying for Canadian visas and start arriving in Vancouver in large numbers. Property prices soar.

1992 Vancouver celebrates the bicentennial of Captain Vancouver's arrival.

1995 Vancouver adds the new Vancouver Grizzlies of the National Basketball Association to its roster of professional sports teams.

1996 Statistics Canada announces that fewer than half of Vancouver's residents speak English at home.

1997 Environment Canada reports the highest rainfall in Vancouver's recorded weather history.

1999 A Treaty-in-Principal is signed with the Nisga'a First Nation of the Nass River Valley, the first such treaty to be signed in the modern era.

2000 Vancouver submits its bid to host the 2010 Olympic Winter Games.

2001 The Vancouver Grizzlies franchise is sold and moved to Memphis, Tennessee.

2 The Best Experiences with Kids Just Outside Vancouver

The areas around Vancouver are as jam-packed with things to do as Vancouver itself. Take an adventure into the rest of BC, with these activities topping the list. See chapter 11, "Easy Side Trips from Vancouver" for more information.

- **Building a sand castle at Rathtrevor Beach:** You have your pick of spots on this 5 kilometer (3 mile) long sandy beach, which goes out about a mile when the tide is out. That's when you bring adult-sized spades and build a sand castle and a moat, and then wait until the tide comes in and washes it all away. See chapter 11.

- **Strolling along the waterfront in Victoria:** Horse-drawn carriages, the Empress Hotel, and the Parliament Buildings are in the background, the ocean is in front of you, and a boardwalk full of artists, buskers, and an assortment of characters provides plenty of entertainment. See chapter 11.

- **Sitting in a hot pool in the winter at Harrison Hot Springs:** Winter is also off-season, which means you can snare a great deal at the Harrison Hot Springs Resort. With this in mind you get a choice of 2 indoor and 3 outdoor natural mineral hot spring pools. See chapter 11.

- **Taking a BC Ferry just about anywhere:** Taking a BC Ferry is still a pretty inexpensive way to see magnificent scenery like Active Pass. It's fairly fast and roomy (unless it's a fast ferry), and letting the kids play or wander on the deck, play in the kids' play area, or even check out the games arcade is much more pleasant than the invariable "are we there yet?" you hear on a car trip. See chapter 11.

3 The Best Hotel Bets for Families

See chapter 4, "Family-Friendly Accommodations" for full reviews.

- **Best All-Round Family Hotel:** The **Pacific Palisades** (1277 Robson St. ✆ **800/663-1815** or 604/688-0461) has color, pizzazz, large rooms with toys, and kid-friendly snacks in the mini-bar, a great view, a complimentary wine and pop hour, a fantastic pool with a play area for kids, and, to top it all off, a killer location.

- **Best Service:** The **Four Seasons** (791 W. Georgia St. ✆ **800/332-3442** or 604/689-9333) hasn't won the AAA Five Diamond award every year since it opened in 1976 for nothing. Of course, I assume price is no object, and you'll be staying in a suite, not a puny little C$455-a-night double.

- **Best Pool:** The **Four Seasons** (791 W. Georgia St. ✆ **800/332-**

3442 or 604/689-9333) wins again. Can't beat a year-round pool that's half indoor and half outdoor and has a patio for the oldies. The pool is also fairly shallow and has on hand for the kids a bunch of interesting kick boards, goggles, and toys to dive for.

- **Best Surprise:** This downtown **YWCA** (733 Beatty St. ✆ **604/895-5840**) is no youth hostel. Neither is it the Ritz, but you'll find good clean accommodations, many with private bathrooms— and a television set—for a great price. You can even cook here.

- **Best Deal:** A West End hotel with a fabulous Robson Street location, the **Riviera Hotel** (1431 Robson St. ✆ **888/699-5222** or 604/685-1301) has two types of suites and both are huge with large kitchens. It has balconies where you can either watch great views or the people, and a coin-operated laundry.

- **Best Heritage:** The **Fairmont Hotel Vancouver** (900 W. Georgia St. *Ⓒ* **800/441-1414** or 604/684-3131) spent C$65 million in renovations in the late '80s and early '90s, and a chunk of it was to restore the original 1939 architecture where it had been modernized over the years to its former glory.
- **Best Family Suite:** There's only one, but it's a doozy. The **Rosedale on Robson** (838 Hamilton St. *Ⓒ* **800/661-8870** or 604/689-8033) has a two-bedroom family suite that comes with bean bags, kid art, a bunk bed, a Canucks bedspread, a blackboard and chalk, a box of toys in the cupboard, and books on the shelf.
- **Best Kids' Program:** Kids get to walk up a flight of stairs to their own check-in at this Richmond hotel. The **Delta Pacific Resort and Conference Centre** (10251 St. Edwards Dr., Richmond *Ⓒ* **800/268-1133** or 604/278-9611) sees children as the key to return visits, and lavishes them with toys, personalized cards, tiny terry robes, and cookies. It has a three-story water slide, a creative center with free Nintendo, and organized kids programs in the holidays.
- **Best Pet Program:** The **Sutton Place Hotel** (845 Burrard St. *Ⓒ* **800/961-7555** or 604/682-5511) got a lot of press when it introduced its VIP program for pets. For C$95 (US$63) Fido or Fifi cops a gourmet T-Bone or caviar served on porcelain dishes with Evian water served on the side.
- **Best Chance to Spot a Celebrity:** The penthouse suite was named after Katharine Hepburn, who has stayed at this hotel for up to 6 months at a time. Located just half a block from Stanley Park, the **Rosellen Suites** (2030 Barclay St. *Ⓒ* **888/317-6648** or 604/689-4807) has a location and privacy that appeal to celebrities, and the pictures to prove it.
- **Best Added Value for Visitors:** The **Quality Hotel, the Inn at False Creek** (1335 Howe St. *Ⓒ* **800/663-8474** or 604/682-0229) came up with the innovative idea to offer its guests a *Vancouver City Passport,* which for C$15 (US$10) gives them more than C$500 (US$330) in discounts on various destinations, restaurants, and museums, as well as a CD by Michael Conway Baker, one of the foremost Canadian composers of classical music.
- **Best Views:** Sitting on the edge of Stanley Park, the **Westin Bayshore Resort and Marina** (1601 Bayshore Dr. *Ⓒ* **800/WESTIN-1** or 604/682-3377) can't help but have stunning views. There are no other downtown hotels or high-rises to obstruct panoramic views of the park, Coal Harbour, and the North Shore mountains.
- **Best Art:** Much of the art in the lobby and in the rooms of the **Listel Vancouver** (1300 Robson St. *Ⓒ* **800/663-5491** or 604/684-8461), is supplied by the Buschlen Mowatt Galleries, a large Vancouver private art dealer. On other floors, you'll see work on loan from the Museum of Anthropology.
- **Most Eccentric:** Accommodations at **Pillow Suites** (2859 Manitoba St. *Ⓒ* **604/879-8977**) is unforgettable. One of the apartments, now painted bright purple, was a 1910 corner grocery store. Others are done out in themes from Central America to West Coast.

- **Best Weekend Getaway: Harrison Hot Springs Resort** (100 Esplanade, Harrison Hot Springs *C* **800/663-2266** or 604/796-2244) is a kid's dream. It has five pools, a game room, activities in the restaurants, buckets and digging toys for the beach, and Nintendo in the bedrooms.

4 The Best Dining Bets for Families

See chapter 5, "Family-Friendly Dining" for full reviews.

- **Best All-Round Family Restaurant:** The fish and chips at **Troll's** (6408 Bay St., West Vancouver *C* **604/921-7755**) are excellent and so are the other seafood dishes on the menu. It's the place we go when we want to have a treat and be well looked after. The bonus is fabulous views of Horseshoe Bay, BC Ferries, and a playground with a water park across the road where we can work off our meal.

- **Best Child-Centric:** How can you beat a Japanese restaurant that has a large room filled with toys for kids, a climbing structure, and a video of Pokémon in Japanese? **Fukuroku Sushi** (4260 No. 3 Rd., Richmond *C* **604/273-0622**) also has a huge bar where sushi of different types and configurations sail by, and the food is good.

- **Best View:** From the deck of **Bridges Restaurant** (1696 Duranleau St., Granville Island *C* **604/687-4400**), named because it sits between the Burrard and Granville street bridges, you can watch the boats sail by on English Bay, and the foot traffic at the Granville Island Public Market.

- **Best Value:** A trendy Kitsilano restaurant, **Sophie's Cosmic Cafe** (2095 W. 4th Ave., Vancouver *C* **604/732-6810**) still boasts lineups after more than a decade in business, because its food is great, portions are huge, and prices are very reasonable. It also has a bunch of toys in the corner and crayons to keep kids occupied, and lots of garage sale-type fixtures to stare at.

- **Best Eye Candy: Planet Hollywood** (969 Robson St., Vancouver *C* **604/688-7827**), the American chain owned by a bunch of actors, is packed with movie paraphernalia, life-size replicas of actors, and film clips. Kids are encouraged to wander about while they wait for their food. The food is forgettable, but so what, the kids are happy.

- **Best Chinese: Hon's Wun-Tun House** (1339 Robson St., Vancouver *C* **604/685-0871**) started off as a small Chinatown restaurant. Its reputation for great food and prices grew quickly and the restaurant has spread to other locations, including, of course, this one. You can choose from hundreds of dishes from the menu or dim sum at lunch. It has a terrific vegetarian section.

- **Best Pizza: Lombardo's Pizzeria** (1641 Commercial Dr., East Vancouver *C* **604/251-2240**) serves pizza made with fresh ingredients and baked in a traditional Sicilian wood-burning oven. It shows. Lombardo's also has a large box of toys to keep kids busy while they wait.

- **Best Burger: White Spot** is a British Columbia institution, along the lines of Mom and apple pie, that has served up burgers topped with its famous Triple O sauce now for a couple of generations of families. Kids love the Pirate Pack and the crayons, and service is usually fast and friendly. Locations are everywhere.

- **Best Cafe: Urban Fare** (177 Davie St., Vancouver. ℂ **604/975-7550**) is actually a supermarket, but its location and fast and decent food have turned it into a meeting place for people who live and work in Yaletown. Good food, fast delivery, and reasonable prices make this bustling cafe a great place for families and the pickiest of eaters. Its noisy, bustling atmosphere also works well with kids, and after you eat you can browse through the rest of Urban Fare, which is actually a rather unusual kind of supermarket.
- **Best Dim Sum:** It's not cheap, but the **Pink Pearl** (1132 E. Hastings St., East Vancouver ℂ **604/253-4316**) is our choice when we want to splurge a little. The staff love kids, and the food comes fast and furious. There's also a huge selection of dim sum.
- **Best Patio: The Beach House** (150 25th St., West Vancouver ℂ **604/922-1414**) has a huge and lovely patio that gives you sweeping views of Burrard Inlet, the Lions Gate Bridge, Stanley Park, and killer sunsets. Because it's heated you can sit out here in the winter. In the summer, there's a sandy beach, a playground, and a toddler's wading pool.
- **Best When You Have a Babysitter:** I can't imagine anything better than a super restaurant that offers changing scenery, and BC Rail's **Pacific Starlight Dinner Train** which leaves from Pemberton Station, North Vancouver (ℂ **604/984-5246**), does this spectacularly. The whole trip, through Howe Sound and up to Porteau Cove and back, takes about 4 hours and includes three sumptuous courses.
- **Best Breakfast:** The tiny **Tomahawk** (1550 Philip Ave., North Vancouver ℂ **604/988-2612**) is a North Vancouver fixture that has

served up enormous helpings of eggs, pancakes, and hash browns since the late 1920s. Staff are great with the kids. There is a small gift shop and a collection of West Coast First Nations artifacts to look at. In summer you can sit on the patio.
- **Best Hotel Restaurant: Griffins Restaurant** at the Hotel Vancouver (900 W. Georgia St., Vancouver ℂ **604/662-1900**) does a roaring lunchtime business with the office crowd, but it's also a great family restaurant. There is a daily buffet with endless choices, a kids' menu, and the decor—meant to look like a West Coast brasserie—is bright and cheerful.
- **Best Vegetarian:** You know you're at **Cafe Deux Soleils** (2096 Commercial Dr., East Vancouver ℂ **604/254-1195**) when you see the lineups on a weekend. This is a small, funky restaurant that serves up huge meals and very affordable prices. Even if you're not vegetarian, you won't miss the meat. Really. And the kids can play with the toys on the elevated stage, while you sip coffee served in giant mugs.
- **Best Ice Cream: La Casa Gelato** (1033 Venables St., East Vancouver ℂ **604/251-3211**) serves up 168 flavors from its pink palace. My niece tells me it's The Place to take someone you are trying to impress on a first date. Try the curry or the pear, gorgonzola, and blue cheese flavors—go on, I dare you.
- **Best Outside Vancouver:** The **Harrison Hot Springs Resort Hotel** (100 Esplanade, Harrison Hot Springs ℂ **800/663-2266** or 604/796-2244) serves up an incredibly good brunch in its signature restaurant, The Copper Room. The only problem is keeping the kids away from the dessert table before they've had anything else to eat.

10 Famous British Columbians

- **Bryan Adams** An international superstar, Adams was born in Kingston, ON, but spent most of his formative years in British Columbia and still has a residence in West Vancouver. Hits include "Have You Ever Loved a Woman" and "(Everything I Do) I Do It For You."
- **Pamela Anderson** Star of those classy television dramas *Baywatch* and, most recently, *VIP*, and a former *Playboy* centerfold, Anderson was born in Ladysmith, BC, in 1967.
- **Emily Carr** Born in Victoria in 1871, Carr was a contemporary of the Group of Seven, a gifted writer, and an artist who had a passion for native culture.
- **William Deverell** A former Vancouver lawyer, Deverell has produced several bestselling thrillers, including *Dance of Shiva* and *Needles*, some based on his own cases. He lives on one of the Gulf Islands.
- **Arthur Erickson** The Vancouver architect designed the Museum of Anthropology, Simon Fraser University, the Provincial Law Courts, and Robson Square.
- **David Foster** Fourteen-time Grammy Award winner, Victoria-born Foster has written songs for dozens of musical heavyweights, including Phil Collins, Barbra Streisand, and Paul McCartney, as well as the award-winning soundtrack to *The Bodyguard* sung by Whitney Houston.
- **Michael J. Fox** After spending most of his formative years in Burnaby, BC, Fox moved to Los Angeles at 18, starred in the television series *Family Ties*, acted in the *Back to the Future* series, and, most recently, had a starring role in *Spin City*, a hit television show.
- **Terry Fox** With one leg already lost to cancer, Fox ran the Marathon of Hope in 1980 to raise money for research. He died the next year one month before his 23rd birthday. The 20th Terry Fox Run in September 2000 raised C$270 million for cancer research.
- **Joni Mitchell** Mitchell has been described as one of the most important and influential recording artists of the late 20th century. Her work has covered folk, pop, jazz, and avant-garde.
- **David Suzuki** Vancouver-born Suzuki is an internationally known scientist. He is a professor of genetics at the University of British Columbia and host of the television show *The Nature of Things*.

5 The Best Views

- **Cypress Bowl:** A West Vancouver mountain less than 30 minutes from downtown, this is our absolutely favorite viewpoint to take visitors. Halfway up the mountain there is a spot that has panoramic views from Vancouver Island to Mount Baker in Washington, and all the city's features are laid out in front of you. See chapter 7, p. 147.
- **Canada Place:** Head up to the prow of Canada Place and you can really get a good lay of the land

from just above water height—
with the North Shore mountains
straight in front of you, Stanley
Park to the west, and the Port of
Vancouver, North America's busiest
port, all around you. See chapter
8, p. 156.

- **Lonsdale Quay:** Take the SeaBus
from Waterfront Station for a cruise
of Burrard Inlet and get up close to
those ships. At the other side you
can look back at a different angle
of Canada Place. See chapter 6,
p. 131.

- **Prospect Point:** You'll have to
fight the tour buses for position,
but if you're pressed for time, this
is a beautiful part of Stanley Park
with wonderful views of the North
Shore mountains. See chapter 6,
p. 103.

- **Queen Elizabeth Park:** Known as
Little Mountain because it's a
pretty puny 150 meters (500 ft.),
it's still a great place to view the
downtown skyline and the North
Shore mountains. It also has beautiful gardens and two pieces of
sculpture by Henry Moore and
Seward Johnson, worth the trip
alone. See chapter 7, p. 139.

- **Cleveland Dam:** You can't see the
ocean from here, but what you get
is a very close-up view of the
majestic Lions peaks, which are
capped with snow for most of the
year. Walk a little further and you
get a fabulous view of 100 million
gallons of drinking water rushing
down the steep canyon walls each
day. See chapter 7, p. 137.

- **The Lookout! At Harbour
Centre:** You have to pay for this
one, but this is the tallest building
in BC and will give you a fabulous
undercover 360-degree look at
Vancouver and includes a ride up
in a glass elevator. See chapter 6,
p. 126.

- **Grouse Mountain:** Another view
you must pay for unless you hike
the Grouse Grind. Riding the
gondola up a mile may be worth
the price of admission to some,
but the view is definitely worth it
to all. Once on top, you can take in
the view again from 1,100 meters
(3,700 ft.) above sea level while
sipping on a latte or a pop at the
top. See chapters 6 and 7, pp. 111
and 147.

2

Planning Your Family Trip to Vancouver

Not surprisingly, most families visit Vancouver in the summer months when our city is in full bloom, in both a natural and a cultural sense. But Vancouver is truly a year-round city with moderate temperatures. So whether you are here for the summer or joining us for winter skiing, fall colors, or warm spring days and cherry blossoms, here are some tips to help you plan your trip.

1 Visitor Information & Entry Requirements

VISITOR INFORMATION

You can get Canadian tourism information at consulate offices in most major American cities. The provincial and municipal Canadian tourism boards are also great sources of travel information. For free BC travel information and reservations call **Super Natural British Columbia** toll-free from anywhere in North America at ✆ **800/HELLOBC (435-5622)** or from Vancouver at ✆ **604/435-5622.** International visitors can call ✆ **250/ 387-1642.** Reservations and information are also available through www. hellobc.com. Mailing address Box 9830 Stn. Prov. Government, Victoria, BC V8W 9W5. In England: Tourism BC, 3 Regent St., London, England SW1Y 4NS. From within the UK, visitors can call ✆ **0891 715000** (premium rate line).

For specific information on Vancouver and the North Shore contact **Tourism Vancouver**'s Information Centre, 200 Burrard St., Vancouver, BC V6C 3L6 (✆ **604/683-2000;** www.tourismvancouver.com). If you're planning to spend time outside the cities, you might also wish to call or write the **Vancouver Coast and**

Mountains Tourism Region, 205-1508 W. 2nd Ave., Vancouver, BC V6J 1H2 (✆ **604/739-9011**).

ENTRY REQUIREMENTS

If you're driving from Seattle, you'll clear customs at the Peace Arch crossing (open 24 hours a day) in Blaine, Washington. To enter Canada you will pass through **Canadian Customs** (✆ **800/ 461-9999** from within Canada and ✆ **204/983-3500** from outside Canada), and **U.S. Customs** (✆ **360/332-5771**) on your departure. Duty-free shops are located at the Pacific Highway crossing only, both in Canada and the United States (the duty-free store at Douglas/ Peace Arch has closed).

If you fly directly into Vancouver International Airport from another country, you'll clear customs in the new International Terminal. Once you get through Canada Customs passport control, you and your luggage will go through Customs before you leave the terminal. (Even if you don't have anything to declare, Customs officials randomly select a few passengers and search their luggage.)

DOCUMENTS FOR U.S. CITI-ZENS U.S. citizens or permanent U.S. residents don't require visas to enter Canada. American citizens need to show proof of citizenship and residence; a passport or birth certificate plus a driver's license is sufficient. Naturalized citizens should carry their naturalization certificate.

Permanent U.S. residents who are not U.S. citizens should carry their passport and Resident Alien Card (U.S. form I-151 or I-551). Foreign students and other noncitizen U.S. residents should carry their passport or Temporary Resident Card (form 1688) or Employment Authorization Card (1688A or 1688B); a visitor's visa; I-94 Arrival-Departure Record; a current I-20 copy of IAP-66 indicating student status; proof of sufficient funds for a temporary stay (such as a credit card); and evidence of return transportation. In either case, citizens of other countries traveling to Canada from the United States should check with the Canadian Consulate before departure to see if a visitor's visa is required.

When bringing children into Canada, you must have proof of legal guardianship. Lack of it can cause long delays at the border, because there have been cases of parents involved in custody cases abducting their children and attempting to flee to Canada (despite the fact that the Canadian and U.S. governments cooperate closely to resolve matters of this sort). If you are traveling with a minor of whom you are not the legal guardian, a notarized letter from the parents and contact telephone numbers (day and evening) should be provided. If you're under 18 and not accompanied by a parent or guardian, you should bring a permission letter signed by your parent or legal guardian allowing you to travel to Canada. You will still need proof of sufficient funds and evidence of return transportation.

DOCUMENTS FOR COMMON-WEALTH CITIZENS Citizens of Great Britain, Australia, and New Zealand don't require visas to enter Canada, but they must carry either a valid passport or other recognized travel documents as well as evidence of funds sufficient for a temporary stay (credit cards work well here). Naturalized citizens should carry their passport and resident status card. Foreign students and other residents should carry their passport, temporary resident card, or employment authorization card; a visitor's visa; arrival-departure record; a current copy of student status; proof of sufficient funds for a temporary stay; and evidence of return transportation. Check with the Canadian Consulate before departure to see if you will also need a visitor's visa.

CUSTOMS REGULATIONS

Your personal baggage can include the following: boats, motors, snowmobiles, camping and sports equipment, appliances, TV sets, musical instruments, personal computers, cameras, and other items of a personal or household nature. If you are bringing excess luggage, be sure to carry a detailed inventory list that includes the acquisition date, serial number, and cost or replacement value of each item. It sounds tedious, but it can speed things up at the border. If you are stopped, Customs will help you fill in the forms that allow you to bring in your effects temporarily, but they will require a deposit. If you are entering Canada from the U.S. and have registered the goods with U.S. Customs prior to entering Canada, or if an E29B form was issued, U.S. Customs will need to see this list to check off what you take out of Canada. You will be charged Customs duties for anything left in Canada.

Here are a few other things to keep in mind:

- If you come from the U.S. and bring more than US$10,000 in cash, you must file a transaction report with U.S. Customs.
- Never joke about carrying explosives, drugs, or other contraband unless you want to have your bags and person searched in detail, plus face arrest for conspiracy.
- Canada has strict laws concerning firearms and restricted weapons and if you arrive at the border with guns you will more than likely be sent back home. For more information call ℰ **800/731-4000.**
- Some prescription medicines may be considered contraband across the border. If you're bringing any, it's best to check with your doctor and bring a copy of your prescription, or contact the **Canadian Customs Office,** Regional Information Unit, Pacific Region, 333 Dunsmuir St., Vancouver, BC V6B 5R4 (ℰ **800/461-9999** from within Canada and ℰ **204/983-3500** from outside Canada).

- If you're over 18, you're allowed to bring in 40 ounces of liquor or wine, or 24 12-ounce cans or bottles of beer and ale, and 50 cigars, 200 cigarettes, or 8 ounces of tobacco per person. Any excess is subject to duty.
- Americans returning home after more than 48 hours in Canada can take back US$400 worth of goods without paying duty. If you've been in Canada less than 48 hours, the maximum duty-free amount is US$200.
- Gifts not exceeding C$60 (US$43) and not containing tobacco products, alcoholic beverages, or advertising material can be brought in duty free. Meats, plants, and vegetables are subject to inspection on entry. There are restrictions so contact the Canadian Consulate for more details if you want to bring in produce.
- If you plan to bring a dog or cat that is older than 3 months of age, you must provide proof of rabies

---

Ⓒ Travel Information Online: The Best of What's Around

Tourism BC: www.hellobc.com
Tourism Vancouver: www.tourismvancouver.com
Nature & Wildlife Information: www.travel.bc.ca
Tourism Victoria: www.tourismvictoria.com
In Vancouver: www.vancouver-bc.com
Vancouver & Victoria Directory: www.localdir.com
Discover Vancouver: www.discovervancouver.com
Whistler & Blackcomb Resorts: www.whistler.com
City of Vancouver: www.city.vancouver.bc.ca/
City of Victoria: www.city.victoria.bc.ca
Weather (Environment Canada): www.weatheroffice.com/
TransLink (Buses, SeaBus, and SkyTrain): www.translink.bc.ca
BC Ferries: www.bcferries.com
Frommer's Online: www.frommers.com

inoculation during the preceding 36-month period. You are able to bring up to two pet birds that are not classified as exotic. Other types of animals need special clearance and health certification. You must have owned an exotic pet for at least 90 days. For more information contact the **Canadian Food Inspection Agency,** 101-620 Royal Ave., New Westminster, BC V3M 1J2 (© **604/666-8750).**

- If you need more information concerning items you wish to bring in and out of the country, contact the **Canadian Customs Office,** Regional Information Unit, Pacific Region, 333 Dunsmuir St., Vancouver, BC V6B 5R3 (© **800/461-9999** from inside Canada and © 204/983-3500 from outside Canada; www.ccra-adrc.gc.ca).

- For information on U.S. customs regulations, travelers can contact the **American Citizen Information Services System** in BC at © **604/278-1825** in BC or pay by the minute at © **900/443-3131** from the U.S. Call © **900/451-2778** in Canada or check the website at www.amcits.com.

2 Money

CURRENCY

The Canadian currency system is decimal and resembles both British and U.S. denominations. Canadian monetary units are dollars and cents, with dollars coming in different colors, just like British currency. The standard denominations are C$5 (US$3.30), C$10 (US$6.60), C$20 (US$13.20), C$50 (US$33), and C$100 (US$66). The "loonie" (so named because of the loon on one side) is the C$1 (US66¢) coin that replaced the C$1 bill. A C$2 (US$1.32) coin, called the "toonie" because it's worth two loonies, has replaced the Canadian $2 bill.

Banks and other financial institutions offer a standard rate of exchange based on the daily world monetary rate. The best exchange rates can be had by withdrawing funds from bank ATMs. Hotels will also gladly exchange your notes, but they usually give a slightly lower exchange rate. Almost all stores and restaurants accept American currency, and most will exchange amounts in excess of your dinner check or purchase. However, these establishments are allowed to set their own exchange percentages, and generally offer the worst rates of all.

The exchange rate between Canadian and U.S. dollars should always be kept in mind. The figures charged in hotels and restaurants in Vancouver are often incrementally higher than in comparable U.S. cities; the cost is typically about one-third less. Canada, at the moment, is a bargain.

TRAVELER'S CHECKS

While ATMs are really the most convenient way of obtaining local currency (and usually give the best exchange rate), some people just feel more comfortable carrying traveler's checks.

Traveler's checks in Canadian funds are universally accepted by banks (which may charge a small fee to cash them), larger stores, and hotels. If you are carrying American Express or Thomas Cook traveler's checks, you can cash them at the local offices of those companies free of charge.

ATM NETWORKS

The 24-hour PLUS and Cirrus ATM systems are available in Vancouver. The systems convert Canadian withdrawals to your account's currency within 24 hours, so don't panic if you call your bank and hear a one-to-one balance

The Canadian Dollar, the U.S. Dollar & the British Pound

The prices cited in this guide are given in both Canadian and U.S. dollars. Note that the Canadian dollar is worth 30% less than the U.S. dollar, but buys nearly as much. As we go to press, C$1 is worth US66¢, which means that your C$200-a-night hotel room will cost only US$168 and your C$8 breakfast only US$5.

Here's a table of equivalents:

C $	U.S. $	UK £	U.S. $	C $	UK £
1	0.66	0.48	1	1.51	0.73
5	3.30	2.40	5	7.58	3.65
10	6.60	4.80	10	15.15	7.30
20	13.20	9.60	20	30.30	14.60
50	33.00	24.00	50	75.75	36.50
80	52.80	36.00	80	121.21	58.40
100	66.00	48.00	100	151.52	73.00

immediately after conducting a transaction. Cirrus network cards work at ATMs at the Bank of Montreal (© 604/665-2703), CIBC (© 800/465-2422), HSBC Bank of Canada (© 604/685-1000), Royal Bank (© 800/769-2511), and Toronto Dominion (© 800/983-2265), and at all other ATMs that display the Cirrus logo. None of these ATM systems provides your current balance. You must have a 4-digit PIN to access Canadian ATMs.

CREDIT & DEBIT CARDS

Major U.S. credit cards are widely accepted in British Columbia, especially American Express, MasterCard, and Visa. British debit cards such as Barclay's Visa debit card are also accepted. Diner's Club, Carte Blanche,

GST REFUNDS

The 7% goods and services tax (GST) is refundable on many items for nonresidents.

The **Mapleleaf GST Refund Service** at the Hotel Vancouver, 900 W. Georgia St. (© 604/893-8478), will give you cash back before you leave for individual purchases over C$50 (US$33) before taxes. You will need to provide two pieces of identification, one with a photo and one with your home address, together with the airline ticket you plan to use to leave Canada. You will also need to bring the goods you have purchased with the receipts. Mapleleaf will charge you 18% of the total refund or a minimum of C$7 (US$4.62) cash or C$10 (US$6.60) for a credit card refund.

If you would like to avoid paying a fee for this convenience and you are leaving Canada by car, you can also receive a GST refund through most duty-free shops before the border. However, the cash refund for eligible claims cannot exceed C$500 (US$330) and you will have to provide proof that you are a nonresident, the goods that go with the original receipts, and proof that you are leaving Canada. The duty-free shops in the Vancouver International Airport do not provide the GST refund service.

Once you have left Canada, you can still apply for the GST rebate. You will need form GST 176 Application for Visitor Tax Refund, which is included in the publication *Tax Refund for Visitors to Canada* and is available at most hotels, many stores in downtown Vancouver, and some duty-free shops and through the CCRA's website at **www.ccra-adrc.gc.ca**. You will need to mail the original receipts and proof of departure from Canada, such as your boarding pass of the flight out of Canada or receipts validated by a Canadian land-border customs officer. There is no charge for the processing of your refund application through the CCRA, but the procedure normally takes 4 to 6 weeks.

Note that accommodation (including camping) is also refundable, but transportation and food is not. For more information on the rebate program, contact Visitor Rebate Program Summerside Tax Centre, Canada Customs and Revenue Agency, 275 Pope Rd., Suite 104, Summerside, PEI C1N 6C6. From within Canada call © **800/668-4748,** and from outside Canada © **902/432-5608.**

Discover, JCB, and EnRoute are taken by some establishments, but not as many. The amount spent in Canadian dollars will automatically be converted by your issuing company to your currency when you're billed—generally at rates that are better than you'd receive for cash at a currency exchange.

What Things Cost in Vancouver	C $	U.S. $
Taxi from the airport to downtown Vancouver	25.00	16.50
One-zone bus fare, Adult	1.75	1.15
Child	1.25	0.83
Local telephone call	0.25	0.17
Downtown hotel rooms in the high season:		
Double at the Four Seasons (very expensive)	455.00	300.00
Double at the Quality Hotel, the Inn at False Creek (moderate)	159.00	105.00
Double at the Ramada Inn & Suites (inexpensive)	129.00	85.00
Tall latte at Starbucks	2.80	1.85
Kid's apple juice or hot chocolate at Starbucks	1.00	0.66
Slice of plain pizza	3.75	2.48
Ice-cream cone	2.50	1.03
Medium-sized pop	1.25	0.83
Weekday *Vancouver Sun*	0.60	0.40
Movie ticket, Adult	9.75	6.44
Child	5.50	3.63
Admission to the Vancouver Aquarium, Adult	13.85	9.14
Child	9.15	6.04

3 When to Go

Families often don't have much choice—we have to pick our holidays around the school year's summer holidays. And that's just fine in Vancouver: it's when you'll find the best weather and the least rain, the days stay light until 10pm, and, aside from all our year-round attractions, there are concerts in the parks, plays on the beach, and a variety of festivals and great family entertainment happening daily. If you do come in summer, make sure to plan your trip ahead of time. It's fine to drop in on us in the low season—we love unexpected visitors—but during summer our hotels are booked and everything is just a little more crowded than in other times of the year.

THE WEATHER

A sense of playfulness descends on locals around the end of March, as the cherry trees explode with pink and white blossoms and spring flowers start to appear. Skiers enjoy longer, warmer days, and, especially if we've had a long rainy season, sunny days bring out the best in us. Speaking of rain, we do get a lot of it—about 1,068 millimeters (42.7 in.) each year—and while it can strike at any time, it tends to rain more frequently between October and March.

Summer never really gets particularly hot, but you will hear Vancouverites complaining about high temperatures when the gauge hits the mid-20s °C (high 70s °F).

For a recorded daily report on Vancouver's weather call ✆ 604/664-9032.

Daily Mean Temperature & Total Precipitation for Vancouver, BC

	Jan	Feb	Mar	Apr	May	June	July	Aug	Sept	Oct	Nov	Dec
Temp. (°F)	42	44	50	58	65	69	74	74	65	58	48	43
Temp. (°C)	5	7	10	14	18	21	23	23	18	14	9	6
Precip. (mm)	150	124	109	75	62	46	36	38	64	115	169	178

HOLIDAYS

BC has one public holiday every month in January, April, May, July, August, September, October, November, and December. Banks and most nonretail businesses close for the holiday. Many businesses and services also shut on the Easter Monday, although it is not an official holiday.

Public holidays include January 1 (New Year's Day), late March or early April (Good Friday and Easter Sunday), third Monday of May (Victoria Day), July 1 (Canada Day), first Monday in August (BC Day), first Monday in September (Labour Day), second Monday in October (Thanksgiving), November 11 (Remembrance Day), December 25 (Christmas), and December 26 (Boxing Day).

KIDS' CALENDAR OF EVENTS

If you are traveling through British Columbia you'll find all sorts of events and glimpses into the culture of the province. There's an eagle count in Squamish, an ice-cream festival in McBride, and a chicken flying contest in Lumby. And there is also a variety of entertainment, festivals, and just plain weird stuff happening year-round in Vancouver. Check the Tourism Vancouver website at www.tourismvancouver.com for an up-to-date calendar of events, and other sources include *WestCoast Families* magazine (www.westcoastfamilies.com), *BC Parent Newsmagazine* (www.bcparent.com), the *Georgia Straight* (www.straight.com), the *Vancouver Sun* (www.vancouversun.com), and *Vancouver Magazine* (www.vanmag.com).

You can also email *Where Vancouver* at info@wherevancouver.com or call © 604/736-5586 for a free copy of its excellent annual *Kids' Guide*.

In almost all instances, you can buy tickets through TicketMaster (© 604/280-4444) or order online at www.ticketmaster.ca. Tickets are also usually available on-site before the performance, but it's always best to call first.

January

Polar Bear Swim. See a couple of thousand people, many dressed in elaborate costumes, take a dip in the icy waters of English Bay. Takes place at 2:30pm on January 1 at English Bay Beach.

Annual Bald Eagle Count. Every January, the town of Brackendale celebrates the arrival of thousands of bald eagles with a month-long festival that includes art displays, workshops, and, of course, the official Sunday eagle count. © **604/ 898-3333.**

February

Chinese New Year. Activities such as fireworks, dragon parades, and other festivities take place in and around Chinatown and the Plaza of Nations for 2 weeks starting in late January/early February.

March

Reel to Real Film Festival. An international film festival geared entirely to kids aged 8 and up, this festival also has filmmaking activities for kids to do when not actually watching the movies. Held first Wednesday in March. Tinseltown and International Village, 88 W. Pender St. (at Abbott St.), Vancouver. © 604/224-6162.

Spring Break Theatre Festival. Here is a chance to see work from local professional theater companies that is usually only seen in the schools. Geared to ages 4 and up, this annual festival has two to three shows a day from Green Thumb Theatre, Hooked on Books, Axis Theatre, and other local companies. Held each spring break at Granville Island, Shadbolt Centre for the Arts in Burnaby and the Surrey Arts Centre. © **604/738-7013.**

April

Easter Egg Hunts. Check local papers and websites (in this chapter) for local hunts as well as Easter activities at Granville Island and many other local attractions and destinations.

Vancouver Sun Run. Join more than 44,000 runners, joggers, walkers, strollers, and kids in Canada's biggest 10 kilometer (6.2 mile) race through downtown Vancouver and Stanley Park, finishing up at BC Place Stadium. For kids (and anyone who wants a shorter course), there is a 1.5 kilometer (1 mile) mini-run that starts 30 minutes before the race at 8:30am. Register by phone or online. Cost is C$25 (US$16) for early registration, C$35 (US$23) for last-minute registration for the 10 kilometer run, and C$15 (US$9.90) for early registration, C$20 (US$13.20) for late registration for the 1.5 kilometer run. You must register to participate and the cost includes a T-shirt and your name in the paper. © **604/ 689-9441;** www.sunrun.com.

Farmers' and Gardeners' Truck Market. Every Thursday afternoon behind the Arts Club Theatre on Granville Island, farmers and local growers bring their trucks of produce and sell directly to the public. April to October. © **604/666-6477.**

May

Cloverdale Rodeo & Exhibition. At this Surrey rodeo with a true country-fair atmosphere, see cowboys from all over North America compete in various roping and bull- and bronco-riding events. There are also pony rides, children's entertainers, and interactive activities for the whole family. Held on the Victoria Day long weekend. © **604/576-9461;** www.cloverdalerodeo.com.

Vancouver International Children's Festival. The festival celebrates its 25th anniversary in 2002 and it will be bigger and better than ever. See the best children's performers from all over the world as well as 20-plus educational and activity tents; dance, music, and storytelling workshops; and crafts to make and take. Suitable for kids aged 2 up to teens. Starts last Monday in May and runs for 1 week. You can buy advance tickets to performances through TicketMaster (which also gives you free admittance to the site). The weekend before the festival there are free performances 11:30am to 4pm at Granville Island on the stage behind the public market. Vanier Park (Ogden Ave. at Chestnut St.), Vancouver. © **604/708-5655.**

Haywood Bandstand. Enjoy a mix of professional and community-based live music aimed at all age groups and representing a cross-section of Vancouver's ethnic communities. Held every Sunday, weather permitting, 2 to 4pm, Victoria Day long weekend to Labour Day in September. Free. Haywood Park (across from English Bay at Bidwell St. and Beach Ave.). © **604/257-8400.**

Theatre under the Stars. Most plays are family friendly and *Annie Get Your Gun*, *Oklahoma*, *West Side Story*, and *Little Orphan Annie* are just a few of the past productions. Runs from mid-July to mid-August. Malkin Bowl, behind the Pavilion at Stanley Park. © **604/687-0174.**

Hyack Festival. Bands, parades, a petting zoo, and carnival rides are available at this 9-day annual festival. Starts on the Victoria Day long weekend. Queens Park (at 1st and 3rd aves.), New Westminster. © **604/522-6894.**

Maplewood Farm. An annual sheep fair celebrates the "rites of spring." Kids can see sheep shorn and herding demonstrations by working dogs, as well as demonstrations of spinning and weaving, food, and pony rides. Held on a Sunday toward the end of May. 405 Seymour River Place (at Seymour Mount Pkwy.), North Vancouver. © **604/929-5610.**

June

SlugFest. Bring your own slug to this event and pick up an award for the smallest or the slimiest or the most beautiful slug. Grand finale is a slug race. There are also carnival games, face painting, and guided walks. Held in early June. Richmond Nature Park, 11851 Westminster Hwy. (at No. 5 and Shell rds.) Richmond. © **604/273-7015.**

Fraser River Festival. This 1-day festival celebrates river life with paddle-boat rides, live entertainment, wooden boat building workshops, and paper-making crafts. First Sunday in June. Deas Island Regional Park, Deas Island, off River Road, south of Richmond. © **604/432-6350.**

The VanDusen Flower and Garden Show. This is North America's largest gardening exhibition and attracts thousands of visitors from around Canada, the United States, and the world. There are more than 200 displays on everything from flowers to furniture and garden gnomes to gargoyles. Open 9am to 6pm. C$12 (US$8) adults, C$10 (US$6.60) kids. Early June. Van-

Dusen Botanical Garden, 5251 Oak St. (at 37th Ave.), Vancouver. © 604/878-9274; www.vandusen garden.org.

Bard on the Beach Shakespeare Festival. Even if you're not a fan of Shakespeare, you have to love the location. Held in a 520-seat open-ended tent, with fabulous sea, mountain, and city views. Some plays suitable for children aged 6 and up. Runs from mid-June until late September. Vanier Park (Ogden Ave. at Chestnut St.), Vancouver. © 604/737-0625; www.bardonthebeach.org.

Dance at Dusk at Ceperley Park. Programming highlights are Scottish country dancing, international folk dancing, ballroom dancing, and West African dance. Instruction is provided and all ages are welcome. Runs Monday to Thursdays 7 to 9.30pm, weather permitting, mid-June to mid-August. Free. Stanley Park. © 604/257-8400.

Festival d'été francophone de Vancouver. Various venues, includes street festival. This week-long festival celebrates French music from around the world. Performers often include well-known Quebec artists. While the festival targets an adult audience, some of the street festival entertainment may be of interest to older children. Mid-June. © 604/736-9806.

Alcan Dragon Boat Festival. Traditional dragon-boat racing is part of the city's cultural scene. You can watch the races from False Creek. Singers and dancers perform on stage throughout the festival. Third week of June. Plaza of Nations, Vancouver. © 604/688-2382.

Kitsilano Showboat. Everything from square dancing to martial arts and Hawaiian dancing takes place in an open-air theater at the beach. Runs from late June to late August,

weather permitting, Monday, Wednesday, and Friday nights 7:30 to 9:30pm. 2300 Cornwall Ave. (at Kitsilano Park), Vancouver. © 604/734-7332 or 604/733-7297.

Kitsilano Soap Box Derby. Kids aged 9 to 13 (with help) build their own car and compete for best engineered car, best paint job, and best design. Fastest car wins the derby. Heats run in groups of three. Held last Sunday in June. 4th Ave. at Balsam Street, Vancouver. © 604/263-6443.

Vancouver International Jazz Festival. This 10-day festival features more than 1,500 musicians from Canada and around the world performing at 40 venues around the city and playing all sorts of jazz as well as blues, funk, and Latin fusion. The main event happens at the David Lam Park off Pacific Boulevard in Yaletown and next to the Roundhouse Community Centre, which holds more indoor stages and Kid.calm, an area where kids get face painting, play board games, and make their own instruments. Last week of June. © 604/872-5200.

July

Canada Day Celebrations at Canada Place. This all-day celebration has live entertainment throughout the day and finishes with a fireworks display. Wear red and white for the chance to win prizes. Other Canada Day events are at Granville Island, Lonsdale Quay, Steveston, and Grouse Mountain. Foot of Howe Street, Vancouver. © 604/666-7200.

Kids' Market. Magic shows, arts and crafts, and other free events happen throughout the summer holidays for kids aged 5 and up. On the lawn outside the market 10am to 6pm. Granville Island, Vancouver. © 604/689-8447.

Vancouver Folk Music Festival. Folk music performances from around the world on a weekend in mid-July. Jericho Beach Park, Vancouver. ℂ **604/602-9798.**

Illuminares. Starting at dusk, families gather to light paper lanterns and listen to music. See serpents, fire sculptures, torch choreography, and fireworks. Held in late July. Trout Lake, East Vancouver. ℂ **604/879-8611;** www.thedrive.net/publicdreams.

Vancouver International Comedy Festival. This 10-day festival has free outdoor busking during the day and indoor evening performances at various prices. About three or four of the evening shows are suitable for children. Held late July, early August. Granville Island, Vancouver. ℂ **604/683-0883.**

August

Festival Vancouver. Programming and venues were still to be determined at the time of publication, but the second bi-annual festival will include downtown lunchtime and early evening concerts at various venues and weekend performances of everything from classical to jazz and world music. Perhaps the best for children will be the weekend concerts at the First Nations Longhouse at UBC, August 1 to 11, 2002. ℂ **604/221-0080;** www.festivalvancouver.bc.ca.

Abbotsford International Air Show. This is one of the world's largest air shows and has 3 days of planes and live entertainment. See the Canadian Snowbirds, model aircraft, demonstrations of F15s and F16s, B52s, and military displays. It can get really crowded and hot on the tarmac, so dress accordingly and take lots of water. First full long weekend in August. Abbotsford Airport. ℂ **604/852-8511.**

Powell Street Festival. At this annual 2-day Japanese festival, you can enjoy music, dance, food, a children's tent, and a small stage with performers geared especially to children. BC Day long weekend in August. Free. Oppenheimer Park, Powell St. (at Jackson St.), Vancouver. ℂ **604/739-9388.**

Circus of Dreams. This circus parade has clowns, fire performers, and stilt performers. Held at the end of August. Maclean Park, Strathcona, East Vancouver. ℂ **604/879-8611;** www.thedrive.net/public dreams.

Vancouver Wooden Boat Festival. This 4-day festival includes free toy boat building for kids up to 12. It also includes family boat building that costs C$300 (US$200), but at the end you can take home a 3.5 meter (12 ft.) sea-worthy dinghy with oars. (In addition to the price tag, you have to enter a contest to win a place in the boat-building workshop.) Late August. Granville Island, Vancouver. ℂ **604/688-9622.**

September

Maplewood Farm. Enjoy a full weekend of farm activities, pony rides, coloring contest, straw play area, and music and dancing. Also hand-milking demonstrations and butter making, and kids can milk a goat. 405 Seymour River Place (at Seymour Mount Pkwy.), North Vancouver. ℂ **604/929-5610.**

Harvest Festival. Celebrate the fall harvest, and meet local growers and taste their produce. Granville Island, Vancouver. ℂ **604/666-6477.**

Mid-Autumn Moon Festival. Experience an outdoor Chinese cultural celebration with lanterns, myth telling, music, and free tea and mooncakes. Early to mid-September according to the lunar cycle (15th day of the 8th month of the Chinese calendar). Dr. Sun Yat-sen Classical Garden, Chinatown. ✆ 604/662-3207.

World Championship Sand Sculpture Competition. This event is held each year around the Labour Day weekend. Main Beach, Harrison Hot Springs. ✆ 604/796-3425.

October

Vancouver International Writers Festival. Attend public readings conducted by international and Canadian authors and writer's workshops. Two of the five days of readings, discussions, and book signing are aimed at kids aged 5 to high school age. Around the second and third weeks of October. Granville Island, Vancouver. ✆ 604/681-6330; www.writersfest.bc.ca.

Parade of the Lost Souls. An annual neighborhood celebration to honor the dead, wake the living, and chase away bad luck, with a torch-lit procession through streets and alleys as well as fireworks. Held at the end of October. Grandview Park on Commercial Drive, East Vancouver. ✆ 604/879-8611; www.thedrive.net/publicdreams.

Maplewood Farm. First 101 families to arrive in costume get a free pumpkin. Home-grown pumpkin judging and pony rides. Open 10am to 4pm. 405 Seymour River Place (at Seymour Mount Pkwy.), North Vancouver. ✆ 604/929-5610. The **Pumpkin Patch** operates all month and families can pick their pumpkins, go on a hayride, eat lunch, and watch the country-style entertainment. Also check local papers and community centers for Halloween events. Richmond. ✆ 604/274-0522.

Stanley Park Ghost Train. Steel yourself for a spooky 12-minute ride through the park. Runs October 7 to 31. Stanley Park Train, Stanley Park. ✆ 604/257-8531.

November

Bear Creek Park Train. Take a train ride through the Christmas light display, which runs every day 10am to 10pm in covered coaches. From the end of November see Santa from 5pm. 13750-88th Ave., Surrey. ✆ 604/501-1232; www.bctrains.com.

The Vancouver Storytelling Festival. Each year the festival includes more children's programming—and it usually sells out. Events take place at various venues at the end of November. ✆ 604/876-2272.

Burnaby Village Museum. The village is transformed into a Christmas scene with costumed townsfolk, carolers, and craft making for the kids. Runs from the end of November to the first week of January. 6501 Deer Lake Ave., Burnaby. ✆ 604/293-6500.

December

Christmas at Canada Place. Dress warmly and wander the outside of this building to look at more than 200 animated characters from the old Woodward's Department store Christmas display windows. Kids can also mail their letters to Santa here. Open daily 10am to 10pm December 1 to January 1. Canada Place, Vancouver. ✆ 604/666-8477; www.canadaplace.ca.

Bright Nights. The 12-minute miniature train takes you through a spectacular Christmas lights display. But be warned, this is a tremendously popular event, so dress warmly and expect to wait. Runs December 8 to January 7 3 to 10pm daily, weather permitting. Stanley Park Train, Stanley Park, Vancouver. ✆ 604/257-8531.

Festival of Lights. Enjoy a beautiful Christmas light display complete with a Santa's workshop. VanDusen Botanical Garden, 5251 Oak St. (at 37th Ave.), Vancouver. ℭ **604/878-9274;** www.vandusen garden.org.

Winter Solstice Lantern Procession. Annual parade to celebrate the coming of winter. Starts around dusk, December 21. Granville Island. ℭ **604/257-8195.**

4 What to Pack

Vancouver is a casual city and we like to think of ourselves as urbanites who might at any moment change our minds. We just might dive off into those mountains for a bit of hiking or mountain biking or perhaps have a quick sail during the day and a ski after dinner. Anyway, that's the myth, but we do dress accordingly.

In the summer, shorts and T-shirts, summer dresses, and jeans are all okay and will take you from breakfast through to evening. Whether it's a hike in the mountains, a stroll around Stanley Park Seawall, or just checking out the shops along trendy Robson Street, prepare to walk and pack comfortable worn-in shoes for everyone. Those sports water bottles are a terrific thing when kids say "I'm thirsty" and there's not a fountain, stream, or cafe for miles. Consider a Snugli—those small cloth carrier packs for babies—and for small children an easily foldable stroller that can double as a high chair or a makeshift cot. Also don't forget sunscreen, swimsuits, hats, and beach towels if you can fit them in. Even on our warmer days, the nights tend to cool off quickly, so don't forget to pack at least one jacket or sweater.

As the weather cools in the autumn, Gore-Tex or fleece, jeans or sweats, gloves, scarves, and hats will pretty much take you up a mountain, out to walk the dog, or off to take the kids grocery shopping. Hiking boots, running shoes, or boots are also okay, and the kids can dress in pretty much anything they like as long as they are warm and dry. Speaking of dry, rain gear is a necessity from November through March, and think of it as insurance during the rest of the year. Throw in one of those small foldable umbrellas or, if you hate umbrellas like I do, just bring those light rain pants and jackets with the hoods. Of course, I never follow my own advice, and tend just to throw in an extra change of clothes for the kids if they do happen to get wet. It rarely snows in the city, but if you're heading up to the mountains in winter, pack snow boots and snowsuits.

In Vancouver, eating out is casual so you can leave the ball gown and tux in the cupboard, but if you get the opportunity to try our fine dining restaurants, the theater, or the opera, you may want to replace the sweats and hiking boots with something more upmarket.

It seems that every time we have been away on holidays, at least one child has either thrown up in the plane or the back seat of the car. We now take at least one change of clothes on the plane (each) in case they've thrown up all over us (or in case the airline loses our bags) and keep clothes in the car as well as a bowl, diapers, diaper wipes, and receiving blankets (the last two are great things with or without a baby). Also, Chapstick is handy for long flights, and don't forget to take a sweater on the plane as those airline blankets are mighty small and often scarce.

Online Parent Magazines/Newspapers and Other Kid-Friendly Websites

Westcoast Families magazine: www.westcoastfamilies.com

BC Parent magazine: www.bcparent.com

Vancouver Sun: www.vancouversun.com

Vancouver Magazine: www.vanmag.com

Georgia Straight: www.straight.com

Where Vancouver magazine: www.wherevancouver.com

In Vancouver!: www.vancouver-bc.com

MyBC: www.mybc.com

VancouverPlus: www.vancouverplus.ca

Vancouver Today: www.vancouvertoday.com

KidFriendly: www.kidfriendly.org

Family Fun Magazine: www.familyfun.com

I always overpack for the kids, but sometimes, when a washer and dryer are not readily available, it's a huge relief. Throw in some laundry soap for rinsing out clothes in the bathtub if you're desperate, and if you are here for more than a couple of days, and your hotel doesn't come with one, sniff out the coin-operated laundry closest to you. You've always got to balance doing laundry against packing light, and with a family of three small children, we find a combination of the two works best for us.

5 Health & Safety

If any of your family members take medication, bring plenty in a carry-on bag and include prescriptions. I find Gravol for motion sickness can be a boon for kids who tend to get car sick on long drives or may be queasy on a flight. If you are flying, have little ones suck on a bottle or a candy on takeoff, or if anyone has a cold, some decongestant before the flight will save a lot of discomfort. Even if everyone is healthy, someone usually manages to get a cold, earache, or sore throat and it's convenient at 3am to have some children's aspirin or Tylenol, a thermometer, cough syrup, a little plastic cup or spoon, and Chapstick. Pack a first-aid kit for traveling and for any sightseeing misadventures.

Keep a list of children's inoculations with dates with you. It may save a lot of time if they require medical attention.

If you become separated from your children, them knowing their home address and phone number won't help a lot. Some people suggest putting a nametag on young children with their name and the hotel's address, but that makes me quite uncomfortable. I keep a tight handle on the little ones, dress others in bright yellow, and work out a clear meeting place should older ones become separated. If your kids can be trusted to use it only in an emergency, then a security whistle is a good idea when traveling in crowded areas. I've also told my kids if they ever did become separated in a crowded place to approach another mother with children and ask for help.

There are some areas of otherwise safe Gastown and Chinatown that can be shady. Keep an eye out as a turn around a seemingly innocuous corner can land you in the middle of skid row. The areas of Hastings and Main streets can make you uncomfortable during the day, and it's best to avoid Hastings Street between Abbott and Main streets at night.

Canada's health care is similar in quality to that of the United States, and while no one would be refused emergency medical treatment, it's always wise to check that you have travel insurance before you leave home. If you're Canadian, make sure you have your provincial health card with you as well.

When you check into your room, find out where the nearest fire exits are and discuss dos and don'ts of fire safety. You may even want to keep a small kit of emergency items: a flashlight, cash, and other essentials. This will also serve you well in the event of an earthquake. Vancouver is situated in an earthquake zone and we experience tremors daily. While we rarely feel these tremors, learning about earthquakes and earthquake preparedness is a family project that Vancouverites know well. The front pages of the Vancouver telephone directory have a quick course in emergency procedures, but if you do feel a tremor while you are inside a building remember to stay out of elevators and away from windows. In fact, experts recommend that you either head for a doorway or the inside wall or climb under a sturdy table. If you are outside, get into an open area away from trees, buildings, walls, and power lines.

6 Tips for Travelers with Disabilities

According to *We're Accessible,* a newsletter for travelers with disabilities, Vancouver is "the most accessible city in the world." There are more than 14,000 sidewalk wheelchair ramps and motorized wheelchairs are a common sight in the downtown area. Most major attractions and venues have ramps or level walkways for easy access. In 1990, Vancouver was the first city in Canada to provide scheduled bus service to people with disabilities. More than half of all Lower Mainland buses are accessible and all SkyTrain stations with the exception of Granville Street are accessible. For more information about public transit call ℭ 604/521-0400, or go to www.translink.bc.ca.

The **Vancouver International Airport** features ticket and service counters with amplified handsets, low-mounted flight information monitors, visual paging monitors, and accessible washroom and public telephone facilities.

Vancouver and other large BC centers have accessible taxi services (**Vancouver Taxi** ℭ 604/255-5111, 604/669-5555, or 604/871-1111). For airport service in Vancouver, call the **Airporter** bus (ℭ 800/668-3141 or 604/273-8436).

The **Vancouver Aquarium, Science World,** the **Vancouver Zoo,** and many other attractions offer wheelchair access. The free trolley ride around Stanley Park (ℭ 604/801-5515) and the horse-drawn tours of Stanley Park are wheelchair accessible. **Grouse Mountain Skyride** can arrange wheelchair accessibility on the gondola if you call the sales department at least 24 hours in advance (ℭ 604/984-0661).

The **Queen Elizabeth Theatre** and **Playhouse Theatre** in Vancouver and the **Centennial Theatre** in North Vancouver all offer wheelchair-accessible spaces.

Many hotels and theaters are wheelchair accessible and some downtown hotels are equipping rooms with visual smoke alarms and other facilities for hearing-impaired guests. You'll also notice that downtown sidewalks are equipped with ramps, though very few intersections have beeping crosswalk signals for the visually impaired.

For renting lift-equipped vans, call the **BC Paraplegic Association** at ✆ **604/324-3611.**

For **BC Ferries** call ✆ **888/223-3779** in BC, or out of province at ✆ **250/386-3431.** Wheelchair users should request parking near the elevator when they buy their ferry ticket. All washrooms and deck areas are accessible.

Greyhound Bus Lines (✆ **800/661-8747**) has lift-equipped service from Vancouver to Kelowna, Calgary, and Prince George, with stops in major centers along the way. Book 24 hours in advance. **Pacific Coach Lines** (✆ **604/662-7575**) offers accessible service between Vancouver and Victoria.

The **BC Sport and Fitness Council for the Disabled** (✆ **604/737-3039**) in Vancouver is a group of associations offering competitive and recreational opportunities for disabled skiing, horseback riding, sailing, sledge hockey, ice picking, and track and field. The **Mobility Opportunities Society** (✆ **604/688-6464**) also offers disabled sailing and other recreational opportunities.

For a complete list of facilities for disabled travelers, or to subscribe to a quarterly newsletter, call Penny and Ken Bartel at *We're Accessible.* (✆ **604/588-3731**).

7 Getting the Kids Interested

I can't think of a better way of getting kids interested in a foreign city than having them read up about it or, depending on their age, reading to them about it. Local writers and artists will help give your kids a connection to our city and its culture (see "Set in Vancouver and BC," a list of picture books and stories for kids from 2 years and up on p. 34).

You can also receive an awful lot of useful information through **Tourism Vancouver** (✆ **604/683-2000;** www.tourismvancouver.com), but a more interesting exercise might be to get your kids to write to the information center at 200 Burrard St., Vancouver, BC V6C 3L6 and request kid-friendly attractions brochures and maps (and they can look forward to receiving a personally addressed package in the mail). You can also contact *Where Vancouver* at **info@wherevancouver.com** or ✆ **604/736-5586** for a free copy of its excellent annual *Kids' Guide.*

If you are not from Canada, use an atlas to try to give the kids a good understanding of where Vancouver is in Canada and in relation to North America. Get them to look for references to both Vancouver and Canada in the newspaper, in magazines, and at the local library.

Gone are the days when you can leap on a plane or in the car and arrive at your destination with little or no planning. With kids, successful holidays, whether 2 days or 4 weeks, need careful thought and preparation. Involve the kids in planning your itinerary and remember, think small. The best advice I've been given is to plan out the itinerary and then cut it in half. Make sure there is a park or beach close by for a break and schedule in plenty of time to chase squirrels, splash in water parks, and eat ice-cream cones.

8 Getting to Vancouver

BY PLANE

THE MAJOR AIRLINES The Open Skies agreement between the United States and Canada has made flying to Vancouver easier than ever. Daily direct flights between major U.S. cities and Vancouver are flown by **Air Canada** (© 888/247-2262, 800/661-3936, or 800/776-3000; www.aircanada.ca), **United Airlines** (© 800/241-6522; www.ual.com), **American Airlines** (© 800/433-7300; www.americanair.com), **Continental Airlines** (© 800/231-0856; www.continental.com), **Alaska Airlines** (© 800/252-7522; www.alaskaair.com), **Horizon Air** (© 800/547-9308; www.horizonair.com), and **Northwest Airlines** (© 800/447-4747; www.nwa.com). Direct flights on major carriers serve Los Angeles, Boston, Atlanta, Las Vegas, Chicago, Seattle, Phoenix, Dallas, New York, Houston, Minneapolis, Reno, San Francisco, and many other cities.

FINDING THE BEST AIRFARE The best advice we can give you on shopping for an airfare bargain is to call travel agencies or the major airlines 30 or more days before your departure. That's when you'll find the best discounted seats on flights. Most airlines offer restricted ticketing on these deals. You cannot change dates without paying extra, and the tickets are usually nonrefundable.

If you have access to the Internet, check out **www.airfare.com** or search "discount airfare" on google.com for a listing of other companies offering discount air packages. See the box "Travel-Planning Websites" for more ideas on how to find cheap air fare.

VANCOUVER INTERNATIONAL AIRPORT The airport is 13 kilometers (8 miles) south of downtown Vancouver on Sea Island in Richmond. The new International Terminal features an extensive collection of First Nations sculptures and paintings set amid grand expanses of glass under soaring ceilings. Turn around and look up, or take the up escalator on your right just before you leave the International Terminal to catch a glimpse of Bill Reid's huge jade canoe sculpture, the *Spirit of Haida Gwaii.*

More than 10 million passengers pass through this airport annually on Canadian, U.S., and international carriers, including British Airways, Cathay Pacific, China Airlines, Continental, Japan Air Lines, KLM Royal Dutch Airlines, Lufthansa, Qantas, and Singapore Airlines.

Airport services include restaurants, cocktail lounges, bookstores, newsstands, florists, duty-free shops, food specialty shops, ATMs, currency exchanges, a post office, a barber shop, and hotel reservation telephones. There are several unsupervised **play areas** in the departure gates areas as well as in the connecting corridor between the two terminals. There is also a **nursery** located next to the children's play area in the connecting corridor between the two terminals. It's an unsupervised room designed to offer a refuge for families and has cribs, a playpen, a highchair, and a rocking chair on hand. **Shower** facilities are available at the Fairmont Vancouver Airport Fitness Centre, located at the U.S. departures level. **Tourist Information Kiosks** on Level 2 of the Main and International Terminals (© 604/303-3601) are open daily from 8am to 11:30pm.

Parking is available at the airport for both loading passengers and long-term stays (© 604/276-6106). **Courtesy buses** to the airport hotels are available, and a **shuttle bus** links the Main and International Terminals to

Travel-Planning Websites

If you're a Net surfer, it's possible to get some great cyber deals on air-fare, hotels, and car rentals.

www.frommers.com   Arthur Frommer's Budget Travel Online is a good place to start. You'll find indispensable travel tips, reviews, monthly vacation giveaways, and online booking services. One of the most popular features of this site is the regular "Ask the Expert" bulletin board, where you can post questions and have them answered online by Frommer's authors. You can also sign up for an electronic newsletter to receive the latest travel bargains and insider travel secrets in your e-mailbox every day. The Destinations Archive lists more than 200 domestic and international destinations, with information on great places to stay, traveling tips, and things to do while you're there.

www.travelocity.com; www.previewtravel.com; www.frommers. travelocity.com   Travelocity is Frommer's online travel-planning and booking partner. Travelocity uses the SABRE system to offer reservations and tickets for more than 400 airlines, plus reservations and booking services for more than 45,000 hotels and 50 car-rental companies.

www.expedia.com   Expedia is Travelocity's major competitor. It offers several ways to obtain the best possible fares. Expedia focuses on the major airlines and hotel chains, so don't expect to find many budget airlines or one-of-a-kind B&Bs here.

www.trip.com   TRIP.com began as a site geared toward business travelers, but its innovative features and highly personalized approach have broadened its appeal to leisure travelers as well. It is the leading travel site for those using mobile devices to access Internet travel information.

www.travel.yahoo.com   Yahoo! is currently the most popular of the Internet information portals, and its travel site is a comprehensive mix of online booking, daily travel news, and destination information.

---

the South Terminal, where smaller and private aircraft are docked.

The airport is easily accessible via three bridges. Travelers heading into Vancouver take the Arthur Laing Bridge, which leads directly to Granville Street, the most direct route to downtown.

DEPARTURE TAX Passengers departing Vancouver International Airport are required to purchase an Airport Improvement Fee ticket. Children under 2 and passengers connecting through Vancouver Airport on the same day are exempt. AIF tickets must be presented along with airline tickets and boarding passes as you pass through the airport security checkpoint on your way to the flight gate. The departure tax is C$15 (US$9.90) per person for international air travelers outside of North America, C$10 (US$6.60) for passengers traveling within North America (including Hawaii and Mexico), and C$5 (US$3.30) for passengers departing on flights within BC or to the Yukon.

LEAVING THE AIRPORT The pale-green YVR Airporter (© **604/ 946-8866**) provides **airport bus serv-**

Tips Airport Tip

Unlike many other airports around the world, Vancouver does not gouge. All retail shops run under a system called street pricing, which means if a Starbucks sells a latte for C$2.80 at its suburban location, it must also sell a latte for C$2.80 at the airport outlet.

---

ice to downtown Vancouver's major hotels. It leaves from level 2 of the Main Terminal every 15 minutes daily from 6:30am to 10:30pm and every 30 minutes from 10:30pm, with a final run at 12:10am. The 30-minute ride to the downtown area whisks you through central Vancouver before taking the Granville Bridge into downtown Vancouver. The one-way fare is C$12 (US$7.92) for adults, C$9 (US$5.94) for seniors, C$5 (US$3.30) for children; the round-trip fare is C$18 (US$11.88) for adults, C$17 (US$11.22) for seniors, C$10 (US$6.60) for children. Bus service back to the airport leaves from selected downtown hotels every half hour between 5:35am and 10:55pm. Scheduled pickups serve the bus station, the Hotel Vancouver, Waterfront Centre Hotel, Georgian Court, Sutton Place, Landmark, and others. Ask the bus driver on the way in or ask your hotel concierge for the nearest pickup stop and time.

Getting to and from the airport by **public transit** is a pain. Buses are slow, and you have to transfer at least once to get downtown. Given that the YVR Airporter bus costs only C$10 (US$6.60), the hassle probably isn't worth the savings. If you insist, however, bus no. 100 stops at both terminals. At the Granville/West 71st Street stop get off and transfer to bus no. 8 to downtown Vancouver. TransLink fare from the airport to downtown Vancouver is 3 zones and costs C$3.50 (US$2.31) adults and C$2.50 (US$1.65) children 5 and over, and C$1.75 (US$1.16) adults and C$1.25

(US83¢) children after 6:30pm, on weekends, and public holidays. But transfers are free in any direction within a 90-minute period. TransLink also offers a Daypass of unlimited travel for C$7 (US$4.62) adults and C$5 (US$3.30) children.

The average **taxi** fare from the airport to a downtown Vancouver hotel is approximately C$25 (US$16.50) plus tip. Because the meter charges for time when the cab is stuck in traffic and some hotels are closer to the airport than others, the fare can get as high as C$40 (US$26). Nearly 400 taxis service the airport. AirLimo (© **604/273-1331**) offers flat-rate stretch-limousine service. AirLimo charges C$29 (US$19) per trip to the airport (not per person), plus tax and tip. The drivers accept all major credit cards.

Most major **car-rental firms** have airport counters and shuttles. Make advance reservations for fast check-in and guaranteed availability—especially if you want a four-wheel-drive vehicle. See chapter 3, "Getting to Know Vancouver," p. 46 for a list of rental car companies and their contact information.

BY TRAIN

The main Vancouver railway station is at 1150 Station Street, near Main Street and Terminal Avenue just south of Chinatown. You can reach downtown Vancouver from there by cab for about C$7 (US$4.60). There are plenty of taxis at the station entrance. One block from the station is the Sky-Train's Main Street Station. Within minutes, you're downtown. The Granville and Waterfront stations are two and four stops away, respectively.

VIA Rail Canada, 1150 Station St. (✆ **800/561-8630;** www.viarail.ca), connects with Amtrak at Winnipeg, Manitoba. From there, you travel on a spectacular route that runs between Calgary and Vancouver. Lake Louise's beautiful alpine scenery is just part of this enjoyable journey. **Amtrak** (✆ **800/872-7245;** www.amtrak.com) has regular service from Seattle and also has a direct route from San Diego to Vancouver. It stops at all major U.S. West Coast cities, and takes a little under 2 days to complete the entire journey. Fares are US$232 to US$440 depending on the season and availability. Non-U.S. and non-Canadian travelers can buy a 15- to 30-day USA Railpass for US$295 to $US485. The pass can be used for rail connections to Vancouver.

BC Rail, 1311 W. First St., North Vancouver, BC V7P 1A6 (✆ **800/663-8238** or 604/631-3500; www.bcr.com), connects Vancouver to other cities throughout the province. The Cariboo Prospector offers a daily service leaving North Vancouver at 7am and arriving in Whistler at 9:45am. A return ticket, which includes tax and breakfast and dinner, is C$69 (US$46) adults, C$44 (US$29) seniors and children under 12. In May 2001, BC Rail introduced a luxury train service called the Whistler Northwind. The train runs between North Vancouver, Whistler, 100 Mile House, and Prince George from May to October.

Rocky Mountaineer Railtours (✆ **800/665-7245**) offers scenic daylight trips from Vancouver to Jasper, Banff, or Calgary in Alberta. The trip takes 2 days with an overnight stay in Kamloops. One-way fares in the Red Leaf service are C$660 (US$436) adults and C$560 (US$370) children in the high season and C$490 (US$323) adults and C$390 (US$258) children in the low season. In the more up-market Golf Leaf, high-season fares are C$1,190 (US$785) adults and C$1,010 (US$667) children and low-season fares C$880 (US$581) adults and C$700 (US$462) children. Perhaps the best time for families considering a luxury train trip is at Christmas. Between December 20 and 30, the company offers a Christmas train with coaches just for kids, Santa, and various entertainment. Cost one-way is Red Leaf C$510 (US$337) adults, C$199 (US$131) children, and Gold Leaf C$1,010 (US$667) adults, C$399 (US$263) children.

BY BUS

Greyhound Bus Lines (✆ **604/482-8747**) and **Pacific Coach Lines** (✆ **604/662-8074**) also have their terminals at the Pacific Central Station, 1150 Station St. Greyhound Canada's **Canada Pass** offers 7, 10, 15, 21, 30, 45, and 60 days of unlimited travel for C$266 to $640 (US$176 to $422) and the family fare (Canada only), which needs to be booked 7 days in advance and allows one child under 16 to travel free when accompanied by a full-fare passenger. Pacific Coach Lines provides service between Vancouver and Victoria. The cost is C$54 (US$36) for a round-trip adult fare and includes the ferry. There are seven daily departures in winter and more are added in the peak season. **Quick Coach Lines** (✆ **604/940-4428**) connects Vancouver to the Seattle-Tacoma International Airport. The bus leaves from the Holiday Inn, 1110 Howe St., Vancouver, picks up passengers from most major hotels, and stops at the Vancouver International Airport. The 4-hour one-way ride costs C$42 (US$28) adults, C$22 (US$15) children 5 to 12; and round-trip C$76 (US$50) adults, C$40 (US$26) children 5 to 12.

BY CAR

You'll probably drive into Vancouver along one of two routes. U.S. Interstate 5 from Seattle becomes **Highway 99** when you cross the border at the Peace Arch. The 210 kilometer (130 mile) drive takes about 2½ hours. You'll drive through the cities of White Rock, Delta, and Richmond, pass under the Fraser River through the George Massey Tunnel, and cross the Oak Street Bridge. The highway ends there and becomes Oak Street, a very busy urban thoroughfare. Turn left onto 70th Avenue. (A small sign suspended above the left lane at the intersection of Oak Street and 70th Avenue reads CITY CENTRE.) Six blocks later, turn right onto Granville Street. This street heads directly into downtown Vancouver on the Granville Street Bridge.

Trans-Canada Highway 1 is a limited-access freeway, running all the way to Vancouver's eastern boundary, where it crosses the Second Narrows Bridge to North Vancouver. When coming on Highway 1 from the east, exit at Cassiar Street and turn left at the first light onto Hastings Street (Highway 7A), which is adjacent to Exhibition Park. Follow Hastings Street 6 kilometers (4 miles) into downtown. When coming to Vancouver from Whistler or parts north, take Exit 13 (the sign says TAYLOR WAY, BRIDGE TO VANCOUVER) and cross the Lions Gate Bridge into Vancouver's West End.

BY SHIP & FERRY

The Canada Place cruise-ship terminal at the base of Burrard Street (© **604/ 665-9085**) is a city landmark. Topped by five eye-catching white Teflon sails, Canada Place pier juts out into the Burrard Inlet and is at the edge of the downtown financial district. **Princess Cruises, Holland America, Royal Caribbean, Crystal Cruises, Nor-** wegian **Cruise Lines, World Explorer, Majesty Cruise Line, Hanseatic, Seabourne,** and **Carnival** Cruise lines dock at Canada Place and the nearby Ballantyne Pier to board passengers headed for Alaska via British Columbia's Inside Passage. They carry approximately 700,000 passengers annually on more than 250 cruises a year from mid-May to early October. Public-transit buses and taxis greet new arrivals, but you can also easily walk to many major hotels, including the Pan Pacific, Waterfront Centre, and Hotel Vancouver. (If you're considering an Alaska cruise, late May and all of June generally offer the best weather, the most daylight, and the best sightseeing opportunities.)

BC Ferries (© **888/223-3779** or 888/724-5223 automated; www. bcferries.bc.ca) has three Victoria–Vancouver routes. Its large ferries offer on-board facilities such as restaurants, snack bars, gift shops, inside and outside seating, a video arcade, and kids' play area. The one-way fare is C$9 (US$6) adults, C$4.50 (US$3) children 5 to 11, and C$28.50 (US$18.81) per car Monday to Thursday and C$30.25 (US$19.97) Friday to Sunday. Children under 5 ride free. In the summer it is advisable to reserve a space when traveling with a vehicle, especially on long weekends and to and from the Gulf Islands. The cost to reserve a one-way space is C$15 (US$9.90).

The most direct route between the cities is the **Tsawwassen-Swartz Bay** ferry, which operates daily between 7am and 9pm. Ferries run every 2 hours. Check for extra sailings on holidays or during the peak travel season. The actual crossing takes 95 minutes. However, schedule an extra 2 to 3 hours for travel to and from both ferry terminals, including waiting time at the docks. Driving distance from Tsawwassen to Vancouver is about 19 kilometers (12 miles). Take Highway 17 from Tsawwassen until it merges with Highway 99 just before the George Massey Tunnel, then follow the driving directions to Vancouver given in "By Car," above. If you prefer to travel by public transit, TransLink has regular bus service to both terminals. From Swartz Bay, there's regular bus service to Victoria.

The **Mid-Island Express** operates between Tsawwassen and Duke Point, just south of Nanaimo. The 2-hour crossing runs eight times daily between 5:15am and 10:45pm.

The **Horseshoe Bay-Nanaimo ferry** has eight daily sailings, leaving Horseshoe Bay near West Vancouver and arriving 95 minutes later in Nanaimo. From there, passengers bound for Victoria board the E&N Railiner or drive south to Victoria via the Island Highway (Hwy. 1).

To reach Vancouver from Horseshoe Bay, take the Trans-Canada Highway (Highways 1 and 99) east and then take Exit 13 (Taylor Way) to the Lions Gate Bridge and downtown and Vancouver's West End.

BY PACKAGE TOUR

Air Canada (✆ **800/247-2262;** www.aircanada.ca) offers a number of fly/drive packages. And **SNV International,** 402-1045 Howe St., Vancouver (✆ **604/683-5101**), specializes in vacation packages to Vancouver and Victoria.

9 Keeping the Kids Entertained While Traveling

"Are we there yet?" must be a universal question in any language and it can be especially trying when you are anything but there yet. On long drives especially, keeping younger children entertained with their minds off the trip is a real challenge and I clearly remember the looks of fellow passengers as I walked toddlers endlessly up and down those narrow aisles on the plane. When driving, we always try to time the drive around an afternoon nap and a stop for lunch or just to kick a ball around in a park. We pack a large cooler full of snacks and drinks, everything from crackers and carrots to candy and pop that they are not normally allowed. Those water bottles with the sports tops are the greatest invention, and throwing food and drink to those in the back at regular intervals, especially on long trips, works well as entertainment and bribery. Diaper wipes are a great tool also, with or without a baby, as are paper towels and plastic bags. Before the trip we often go to a dollar shop or bargain bin and grab a bunch of small cheap and light toys, gift wrap them, and hand them out every hour or so. The knowledge that those gifts were coming kept them quiet for a while, and the novelty of the toy kept them busy. My husband keeps balloons in his pocket and finds he can keep little ones entertained for ages, blowing them up and kicking them around.

For older children, books are great on planes, though they don't work well in the car. Coloring books, activity books, and crayons are a great diversion, as are cards, magnetic games, "I Spy," and travel-size board games. Cassette tapes of music and books are a good idea.

Older children may be interested in a travel diary or just to write their own story in a blank notebook. For teenagers a radio/cassette with headphones and music you hate will keep them entertained.

Set in Vancouver & BC

Picture Books
Ages 2 to 5
Who Hides in the Park? by Warabe Aska (Tundra Books). A wonderfully illustrated book with a First Nations story set in Stanley Park. Written in English, French, Japanese, and Chinese.

Putting up with Mitchell: My Vancouver Scrapbook by Sarah Ellis, illustrated by Barbara Wood (Brighouse Press). A little dated—there is no longer a Stanley Park Zoo—but still a great story about two kids visiting Vancouver with their grandparents and their thoughts on Chinatown, the Aquarium, and many other local attractions.

The Ferryboat Ride by Roberta Perry, illustrated by Greta Guzek (Nightwood). If you're planning a trip to Victoria this is a great book, written in verse, for little ones. Takes you through illustrations of Active Pass and whales and seagulls.

Melted Star Journey by Nancy Hundal, illustrated by Karen Reczuch (HarperCollins). Luke is driving home from the North Shore with his family, trying not to fall asleep on a rainy Vancouver night.

Ages 4 to 7
Mister Got to Go: The Cat that Wouldn't Leave by Lois Simmie, illustrated by Cynthia Nugent (Northern Lights). Based on a true story about a cat that lived at the Sylvia Hotel in Vancouver's West End and became a local fixture.

Hound without Howl by Deborah Turney-Zagwyn (Orca Book Publishers). The story about an opera lover and his new dog could be set anywhere, but the pictures are definitely Vancouver.

A Present for Mrs. Kazinski by Marilynn Reynolds, illustrated by Lynn Smith-Ary (Orca Book Publishers). Set in Commercial Drive—known as "the Drive" to locals in East Vancouver.

Ages 6 to 12
Wow Canada! Exploring this Land from Coast to Coast by Vivien Bowers (Owl Books). Won the 2000 BC Book Prize, because it's such a wonderfully written and uniquely illustrated book written from a child's perspective as he and his family drive across Canada starting from Victoria. Kids won't even realize they are learning stuff.

Mr. McUmphie of Caulfield Cove by Ainslie Manson, illustrated by Janet Stethem (Queenston House Publishing). A brother and sister befriend an old sea captain now living in a cave near their West Vancouver house.

Raymond's Raindance by Harrill Bjornson, illustrated by Roy Peterson (Skoal House). Set in North Vancouver's Lynn Valley, a young boy is bedridden for 2 months and learns all about the birds who visit his home. Pictures are by one of Canada's best-known editorial cartoonists.

Ages 8 to 12
What's a Daring Detective Like Me Doing in the Doghouse? by Linda Bailey (Kids Can Press). A Stevie Diamond mystery about a girl living in Vancouver who works at a doggie daycare during spring break and finds the dog that was stolen from the President of the United States who was visiting the Canadian Prime Minister at a summit.

10 and up

Tales from Gold Mountain: Stories of the Chinese in the New World by Paul Yee, illustrated by Simon Ng (Douglas & McIntyre). The author, a historian who grew up in Vancouver's Chinatown, has written a collection of stories about the role of the Chinese immigrant in Canadian history.

Vancouver Short Stories edited by Carole Gerson (UBC Press). Stories of our city's social and cultural life described by famous Canadian writers and spanning a period of 80 years.

3

Getting to Know Vancouver

As cities go, Vancouver is pretty new. Since Expo 86 it has reinvented itself as a more cosmopolitan city with a thriving multicultural population and the restaurants, entertainment, and shopping that it deserves. Don't restrict yourself to downtown Vancouver; many diverse neighborhoods across the city are well worth exploring. If you have trouble with your sense of direction, look to the mountains—they are always pointing north. If you're facing them, east is right, west is left, and turn around and you're pointing south.

1 Orientation

VISITOR INFORMATION

The **Vancouver Tourist InfoCentre,** 200 Burrard St. (© **604/683-2000;** www.tourismvancouver.com), is your single best travel information source about Vancouver. You can buy bus passes and pick up maps, brochures, and travel guides here. The staff is outgoing and can be very helpful if you need directions or recommendations. The InfoCentre will make hotel reservations for you, and there is a phone where you can book bed-and-breakfasts yourself. The Info-Centre is open daily from May to Labour Day from 8am to 7pm; the rest of the year, it's open Monday to Friday from 8:30am to 5pm, and Saturday 9am to 5pm.

For the North Shore, the **Chamber of Commerce,** 131 East 2nd St. (at Lonsdale Ave.), North Vancouver (© **604/987-4488**), is open Monday to Friday 9am to 5pm year-round. From mid-May to mid-September the North Vancouver Visitor Information Centres are open daily 9am to 6pm at the foot of Lonsdale Street, next to Lonsdale Quay (© **604/984-8588**), and at the southeast corner of Capilano Road, just as you come off the Lions Gate Bridge (© **604/980-5332**).

Tourism Richmond, 11980 Deas Thruway (© **604/271-8280**), has information about the Richmond area, including the heritage fishing village of Steveston. It's open daily from 9am to 7pm in July and August and daily from 10am to 4pm September through June. The office is located north of the George Massey Tunnel.

Tourist Information Delta, 6201-60 Ave., Ladner (© **604/946-4232**), has information about Tsawwassen, Delta, and Ladner. It's open Monday to Friday 8:30am to 4:30pm.

If you plan to see more of British Columbia, **Super, Natural British Columbia** (© **800/HELLOBC;** www.hellobc.com) can help you.

The two local parent monthlies have calendars of upcoming events and entertainment options for kids, and you can pick up *WestCoast Families* magazine and *BC Parent Newsmagazine* free at public libraries, recreational centers, malls, and just about anywhere kids hang out. The annual *Kids' Guide* put out by *Where* magazine is an excellent resource and you can find it at tourist information centers, hotels, and border crossings. For more information check the *Vancouver Sun,* the city's largest daily newspaper, the *Georgia Straight,* a free weekly found at most of the same places as the parenting magazines, and *Vancouver Magazine,* a monthly fashion and city magazine available at the newsstands. A full list of websites is included in chapter 2, "Planning Your Trip," p. 25.

CITY LAYOUT

If you were looking for the core of Vancouver you would find it about where Granville Street intersects Georgia Street. Here you are flanked by two large department stores, at the pulse of underground shopping malls, and in the financial district of Vancouver. Move to the east toward BC Place Stadium and General Motors Place and you are in the entertainment district. To the west is Vancouver's residential area, the West End. Turn northwest and you'll enter Stanley Park, and due north you'll see the mountains and the North Shore of Vancouver. To the south is Yaletown and further still, False Creek.

MAIN ARTERIES & STREETS

If you are coming from the airport, most likely you will take the Arthur Laing Bridge and enter Vancouver by **Granville Street.** Granville Street snakes through West Side neighborhoods, crosses False Creek at the Granville Street Bridge, and cuts right through the core of the city until it ends at the Burrard Inlet near Waterfront Station. In the downtown area the street turns into a mall and is no longer accessible by car, so if you are driving, you'll most likely enter downtown by Seymour Street. Once downtown there are four key east-west streets. **Robson Street** starts at BC Place Stadium on Beatty Street and ends at Lagoon Drive, at the tip of Stanley Park. While walking is most pleasant on Robson Street, **Georgia Street,** which runs parallel to Robson, is the main thoroughfare for drivers. It runs from the Georgia Viaduct on the eastern edge of downtown, through Vancouver's commercial core, and continues through Stanley Park and over the Lions Gate Bridge to the North Shore. Three blocks north of Georgia is **Hastings Street,** which begins in the West End, runs east through downtown and along Gastown, and then heads east to the Trans-Canada Highway. **Davie Street** starts at Pacific Boulevard near the Cambie Street Bridge, travels through Yaletown, through the West End, and ends at English Bay Beach.

Two blocks east of Stanley Park is **Denman Street,** which runs from West Georgia Street at Coal Harbour to Beach Avenue at English Bay Beach. It's the shortest north-south route between the two ends of the Stanley Park Seawall, the quickest route from the West Side of the city to the North Shore, and is dotted with restaurants, ice-cream parlors, and coffee shops.

Eight blocks east of Denman is **Burrard Street,** which starts near Canada Place and runs south through downtown, crosses the Burrard Street Bridge, and angles sharply to enter the West Side of Vancouver. Burrard Street passes **West Fourth Avenue** and **Broadway Avenue,** two main shopping areas in Kitsilano, and ends at **West 16th Avenue.** If you were to continue across Burrard Street and hug the coast, you would head along **Cornwall Avenue,** skirt **Vanier Park,** and head west until the road changes to **Point Grey Road** and then **Northwest Marine Drive** and enters the campus of the University of British Columbia.

On the mainland portion of Vancouver, the city's east-west roads are numbered from First Avenue closest to False Creek to 77th Avenue by the banks of the Fraser River. **Broadway** (which substitutes for 9th Avenue) is the most important east-west route and starts a few blocks from the University of British

Greater Vancouver

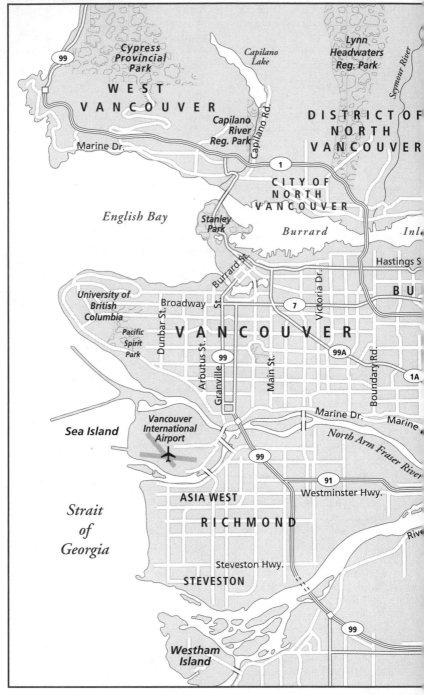

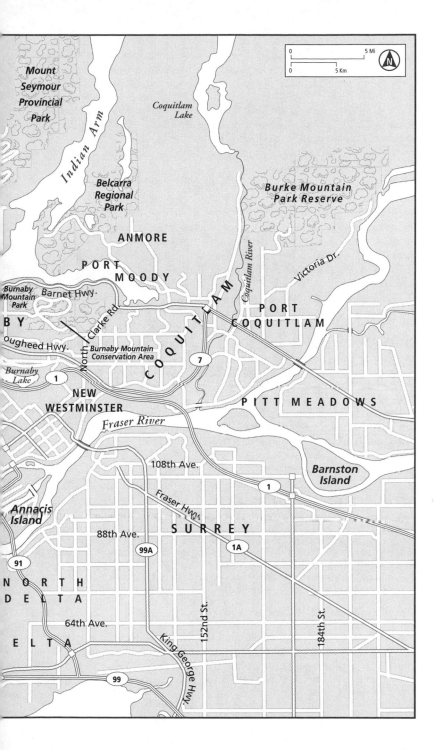

Mount
Seymour
Provincial
Park

Indian Arm

*Coquitlam
Lake*

Belcarra
Regional
Park

Burke Mountain
Park Reserve

ANMORE

Coquitlam River

Victoria Dr.

P O R T
M O O D Y

Burnaby
Mountain
Park

Barnet Hwy.

P O R T
C O Q U I T L A M

B Y

North Clarke Rd.

C O Q U I T L A M

ougheed Hwy.

Burnaby Mountain
Conservation Area

7

*Burnaby
Lake*

1

NEW
WESTMINSTER

P I T T   M E A D O W S

Fraser River

108th Ave.

*Barnston
Island*

1

*Annacis
Island*

Fraser Hwy.

S U R R E Y

88th Ave.

99A

1A

91

N O R T H

D E L T A

64th Ave.

King George Hwy.

152nd St.

184th St.

E L T A

99

0 _____ 5 Mi
0 _____ 5 Km

N

Columbia (UBC) and extends across the length of the city to the border of neighboring Burnaby, where it becomes the Lougheed Highway. In Kitsilano, **West Fourth Avenue** is also an important east-west shopping and commercial corridor. Intersecting with Broadway at various points are a number of important north-south commercial streets, each of which defines a particular neighborhood. The most significant of these streets are (from west to east) **MacDonald Street** in Kitsilano; **Granville Street, Cambie Street,** and **Main Street** downtown; and **Commercial Drive** in East Vancouver.

FINDING AN ADDRESS   In downtown Vancouver, Chinatown's Carrall Street is the east-west axis from which streets are numbered and designated. Westward, numbers increase progressively to Stanley Park; eastward, numbers increase heading toward Commercial Drive. For example, 400 W. Pender St. would be about 4 blocks from Carrall Street heading toward downtown; 400 E. Pender St. would be 4 blocks on the opposite side of Carrall Street.

Similarly, the low numbers on north-south streets start on the Canada Place Pier side and increase southward in increments of 100 per block (the 600 block of Thurlow Street is 2 blocks from the 800 block) toward False Creek and Granville Island.

Off the peninsula, the system works the same, but Ontario Street is the east-west axis. Also, all east-west roads are avenues (for example, 4th Avenue), while streets (for example, Main Street) run exclusively north-south.

STREET MAPS   The Travel Information Centres (see "Visitor Information," above) and most hotels can provide you with detailed downtown maps. A good all-around metropolitan area map is the Rand McNally Vancouver city map, which is available for C$3 (US$2) at the Vancouver Airport Tourism Centre kiosk. If you're an auto club member, the Canadian Automobile Association (CAA) map is also good. It's not for sale, but is free to both AAA and CAA members and is available at AAA offices across North America. **International Travel Maps and Books,** 552 Seymour St. (© **604/687-3320**), has the city's most extensive selection of Vancouver and British Columbia maps and specialty guide books.

NEIGHBORHOODS IN BRIEF

If you look at a map of the Lower Mainland, the City of Vancouver stands out like a giant mitten. At the tip of the thumb is Stanley Park and the West End, leading to the downtown core, and just before the thumb joins the rest of the hand is East Vancouver. The University of British Columbia (UBC) is at the finger tips. The West Side is the rest of the hand. At about the sleeve line is Burnaby, and New Westminster and Coquitlam then follow down the arm. The Vancouver International Airport and Richmond fall to the left of the mitten.

If you were looking at a highly detailed map of the city, you would see 22 "local areas" within the city limits. I've highlighted a few of them below. But, for simplicity's sake, we can pretty much carve the city of Vancouver up into east and west. East is easy; it's west that becomes confusing. However, visitors to the city are most likely going to be concerned about west—it's the downtown of the city, the bustling West End, and the West Side with its beaches, and that's where I've chosen to give a glimpse of these neighborhoods.

There's West, and Then There's West

When you hear people discussing the West Side, the West End, and West Vancouver, they mean three quite different areas. If you go back to the map you'll see the West End as an extension of the downtown area spreading out to Stanley Park to the northwest. It's a high-rise residential neighborhood described below, whereas the West Side is roughly a half of Vancouver, stretching from Ontario Street west to the University of British Columbia. West Vancouver and North Vancouver form the North Shore, and West Vancouver is really west of North Vancouver, rather than west of downtown Vancouver. Whew.

Downtown   Unlike residents of many North American cities, a lot of us tend to stick around downtown once business hours are over. We often choose to live near our work, in the hub of the city, and for that reason, it never really empties and it's always fairly safe. Part of the reason is that the central business district is bordered on two ends by stretches of water—the Burrard Inlet to the north and False Creek to the south. The core, where Georgia Street intersects Granville Street, is where you find the two largest department stores—Eatons and the Bay facing off each other—and the major underground shopping centers of Pacific Centre and Vancouver Centre. The rest of the central business district runs from Burrard Street to Homer Street at its eastern edge. Howe Street has long been home to the brokerage and finance community and there are hotels and restaurants throughout this area.

Gastown   Minutes from the downtown core, Gastown was originally the pulse of the city when it was incorporated as the City of Vancouver in 1886. It got its name from former steamship operator John "Gassy Jack" Deighton, obviously a chatty fellow who owned the first bar, a wooden shack at the corner of what is now Carrall and Water streets. In those days it was a hard-living kind of town, home to hotels, saloons, and shops that served the lumberjacks and speculators, and in the same year of its incorporation, it burned to the ground. Now it sells great art and not-so-great curios, but it has some really distinctive architecture and its cobblestone streets,

its gas lamps, and the steam clock put it on just about every visitor's list. While Gastown is quite safe to wander around during the day, be a little more cautious at night. Gastown borders on the downtown East Side, one of the poorest areas in Canada, and has a significant drug and homeless problem. Be careful about going too far east on Hastings Street toward Main Street.

Chinatown   Located south of Hastings Street, between Gore and Carrall streets to the east and west, and Keefer Street to the south, you can take your time discovering this area, or just drop in for a meal. It's a noisy sensory experience with all the mystique of the east. Chinatown is always bustling. There is the sound of foreign and exotic languages, the smells wafting from the restaurants, the appearance of vegetables like durian and the clam-like phallic-looking geoduck, giant crabs, dried oysters, and eels, which you normally don't encounter in the neighborhood grocery store. There are novelty gifts, bamboo and rattan furniture, trading companies, fresh vegetables, and, before the government cracked down on such things, tiger testicles and bear bladders found in musty Chinese pharmacies. Again, Chinatown is perfectly safe but it borders on a problem area. Try to avoid the Hastings and Main streets intersection.

Yaletown   You could be forgiven for thinking you've landed in Europe. Yaletown is quite unlike the rest of the city. Bounded by Nelson, Homer, and Drake streets and Pacific Boulevard, Yaletown was once a warehouse district. Rather than rip them down, city planners found that the loading docks transformed into terraces and outdoor cafes and the low brick buildings made offices and condos. Soon young singles mostly with large incomes began to move in to the area and were followed, or preceded (it's like the chicken and the egg) by tony furniture stores, leading-edge designers, and advertising agencies. At one time the area was dubbed the Internet capital of Canada, with dot-coms housed in offices built of exposed bricks and sticks. You can still see early rooming houses and late 19th-century warehouses, but now it has a residential population of more than 20,000 and some of the city's better restaurants, art galleries, and a lot of loft-style living.

The West End   Shaped like a large triangle, the West End stretches from Coal Harbour to English Bay with Stanley Park on one side and Burrard Street on the other. It is a vibrant urban center, alive day and night, and is the most densely populated area in Canada, and perhaps in North America. You'll find highrise condos mixed with magical turn-of-the-century Queen Anne homes, wonderful restaurants, bookshops, an active community center, and the world's best ice cream. There are three major streets, each seven blocks long: Denman Street, a strip that seems to be mostly about eating, Davie Street with more restaurants, nightlife, and shopping, and Robson Street with its coffee houses and designer shops. English Bay Beach, where Denman and Davie streets intersect, is a sandy swimming beach with some of the most incredible views in the world. And then, of course, there is Stanley Park, a rain forest in the middle of the city filled with treasures for any age to explore.

The East End   Known to locals as East Van, there are beautiful old neighborhoods with tree-lined streets, the waterfront that skirts the Burrard Inlet, lovely parks, Trout Lake, and people who would never live anywhere else. But whereas property values began to skyrocket on the West Side following Expo 86, East Van remained largely the working class district, or Vancouver's poorer cousin. The East Side covers the mainland portion of the city, from Ontario Street east to Boundary Road and over to Grandview Highway to the south. It is also home to Commercial Drive, a long strip of street that locals have dubbed "the Drive," and the colorful home to an assortment of immigrant groups that have arrived in Vancouver. You can see a bit of the history in the restaurants—Italian espresso and pizza, Portuguese, Honduran, Guatemalan, and, more recently, trendy organic and vegetarian.

Granville Island   It's come a long way from the early part of the last century, when False Creek was little more than an industrial sewer. Now Granville Island is one of Vancouver's biggest tourist attractions, and an equally important place to locals. The idea of an island conjures up a lot of images that Granville Island is not, and it's hard to describe, because it really has so much. The enormous public market offers up entertainment and sustenance to everyone; there is a lively arts and crafts community, much of it visible to a visitor. In summer, there is the gargantuan waterpark, and year-round there are the Kids' Market, the parks, and all the interesting discoveries along the waterfront. Much of the entertainment is free behind the market, but Granville Island also has three theaters that stage some fine productions.

Kitsilano Known to locals as Kits, the area comprises Kitsilano Beach and Vanier Park (home of the Vancouver Children's Festival in the spring and Bard on the Beach, a summer-long Shakespeare Festival), as well as the Vancouver Museum, Maritime Museum, and H.R. MacMillan Planetarium. In the 1960s, Kitsilano was Canada's Haight-Ashbury, home to hippies and other recent arrivals to the city. It's no longer a cheap place to find a room, and has long since been left to singles and families who live in the many townhouses or can afford some of the beautiful old rambling houses along the tree-lined streets. Along the stretch of Cornwall Street that's closest to Kits Beach is a lively area of restaurants and nightspots. Most of the older houses have succumbed to denser apartment living. The main streets for eating and shopping in designer boutiques, upscale furniture stores, and interesting restaurants are West 4th Avenue and West Broadway with most of the action between Burrard and MacDonald streets. The boundaries are from Blenheim Street east to Main Street north of 33rd Avenue.

Shaughnessy The Canadian Pacific Railway first developed this neighborhood, which stretches from 16th to 41st avenues, for the city's elite in 1907, and it remains the city's poshest residential suburb. Shaughnessy has an estate-like character with large lots, curving streets, and manicured lawns. Hidden away behind tall trees and high gates, it takes a determined effort to see the stately homes and mansions, many

of which are now featured in film shoots. The center of opulence is the Crescent, a street that wraps itself around a park on the southwest of Granville and 16th Avenue. It's worth a drive through on your way to or from the airport. If you're coming from downtown Vancouver, turn left at Angus Drive, just past West 16th Avenue. If you're looking for a lay of the land, visit the VanDusen Gardens, also part of Shaughnessy.

Southlands This is a rural equestrian paradise virtually in the middle of the city. Southlands is bounded by Southwest Marine Drive to the north and the Fraser River to the south and bookended by two golf courses. In fact, the neighborhood has six parks, two public and three championship-rated private golf courses, the Southlands Riding Club, the Musqueam Reserve, and a trail network used by hikers and equestrians that begins at Musqueam Park and runs along the Fraser River. Here you'll find a mixture of multimillion dollar mansions, tumbled-down houses, shipyards, and secluded river lookouts. Enter from either Southwest Marine Drive or 49th Avenue, watch out for horses and flying golf balls, and amble your way down there.

The North Shore Drive over the Lions Gate Bridge and to your right stretches North Vancouver, which runs east to Deep Cove, a spectacularly beautiful village where mountains, trees, and ocean converge. (For those with a literary bent, the Cates Park end was the home of Malcolm Lowry in the 1940s.) To the north is Grouse Mountain, to the east is Lynn Canyon Park with its many hiking trails and roaring creeks, the Mount Seymour Provincial Park, and much to explore in between. If you turn left at the Lions Gate Bridge, you are in West Vancouver, an area that consistently seems to record the highest per capita income in Canada. To the west are Horseshoe Bay and the ferry terminal to the Sunshine Coast and Nanaimo, on Vancouver Island. Along windy Marine Drive are breathtaking views, cliff-hugging mansions, the beaches of Ambleside and Dundarave, and the little seaside-village-like treats of Caulfield Cove and Whytecliffe Park. Above are the stunning city views from Cypress Mountain.

Burnaby   Bounded by the Burrard Inlet on the north and the north arm of the Fraser River on the south, and just 10 kilometers (6 miles) east of downtown Vancouver, Burnaby is the mountain home to Simon Fraser University (on Burnaby Mountain) and houses the huge Burnaby Lake Regional Park and a wildlife sanctuary, beaches, old-growth forests, and a mega shopping center complex. The third largest city in British Columbia, Burnaby is also gaining an artistic reputation, as Deer Park Lake is home to the Burnaby Art Gallery, the Burnaby Arts Council, the Burnaby Arts Centre, and Shadbolt Centre for the Arts. Next door is the Burnaby Village Museum, a historical village set on 5 acres of beautiful gardens. Central Park, at Boundary Road and Kingsway, has a lake, pitch'n'putt, tennis courts, swimming pool, jogging trails, and sports events at Swangard Stadium.

New Westminster   Sitting on the banks of the Fraser River, New Westminster is just 9.6 square kilo-meters (3.7 sq. ft.) in size and was once, albeit briefly, the capital of British Columbia. It has the distinction of being the oldest Canadian city west of the Great Lakes, and you can still see much of its history. The city began as a result of the gold rush on the Fraser River, and as the gold rush moved on, it forged out a strong industrial position in fish, lumber, and shipbuilding. If you stroll on the esplanade along the Fraser River you can watch the working tugs, fish boats, log booms, and tour boats, maybe even a seal. Westminster Quay offers a public market, a hotel, a maritime museum, and river cruises of the Fraser River.

Richmond   As you enter Richmond you'll see the sign that says ISLAND CITY, BY NATURE. It's cradled between the north and south arms of the Fraser River and was not so very long ago a farming and fishing community. In the last 20 years, Richmond has seen a population explosion and although it still has agricultural land and cranberry fields, much has turned into high-rise towers, lavish Asian shopping centers, hotels, and restaurants. Behind its urban center, though, are over 50 kilometers (31 miles) of trails, dikes and beaches, and Minoru Park, where you can swim, ice skate, bowl, or see a play. Richmond can also thank its tenant, the Vancouver International Airport, and the large and recent Chinese immigration for its huge growth. At the southwestern corner is the fishing port of Steveston, a quaint village with a small-town atmosphere and lots of restaurants and shops to poke around in.

2 Getting Around

BY PUBLIC TRANSPORTATION

The TransLink system includes electric buses, SeaBus catamaran ferries, and the driverless SkyTrain, and connects most places in the Greater Vancouver area from A to B including the beaches and the ski hills. Regular service on the main routes runs from 5am to 2am.

Schedules and routes are available at the Travel Info Centres, at many hotels, the public libraries, www.translink.bc.ca, and on the buses or by calling **TransLink** (© **604/521-0400**). Pick up a copy of *Discover Vancouver on Transit* at one of the Travel Info Centres (see "Visitor Information," earlier in this chapter). This publication gives transit routes for many city neighborhoods, landmarks, and attractions.

FARES   Fares are the same for the buses, SeaBus, and SkyTrain. One-way, all-zone fares are C$1.75 (US$1.15) for adults and C$1.25 (US83¢) for children 5 to 13, students, and seniors, after 6:30pm on weekdays and all day on weekends and holidays. At other times, a one-zone fare costs C$1.75 (US$1.15) for adults and C$1.25 (US83¢) for children 5 to 13, and covers the entire city of Vancouver. A two-zone fare—C$2.50 (US$1.65) for adults, C$1.75 (US$1.15) for children 5 to 13—is required to travel to nearby suburbs such as Richmond or North Vancouver, and a three-zone fare—C$3.50 (US$2.30) for adults, C$2.50 (US$1.65) for children 5 to 13—is required to travel further afield, say Surrey. Children under 5 travel free. Free transfers are available on boarding and are good for travel in any direction and for the SkyTrain and SeaBus, but they do have a 90-minute expiration. **DayPasses,** which are good on all public transit, are C$7 (US$4.62) adults, C$5 (US$3.30) children 5 to 13, and free for children under 5. They can be used for unlimited travel on weekdays or weekends and holidays. Tickets and passes are available at Travel Info Centres, both SeaBus terminals, convenience stores, drugstores, credit unions, and other outlets displaying the "FareDealer" symbol.

BY SKYTRAIN   The SkyTrain is a computerized, magnetic-rail train that services 20 stations along its 35-minute trip from downtown Vancouver east to Surrey through Burnaby and New Westminster. Construction of a new SkyTrain line—the Millennium Line—is expected to be complete by the end of 2001.

BY SEABUS   The *Burrard Beaver* and the *Burrard Otter* catamaran ferries annually take more than 700,000 passengers, cyclists, and wheelchair riders on a scenic 12-minute commute between downtown's Waterfront Station and North Vancouver's Lonsdale Quay. On weekdays a SeaBus leaves each stop every 15 minutes from 6:15am to 6:45pm, then every 30 minutes until 12:30am. SeaBuses depart on Saturdays every half-hour from 6:15am to 10:15am, then every 15 minutes until 6:15pm, then every half-hour until 12:30am. On Sundays and holidays, runs depart every half-hour from 8:30am to 11pm; however, there are increased sailings during the peak summer months.

BY BUS   There are some key routes to keep in mind if you're touring the city by bus: no. 5 (Robson Street), no. 22 (Kitsilano Beach to downtown), no. 50 (Granville Island), no. 35 or 135 (to the Stanley Park bus loop), no. 240 (North Vancouver), no. 250 (West Vancouver-Horseshoe Bay), and buses nos. 4 and 10 (UBC to Exhibition Park via Granville Street downtown). In the summer months from mid-June until mid-September, the Vancouver Parks Board operates the Stanley Park Shuttle, a free bus service through Stanley Park. The run starts at the Children's Miniature Railway and there are 14 stops around the park. You can get on and off whenever you want. The bus runs every 15 minutes between 10am and 6:30pm daily (© **604/257-8400**).

BY TAXI   Cab fares start at C$2.30 (US$1.52) and increase at a rate of C$1.25 (US83¢) per kilometer, plus C30¢ (US20¢) per minute at stoplights. It's a little lower than in most other major cities, but it still adds up pretty quickly. In the downtown area, you can expect to travel for less than C$6 (US$4) plus tip. The typical fare for the 13 kilometer (8 mile) drive from downtown to the airport is C$25 (US$16.50). Other approximate fares are downtown to Stanley Park C$7 (US$4.62); downtown to Tsawwassen ferry terminal C$53 (US$35); downtown to Horseshoe Bay ferry terminal C$32 (US$21); and downtown to the University of British Columbia (UBC) C$21 (US$14).

Taxis are easy to find in front of major hotels, but flagging one can be tricky. Most drivers are usually on radio calls. Thanks to built-in satellite positioning systems, if you call for a taxi, it usually arrives faster than if you go out and hail one. Call for a pickup from **Black Top** (© **604/731-1111**), **Yellow Cab** (© **604/681-1111**), **Vancouver Taxi** (© **604/871-1111**), or **MacLure's** (© **604/731-9211**). **AirLimo** (© **604/273-1331**) offers flat-rate stretch limousine service. AirLimo charges C$32 (US$21) per trip to the airport (not per person), plus tax and tip. The drivers accept all major credit cards.

BY CAR   Vancouver has nowhere the near-permanent gridlock of northwest cities like Seattle, but neither are the roads exactly empty. Fortunately, if you're just sightseeing around the downtown area, public transit and cabs should see you through. However, if you are planning to visit the North Shore or other places that are further afield, a car is a great time saver and much easier when you have small children who need strollers and diapers and snacks and changes of clothes and all the other paraphernalia required.

Gas is sold by the liter, and the average is C70¢ (US46¢) for a liter of regular. Speeds and distances are posted in kilometers.

RENTALS   Rates vary widely depending on demand and style of car. Most rental companies also have a line of minivans and sports utility vehicles. If you're over 25 and have a major credit card, you can rent a vehicle from **Avis,** 757 Hornby St. (© **800/879-2847** or 604/606-2847; www.avis.com); **Budget,** 501 W. Georgia St. or 1705 Burrard St. (© **800/472-3325,** 800/527-0700, or 604/ 668-7000; www.bc.budget.com); **Enterprise,** 585 Smithe St. (© **800/736-8222** or 604/688-5500; www.enterprise.com); **Hertz Canada,** 1128 Seymour St. (© **800/263-0600** or 604/688-2411; www.hertz.com); **National Car Rental,** 1130 W. Georgia St. (© **800/387-4747** or 604/685-6111; www.nationalcar .com); or **Thrifty,** 1015 Burrard St. or 1400 Robson St. (© **800/847-4389** or 604/606-1666; www.thrifty.com). These firms all have counters and shuttle service at the airport as well. To rent a recreational vehicle, contact **CC Canada Camper RV Rentals,** 4431 Vanguard Rd., Richmond (© **604/270-1833;** www.canada-camper.com). Not exactly my idea of a family sedan, but at **Exotic Motorcycle & Car Rentals,** 1820 Burrard St. (© **877/327-3003** or 604/644-9128; www.exoticcars.com), you can rent a Ferrari, Viper, Porsche, Hummer, Jaguar, or Corvette. A wide selection of Harley-Davidson motorcycles is also available by the day (C$227/US$150, which includes helmets, gloves, and leather jackets for two).

PARKING   All major downtown hotels have guest parking; rates vary from free to C$20 (US$13) a day. There's public parking at **Robson Square** (enter at Smithe and Howe streets), the **Pacific Centre** (Howe and Dunsmuir streets), and **The Bay** department store (Richards near Dunsmuir Street). You'll also find parking lots at Thurlow and Georgia streets, Thurlow and Alberni streets, Robson and Seymour streets, and at the Vancouver Public Library (entrance is on Hamilton Street and you enter from West Georgia). Public parking is approximately C$2 (US$1.32) for a half-hour or C$10 (US$6.60) for the day.

Metered street parking isn't impossible to come by, but it may take a trip or three around the block to find a spot. Rules are posted on the street and are invariably strictly enforced. (Drivers are given about 2 minutes' grace before their cars are towed away when the 3pm no-parking rule goes into effect on many major thoroughfares.) Unmetered parking on side streets is often subject to neighborhood residency requirements. Check the signs. If you park in such an area without the appropriate sticker on your windshield, eventually you'll get ticketed, then towed. If your car is towed away or if you need a towing service and aren't a member of CAA, BCAA, or AAA, call **Unitow** (✆ **604/251-1255**) or **Busters** (✆ **604/685-8181**).

SPECIAL DRIVING RULES   Canadian driving rules are similar to those in the United States. Stopping for pedestrians is required even outside crosswalks. Seat belts are mandatory. Children under 5 must be in child restraints. Motorists must yield to buses. Motorcyclists must wear helmets. It's legal to turn right at a red light after coming to a full stop unless posted otherwise. Unlike in the United States, however, daytime headlights are required. Finally, the police have recently discovered the joys of automated ticketing: photo radar is used extensively in Vancouver, and photo-monitored intersections are becoming more common. If you speed or go through a red light, you may get an expensive picture of your vacation from the Royal Canadian Mounted Police. Fines start at C$100 (US$66).

AUTO CLUB   Members of the American Automobile Association (AAA) can get assistance from the **British Columbia Automobile Association** (BCAA), 999 West Broadway, Vancouver (✆ **604/268-5600,** or for road service 604/293-2222).

BY BIKE

Especially if you stick to the designated bike routes, the trails, and the seawalls, you'll find that Vancouver is a bicycle-friendly city and touring by bike is a great way to experience it. There are plenty of places to rent a bike along Robson and Denman streets near Stanley Park. (For specifics, see "Biking" in chapter 7.) Bike routes are designated throughout the city. Paved paths crisscross through parks and along beaches, and new routes are constantly being added. Helmets are mandatory and riding on sidewalks is illegal except on designated bike paths.

Cycling BC (✆ **604/737-3034;** www.cycling.bc.ca) accommodates cyclists on the SkyTrain and buses by providing "Bike & Ride" lockers at all "Park & Ride" parking lots. The department also dispenses loads of information about events, bike touring, and cycle insurance. Many downtown parking lots and garages also have no-fee bike racks.

You can take your bike on the SeaBus anytime at no extra charge. Bikes are not allowed in the George Massey Tunnel, but a tunnel shuttle operates four times daily mid-May through September to transport you across the Fraser River. From May 1 to Victoria Day (the third weekend of May), the service operates on weekends only.

All the West Vancouver blue buses (including the buses to the Horseshoe Bay ferry terminal) can carry two bikes, first-come, first-served, free of charge. In Vancouver, only a limited number of suburban routes allow bikes on the bus: bus 351 to White Rock, bus 601 to South Delta, bus 404 to the airport, and the 99 Express to UBC.

BY FERRY

Vancouver is a city on the water, and one of the best ways to get around it (and the cheapest) is by one of the mini-ferries. There are two outfits that offer regular commuter service across False Creek to various destinations and depending on the distance, the fares range from C$2 to $5 (US$1.32 to $3.30), and C$1 to $3) (US66¢ to $2) for children 4 to 12. Children under 4 are free. Aquabus runs ferries from Granville Island to Hornby Street and Yaletown, from Hornby Street to Yaletown, from Granville Island to Stamps Landing, from Yaletown to Stamps Landing, from Yaletown to Science World, from Stamps Landing to Science World, and from Granville Island to Science World. **Aquabus** (✆ **604/689-5858;** www.aquabus.bc.ca) also offers a 25-minute mini-cruise at C$6 (US$4) for adults and C$3 (US$2) for children 4 to 12 that leaves from Granville Island dock (beside the Arts Club Theatre) about every 20 minutes daily from 9am to 7pm. Bikes are an extra C50¢ (US33¢) on all routes.

The **Granville Island Ferry** (✆ **604/684-7781;** www.granvilleislandferries.bc.ca) offers a continuous shuttle service between Granville Island, Vanier Park, the Aquatic Centre, Stamps Landing, and Science World. Granville Island Ferries offers an Adventure Pass where you can travel to all stops and get on and off the ferry as you wish at C$12 (US$8) for adults, C$8 (US$5.28) for children under 12. Ferries to Granville Island leave every 5 minutes from 7am to 9pm. Ferries to Vanier Park leave every 15 minutes from 10am to 8pm (in summer).

ⒸⒻ *FAST FACTS:* Vancouver

American Express   666 Burrard St. (corner Hornby and Dunsmuir sts.) ✆ **604/669-2813.** It's open Monday to Friday 8am to 5:30pm, Saturday 10am to 4pm.

Area Codes   The telephone area code for the lower mainland, including greater Vancouver and Whistler, is **604.** The area code for Vancouver Island, the Gulf Islands, and the interior of the province is **250.** By November 3, 2001, 10-digit phone numbers will be mandatory. In other words, dial the area code before the phone number even if you are calling next door. The telephone company is also introducing a new area code (**778**), which will come into effect in November. It means that one household or business could essentially have two different area codes.

Babysitters   Most major hotels can arrange babysitting service and have cribs available. If you need cribs, car seats, playpens, or other baby accessories, **Cribs and Carriages** in North Vancouver (✆ **604/988-2742**) delivers them right to your hotel. This is not cheap. While daily rental fees range from C$3 (US$2) for an infant seat to C$6 (US$3.30) for a jogging stroller, the charge for delivery one-way can be C$20 (US$13.20) or higher.

Business Hours   Vancouver **banks** are open Monday to Thursday from 10am to 5pm and Friday from 10am to 6pm. Some banks, such as Canadian Trust, are also open on Saturday. Retail stores are generally open Monday to Thursday and Saturday 10am to 6pm, Friday 10am to 9pm, and Sunday and public holidays noon to 5pm. Last call at the city's restaurant bars and cocktail lounges is 2am.

Consulates   The U.S. Consulate General is at the 21st Floor, 1095 W. Pender St. (✆ **604/685-4311**). The British Consulate General is at 800-1111 Melville St. (✆ **604/683-4421**). The Australian Consulate is at 1225-888 Dunsmuir St. (✆ **604/684-1177**). Check the telephone book for other countries.

Currency Exchange   Banks and ATMs have a better exchange rate than most foreign exchange bureaus (the latter charge transaction and service fees). See "Money," in chapter 2.

Dentist   Most major hotels have a dentist on call. **Vancouver Centre Dental Clinic,** Vancouver Centre Mall, 11-650 W. Georgia St. (✆ **604/682-1601**), is another option. You must make an appointment. The clinic is open Monday through Wednesday 8:30am to 6pm, Thursday 8:30am to 7pm, Friday 9am to 6pm, and Saturday 9am to 4pm. **The City Square Dental Clinic,** at 5-555 W. 12th Avenue (at Cambie St. and opposite the Safeway) (✆ **604/876-4537**), is open Tuesday to Thursday 8am to 9pm, Friday 8am to 6pm, and Saturday 9am to 5pm.

Doctor   Hotels usually have a doctor on call. **Vancouver Medical Clinic,** Bentall Centre, 1055 Dunsmuir St. (✆ **604/683-8138**), is a drop-in clinic open Monday to Friday 8am to 4:45pm. Another drop-in medical center, **Carepoint Medical Centre,** 1175 Denman St. (✆ **604/681-5338**), is open daily from 9am to 9pm, and the **Seymour Medical Clinic,** 1530 W. 7th Ave. (at Granville St.) (✆ **604/738-2151**), is open Monday to Friday 8:30am to 9pm, and Saturday 8:30am to 5pm. See also "Emergencies," below.

Electricity   As in the United States, electric current is 110 volts AC (60 cycles).

Emergencies   Dial ✆ **911** for fire, police, ambulance, and poison control.

Hospitals   **St. Paul's Hospital,** 1081 Burrard St. (at Davie St.) (✆ **604/682-2344**), is the closest facility to downtown and the West End. West Side Vancouver hospitals include **Vancouver General Hospital Health and Sciences Centre,** 855 W. 12th Ave. (at Oak St.) (✆ **604/875-4111**), and **British Columbia's Children's Hospital,** 4480 Oak St. (between King Edward and 41st aves.) (✆ **604/875-2345**). In North Vancouver, there's **Lions Gate Hospital,** 231 E. 15th (at St. Georges Ave.) (✆ **604/988-3131**).

Internet Access   Free Internet access is available at the **Vancouver Public Library** Central Branch, 350 W. Georgia St. (✆ **604/331-3600**). **London Drugs** at the corner of Granville and West Georgia streets has an Internet cafe downstairs. The store is open Monday to Saturday 8am to 9pm, and Sundays and public holidays 10am to 8pm. **Webster's Internet Cafe,** 340 Robson St. (✆ **604/915-9327**) and just across from the main library, is open daily 9am to midnight. And in Kitsilano, **Dakoda's Internet Cafe,** 1602 Yew St. across from Kits Beach (✆ **604/731-5616**), is open daily 7:30am to 9pm.

Laundry & Dry Cleaning   **Davie Laundromat,** 1061 Davie St. (at Thurlow St.) (© **604/682-2717**), offers self-service, drop-off service, and dry cleaning. **Metropolitan Laundry and Suntanning,** 1725 Robson St. (at Denman St.) (© **604/689-9598**), doesn't have dry-cleaning services, but you can have a coffee or work on your tan while you wait.

Liquor Laws   The legal drinking age in British Columbia is 19. Spirits are sold only in government liquor stores, but beer and wine can be purchased from specially licensed, privately owned stores and pubs. There are 22 LCBC (Liquor Control of British Columbia) stores scattered throughout Vancouver. Most are open Monday to Saturday from 10am to 6pm, and some are open to 11pm.

Lost Property   The **Vancouver Police** have a lost-property room (© **604/717-2726**), which is open during office hours Monday to Saturday. If you think you may have lost something on public transportation, call **TransLink** during office hours at © **604/682-7887.** In West Vancouver call © **604/985-7777** or at the Vancouver International Airport © **604/276-6104.**

Luggage Storage & Lockers   Most downtown hotels will gladly hold your luggage before or after your stay. Just ask at the front desk. Lockers are available at the main Vancouver railway station (which is also the main bus depot), **Pacific Central Station,** 1150 Station St., near Main Street and Terminal Avenue (© **604/661-0328**). Daily rate for a regular locker for a suitcase or duffel bag is C$2 (US$1.32), for skis C$4 (US$2.64), and for oversized luggage $5.35 (US$3.53) per bag.

Mail   Letters and postcards cost C47¢ (US30¢) within Canada, C60¢ (US40¢) to mail to the United States, and C$1.05 (US70¢) to mail overseas. You can buy stamps and mail parcels at the main post office (see "Post Office," below) or at any of the many postal outlets operating inside drugstores and convenience stores. Look for a POSTAL SERVICES sign. You can mail items at any of the tall, red, rectangular mailboxes every few blocks on the street.

Newspapers and Magazines   The two local papers are the *Vancouver Sun* (published Monday to Saturday) and the *Province* (published Sunday to Friday mornings). The free weekly entertainment paper the *Georgia Straight* comes out on Thursday. Other newsworthy papers are the national *Globe and Mail* or the *National Post. Where Vancouver,* a shopping and tourist guide, and another companion publication called *Kids' Guide* is usually provided in your hotel room or can be picked up from Tourism Vancouver. See "Visitor Information" earlier in this chapter for more information.

Pharmacies   **Shopper's Drug Mart,** 1125 Davie St. (at Thurlow St.) (© **604/685-6445**), is open 24 hours a day. Several Safeway supermarkets have late-night pharmacies, including the one at the corner of Robson and Denman streets, which is open until midnight.

Police   For emergencies, dial © **911.** Otherwise, the **Vancouver City Police** can be reached at © **604/717-3535.**

Post Office   For **Canada Post** information call ℭ **800/267-1177** or for rate information call ℭ **888/550-6333**. The main post office is at West Georgia and Homer streets (349 W. Georgia St.). It's open Monday to Friday from 8am to 5:30pm.

Postal outlets are usually open Saturday and Sunday as well as later in the evening and can be found in souvenir stores, 7-11 stores, and drugstores displaying the red-and-white CANADA POST emblem.

Provincial Government   Tracking down information in government offices can be a headache, especially for visitors, but fortunately the BC Government has set up one convenient number to find just about everything. Call **Enquiry BC** at ℭ **800/663-7867**.

Restrooms   Hotel lobbies are your best bet for downtown facilities. The shopping centers like Pacific Centre and Sinclair Centre, as well as the large department stores like the Bay, also have restrooms.

Safety   Overall, Vancouver is a safe city; violent crime rates are quite low. However, property crimes and crimes of opportunity (such as items being stolen from unlocked cars) do occur with troubling frequency, particularly downtown. Vancouver's downtown East Side, between Gastown and Chinatown, is a troubled neighborhood and should be avoided at night.

Snow   For Grouse Mountain call ℭ **604/986-6262**; for Blackcomb/Whistler ℭ **604/664-5614**; for Cypress Mountain ℭ **604/419-7669**; and for Seymour Mountain ℭ **604/718-7771**.

Taxes   Hotel rooms are subject to a 10% tax. The provincial sales tax (PST) is 7% (excluding food, restaurant meals, and children's clothing). For specific questions, call the BC Consumer Taxation Branch at ℭ **604/660-4500**.

Most goods and services are subject to a 7% federal good and services tax (GST). You can get a refund on short-stay accommodations and all individual shopping purchases over C$50 (US$33). See "GST Refunds" in chapter 2, p. 16 for more information.

Telephone   Phones in British Columbia are identical to phones in the United States. The country code is the same as the U.S. code (1). Local calls normally cost C25¢ (US17¢). Many hotels charge up to C$1.50 (US$1) per local call and much more for long-distance calls. You can save considerably by using your calling card. You can also buy prepaid phone cards in various denominations at grocery and convenience stores. If you need a cellular phone, **Cell City,** 105-950 W. Broadway (ℭ **604/656-2311**), rents them for C$19 (US$13) per day, plus C70¢ (US46¢) per minute, or C$39 (US$26) per week, plus C65¢ (US43¢) per minute.

Time Zone   Vancouver is in the Pacific Standard Time zone, as are Seattle and San Francisco. Daylight saving time applies from April through October.

Tipping   Tipping etiquette is the same as in the United States: 15% in restaurants, C$1 (US66¢) per bag for bellhops and porters, and C$1 (US66¢) per day for the hotel housekeeper. Taxi drivers get a sliding-scale tip— fares under C$4 (US$2.64) deserve a C$1 (US66¢) tip; for fares over C$5 (US$3.30), tip 15%.

Useful Telephone Numbers   You might find the following telephone numbers useful during your stay:

BCAA 24-Hour Road Service ✆ **604/293-2222**

BC Coalition for People with Disabilities ✆ **604/875-0188**

BC Ombudsman ✆ **800/567-3247**

BC Road Conditions ✆ **604/299-9000 ext. 7623**

Crisis Centre ✆ **604/872-3311**

Multilingual Helpline ✆ **604/572-4060**

Poison Control Centre ✆ **604/682-5050**

Sexual Assault Centre ✆ **604/255-6344**

Tourism Info Centre ✆ **604/683-2000**

TransLink (public transit) ✆ **604/521-0400**

Weather ✆ **604/664-9010**

4

Family-Friendly Accommodations

In the last few years there has been a flurry of activity in Vancouver's hotel industry. New hotels are popping up in all price ranges, and older ones have poured millions into facelifts, overhauling their rooms, buying new furnishings, and creating new decor, and facilities. This is great news for families as rates have stayed reasonable and it means far more accommodation styles and choices. Demand remains strong in the summer months.

LOCATION

At the end of 2000 there were close to 13,000 rooms in the downtown and West End areas. Staying here puts you close to everything—public transportation, the beaches, restaurants, shopping, Stanley Park, and the routes that will take you out of the city to other areas and destinations.

If you have a car, the North Shore is a cheaper alternative to downtown and still close to the city. The West Side also offers several hotels and alternative accommodations. In Richmond, where Vancouver International Airport is located, there are super deals and it is still less than 30 minutes from downtown.

HOUSEKEEPING

Quoted prices do not include the hefty 17% **tax**. This is made up of the 7% federally applied GST (goods and services tax), which is refundable to non-Canadian residents (see chapter 2, "Planning Your Family Trip to Vancouver," p. 16), and a 10% provincial room tax, which is not.

Many hotels have the audacity to charge a dollar or more for an otherwise free local phone call. It's worth checking this out before the kids start calling around to dozens of friends, restaurants, and destinations.

Pay movies, Internet connections, Nintendo, snacks, and other entertainment options quickly add up. Delighted that our children were quietly watching television in the adjoining hotel room, we didn't notice that our 6-year-old was activating C$40 worth of pay movies and Nintendo. With the 20/20 clarity of hindsight, we now know that most hotels will lock off movies and games if you ask and give you a key to the minibar. However, if you do forget, it's worth throwing yourself on the mercy of the hotel; quite often they will understand and erase the bill.

If you have a family with more than one child, make sure you check the **maximum number of bodies** allowed in a room. Many allow only four people and some just three.

Hotels do not provide their own babysitters; however, if **babysitting** is listed in the amenities, it means that the hotel has a list of sitters that it can call on. Prices vary, but in general you will be expected to pay for a 4-hour call at C$10 to $20 (US$6.60 to $13.20) per hour, depending on the time, the notice, and the number of children. Most will also require travel time and/or cab fare. A few hotels have kids' programs of one sort or another, but generally kids' camps and the like are found only in resorts outside the city area.

A full **breakfast** is defined as one being along traditional English lines, includ- ing eggs and/or meat as well as breads, toast, juice, and coffee. A continental breakfast is usually coffee, juice, and a choice of several breads and pastries.

FOUR-FOOTED FRIENDS

To my pleasant surprise many hotels will now take pets. However, while some will roll out the red carpet for your 300-pound Rottweiler, others will accept only small pets—the size of a Chihuahua or a large house cat. Many will also allow you to bring pets, but not to leave them unattended in the room. Others have full pet programs complete with sirloin steak or caviar, hand-painted bowls, and dog walkers—all for a hefty fee of course. Prices also vary wildly. Some won't charge a dime, but will put you in a smoking room or separate area of the hotel, and others will charge anywhere from C$10 to $50 (US$6.60 to $33) a night, while others will charge a flat cleaning charge of up to C$150 (US$99) a visit.

PRICES

I've based the categories from very expensive down to inexpensive on a family of four staying in high season. Roughly it works out that a hotel that lists a double room at the bottom of the range at C$130 (US$85) or under is inexpensive, between C$130 to $200 (US$85 to $132) moderate, between C$200 to $280 (US$132 to $185) expensive, and more than C$280 (US$185) very expensive.

Of course, price is all relative—compared to most large American cities and with a more than 30% discount thanks to our Canadian dollar, even our priciest hotels are a steal.

A WORD ABOUT RACK RATES AND HOW TO AVOID THEM

Rack rates are the prices that are listed in this guide and what the hotel will give you if you walk in the door without a prior booking. Few people pay these rates and there's no reason why you should either.

October 1 to April 30 is the "Entertainment Season" in Vancouver or, in other words, the winter or low season when you will find the best deals and save up to 50% on the cost of a room. If you plan to travel during this time, there are all sorts of packages, specials, and promotions on offer. Many hotels team up with attrac- tions such as Grouse Mountain to offer a "snowsports package," which could include lodging, transportation, and lift tickets. Hotels may offer breakfast pack- ages that either give you a luscious breakfast buffet, breakfast in bed, or a coupon for a meal at a nearby restaurant. Other packages include bonuses such as free valet parking, spa treatments, tickets to the game or to a movie, or an upgrade to a suite. And, while hotels are far less flexible in the summer, there are packages, and you can get considerable savings booking months in advance. In the past, May to September was dubbed "Vancouver's Summer Cruise Season," when hotels join forces with attractions to offer free or discounted passes and other perks.

Always check the website of the individual hotel—not the chain—before you book. Here you will find promotions and other offers. Even in the peak summer period, it's worth checking again because you can often pick up a last-minute deal or an upgrade when hoteliers find beds in need of bodies.

Hotels offer **discounts** of all sorts—off-season discounts and web special discounts, weekend discounts, AAA and seniors discounts, corporate and military discounts, airline and Girl Guide discounts (okay, I'm sort of kidding on the last one, but the point is it pays to ask).

When you book the hotel, always ask if they are running any packages, specials, or promotions for the time that you want to stay. Ask if there are upgrade possibilities at no extra charge. Remember, if you don't ask, they usually won't offer. It is also their job to "upsell" you—"Sure, we have rooms at $75 a night, but wouldn't you rather have a premium room with a duvet and a rubber duckie for $150?" Kids under certain ages stay in parents' rooms for free. It varies with the hotel, so ask. Your last question should always be along the lines of "Are you sure that's the best you can do?" It doesn't hurt and you may well save up to 50% on the cost of your accommodation.

HANDY CONTACTS

Reservations are always an excellent idea if you are traveling to Vancouver between June and September. However, if you find your hotel has lost your reservation, or you like to travel dangerously, call **Tourism BC** at ✆ **800/HELLOBC** outside Vancouver or 604/435-5622 in Vancouver. You can also find their website with lots of useful information on last-minute bookings and tourist information at www.hellobc.com. The folks at **Tourism Vancouver** are also very helpful (✆ **604/682-2000;** www.tourismvancouver .com). If you are looking for a B&B try the **Western Canada Bed and Breakfast Innkeepers Association** (✆ **604/255-9199;** www.wcbbia.com) or the **British Columbia Bed & Breakfast Association** (✆ **604/734-3486**). Another useful website for local accommodation is www.vancouver-bc.com/accommodations.

1 Downtown

The downtown area stretches from Thurlow Street to encompass Yaletown, the entertainment district where the sports arenas and theaters cluster, right down to False Creek. Not surprisingly, hotels tend to be fairly expensive. Decent budget hotels can be found on or around the south end of Granville Street, and while the area is quite safe during the day, it can get a little seedy after dark, filling up with street kids and pan handlers. I have intentionally not included hotels in the East Hastings Street area. Known as "skid row," this has some of Canada's highest crime rates and is not worth the savings.

VERY EXPENSIVE

Fairmont Hotel Vancouver ⭐⭐⭐ If your family is seeking elegance and old-world charm, then this beautiful hotel built in 1939 will fill your needs. This hotel is in business to pamper your family with luxury, and after receiving a package with coloring book and a Kid's Guide to Vancouver, your kids will find pint-sized terry bathrobes in their room, chocolates, and large feather pillows. A card will ask them to phone housekeeping to bring up their free milk and cookies. If you've brought the family pet, you'll find treats for it too. In July 2000 the hotel opened a spa to pamper parents and give haircuts to everyone. Children will love the second-floor glass-covered swimming pool, where there's even a small wading pool for toddlers. You can request to stay on this level.

Kids will also like to watch letters whizzing down the 1939 glass mail chute by the elevators, which shoots down all 14 floors.

Family-Friendly Vancouver Accommodations

Best Western Exhibition Park **1**
Blue Horizon Hotel **2**
Bosman's Hotel **3**
Buchan Hotel **4**
Burnaby Cariboo RV Park **5**
Canyon Court Inn & Suites **6**
Capilano R.V. Park **7**
Century Plaza Hotel & Spa **8**
Comfort Inn Vancouver Airport **9**
Delta Pacific Resort and Conference Centre **10**
Delta Vancouver Suites **11**
Fairmont Hotel Vancouver **12**
Four Seasons Hotel **13**
Greenbrier Hotel **14**
Grouse Inn **15**
Holiday Inn [Cambie Rd.] **16**
Holiday Inn [West Broadway St.] **17**
Holiday Inn Hotel & Suites [Howe St.] **18**
Holiday Inn Hotel & Suites [Old Lillooet Rd.] **19**
Hyatt Regency Vancouver **20**
Listel Vancouver **21**
Lonsdale Quay Hotel **22**
Manor Guest House **23**
Oceanside Hotel **24**
Pacific Palisades **25**
Parkhill Hotel **26**
Pillow & Porridge Guest Suites **27**
Quality Hotel, the Inn at False Creek **28**
Ramada Inn & Suites **29**
Riviera Hotel **30**
Robsonstrasse Hotel **31**
Rosedale on Robson Suite Hotel **32**
Rosellen Suites at Stanley Park **33**
Sunset Inn Travel Apartments **34**
Sutton Place Hotel **35**
Sylvia Hotel **36**
2400 Motel **37**
Westin Bayshore Resort and Marina **38**
Westin Grand **39**
YWCA Hotel/Residence **40**

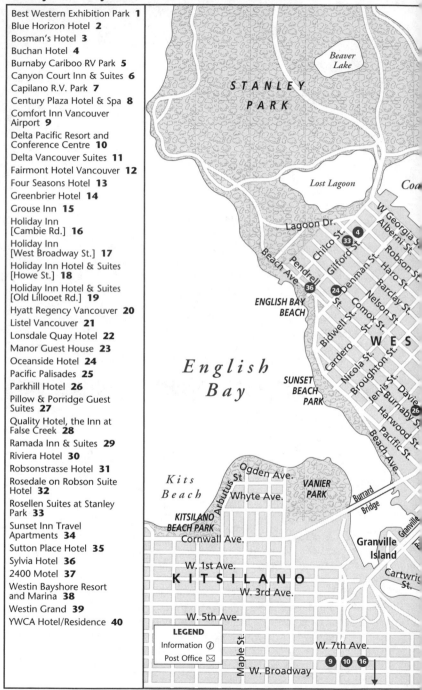

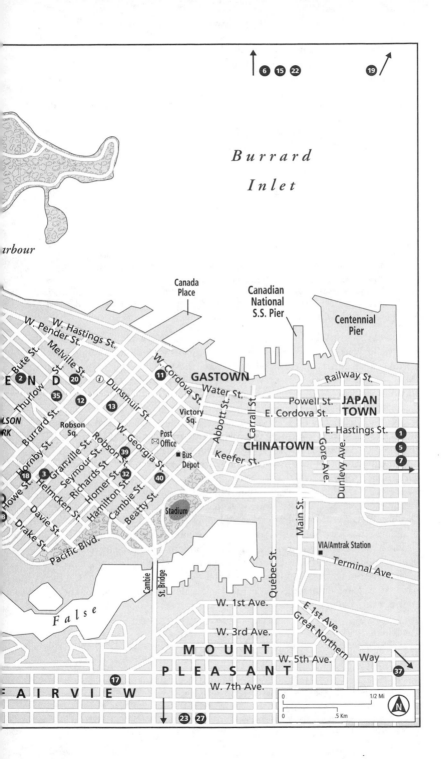

Burrard Inlet

Harbour

False

Canada Place

Canadian National S.S. Pier

Centennial Pier

W. Hastings St.
W. Pender St.
Melville St.
Bute St.
Thurlow St.
Burrard St.
Hornby St.
Howe St.
Helmcken St.
Davie St.
Drake St.

E N D

Dunsmuir St.
W. Cordova St.
GASTOWN
Water St.
Abbott St.
Carrall St.
Powell St.
E. Cordova St.
JAPAN TOWN
Railway St.
E. Hastings St.
Robson Sq.
Granville St.
Seymour St.
Richards St.
Homer St.
Hamilton St.
Cambie St.
Beatty St.
W. Georgia St.
Robson St.
Victory Sq.
Post Office
Bus Depot
Keefer St.
CHINATOWN
Gore Ave.
Dunlevy Ave.
Main St.

Stadium

Pacific Blvd.

Cambie
St. Bridge

Québec St.

VIA/Amtrak Station
Terminal Ave.

W. 1st Ave.
W. 3rd Ave.

E 1st Ave.
Great Northern
Way

M O U N T
P L E A S A N T
W. 5th Ave.
W. 7th Ave.

F A I R V I E W

0   1/2 Mi
0   .5 Km

The hotel has two family suites available at the same price as a regular room, so it's definitely worth asking when you book.

According to the press material, this is the hotel of choice for visiting royalty and celebrities—everyone from Queen Elizabeth and Indira Gandhi to Bryan Adams, Charlie Chaplin, Richard Gere, and John Travolta have put their heads down here at some time.

Since 1989 the hotel has spent C$65 million on renovations and restoring the hotel to its original architecture, which had been modernized over the years. Downstairs there is a small shopping arcade and the Maple Leaf GST, a handy on-site store for GST rebates.

The hotel is smack in the middle of downtown Vancouver and is clearly recognizable by its green copper roof and gargoyles.

900 W. Georgia St. (at Hornby St.), Vancouver, BC V6C 2W6. ✆ 800/441-1414 or 604/684-3131. Fax 604/662-1929. www.fairmont.com. 556 units. May 1–Oct 31 C$299–$489 (US$197–$323) double. Suites from C$499 (US$329). Nov 1–Apr 30 C$229–$339 (US$151–$224) double. Suites from C$359 (US$237). Crib free. Children under 18 stay free in parents' room. AE, DC, DISC, MC, V. Underground valet parking C$19 (US$12.55). Pets accepted C$20 (US$13.20). **Amenities:** Restaurant (West Coast), kids' menu; wine bar & lounge; indoor lap pool; health club with Jacuzzi; sauna; steamroom; full spa; concierge; small shopping arcade; salon; 24-hour room service; babysitting; same-day laundry/dry cleaning; nonsmoking rooms. In room: A/C, TV w/ pay movies, VCR & Nintendo, dataport, fax, minibar, coffeemaker, hairdryer, iron, adult- and children-sized terry robes, umbrellas.

Four Seasons Hotel ⭐⭐⭐   If you are seeking luxury and a staff devoted to servicing your family's every whim, look no further than this centrally located 28-floor hotel. After all, the hotel hasn't won the AAA Five Diamond award every year since it opened in 1976 (and the only hotel in the country to attain this) for naught.

Children are well taken care of through the hotel's Very Important Kids program, which includes a huge chocolate cookie and milk, activity book, crayons, and access to the complimentary video library. There are kid-sized bathrobes in the rooms and the hotel has a huge list of things available in case you have forgotten baby bottles, bibs, or swimsuits or need a baby bathtub, bottle warmer, car seat, or stroller.

The hotel also has a fabulous indoor/outdoor swimming pool and plenty of kickboards, goggles, and other water toys to splash around with. Bored kids can also borrow Lego, Monopoly, puzzles, and other games and toys, and plans are in the works to have Sony PlayStations in every room.

The hotel has also recently sunk C$10 million into renovating its rooms, the lighting, and the bar and refurbishing its very grand Chartwell Restaurant.

If you've brought the family pet, the hotel makes its own dog biscuits—the recipe is available on request—served in handmade dog and cat bowls, and of course, a dog-walking service.

791 W. Georgia St. (at Hornby St.), Vancouver, BC V6C 2T4. ✆ 800/332-3442 in the U.S. or 800/268-6282 in Canada or 604/689-9333. Fax 604/684-4555. www.fshr.com. 385 units. May 1–Oct 31 C$455–$485 (US$300–$320) double, C$505–$1,320 (US$333–$871) suite. Nov 1–Apr 30 C$320–$350 (US$211–$231) double, C$370–$915 (US$244–$604) suite. Children under 18 stay free in parents' room. Crib free. AE, DC, DISC, MC, V. Valet underground parking C$20 (US$13.20). Pets accepted free. **Amenities:** Restaurant (Continental) and the Garden Terrace, kids' menu; one bar; indoor/outdoor pool and watersports equipment; health club with Jacuzzi; sauna; exercise room; Very Important Kids program; concierge; Pacific Centre shopping arcade; 24-hour room service; babysitting; same-day laundry/dry cleaning; nonsmoking rooms. In room: A/C, TV w/ pay movies, VCR, fax, dataport, minibar, hairdryer, safe, phones in some of the bathrooms, adult- and children-sized terry robes.

The Westin Grand ✴✴✴   Right in the heart of the entertainment district, the Grand is across the street from the Coliseum-like Vancouver Public Library and within minutes of GM Place, Robson Street shopping, and Yaletown. This magnificent hotel opened in 1999 and is shaped like a baby grand piano. Carrying on the theme, it has a sweeping marble staircase, and piano stool-like benches in the lobby. Those who have seen it from the air say that the next-door (and now shut) Ford Centre for the Performing Arts looks like a giant stage with the Westin as its piano. The hotel is part of the Westin Kids Club, which starts at check-in with a pack for the kids—depending on the child's age this could include soap, sponges, and coloring book, or a hat. There is a special children's menu, laundry prices for children's clothes, one free kids movie during your stay, and the Story Line, a selection of 30 bedtime stories in English, French, or Japanese that you dial up free from your room. Strollers, bottle warmers, and other amenities that you may need during your stay are there for the asking. The minibar has all the usuals as well as Oreos, jellybeans, and other kid-friendly treats. The hotel is frequented by film and television producers, actors, and often animals. And, while the hotel will take any size dog you may bring, they have been known to draw the line at 20 ducks that a producer once wanted to use in a TV commercial. Who knows? Little Johnny or the family dog may be discovered in the elevator. Every room is a spacious suite with floor-to-ceiling windows, a sitting room, and kitchenette stocked with a microwave convection oven, dishwasher, dishes, cutlery, sink, and fridge. The large bathroom with warmed gleaming black floor tiles has a separate shower and oversized bath and two entrances. Some rooms have balconies. If you're off on a bike ride or perhaps a drive to Whistler, the chef will make up a picnic box for between C$9.95 (US$6.55) and C$16 (US$10.55) per person.

433 Robson St. (at Homer St.), Vancouver, BC V6B 6L9. (℃) **888/680-9393** or 604/602-1999. Fax 604/647-2502. www.westingrandvancouver.com. 207 units (all suites). May 15–Dec 30 C$359–$399 (US$237–$264). Jan 1–May 14 C$349–$389 (US$230–$257). Children under 18 stay free in parents' room, children under 12 eat free. Crib free. Pets C$50 (US$33) for stay. AE, DC, MC, V. Underground valet parking C$15 (US$9.90). **Amenities:** Restaurant (West Coast); bar; large heated outdoor pool; exercise facilities; whirlpool; sauna; nonsmoking rooms; concierge; 24-hour room service; babysitting; same-day laundry/dry cleaning. *In room:* A/C, TV w/ pay movies in bedroom and living room, Nintendo, fax, dataport, high-speed Internet access C$13 (US$8.60), full kitchenette in all rooms, coffeemaker, toaster, hairdryer, iron, bathrobes, safe, and heavenly beds.

EXPENSIVE

Delta Vancouver Suites ✴✴   While this suite hotel does not have kitchens, it does have a variety of large rooms perfect for families. Located just minutes from the SeaBus Terminal, Gastown, and downtown shopping, this sleekly modern 23-story hotel is built to resemble a New York–style establishment. It has a large lobby with lots of black marble and a 3-story atrium that lets in the light on even the darkest Vancouver day.

On check-in your kids will receive a package that includes bubble bath, activity and sticker books, crayons, a plastic water bottle, and various attractions coupons. As the name suggests, all the rooms are suites with a separate bedroom and parlor, but the configurations are quite different. Depending on the size and age of your children, you can choose between a standard suite, in which the bedroom has a Japanese-looking door and is not completely separated from the rest of the suite. There is the executive suite, which has a separate bedroom, and another with a completely open plan, where the television swivels between the bedroom, with queen, king, or two double beds, and a sitting area. There are only 23 rooms with two double beds and a pullout couch, so be sure to ask for this when you book. The rooms have sweeping floor-to-ceiling windows and there are stunning water views and mountain views at no extra charge from the 13th floor up. Suites on the Signature Club Floor are an extra C$30 (US$20), but offer concierge service as well as a goose-down duvet, turn-down service, a deluxe continental breakfast, evening hors d'oeuvres, and access to an airline business class–style lounge with a large balcony.

550 W. Hastings St. (entrance off Seymour St.), Vancouver, BC V6B 1L6. ℂ **800/268-1133** or 604/689-8188. Fax 604/605-8881. www.deltahotels.com. 226 units. May–Oct C$245–$400 (US$162–$264); Nov–Dec C$195–$370 (US$129–$244); Jan–Apr C$185–$370 (US$122–$244) double. 15% discount on stays of more than 3 nights. Children under 18 stay free in parents' room. Children under 7 eat free. Cribs and rollaway free. AE, DC, DISC, MC, V. Valet underground parking C$15 (US$9.90). Small pets accepted free. **Amenities:** Restaurant (West Coast), kids' menu; bar; indoor heated lap pool; exercise facilities; Jacuzzi; concierge; 24-hour room service; babysitting, same-day laundry service; nonsmoking rooms. *In room:* A/C, TV w/ pay movies, Nintendo, high-speed Internet C$9.95 (US$6.55), dataport, minibar, coffeemaker, hairdryer, iron, robes, pool bag.

Hyatt Regency Vancouver ⚹

This is the largest convention hotel in Western Canada, which will give you a clue to its clientele. It also seems to be the hotel of choice for politicians—Henry Kissinger, George Bush, Mikhail Gorbachev, and Bill Clinton have all booked rooms here at one time or another. It does have some good features for families. At check-in kids get an activity book about Vancouver with a kids' menu for those 12 and under. And it's a super location—close to all Vancouver's other downtown areas and attractions and within walking distance of Stanley Park. It also has a large shopping mall that you can access through the lobby. The 34-story hotel tower was built in 1974 and plans are to have a major overhaul of the public areas, including the rather dramatic looking 3-story atrium lobby, in 2002. It needs it. However, the guest rooms were renovated in 1999—they are larger than your typical hotel room and pleasantly decorated and comfortably furnished. If you are interested in a standard double room, ask for one of the 80 corner rooms. It's the same price, but the rooms are quite a bit larger with a hallway and two vanity sinks—one outside the bathroom. They are also connected to a parlor with a Murphy bed, which is available at 50% off the normal room rate.

655 Burrard St. (at Georgia St.), Vancouver, BC V6C 2R7. ℂ **800/233-1234** or 604/683-1234. Fax 604/689-3707. www.hyatt.com. 644 units. May 1–Oct 31 C$249–$465 (US$164–$307) double. Nov 1–Apr 30 C$149–$320 (US$98–$211) double. Camp Hyatt rate 50% off an adjoining room. Suites start at C$625 (US$412). Children under 17 stay free. Cribs and rollaway free. AE, DC, DISC, MC, V. Valet underground parking C$18.50 (US$12.20). **Amenities:** Restaurant (seafood), cafe, kids' menu; bar; outdoor heated swimming pool; exercise facilities; concierge; Royal Centre shopping arcade; limited room service; babysitting; same-day laundry/dry cleaning; nonsmoking rooms. *In room:* A/C, TV w/ pay movies, dataport, minibar, hairdryer, iron, safes in some rooms, umbrellas, terry robes.

Rosedale on Robson Suite Hotel ⚹⚹⚹ *Finds*

The Rosedale is a perfect family hotel. Among its treasures is the second floor, which has a huge outdoor patio, landscaped garden, and children's play area with slide and swings. The suites vary in size, but most have a separate sitting area and full kitchen equipped with oven, stove top, sink, microwave, and fridge. Dishes, cutlery, pots, and pans are also provided and there is a convenience store right outside the entrance accessible through a covered driveway. All the suites have floor-to-ceiling windows, many with sweeping city views. One 2-bedroom suite is dedicated to families and comes with bean bags, colorful children's art, and a kids' room with a bunk bed complete with a Grizzlies bedspread and a Canucks lampshade. There is a box filled with toys in the closet, kids' books and crayons, and a blackboard fixed to one wall. Those who stay on the third floor will find that for no extra charge, the sitting room doors open out onto a large and private courtyard. Most suites have two televisions and all have Nintendo. Both kids and parents will love the pool, the lounge chairs, and the surfing mural backdrop. Note that the pool closes for repairs during the month of April. As the pool also closes for cleaning for 1 hour each day, it's a good idea to check the schedule with the front desk before heading down there.

838 Hamilton St. (at Robson St.), Vancouver, BC V6B 6A2. ℂ **800/661-8870** or 604/689-8033. Fax 604/689-4426. www.rosedaleonrobson.com. 275 units, 265 with separate living rooms. May 1–Oct 31 C$225–$295 (US$149–$195). Nov 1–Apr 30 C$200–$270 (US$132–$178). Rates include a light breakfast served in the pool area. Children under 16 stay free in parents' room. Crib free. Pets C$10 (US$6.60). AE, DC, MC, V. Valet underground parking C$8 (US$5.30). **Amenities:** Restaurant (West Coast); kids' menu; bar; bright and airy indoor pool; exercise facilities; Jacuzzi; sauna; steam room; limited room service; babysitting; coin-op washers and dryers; same-day laundry/dry cleaning; nonsmoking rooms. *In room:* A/C, TV w/ pay movies & Nintendo, fax, dataport, high-speed Internet access C$10 (US$6.60), full kitchens in all rooms, coffeemaker, hairdryer, iron.

Sutton Place Hotel 🄅 This luxurious pink place has been dubbed "Grandma's Hotel" by competitors because of all the marble, chandeliers, and antiques that look gorgeous, but don't exactly give you the feeling of putting your feet up and kicking back. But this European boutique-style hotel built in 1986 does go the extra mile in making children feel welcome. The kids' program includes cookies and milk in the room on the first night, a kids' registration card, an activity book and crayons, free videos, and a newsletter with shopping tips for kids. There are also complimentary bottle warmers, safety gates, baby bathtubs, and strollers for the asking. On Sunday nights if you are eating in the hotel's upmarket restaurant, kids aged 6 to 12 can book a pastry lesson under the tutelage of the hotel's chefs. It costs an extra C$10 (US$6.60) and you need to book this 48 hours in advance. The kids make and serve the family a chocolate brownie dessert and get to wear a chef's hat and apron. Kids receive a diploma, keep the apron, and eat the dessert, of course. The Sutton got a lot of media attention a couple of years ago when it launched its Five Diamond service for pets. For C$95 (US$63) the family dog or cat gets a gourmet T-Bone or fresh tuna and caviar served on porcelain dishes with Evian water and a bedtime story book.

There are three room types: deluxe guest rooms, junior suites, and large suites. The suites offer a separate parlor area with French doors, but note that all rooms and suites will allow only three people (including children) in one room.

845 Burrard St. (near Robson St.), Vancouver, BC V6Z 2K6. ℂ **800/961-7555** or 604/682-5511. Fax 604/682-5513. www.suttonplace.com. 397 units. May 1–Oct 31 C$239–$450 (US$158–$297) double. Suites from C$339 (US$224). Nov 1–Dec 30 C$179–$299 (US$118–$197) double. Suites from C$249 (US$165). Jan 1–Apr 30 standard rooms C$169–$289 (US$112–$190) double. Suites from C$239 (US$158). Children under 18 stay free. Cribs and rollaway free. AE, DC, DISC, MC, V. Valet underground parking C$15 (US$9.90). Small pets accepted C$150 (US$99) cleaning fee. **Amenities:** Restaurant (French Continental); bar; indoor lap pool; European health fitness and beauty spa; Jacuzzi; sauna; kids' programs; concierge; 24-hour room service; babysitting; complimentary bikes; same-day laundry/dry cleaning; nonsmoking rooms. *In room:* A/C, TV/VCR w/pay movies & Sony PlayStation, high-speed Internet C$14.95 (US$9.85), fax, dataport, minibar, hairdryer, iron, safe in suites, umbrellas, robes.

MODERATE

Century Plaza Hotel & Spa   Right across from St. Paul's Hospital and close to the Burrard Street Bridge, this 30-floor tower was originally built in 1972 as an apartment building. For families this means much larger rooms than your average hotel and all with fully equipped kitchens including stove, fridge, microwave, and sink. The studio rooms, which comprise a large living room and bedroom, have all the amenities of the one-bedroom except for the microwave and pullout sofa bed. Rooms from the 13th floor up have a decent mountain, city, or water view. For further pampering, Absolute Spa is located off the lobby. The hotel also acts as the stage for Tony n' Tina's Wedding—Vancouver's longest running dinner theater performance.

1015 Burrard St. (at Comox St.), Vancouver, BC V6Z 1Y5. ℂ **800/663-1818** or 604/687-0575. Fax 604/682-5790. www.century-plaza.com. 236 units. May 1–Oct 14 C$159–$189 (US$105–$125) 1-bedroom studios, C$209–$229 (US$138–$151). Oct 15–Apr 30 C$149–$169 (US$98–$116) 1-bedroom studios, C$189–$209 (US$125–$138). Children under 17 stay free in parents' room. Crib free, rollway C$15 (US$9.90). AE, DC, MC, V. Underground parking C$7 (US$4.60). **Amenities:** Restaurant, cafe, kids' menu; bar; indoor pool; full-service European day spa; eucalyptus steam room; concierge; Thrifty Car Rental desk; limited room service; coin-op laundry; same-day laundry/dry cleaning; nonsmoking rooms. *In room:* TV w/ pay movies & Sony PlayStation, kitchen, utensils C$5 (US$3.30), coffeemaker, tea kettle, hairdryer.

Holiday Inn Hotel & Suites *(Value)*   This is an unglamorous but centrally located hotel in the downtown area that actually spends some time thinking about families. On the third floor the hotel has turned a full-sized hotel room into a play area for kids aged 2 to 13. It is done in a jungle theme and has a climbing structure, toys, games, books, and televisions with videos and Nintendo, a chalk-board, a mini-kitchen, and a lounge chair for adults. If you can get a room on this floor you are also close to the second-floor pool, which is shaped like a whale and even has a killer whale painted inside it. The area is airy and bright with cabana lounge chairs to relax in.

The standard rooms are simple but clean and there are two types of suites. The King Suite is the size of two rooms with a full bedroom, sitting area, and pullout couch. The Tower Suite has a separate bedroom and a kitchenette with hot plate, microwave, fridge, sink, toaster, and tea kettle. Dishes and cutlery are provided.

Originally built in the 1960s, the hotel was added onto in the 1970s and again in 1989. The lobby and public areas and many of the guest rooms were renovated in 1999.

The hotel is just a few blocks from the downtown core and trendy Yaletown. And although it is quite safe to wander around in daylight, Granville Street, one block to the east, can be quite seedy after dark.

1110 Howe St. (at Helmcken St.), Vancouver, BC V6Z 1R2. ℂ **800/663-9151** or 604/684-2151. Fax 604/684-4736. www.vancouverholidayinn.com. 245 units. May–Sept C$179–$219 (US$118–$145) double, C$259–$349 (US$171–$230) suite. Oct–Apr C$99–$159 (US$65–$105) double, C$159–249 (US$105–$164) suite. Children under 19 stay free in parents' room. Children under 12 eat free from the kids' menu. Cribs free; rollaways C$15 (US$9.90). AE, DC, DISC, MC, V. Valet underground parking C$10.95 (US$7.25), self-parking C$9.95 (US$6.55). Small pets accepted free. **Amenities:** Restaurant (International), kids' menu; bar; indoor pool; exercise room; sauna; Kids Activity Centre; concierge; Gray Line tour desk; 24-hour room service; babysitting; coin-op washers and dryers; same-day laundry/dry cleaning; nonsmoking rooms. *In room:* A/C, TV w/ pay movies & Nintendo, fax, dataport, kitchenettes in Tower Suites, minibar, coffeemaker, hairdryer, iron.

Quality Hotel, the Inn at False Creek ⊛ With its bright open lobby, Mexican art, pottery and rugs, and classical music, this Mediterranean boutique hotel has a real holiday feel. It's about as far from the downtown core as you can get, but it's close to Granville Island and the False Creek commuter ferries as well as the Aquatic Centre, Vanier Park, and Science World. Originally built in 1975, the hotel was totally refurbished in 1998. All the rooms are beautifully decorated and have a brick wall. A one-bedroom family room has a sofa bed in the living room and most have adjoining rooms with 50% off the second room in the winter (though it doesn't hurt to ask in summer). Stay on the top floor (seventh) if available. These rooms came about because of a weird zoning law that forced the hotel to glass in its balconies. What they are left with is a glassed inside section that runs the length of the room and a perfect—and soundproof—area for kids to play in. The hotel won a Tourism Vancouver Service Award for its exclusive Vancouver City Passport program, which is well worth the price if you are staying in the city for a few days. For C$15 (US$9.90) the passport gives you over C$500 (US$330) in discounts on destinations, restaurants, and museums as well as a CD by Michael Conway Baker commissioned for the BC Pavilion at Expo 86. The program has its own website at www.vancouvercitypassport.com.

1335 Howe St. (at the foot of the Granville St. Bridge), Vancouver, BC V6Z 1R7. © **800/663-8474** or 604/682-0229. Fax 604/662-7566. www.qualityhotelvancouver.com. 157 units. May 1–Sept 30 C$159–$179 (US$105–$118) deluxe, C$189–$209 (US$125–$138) suite. Oct 1–Apr 30 C$99–$119 (US$65–$79) deluxe, C$129–$149 (US$85–$98) suite. 7th-floor family suites extra C$20 (US$13.20), full kitchens extra C$20 (US$13.20); packages available all year. Pets accepted C$10 (US$6.60). **Amenities:** Restaurant (Continental), kids' menu; bar; L-shaped outdoor heated pool (closed Nov–Mar); concierge; limited room service; babysitting; same-day laundry/dry cleaning; 80% nonsmoking rooms. *In room:* A/C, TV w/ pay movies, high-speed Internet connection C$12.95 (US$8.55) in executive rooms, fax, dataport, 5 units with full kitchens, coffeemaker, hairdryer, iron.

INEXPENSIVE

Bosman's Hotel Not much has changed since this hotel was built in the 1970s. It's on the gaudy side and there are no frills, but it's clean, the price is reasonable, and the hotel is close to Granville Island, Yaletown, the Aquatic Centre, and downtown restaurants. It also has an outdoor kidney-shaped pool that's open in the summer months. The area is quite safe during the day, but Granville Street—one block to the east—can be quite seedy after dark.

1060 Howe St. (at Helmcken St.), Vancouver, BC V6Z 1P5. © **888/267-6267** or 604/682-3171. Fax 604/684-4010. www.bosmanshotel.com. 102 units. May 1–Sept 30 C$109–$129 (US$72–$85) double. Oct 1–Apr 30 C$79 (US$52). Children under 12 stay free. Cribs and rollaways free. AE, DC, DISC, MC, V. Free parking. **Amenities:** Bar and grill (American); bar; outdoor pool; limited room service; coin-op laundry; same-day laundry/dry cleaning; nonsmoking rooms. *In room:* A/C, TV, fax, dataport, hairdryer, iron.

Ramada Inn & Suites Built at the turn of the last century, the Ramada is one of the older buildings in Vancouver, but its six floors have recently had a complete renovation and the room fittings and fixtures look clean and fresh. The bright hotel lobby has floor-to-ceiling windows and lots of wood, and stairwells and hallways are wide and well lit. The hotel is shaped like an E, giving a choice of interior or exterior rooms. The interior rooms are darker and look out largely onto other buildings, while the exterior rooms are very bright but are quite a bit noisier and can heat up in summer. There are various room configurations and while the double rooms will accommodate a small family, the mini-suites have a bedroom that, although not entirely closed off, is separated from the rest of the room, and there is a pullout sofa in the living-room area. The one-bedroom suite has a full kitchen with fridge, microwave, hot plate, sink and dishes, cutlery, pots, and pans provided. Not all rooms have a bath. The front desk hands out complimentary passes to nearby Fitness World for those 17 and over. Kids will also like the hotel's Irish restaurant. It has a dart board, a large stone fireplace, television screens, and a full-size suit of armor. Buses to all over Vancouver are directly outside the door, and the only downside to the location is that Granville Street, with its tattoo parlors and adult-video stores, can get pretty seedy after dark.

1221 Granville St. (at Davie St.), Vancouver, BC V6Z 1M6. ⓒ **888/835-0078** or 604/685-1111. Fax 604/685-0707. www.ramadavancouver.com. 116 units. May 1–Sept 30 C$129–$199 (US$85–$131), Oct 1–Apr 30 C$69–$119 (US$46–$79). Children under 18 stay free in parents' room. Playpens free. AE, DC, DISC, MC, V. Valet parking C$10 (US$6.60). Pets accepted C$20 (US$13.20) daily. **Amenities:** Bar and grill (American); bar; limited room service; babysitting; same-day laundry/dry cleaning; nonsmoking rooms. *In room:* A/C, TV w/ pay movies & Nintendo, fax, dataport, minibar in most rooms, coffeemaker, hairdryers in most rooms, iron.

YWCA Hotel/Residence ⓐ *Value* If you have preconceptions of a YWCA as a youth hostel with a large dorm, this facility will break them. Housed in a nondescript brown brick building built in 1995, it is certainly spartan, but the rooms are varied, well equipped, and sparkling clean. There are semi-private rooms with a shared hall bathroom, but also completely private rooms with clock radios, hairdryers, and televisions. Some rooms come with two double beds and another, called the Quint, has five single beds. There are also three lounges with television sets and comfortable couches and a table for games, and three shared kitchens and eating areas where you can meet up with fellow travelers. The front desk has cookware and cutlery available for a nominal rental fee or will direct you to a cheap store to buy them. There is a Java Express off the lobby that sells coffee, juices, and muffins and also has Internet access. The hotel is within reasonable distance to two supermarkets and a convenience store, and there are several suitable restaurants within a block's walk. The hotel is also close to Stadium Street SkyTrain Station, across the street from BC Place Stadium, three blocks to Yaletown, and close to Robson Street, Gastown, and Chinatown. Guests over 15 also get free use of YWCA's nearby fitness center.

733 Beatty St. (at Georgia St.), Vancouver, BC V6B 2M4. ⓒ **604/895-5840.** Fax (604) 681-2550. www.ywcahotel.com. 155 units. June 1–Oct 15 C$69–$97 (US$46–$64), May C$64–$92 (US$42–$61), Oct 16–Apr 30 C$54–$72 (US$36–$48) double with shared bathroom. June 1–Oct 15 C$111–$132 (US$73–$87), May C$98–$113 (US$65–$75), Oct 16–Apr 30 C$74–$84 (US$49–$55) double with private bathroom. June 1–Oct 15 C$145 (US$96), May C$128 (US$85), Oct 16–Apr 30 C$99 (US$65) 5 single beds with private bathroom. Weekly rates available in low season. Playpens no charge. Children under 12 stay free in parents' room. AE, MC, V. Underground parking (24 spots) C$5 (US$3.30). **Amenities:** Coin-op washers and dryers; nonsmoking rooms. *In room:* A/C, TV in some rooms, dataport, mini-fridge, wheelchair accessible rooms, hairdryers in rooms with private bathrooms.

2 The West End

If I were traveling to Vancouver with my family, this is where I would want to stay. It's cheaper than downtown, although only about a 10-minute walk away, close to Stanley Park, English Bay, and dozens of restaurants and shops. It's still largely residential and many of the buildings are in lovely tree-lined streets. You are also much more likely to find a suite or a kitchen for the same or less money than a standard double room downtown.

VERY EXPENSIVE

Westin Bayshore Resort and Marina *(★(★(★*   On the doorstep of Stanley Park with majestic views of the North Shore mountains and looking out onto Coal Harbour, this hotel has been busy reinventing itself into a resort with a C$55 million facelift for its rooms, its public areas, and the outside green space, completed in June 2000. Built in 1961, the Westin is still the largest convention center in Western Canada, and while it has its share of business traffic, its killer location has made it a favorite with families. Mainly because of its proximity to the Stanley Park Seawall and downtown Vancouver, the hotel has recently added a bike and roller-blade rental service. In summer, a DJ and various bands liven up the outside pool area. Flying under the Westin flag, the hotel has the Westin Kids Club for kids 12 and under; they get a gift bag on check-in, which, depending on their age, can include crayons and activity books, bath toys, a hat, a sports bottle, free movie passes, and a cup that gives kids free refills of pop at any of the restaurants for the duration of their stay. They also have access to the Story Line, a selection of 30 bedtime stories in English, French, or Japanese that you dial up free from your room. Strollers—jogging or conventional, car seats, bike seats, games, bottle warmers, and other amenities that you may need during your stay are there for the asking.

The 19th and 20th floors are named after Howard Hughes, who once stayed at the hotel for 6 months.

1601 Bayshore Dr. (at W. Georgia St. near Stanley Park entrance), Vancouver, BC V6G 2V4. © 800/WESTIN-1 or 604/682-3377. Fax 604/687-3102. www.westinbayshore.com. 510 units. Apr 29–Nov 24 C$329–$479 (US$217–$316) double, C$459–$1,329 (US$303–$877) suite; Nov 25–Apr 28 C$229–$429 (US$151–$283) double, C$359–$1,229 (US$237–$811) suite. Children under 18 stay free in parents' room. AE, DC, DISC, MC, V. Valet underground parking C$18.50 (US$12.20). Small pets accepted in the tower free. **Amenities:** 2 restaurants (West Coast & bistro); 2 bars; indoor and outdoor pool; exercise room; Jacuzzi; sauna; bike rental; Westin Kids Club; concierge; 24-hour room service; babysitting; same-day laundry/dry cleaning; nonsmoking rooms. *In room:* A/C, TV w/ pay movies, fax, dataport, minibar, coffeemaker, hairdryer, iron, safe in tower rooms, umbrellas, robes.

EXPENSIVE

Listel Vancouver *(★*   This is not my first choice as a hotel to stay with young children as it is very elegant and has beautiful art and furnishings and the hotel disposed of its indoor pool in the last renovation. However, this boutique hotel does offer a fantastic location, and fashion-conscious preteens and early teens will appreciate the proximity to trendy stores, restaurants such as Planet Hollywood, and the Virgin Megastore. Known as O'Doul's Hotel and Restaurant since 1986, the hotel went through a major renovation and name change in 1997. Art lovers will appreciate the paintings and sculptures, as well as the art books in the lobby. Two of the hotel's floors have rooms with original and limited edition art supplied by the Buschlen Mowatt Galleries, a large Vancouver private art dealer. The Art Deco suites have huge soaker tubs that kids would love and chaise lounges built into the bay window. The Museum floor opened in June 2000 with the assistance of the Museum of Anthropology and features raw materials such as BC hemlock and cedar and displays by local artisans.

1300 Robson St. (at Jervis St.), Vancouver, BC V6E 1C5. © 800/663-5491 or 604/684-8461. Fax 604/684-7092. www.listel-vancouver.com. 129 units. May–Sept C$240–$300 (US$159–$198) double. Oct–Apr C$130–$190 (US$86–$125) double, suites from C$600 (US$396). Children under 18 free in parents' room. Cribs free. AE, DC, DISC, MC, V. Valet underground parking C$14 (US$9.25). **Amenities:** Restaurant (Pacific Northwest); exercise facilities; Jacuzzi; limited room service; babysitting; same-day laundry/dry cleaning; non-smoking rooms. *In room:* A/C, TV w/ pay movies, fax, dataport, minibar, coffeemaker, hairdryer, iron.

Pacific Palisades ⟨★⟩⟨★⟩⟨★⟩   This hotel went through a major renovation in the spring of 2000 and now adds a splash of bright orange to an already vibrant street. Although the address is on Robson Street, the lobby is around the corner off Jervis Street and can be hard to find for first timers. The PR bumf calls it "South Beach meets Stanley Park," but I rather think of it as walking into a demented 1950s art gallery. As you look around you'll find a house phone made out of colorful beads and plaster, made by the hotel doorman. He has also created some pretty funky art in the lobby of one of the hotel's two towers. There is always a bowl of fresh fruit at the desk for the taking, and a cozy suspended fireplace, and the paint job has swirling colors that look like bright balloons. Kids will also love the wild color scheme in the rooms, which tend to be a bit larger than your average hotel room. You could play checkers on the green, blue, and yellow carpet; the wallpaper has bright yellow stripes; there are orange shower curtains in the bathroom and a granite counter that matches the floor. There are only four rooms on each floor—some have a stunning view of English Bay while others have beautiful views of the city. One tower has a pillar that runs through the rooms—you can either see this as a room divider or as a waste of space and book accordingly. All rooms have well-equipped kitchenettes with minibars, which include a great selection of kid-friendly Tootsie Rolls and animal crackers. I also saw a pen light, Yahtzee, and an Etch A Sketch in the room. These aren't cheap, but they may be worth it for a few minutes of peace. For C$20 (US$13.20) you can upgrade to a suite with full stove and fridge. If you'd like to meet other guests, you and the kids can drop into the hotel's complimentary wine and pop hour at 5pm every day except Sunday on the Mezzanine level. Directly outside the lobby is a large fenced courtyard with a basketball hoop and the hotel's health club and bike rental. There is a play area with kid-sized tables and Lego, a ping pong table, and a pool that has lap lanes roped off if you want a workout while the kids splash. The hotel also offers a program called "Kid's Night In," which includes pizza, popcorn, and a movie, and will provide a babysitter for C$10 (US$6.60) an hour for two kids on a minimum 4-hour call.

1277 Robson St. (entrance on Jervis St.), Vancouver, BC V6E 1C4. ✆ **800/663-1815** or 604/688-0461. Fax 604/688-4374.www.pacificpalisadeshotel.com. 233 units. May 1–Oct 15 C$225–$375 (US$149–$248) double. Oct 16–Apr 30 C$130–$180 (US$86–$119) double. Children under 18 stay free in parents' room. Cribs, foamies, strollers, and carseats free. Pets free on approval. AE, DC, DISC, MC, V. Valet underground parking C$13 (US$9). **Amenities:** Restaurant (Global); bar; health club with large indoor pool; bike rentals (children's bikes, trailers, and bike seats available); babysitting and kids' program; concierge; 24-hour room service; same-day laundry/dry cleaning; nonsmoking rooms. *In room:* A/C, TV w/ pay movies & Sony PlayStation, fax, dataport, kitchenettes in all rooms or full kitchen C$30 (US$20), minibar, coffeemaker, hairdryer, iron, heavenly beds.

MODERATE

Blue Horizon Hotel   Built at the height of the 1960s, this hotel is indeed blue; it's also tiled and shaped like the Red Cross. The configuration makes it great for families as it provides eight rooms on every floor with a spacious corner room and balcony. Rooms from the 15th floor up have great views of English Bay, although they are a bit more expensive. The guest rooms were refurbished in March 2000 and the pool and small exercise facility underwent an overhaul in the early part of 2001. There is no room service, but step out onto Robson Street and you have a selection of everything the West End has to offer, including close proximity to Stanley Park, shopping, and dozens of restaurants.

1225 Robson St. (near Bute St.), Vancouver, BC V6E 1C3. © **800/663-1333** or 604/688-1411. Fax 604/688-4461. www.bluehorizonhotel.com. 214 units. May 15–Oct 14 C$179–$199 (US$118–$131) double, suites from $235 (US$155). Oct 15–May 14 C$119–$129 (US$79–$85) double, suites from C$149 (US$98). Children under 17 stay free in parents' room. Cribs free. AE, DC, MC, V. Underground parking C$8 (US$5.30). **Amenities:** Bistro (West Coast); bar; small indoor pool; exercise facilities; Jacuzzi; sauna; babysitting; same-day laundry/dry cleaning; 90% nonsmoking rooms. *In room:* A/C, TV w/ pay movies, dataport, minibar, coffeemaker, tea kettle, hairdryer, iron, safe.

Parkhill Hotel   This 24-story hotel was built in 1970, but has been completely remodeled and has large rooms that comfortably fit a family of four. None of the rooms has a kitchen, but the hotel is in a great location with lots of restaurants of all ranges on the doorstep, a supermarket one block away, and a 24-hour drugstore across the road. Every room has a balcony and if you stay on the 19th floor on up, the bay-view rooms have sweeping vistas of English Bay, Stanley Park, and the North Shore mountains. The rooms have floor-to-ceiling windows and about 80% of the rooms have a sofa bed.

1160 Davie St. (between Thurlow & Bute sts.), Vancouver, BC V6E 1N1. © **800/663-1525** or 604/681-0208. Fax 604/685-6706. www.parkhillhotel.com. 192 units. C$180–$220 (US$119–$145). Children under 16 stay free in parents' room. Crib free, rollaways C$10 (US$6.60) for children over 15. AE, DC, DISC, MC, V. Underground parking C$7 (US$4.60). **Amenities:** Restaurant (Japanese), cafe; lounge; exercise room; sauna; heated seasonal outdoor pool in a landscaped garden; limited room service; concierge; babysitting; same-day laundry/dry cleaning; nonsmoking rooms. *In room:* A/C, TV w/ pay movies & Nintendo, fax, dataport, minibar in most rooms, coffeemaker, hairdryers in most rooms, iron.

Robsonstrasse Hotel   Nearly destroyed by fire a few years ago, this hotel tower, built in the 1940s, has had a complete renovation. It now has a colorful tiled lobby, bright stairwells, very large suites, and a terrific location that makes it ideal for families. The rooms at the back of the hotel are the quietest, all the rooms are nonsmoking, and all have fully equipped galley-style kitchens with stove, fridge, and microwave. Some of the suites are one bedroom, others are open plan, some have a separate dining area, and all have pullout sofa beds. The two top-floor penthouses have a sundeck and a Jacuzzi. Step out of the hotel and you are blocks from Stanley Park and downtown Vancouver and in the midst of dozens of restaurants and shops.

1394 Robson St. (at Broughton), Vancouver, BC V6E 1C5. © **888/667-8877** or 604/687-1674. Fax 604/685-7808. www.robsonstrassehotel.com. 48 units. Mar–Oct C$149–$169 (US$98–$112) double, C$179–$309 suite. Nov–Feb C$59–$119 (US$39–$79) double, C$129–$209 (US$85–$138) suite. Children under 7 stay free in parents' room. AE, DC, DISC, MC, V. Free parking on a first-come first-served basis. **Amenities:** Exercise room; coin-op washers and dryers; same-day laundry/dry cleaning. *In room:* A/C, TV w/ pay movies, full kitchen in all rooms, fridge, coffeemaker, hairdryer.

The Rosellen Suites at Stanley Park ★★ *(Finds)*   Don't be disappointed when you see the plain outside of this building, as it hides a beautifully appointed former 1950s apartment building within. It could also quite likely be hiding celebrities, as many choose to stay here incognito, as the signed photos in the office attest. The Rosellen has even named its penthouse suite after Katharine Hepburn, who has stayed at the hotel for up to 6 months at a time. And, as it is just half a block from Stanley Park but only blocks away from the hub of the West End, you couldn't find a much quieter or more beautiful location for your family's Vancouver adventures.

The Rosellen also has some great features. There are the copper-plated doors with the flower motif on all the rooms and the old-fashioned elevator that travels between the four floors.

The suites are all very large and attractively decorated. The larger suites have a fireplace, a full bathroom en suite, and a dining room that is separated from the rest of the apartment by a wall of glass blocks. All the dining tables have elegant table settings for four and the large silk plants add an at-home feel to the rooms. All the suites have large living rooms and fully equipped kitchens with dishes, cutlery, and pots and pans provided.

There is no lobby or front desk, but the office is open between 9am and 5pm. The hotel offers corporate discounts of 20% all year around.

2030 Barclay St., (at Chilco St.), Vancouver, BC V6G 1L5. © **888/317-6648** or 604/689-4807. Fax 604/684-3327. www.rosellensuites.com. 30 units. June 1–Sept 30 C$199 (US$131) 1-bedroom suite, C$229–$299 (US$151–$197) 2-bedroom suite, C$399 (US$263) penthouse. Oct 1–May 31 C$119 (US$79) 1-bedroom suite, C$149–$229 (US$98–$151) 2-bedroom suite, C$325 (US$215) penthouse. Minimum 3-night stay. Weekly & monthly rates available. Cots, cribs, and highchairs free. AE, DC, DISC, MC, V. Limited underground parking C$5 (US$3.30). Pets allowed (cleaning charges may apply). **Amenities:** Babysitting; coin-op washers and dryers; same-day laundry/dry cleaning; nonsmoking rooms. *In room:* A/C in some, TV, fax, dataport, full kitchens in all rooms, coffeemaker, hairdryer, iron.

Sunset Inn Travel Apartments (★) (*Finds*)   Just a couple of blocks from English Bay and close to dozens of restaurants, a supermarket, and a 24-hour drugstore, this hotel is in an ideal location for families. Built in the late 1980s, the hotel is a concrete structure that blends into its otherwise largely residential setting. The one-bedroom suites, which are recommended for families, are really spacious and have a galley-style kitchen with a full-sized fridge, a stove, a microwave, and dishes, cutlery, pots, and pans provided. There is a dining table and a separate living-room area with a sofa bed and floor-to-ceiling windows, and every room has a balcony. The lobby is cheerful with a fireplace and sitting area, and the free coffee and cookies between 8 and 11am should be a hit with both adults and kids.

1111 Burnaby St. (at Thurlow St.), Vancouver, BC V6E 1P4. © **800/786-1997** or 604/688-2474. www.sunsetinn.com. 50 units. June 1–Sept 30 C$138–$168 (US$91–$111) double, C$148–$178 (US$98–$118) 1-bedroom suite. Oct 1–May 30 C$78–$118 (US$52–$78) double, C$88–$128 (US$58–$85) 1-bedroom suite. Children 12 and under stay free. Cribs free, rollaways C$10 (US$6.60). Weekly & monthly rates. AE, DC, MC, V. Parking free. **Amenities:** Exercise room; babysitting; coin-op washers and dryers; same-day laundry/dry cleaning; nonsmoking rooms. *In room:* A/C, TV, full kitchens in all rooms, coffeemaker, hairdryer, iron.

INEXPENSIVE

Buchan Hotel (★) (*Value*)   This is a charming low-rise building with a lovely garden on a tree-lined, largely residential street. While the rooms aren't very big, they are attractively outfitted with floral curtains and bedspreads, and some look over a pretty courtyard, although this side can be a little noisy in the summer.

It's hard to imagine a better location. The hotel is just blocks from Stanley Park in one direction and in the other just blocks from dozens of restaurants, Joe Fortes Library, and the West End Community Centre.

Huge hallways have historic prints of Vancouver and Tiffany lamps. The public areas are recently renovated and there is a large sitting room just off the lobby with a blazing fire in the winter and free coffee all year around. Sit down here in the comfortable overstuffed furniture and grab a novel from the bookcase, the day's newspaper, or a magazine, or simply read about local walks and restaurants. You can book tours at the front desk. There is no elevator in the hotel and there are no phones in the rooms, but you will find three pay phones and the vending machines downstairs. The front desk is open at 7:30am and closes at 11pm so don't forget your keys as there is a C$30 (US$20) call-out charge.

A car is not ideal at this hotel. You can park free on the street for only 2 hours at a time and the nearest 24-hour pay parking lot is at the Coast Plaza Hotel three blocks away. The lot charges C$10 (US$6.60).

1906 Haro St. (at Gilford St.), Vancouver, BC V6G 1H7. © 800/668-6654 or 604/685-5354. Fax 604/685-5367. www.buchanhotel.com. 61 units, 30 with private bathroom. May 1–Sept 30 C$75 (US$50) double with shared bathroom, C$95–$135 (US$63–$89) double with private bathroom. Oct 1–Apr 30 C$45 (US$30) double with shared bathroom; C$70–$110 (US$46–$73) double with private bathroom. Children under 12 stay free in parents' room. Weekly rates. AE, DC, MC, V. **Amenities:** Coin-op washers and dryers; storage room for bikes and skis; and all nonsmoking rooms. In room: TV, no phone.

Greenbrier Hotel (Value)

While not much too look at from the outside, this newly renovated hotel has a killer location, great water views—even from the 2nd floor—and elegantly tiled hallways and bathrooms. The family suites have a huge living room with a pullout sofa bed and separate dining area. The kitchen has a simple dining table and a stove and a fridge, and dishes, cutlery, and cooking utensils are all provided. Step outside and you are on Robson Street, with its restaurants and shopping, and a short walk from Stanley Park and English Bay. Built in the 1960s, this three-story building has no elevator.

1393 Robson St. (at Broughton St.), Vancouver, BC V6E 1C6. © 888/355-5888 or 604/683-4558. Fax 604/669-3109. Greenbrierhotel@aol.com. 32 units. May 1–Oct 15 C$129–$189 (US$85–$125). Oct 16–Apr 30 C$79–$109. (US$52–$72). Children under 12 stay free in parents' room. Cribs free, rollaways C$10 (US$6.60). AE, DC, MC, V. Free parking. **Amenities:** Coin-op washers and dryers, same-day laundry/dry cleaning; non smoking rooms. In room: TV, fax, dataport, full kitchens in all rooms, coffeemaker, hairdryer, iron.

Oceanside Hotel

This is not a classy hotel. You won't find lavish service or decor, a view, frills, or service, but the rooms are clean, the price is right, and the location is unbeatable. Walk out the door and you have dozens of restaurants on Denman Street, and English Bay and Stanley Park are just around the corner. There are basically two room types and both are spacious with pullout sofa beds and full kitchens that include stove, fridge, microwave, toaster, cutlery, and dishes. The three-story hotel was built in the 1970s and there is no elevator.

1847 Pendrell St., (at Denman St.), Vancouver, BC V6G 1T3. © 877/506-2326 or 604/682-5641. Fax 604/687-2340. www.oceanside-hotel.com. 23 units. June 1–Sept 30 C$130 (US$86); Oct 1–May 31 C$90 (US$60). Weekly & monthly rates. Children under 5 stay free. Cribs and rollaways free. AE, DC, MC, V. Free parking. Pets accepted free. **Amenities:** Nonsmoking rooms. In room: TV, fax, dataport, full kitchen in all suites, coffeemaker, iron.

Riviera Hotel (★) (Finds)

This 1970s hotel has two types of suites, both great for families. From the 5th floor up the rooms have a separate bedroom, with a sofa bed in the living room. The rooms on the lower floors have open plans popular with people who have very small children or who just don't want to sleep on a sofa bed. There are fabulous water and mountain views in the quieter rooms at the back of the hotel, or you can do some serious people watching from the Robson Street side. All rooms have balconies with a table and chairs to kick back in the summer and all have a full kitchen with table and chairs and a stove, fridge, dishes, cutlery, and cooking utensils provided. The rooms are very large and well decorated and have an elegant tiled entrance hallway and bathroom. The 11-story hotel was built in the 1970s and the rooms and public areas were updated in 1999. The lobby is small but bright, with a lovely tropical fish tank. And the best thing of all is you are on the doorstep of all of Robson Street's shopping and restaurants and very close to Stanley Park and English Bay.

1431 Robson St. (at Nicola St.), Vancouver, BC V6G 1C1. © 888/699-5222 or 604/685-1301. Fax 604/685-1335. www.rivierahotel@aol.com. 40 units. May 1–Oct 15 C$128–$188 (US$85–$124). Oct 16–Apr 30

C$78–$118. (US$52–$78). Children under 12 stay free in parents' room. Cribs free, rollaways C$10 (US$6.60). AE, DC, MC, V. Free parking. **Amenities:** Coin-op washers and dryers, same-day laundry/dry cleaning; non-smoking rooms. *In room:* TV, fax, dataport, full kitchens in all rooms, coffeemaker, hairdryer, iron.

Sylvia Hotel   This beautiful ivy-covered stone building is right on English Bay and has the comfortable old-fashioned feel of Grandma's house. Even the busy lobby, with its time-worn marble stairs, red carpets, and drop-dead water views, is somehow peaceful. The hotel was originally built as apartments and the suites, with pullout couches and separate kitchens, are great for families. There is no air conditioning, but just open the large windows to let in a very pleasant sea breeze should it ever get hot enough to bother. The rooms at the front of the hotel have a magnificent and unimpeded view of English Bay and are slightly more expensive than those without. There is one top-floor suite—the most expensive listed—that is really large with sweeping views. When the eight-story Sylvia was built in 1912 it was the largest building in Western Canada and remained the tallest building in the West End until the 1950s.

If you do stay here (or even if you don't), spend the C$18 (US$11.90) to pick up a copy of Lois Simmie's *Mister Got to Go: The Cat that Wouldn't Leave.* A beautifully illustrated children's story, it's based on a true story about a stray cat that came to live at the Sylvia and was a hotel fixture until it died in the mid-1990s. The bar, which also overlooks English Bay, is a favorite meeting place for locals and the hotel is a popular one with tourists. Regulars are known to reserve their favorite rooms a year to 18 months in advance.

154 Gilford St. (at Beach Ave.), Vancouver, BC V6G 2P6. © **604/681-9321.** Fax 604/682-3551. www.sylvia hotel.com. 119 units. Apr 1–Nov 1 C$75–$135 (US$50–$89) double, C$145–$205 suite. Nov 2–Mar 31 C$65–$115 (US$43–$76) double, C$105–$115 (US$69–$76) suite. Cribs C$5 (US$3.30) rollaways C$15 (US$9.90). AE, DC, MC, V. Underground parking C$7 (US$4.60). Pets stay free. **Amenities:** Restaurant (Continental), kids' menu; bar; limited room service; babysitting; same-day laundry/dry cleaning; nonsmoking rooms. *In room:* TV, fax, dataport, full kitchen in suites.

3 The West Side

Vancouver's West Side includes the University of British Columbia and the endowment lands, Granville Island, Queen Elizabeth Park, and half a dozen great beaches. While there are several medium-sized hotels in the area, accommodation tends to lean more toward bed-and-breakfasts.

MODERATE

Holiday Inn   This hotel is popular with the business crowd, but it also offers great advantages to families. There is the Holiday Inn Kids Program, which gives kids a package on check-in with an activity book, a toy, coupons to a variety of attractions, and a kids' menu. The desk will also happily provide board games to use in the room. Being removed from the built-up downtown area, the hotel offers breathtaking views of the water, the North Shore mountains, and the downtown core. In the summer you can keep an eye on the kids in the glass-walled pool area from a large patio with million-dollar views, or year-round you can work out in the well-equipped exercise room, which has a glass wall overlooking the pool. You are a 10-minute bus ride from downtown and steps from about 40 restaurants. A large expansion is planned to start in November 2001 and be completed by 2003. It will give the hotel 65 additional rooms, 14 townhouses, a community center, and a grassy courtyard.

711 W. Broadway St. (at Heather St.), Vancouver, BC V5Z 3Y2. ℂ **800/HOLIDAY** or 604/879-0511. Fax 604/872-7520. www.holidayinnvancouver.com. 193 units. June 3–Sept 29 C$189–$200 (US$125–$132) double, Sept 30–June 2 C$149–$169 (US$98–$112) double. Packages available all year; children under 19 stay free in parents' room, children under 12 eat free at the hotel's restaurant. Cribs free, rollaways C$20 (US$13.20). AE, DC, DISC, MC, V. Underground parking C$4 (US$2.65). Pets accepted free. **Amenities:** Restaurant (Continental), bar; well-lit indoor pool; sauna, exercise room; National Tilden car rental desk; limited room service; same-day laundry/dry cleaning; 95% of rooms nonsmoking. *In room:* A/C, TV w/ pay movies, fax, dataport, fridge on request C$10 (US$6.60), coffeemaker, hairdryer.

INEXPENSIVE

Accommodations at Pillow Suites   Right in the middle of the City Hall heritage district and a 5-minute drive or bus ride from downtown Vancouver, these fully equipped apartments are most definitely unforgettable. There are three buildings on a corner lot, the oldest built in 1906 and the most recent, now painted bright purple, originally built in 1910 as a corner grocery store. Each apartment has a different theme, but the corner store is the most arty and feels like you are living inside a giant jumble sale. Kids will love the toy house, the colorful daybed, the Coca Cola lampshades, and the Campbell Soup light fittings. There is a fire-engine red 1940s fridge—next to a more recent white one—a working 1920 General Electric stove, and an old clawfoot bathtub. The other units include in a sun theme, a Central American theme, a West Coast suite complete with original art, an Oriental room, and a smaller country theme with a sleeping loft above the living room and accessible by ladder. All the suites have dishwashers and dishes, cutlery, pots, and pans, and local calls are free. The two- and three-bedroom suites have washers and dryers. The apartments are within walking distance of Granville Island and a variety of restaurants, 20 blocks from Queen Elizabeth Park, and a block from a toddlers' playground, a basketball hoop, and the Mount Pleasant Community Centre and swimming pool.

2859 Manitoba St. (between Cambie & Main Sts. at 13th Ave.), Vancouver, BC V5Y 3B3. ℂ **604/879-8977.** Fax: 604/879-8966. www.pillow.net. 6 units. May 15–Sept 30 C$115 (US$76) 1-bedroom, C$170 (US$112) 2-bedroom, C$255 (US$168) 3-bedroom. Oct 1–May 14 C$85 (US$56) 1-bedroom, C$130 (US$86) 2-bedroom, C$195 (US$129) 3-bedroom. Highchairs, foam mattresses, and rollaways free. No credit cards. 5-night minimum stay. Free parking. **Amenities:** All nonsmoking rooms. *In room:* TV, full kitchens.

The Manor Guest House *(Finds)*   While many bed-and-breakfasts are adult-oriented despite what they might say, this 1902 Edwardian house is a great alternative for families who are looking for a more at-home style of accommodation. In the summer, families are given downstairs suites, which open out to a private patio and a beautifully landscaped garden. Those with children aged 10 and older may want to consider the penthouse suite, which sleeps six. (The reason for the age limit is a large balcony with a small railing.) The penthouse suite has stunning views of the city and North Shore mountains and an attic with a queen-sized bed that the kids will fight over. There is a full-sized kitchen with a sloping picture window, huge bathroom, and walk-in wardrobe. An episode of *The X Files* was filmed in this room. The entire house is beautifully decorated. There is a piano in the downstairs lounge (no Chopsticks allowed), a fireplace, computer with Internet access, and phone (free for local calls). Breakfast is served in a large sunny kitchen and is a full four- to five-course vegetarian buffet that could include quiche, fresh fruit salad, and a selection of cheese, whole wheat or sourdough bread, and copious quantities of orange juice and home-baked muffins. The house is one of the oldest buildings left in Vancouver. It's a block away from City Hall and a few minutes in the car, an easy bus ride, or about a half-hour walk to downtown Vancouver. Brenda Yablon, proprietor, speaks English, French, and German. There is a strict nonsmoking policy. Close by, Yablon also operates a 1909 craftsman-style house. Open to families in summer, it has three suites of varying sizes, all with their own entrances and with fully equipped kitchens.

345 W. 13th Ave. (near Cambie St.), Vancouver, BC V5Y 1W2. © **604/876-8494.** Fax 604/876-5763. www.manorguesthouse.com. 10 units. Family suite (max. 4 people) available summer only C$105 (US$70); adjoining rooms C$95 (US$63) each. Shared bathroom. Penthouse C$95–$190 (US$63–$126). Kids must be 10 or older to stay in the penthouse. Rates include full breakfast.

43 W. 18th St. Vancouver, BC V5Y 2A3. Available summer only: 1-bedroom suite C$145 (US$96), 2-bedroom suite C$195–$250 (US$129–$165). Separate entrance, full kitchen. 3-night minimum. MC, V. Free parking. *In room:* TV, hairdryer, kitchenettes in some, no phone.

4 The East Side

Still relatively close to downtown Vancouver, the East Side offers up good moderate accommodations, some with great views of the North Shore mountains. Known more as a blue-collar working district of the city, it's off the beaten tourist path, but is home to Commercial Drive, one of the more arty and interesting areas of the city.

MODERATE

Best Western Exhibition Park   Situated on busy Hastings Street, this is a no frills, clean place with reasonable prices. It's 15 minutes from downtown, a block from Playland, and walking distance to the New Brighton outdoor pool and Hastings Park, and it has easy access to Highway 1, downtown Vancouver, and the North Shore. There is a McDonald's restaurant with a Playplace across the street, and A&B Sound next door, and a variety of restaurants within walking distance. The rooms at the back of the hotel are quieter and have a view of the mountains instead of the traffic.

3475 E. Hastings St. (at Cassiar), Vancouver, BC V5K 2A5. © **877/296-4751** or 604/294-4751. Fax 604/294-1269. 58 units. June–Sept C$159–$179 (US$105–$118) double, C$220 (US$145) suite. Oct–May C$85–$95 (US$56–$63) double, C$135 (US$89) suite. Rates include continental breakfast. Children under 12 stay free. Rollaways C$10 (US$6.60). AE, DC, DISC, MC, V. Free parking. **Amenities:** Jacuzzi; sauna; coin-op washers and dryers, same-day laundry/dry cleaning; nonsmoking rooms. *In room:* A/C, TV w/ pay movies, fax, dataport, mini-fridge, coffeemaker.

INEXPENSIVE

2400 Motel   This is a bit out of the way, but the price is right and it's a pleasant motel made up of freshly painted white and green bungalows built in the 1940s. It has the feel of a country cabin, and in the units with kitchens you'll find a good-sized old-fashioned kitchen with a table and chairs, a tiled floor, and a separate entrance. The bathroom is also old fashioned but functional, and there is a gas fireplace in the main bedroom. There is a small grassy area out front where the kids can play. There is a coin-operated laundry a block away, and the motel is next door to a Church's Chicken and a 10-minute walk to the Nanaimo Sky-Train Station, which will whip you downtown in about 10 minutes. It is also reasonably close to both Commercial Drive and Metrotown Shopping Centre.

2400 Kingsway (at 33rd Ave. & Nanaimo), Vancouver, BC V5R 5G9. © **888/833-2400** or 604/434-2464. Fax 604/430-1045. 2400motel@bc.sympatico.ca. 65 units. May 1–Sept 30 C$99–$109 (US$65–$72) 1 & 2 bedrooms, C$125–$179 (US$83–$118) with kitchens. Cribs C$5 (US$3.30), rollaways C$8 (US$5.30). AE, MC, V. Free parking. Pets accepted C$4 (US$2.65). **Amenities:** Nonsmoking rooms. *In room:* TV, kitchens in some.

5 The North Shore

Life goes on here at a slightly slower pace and, unless you are traveling at peak traffic periods, downtown is only 15 minutes away. The North Shore is separated from downtown by two bridges or the SeaBus, but the advantages are close proximity to dozens of hiking trails, attractions, and some of the world's best mountain biking. Accommodation is much less expensive than comparable downtown hotels.

EXPENSIVE

Lonsdale Quay Hotel ⊘   Take the glass elevator up to the third floor and you can look down on the Lonsdale Public Market from under the atrium of this hotel's lobby. Built in 1986 for Expo, the hotel underwent extensive renovations in 1998 and in 2000, and it is a lovely hotel for families.

Walk outside and hop on the SeaBus, which is a pleasant 12-minute ride across the Burrard Inlet to the terminal outside Canada Place downtown. There are buses that will take you to all the attractions. The rooms are simple yet cheerfully furnished, and a standard room has two queen-size beds. Rooms on the east side have French doors that open out onto a water view (you can request a view of the tugboats), and on the west side rooms have a small balcony. Two rooms are wheelchair accessible. There are a lot of restaurants in the area and the market has fresh fruit and vegetables, muffins, a soup shop, and a great food court.

123 Carrie Cates Crt. (3rd floor, Lonsdale Quay market), North Vancouver, BC V7M 3K7. ℭ **800/836-6111** or 604/986-6111. Fax 604/986-8782. www.lonsdalequayhotel.com. 70 units. May 1–Oct 31 C$200–$225 (US$132–$149). Nov 1–Apr 30 C$140–$165 (US$92–$109). Children under 18 stay free. Cribs free, rollaways C$20 (US$13.20). AE, DC, DISC, MC, V. Underground parking C$7 (US$4.60), free on weekends and holidays. **Amenities:** Restaurant (West Coast); bar; exercise facilities; whirlpool; concierge; limited room service; babysitting; coin-op washers and dryers; same-day laundry/dry cleaning; nonsmoking rooms. *In room:* A/C, TV, fax, dataport, high-speed Internet C$9.95 (US$6.55), minibar, coffeemaker, hairdryer, iron, watercooler.

MODERATE

Grouse Inn ⊘   A two-level motel-like accommodation built in the 1980s, the Grouse underwent a major renovation in 1999. There are a swing set and picnic area and a great outdoor pool with a slide. The rooms are well appointed and modern, and the ones with kitchens have a tiled floor, full fridge, stove, microwave, dishwasher, sink, table, and chairs. There is a Denny's, a De Dutch Pannekoek House, and an Earl's within walking distance, and its location at the busy intersection of Capilano Road and Marine Drive puts it minutes from the Lions Gate Bridge, Stanley Park, downtown Vancouver, and all the attractions and wilderness that the North Shore has to offer.

1633 Capilano Rd. (at Marine Dr.), North Vancouver, BC V7P 3B3. ℭ **800/779-7888** or 604/988-7101. Fax 604/988-7102. www.grouseinn.bc.ca. 79 units. June 1–Oct 10 C$138–$148 (US$91–$98) double, C$169–C$189 (US$112–US$125) double with kitchen, C$175–$198 (US$115–$131) suite, C$169–$289 (US$112–$191) suite with kitchen. Oct 11–Apr 30 C$89–$99 (US$59–$65) double, C$99–$139 (US$65–$92) double with kitchen, C$99–$128 (US$65–$85) suite, C$99–$165 (US$65–$109) suite with kitchen. Cribs free, rollaways C$20 (US$13.20). AE, DC, DISC, MC, V. Free parking. **Amenities:** Restaurant (Greek); outdoor seasonal pool; children's play area; coin-op washers and dryers; nonsmoking rooms. *In room:* A/C, TV, fax, dataport, kitchenette in some, coffeemaker, hairdryer, iron.

Holiday Inn Hotel & Suites ⊘⊘⊘ *(Finds)*   More like an upmarket ski resort than a city hotel, this chateau-style hotel opened in May 2000 and replaced the Old Coach House building, which was blown up for a *Viper* television show.

The tiled lobby has roaring fireplaces in the winter and a large courtyard, which has a garden sitting area in the summer and also adjoins the large indoor pool. The rooms are large and are fully equipped with stove, fridge, dishes, cutlery, pots, and pans. The Paradise Spa is also a draw for adults in need of some pampering and offers a complete range of services. Recreational vehicles can also park free on the property and film crews have been known to bring zebras and gorillas on occasion. Located at the base of the North Shore mountains, it is 20 minutes from downtown Vancouver, close to Grouse Mountain, Maplewood Farm, and Capilano Suspension Bridge, and minutes from some of the world's finest mountain biking, lakes, and hiking trails.

700 Old Lillooet Rd. (exit 22 off the Trans-Canada Hwy.), North Vancouver, BC V7J 2H5. ℭ **877/985-3111** or 604/985-3111. Fax: 604/985-0857. www.hinorthvancouver.com. 162 rooms. May 1–Sept 30 C$175–$195 (US$116–$129) double, C$205–$225 (US$135–$149) suite. Kitchen C$20 (US$13.20). Oct 1–Apr 30 C$115–$125 (US$76–$83) double, C$135–$150 (US$89–$99) suites. Kitchen C$10 (US$6.60). Discounts of up to 25% if staying 7 days or longer. Cribs free, rollaways C$10 (US$6.60). Children under 18 stay free in parents' room. Children under 12 eat free from the kids' menu. AE, DC, DISC, MC, V. Parking free for cars and recreational vehicles. Small pets accepted only, C$200 (US$132) deposit. **Amenities:** Restaurant (North American), kids' menu; pub, wine & beer store; bright triangular indoor pool; exercise room; Jacuzzi; sauna; spa; concierge; salon; limited room service; babysitting; coin-op washers and dryers; same-day laundry/dry cleaning; nonsmoking rooms. *In room:* A/C, TV w/ pay movies & Nintendo, fax, dataport, high-speed Internet connection C$10 (US$6.60), kitchenette, microwave, fridge, coffeemaker, hairdryer, iron, safe, umbrellas.

INEXPENSIVE

Canyon Court Inn & Suites   Even though this two-story motel is on busy Capilano Road, the rooms are surprisingly quiet and offer families spaciousness with easy access to the Lions Gate Bridge, Stanley Park, and downtown Vancouver. Canyon Court poured C$2 million into renovations in 2000 and sports a new lobby and breakfast eating area and a tranquil private courtyard with a water fountain where you can take your continental breakfast in the summer.

The Canyon Court has done a flurry of remodeling and renovating since it was built in the 1970s and there is little left to recognize from that era. Many of the rooms are completely overhauled, redecorated, and refitted, while others are still a work in progress. There are several different room configurations and some are adjoining—check the website to see which one suits your particular family's size and age. More than a third of the rooms have kitchenettes, which include stove and fridge, and some with microwave. One of the three buildings overlooks the pool and has a balcony that wraps around the second story so you can keep an eye on the kids.

1748 Capilano Rd. (at Marine Dr.), North Vancouver, BC V7P 3B4. ℭ **888/988-3131** or 604/988-3181. Fax 604/904-2755. www.canyoncourt.com. 94 units. June–Sept C$129 (US$85) double, C$159 (US$105) 1-bedroom suite, C$229 (US$151) 2-bedroom suite. Oct–May C$79 (US$52) double, C$89 (US$59) 1-bedroom suite, C$199 (US$131) 2-bedroom suite. Rates include continental breakfast. Weekly rates. Cribs free, rollaways C$10 (US$6.60). AE, DC, DISC, MC, V. Free parking. **Amenities:** Outdoor pool (seasonal); Jacuzzi; coin-op washers and dryers; nonsmoking rooms. *In room:* A/C, TV, some with dataport, 50% with fridge, coffeemaker, 70% with hairdryer.

6 Near the Airport

Richmond is a city on an island surrounded by dikes. You'll find everything from farmland to huge Asian malls, a variety of accommodations, shopping, and great recreational facilities.

MODERATE

Delta Pacific Resort and Conference Centre *(★ ★* *(Value)*   Locals come to the Delta to spend the weekend because of the great facilities for families and the great deals in the off season. As an extra bonus, the resort and its 14 land-scaped acres are close to the airport and about a 20-minute drive to downtown Vancouver. From the moment you check in you can tell this hotel really goes after the kids market; in fact, adults may feel a little neglected. Kids 12 and under have their own check-in with a pint-size staircase, where they register and pick up a gift bag that includes a ball, a yo-yo, bubble bath, and an activity book and crayons. Once in the brightly decorated rooms, kids will find a per-sonalized card with the hotel's Ollie the Orca mascot and a large bowl of cook-ies and Smarties. Kid-sized robes are laid out on the bed. But your kids will most likely be in too much of a hurry to hit the pool with its three-story high water-slide and all the noodles and boards and balls the hotel provides. Right near the pool is the children's creative center, which has, among other attributes, free Nintendo, arts and crafts, toys, and games for kids aged 3 to 9 and is open daily from 9am to 9pm. On Friday and Saturday nights between 6 and 8pm the hotel holds a kids' night: you can drop the kids off for C$5 (US$3.30) to have pop-corn and a special movie and you can go off to eat or hit the running trail or the exercise room, which has cardio equipment, or perhaps enjoy a sauna. There is also a playground and a basketball hoop, and you can rent bikes for C$8 (US$5.30) an hour.

10251 St. Edwards Dr. (at Bridgeport Rd. just off Hwy. 99), Richmond, BC V6X 2M9. © **800/268-1133** or 604/278-9611. Fax 604/276-1121. www.deltapacific.bc.ca. 438 units. May 1–Sept 30 C$139–$300 (US$92–$198), Oct 1–Apr 30 C$99–$250 (US$65–$165). Children under 18 stay free in parents' room. Children under 7 eat free with parents. Cribs free, rollaways C$10 (US$6.60). AE, DC, DISC, MC, V. Small pets accepted C$25 (US$16.50) cleaning fee. **Amenities:** Two restaurants (West Coast & Japanese), kids' menu; two bars and one patio bar in summer; indoor pool with waterslide, 2 outdoor pools (summer only); exercise room; Jacuzzi; sauna; 4 indoor tennis courts; 2 squash courts; children's center programs; bike rentals; concierge; tour desk; massage; 24-hour room service; babysitting; same-day laundry/dry cleaning; nonsmoking rooms. *In room:* A/C, TV w/ pay movies & Nintendo, fax, dataport, minibar, coffeemaker, hairdryer, iron.

INEXPENSIVE

Comfort Inn Vancouver Airport   Aptly named, this simple four-story hotel at a busy intersection is just 5 minutes from the airport and offers good basic accommodation for families. Built in 1956, the hotel poured C$2.5 million into renovating the rooms and public areas. The ground floor rooms have patios that open out onto the outdoor pool and are ideal if you're traveling with older chil-dren. If you prefer a larger room, there is a choice between the family suites on the fourth floor and the business suites. The family suites are huge rooms with two queen-sized beds, a queen-sized pullout sofa, and a dining table and chairs. They also have small windows that you can't see out of, under a vaulted ceiling, which make the rooms seem rather gloomy. At the same price, the 22 business suites seem a better deal. While not nearly as big, they have a small parlor with a television and pullout sofa and a main bedroom with a second television. The hotel offers a 100% satisfaction guarantee and will have Nintendo in every room by 2002. In the summer, there is a free shuttle to the 300-shop Richmond Centre, and the hotel is close to several restaurants, shops, and a golf driving range. Parking is free and the hotel will throw in a free week's parking if you are flying off to someplace else. Prices seem pretty flexible depending on how busy the bookings are. Quote L-FROM (for Frommer's) at the time of booking and receive up to 20% of the rack rate listed below.

3031 No. 3 Rd., (at Sea Island Way), Richmond, BC V6X 2B6. © **800/663-0974** or 604/278-5161. Fax 604/207-2380. www.comfortinnvancouver.com. 130 units. May 16–Sept 30 C$129–$159 (US$85–$105) double. Oct 1–May 14 C$89–C$129 (US$59–US$85) double. Children under 18 stay free in parents' room. Cribs free, rollaways C$10 (US$6.60). AE, DC, MC, V. Free parking. Pets accepted free. **Amenities:** Restaurant (American), kids' menu; one comedy bar; beer & wine shop; outdoor pool (summer only); limited room service; same-day laundry/dry cleaning; nonsmoking rooms. *In room:* A/C, TV w/ pay movies, fax, dataport, coffeemaker, tea kettle, hairdryer.

Holiday Inn   There is nothing fancy about this hotel built in 1997, but its price and location make it a good choice for families, especially if you are only planning to stop over for a day or two. Because it is 15 minutes from BC Ferries, a 20-minute drive to downtown Vancouver, and close to the airport and Richmond business parks, it is a popular hotel with the business crowd. But possibly the hotel's greatest feature is the several kids' rooms. The hotel has cleverly taken a standard double-sized hotel room and, by using a partition, created a kids' room complete with bunk bed and television set with Nintendo (available from the front desk at no charge) next to an area with either a queen- or king-sized bed and a second television. The room has cheery kid-friendly wallpaper and bedspreads and some of the bunks have a double bed in the lower bunk. These rooms (and the efficiency rooms) also have a microwave and fridge.

There is no pool, but the front desk will hand out vouchers to the nearby Watermania complex. The hotel offers special stopover rates, and a free airport shuttle bus stops outside.

10720 Cambie Rd. (at Shell Rd.), Richmond, BC V6X 1K8. © **888/831-3388** or 604/821-1818. Fax 604/207-3170. www.hi-airport.bc.ca. 163 units. May 16–Sept 15 C$115–$145 (US$76–$96) double. Sept 16–May 14 C$95–$125 (US$63–$83) double. Kids' and efficiency rooms C$10 (US$6.60). Children under 18 stay free. Children under 12 eat free. Cribs free, rollaways C$10 (US$6.60). AE, DC, DISC, MC, V. Free parking. **Amenities:** Restaurant and bar (American); exercise room; Jacuzzi; limited room service; same-day laundry/dry cleaning; nonsmoking rooms. *In room:* A/C, TV w/ pay movies, fax, dataport, fridge, coffeemaker, hairdryer, iron.

7 Campgrounds

If the great outdoors is your style, BC has some excellent, well-equipped campgrounds. Here are two that are very close to downtown Vancouver.

Burnaby Cariboo RV Park   This campground has all the feel of the country, but it is close to city essentials and is a 20-minute drive or bus ride to downtown Vancouver. It will also be on the doorstep of a new SkyTrain station planned to open in 2002 and is minutes from shopping and a variety of restaurants. The campground began in 1986 and has a well-equipped convenience store on-site. It also has a great pool, lounge, and sundeck, and a grassy, gated playground with horseshoe pits, tether ball, a climbing area, swings, picnic tables, and a large covered barbecue area. As a bonus you are next door to Burnaby Lake Regional Park, with its miles of meandering walking trails and hundreds of ducks and other interesting water life.

8765 Cariboo Place (take the Gaglardi Way exit 37 from Hwy. 1), Burnaby, BC V3N 4T2. © **604/420-1722.** Fax 800/667-9901 or 604/420-4782. www.bcrvpark.com. 217 sites. C$21 (US$14) for 2 people in a tent, C$32 (US$21) RV hookup, extra person C$3.50 (US$2.30). Cable hookup C$2 (US$1.30) a day or C$6 (US$4) a week. MC, V. Pets accepted free. **Amenities:** Indoor pool; exercise room; Jacuzzi; video arcade; coin-op washers and dryers; RV wash.

Capilano RV Park   Built in 1966, this is a well-appointed park that is privately run on Squamish Band land. You'll find massive totem poles, a Jacuzzi housed in a lovely cedar A-frame building, and an outdoor pool in a grassy fenced-off area, and, in summer, you can watch the salmon run in the nearby Capilano River. There is also a lounge with a television and a playground with a slide and jungle gym. Probably the best deal for campers is this park's incredible location. Situated by the Lions Gate Bridge, the park is minutes away from Stanley Park and downtown Vancouver. The park is also just a few short blocks to West Vancouver's Park Royal Shopping Centre and Ambleside Beach.

295 Tomahawk Ave. (north end of the Lions Gate Bridge), North Vancouver, BC V7P 1C5. © **604/987-4722.** Fax 604/987-2015. www.capilanorvpark.com. June 1–Oct 31 C$40 (US$26) for 2 people with full hook-up, C$35 (US$23) with part hook-up, C$30 (US$20) no hook-up. Nov 1–May 31 C$35 (US$23) with full hook-up, C$30 (US$20) with part-hook-up, C$25 (US$16.50) no hook-up. Children 6 and under stay free. Extra person C$3.50 (US$2.30). MC, V. Pets C$2 (US$1.30) each. **Amenities:** Outdoor pool (seasonal); Jacuzzi; children's playground; coin-op washers and dryers.

5

Family-Friendly Dining

There are more than 3,000 restaurants in Vancouver so you can't go far without stumbling across eateries of all types and sizes, for all budgets and tastes. Vancouver's top restaurants win awards for their fine food and wine lists and deserve even more awards for their fabulous decor. While white linen table cloths and elegant flower arrangements don't always mix well with little hands, the quality has filtered down the ranks. Vancouver is your chance to try new things and tempt those little ones with food that doesn't come out of a cardboard box or come with crayons.

Since Expo 86, Vancouver's Asian population has blossomed and, as a result, some fine Chinese restaurants have emerged. And because children and Chinese food seem to go together like Abbott and Costello, I've tried to include a cross section of restaurants in Chinatown and a few off the beaten track. Dim sum is a favorite in Vancouver. If you've never had it, don't leave town without trying some of these wonderful dishes. It can be a bit imposing at first, but sit down, wait for the carts to wheel past, and don't hesitate to ask what's inside each of the bamboo steamers. My kids are incredibly picky eaters at home, but they will dive into a dish of steaming *hargow* (steamed shrimp dumplings). They love the buns filled with barbecued pork, the sticky rice, spring rolls, and shrimp wrapped in white noodles. For dessert, custards and jello with colorful umbrellas and egg tarts are definitely kid-pleasers.

Don't stop at Cantonese, Mandarin, and Szechwan restaurants—Vancouver also has a great selection of Thai, Mongolian, and Korean. Japanese food especially seems to mix well with children, and mine would happily eat *gyoza* (dumplings), chicken teriyaki, or a kappa roll (sushi with cucumber) any day of the week. I've always thought tempura was a clever way to get kids to eat their vegetables.

All in all, dress is very casual in most restaurants. If you are eating dinner in the more expensive establishments you may want to trade the sweats and hiking boots for something more upmarket, but in general, we live in this city because of its relaxed, kickback lifestyle and we don't get overly fussed about ties or high heels.

While many of Vancouver's best restaurants don't offer special menus for children, they are likely to go out of their way to accommodate their needs. But it is far more pleasant for you and the rest of the customers if you leave restless little ones or bored older ones with a babysitter. If this is not possible, or if your kids are more urbane and gastronomically minded than mine, consider lunching before noon and be seated for dinner between 5 and 6pm. Your efforts will be rewarded by grateful staff, who will lavish you with attention, and you won't have to worry about the offended looks from other diners.

In past years, Vancouver has taken on a more European feel in the summer and many restaurants have outdoor patios where you can relax in the sunshine and do some serious people watching. Of course, part of the reason for this proliferation of outdoor space is that smoking is banned inside all pubs and restaurants, so you may want to take this into consideration before deciding where to sit.

Vancouver's many food courts are also inexpensive and a great alternative to restaurant eating. Most are buried in malls and have a large enough range of food groups to please the entire family. There are also some excellent bakery/cafes scattered around the city. If the sun is shining consider heading to the public markets. Just a bus ride or a SeaBus trip away you can find a whole host of food choices at Granville Island and Lonsdale Quay. Grab some fish and chips and watch fudge being made or buy some local fruit to eat later and watch the boats sail past while the kids chase the pigeons. Further out, Westminster Quay is a fun SkyTrain trip and, as it is perched on the Fraser River, is a different type of water experience.

If you are staying in the city for more than a few days, try not to limit yourself to the downtown and West End. The West Side and the North Shore offer some unique restaurants and are well worth the short drive or bus ride.

A few terms that have recently found their way into the local eating vernacular may be strange to out-of-towners. The terms "West Coast" and "Pacific Northwest" seem to be used almost interchangeably to describe local dishes. As far as I can tell, it means that the restaurant uses local game, seafood, and produce in wonderful and unusual combinations. Tapas is also seen frequently and has made the appetizer portion of the menu more interesting. These finger foods are just the right size for children and give them something more nutritious than fast food to sink their teeth into.

DINING DETAILS   A final note on the bureaucracy of eating. Most restaurants close on Christmas Day, some on New Year's Day, and others on Canadian Thanksgiving. Hours on public holidays often change, and while I've tried to include as much detailed information as possible, things change, so please call ahead to avoid disappointment.

The drinking age in BC is 19, and children under 19 are not allowed in areas that sell only alcohol such as pubs and nightclubs.

The tax on food is 7% GST, which is refundable to non-Canadians upon leaving the country (see chapter 2, p. 16, "GST Refunds").

Average tips for a restaurant meal tend to be around 15%.

And, finally, whatever your food choice, relax, sit back, and enjoy. Eating should always be a great adventure.

1 Restaurants by Cuisine

BAKERY/CAFE

The Bread Garden (chains, *p. 85*)
Calhouns (West Side, $, *p. 92*)
Capers Community Market (West End, West Side, North Shore, $$, *p. 87*)
Indigo Books, Music & Cafe (North Shore, $, *p. 97*)
Urban Fare (Downtown, $, *p. 84*)

BRITISH

Cheshire Cheese Inn (West Side, North Shore, $$, *p. 95*)

BURGERS

Sodas Diner (Gastown, West Side, $, *p. 90*)
White Spot (chains, $, *p. 86*)

2 Downtown

EXPENSIVE

Griffins Restaurant ⍟⍟ WEST COAST   This lovely bright restaurant with its yellow walls, black-and-white checkered tiles, high-arched windows, and open kitchen, is designed to look like a West Coast brasserie. During the week the restaurant fills up with local business people, but on the weekend it's a great place to take the family. Griffins is known for its daily buffets, but the Sunday buffet between 11:30am and 2:30pm is particularly lavish. If you are just after a sweet fix, Griffins offers a dessert buffet for C$9.95 (US$6.57) for adults and C$3.95 (US$2.60) for children. If you order a la carte, the selection is a large range of sandwiches, burgers, pastas, roasts, fish, and pizza.

900 W. Georgia St. (at Hornby St. side of the Hotel Vancouver). ✆ **604/662-1900.** Reservations recommended. Main course lunch C$11.75–$16.50 (US$7.75–$10.90), Mon–Sat buffet C$15–$17.50 (US$9.90–$11.55), Sunday buffet $29.50 (US$19.50), children 5–12 eat for half price at the buffet and children under 4 eat free. Kids' menu C$3.95–$5.75 (US$2.60–$3.80). Main course dinner C$17–$28 (US$11.22–$18.50). AE, DC, DISC, MC, V. Open daily 6.30am–10pm. Highchairs, boosters, kids' menu.

Sutton Place Hotel Chocoholic Bar ⍟ DESSERT   On Thursday, Friday, and Saturday evenings, the hotel's French continental restaurant, the Fleuri, has a dessert-to-die-for night for chocoholics. This is a decadent all-you-can-eat buffet featuring chocolate pizza, exotic fruits dipped in chocolate, chocolate fondues, cakes, pies, eclairs, and the house specialty, fresh Brittany crepes made to order. the buffet has two seatings, 6:30 and 8:30pm.

845 Burrard St. (near Robson St.). ✆ **604/682-5511.** www.suttonplace.com. Reservations recommended. C$18.95 (US$12.50), children 12 and under C$9.50 (US$6.27), children over 12 at half price if they eat dinner in the restaurant. AE, DC, MC, V. Thurs–Sat 6–10pm. Highchairs, boosters.

MODERATE

McKenzie's Cabin NORTH AMERICAN   The first thing you notice about this restaurant is that the overstuffed chairs on the patio look like they've come through more than one second-hand store. There are more disreputable-looking chairs inside, but the place feels like a cabin with its hardwood floors, rough-wood tables, and fireplace. There are also moose heads and antlers, a sewing machine, and a bunch of magazines to read. The menu has lots of ribs, pastas, steaks, and other comfort foods, and while there is no printed kids' menu, staff will make you smaller versions of any of the menu items for about half the price, which is worth it as the portions are huge. They'll also serve up grilled ham and cheese, hot dogs, or peanut butter and jelly sandwiches. The restaurant has a pub-style atmosphere later in the night, but it's great for families for lunch or early in the evening.

310 Robson St. (at Hamilton St. across from the Vancouver Public Library). ✆ **604/602-8100.** www.mackenziescabin.com. Reservations accepted. Main course C$8.95–$15.95 (US$5.90–$9.20), kids' menu C$2.95–$5.95 (US$1.95–$3.93). AE, DC, MC, V. Open daily winter 11am–1am, summer 7am–1am.

Family-Friendly Vancouver Dining

Amato Gelato Cafe **1**
Beach House **2**
Bellaggio Cafe **3**
Bridges Bistro and Dock **4**
Buddhist Vegetarian
Restaurant **5**
C-Lovers **6**
Cafe Deux Soleil **7**
Calhouns **8**
Candy Aisle **9**
Candy Kitchen **10**
Capers Community Market **11**
Charlie's Chocolate Factory **12**
Cheshire Cheese Inn **13**
Chocolate Arts **14**
Coveside Restaurant **15**
Cows **16**
Death by Chocolate **17**
Fish House **18**
Floata Seafood Restaurant **19**
Fukuroku Sushi **20**
Griffins Restaurant **21**
Grove Inn **22**
Hon's Wun-Tun House **23**
Hot Dog Jonny's **24**
House of Brussels
Chocolates **25**
Ice Cream Cafe **26**
Il Giardino **27**
Indigo Books Music
& Café **28**
Joe Fortes Seafood
and Chop House **29**
Kenichi Japanese
Restaurant **30**
La Casa Gelato **31**
Las Margaritas **32**
Lombardo's Pizzeria **33**
McKenzie's Cabin **34**
Mum's Gelato **35**
Nando's **36**
Old Spaghetti Factory **37**
Olde World Fudge Co. **38**
Orca's Favorite
Ice Cream Café **39**
Pacific Starlight
Dinner Train **40**
Park Lock Seafood
Restaurant **41**
Pink Pearl **42**
Planet Hollywood **43**
Raincity Grill **44**
Rosie's on Robson **45**
Sara's Old Fashioned
Ice Cream **46**
Sodas Diner **47**
Sophie's Cosmic Café **48**
Suckers Candy Store **49**
Sugar Mountain **50**
Sutton Place Hotel
Chocoholic Bar **51**
Sweet Factory **52**
Thai House **53**
Tomahawk **54**
Troll's **55**
Urban Fare **56**
Vina **57**
Zin **58**

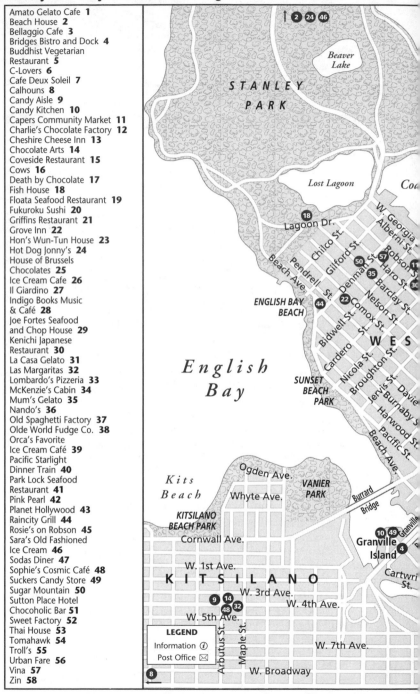

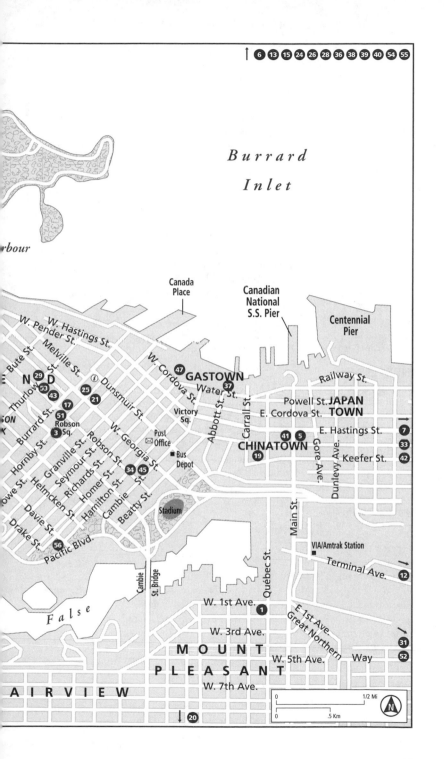

Burrard

Inlet

rbour

Canada
Place

Canadian
National
S.S. Pier

Centennial
Pier

W. Hastings St.

W. Pender St.

Melville St.

W. Cordova St.

GASTOWN
Water St.

Railway St.

E Bute St.

N D

29

53

43

17

25

21

Dunsmuir St.

Thurlow St.

Burrard St.

51

Robson

3 Sq.

SON

Hornby St.

Granville St.

Seymour St.

Richards St.

Robson St.

W. Georgia St.

Homer St.

Hamilton St.

Cambie St.

Beatty St.

Victory
Sq.

Abbott St.

Carrall St.

Powell St. **JAPAN**
E. Cordova St. **TOWN**

41 5

CHINATOWN

19

E. Hastings St.

Keefer St.

Gore Ave.

Dunlevy Ave.

7

33

42

Post
Office

Bus
Depot

34 45

owe St.

Davie St.

Drake St.

Helmcken St.

56

Pacific Blvd.

Stadium

Main St.

VIA/Amtrak Station

Terminal Ave.

12

Cambie

St. Bridge

Québec St.

W. 1st Ave.

1

E 1st Ave.

Great Northern

W. 3rd Ave.

M O U N T

W. 5th Ave.

Way

31

52

P L E A S A N T

A I R V I E W

W. 7th Ave.

↓ 20

False

0   1/2 Mi

0   .5 Km

Planet Hollywood ⋆⋆ NORTH AMERICAN   A kind of museum for Hollywood stars, this restaurant is big, brash, and colorful. Older children will love it. This might not be the place for sensitive tots, but most little ones will enjoy the movie paraphernalia, video clips, and life-size replicas of Arnold Schwarzenegger, Bruce Willis, and others. The restaurant is very child-friendly and staff are happy to let you and the kids wander around while you are waiting for your meal. Little ones are also given crayons and a menu to color. The food is forgettable, and ranges from sandwiches and salads to fajitas, steaks, and pizza. There is a huge patio in the summer that wraps around the outside of the restaurant and is great for people watching and is the only place you can smoke.

969 Robson St. (at Burrard St.). ☎ **604/688-7827.** Reservations for 6 or more only. Sandwiches and burgers C$7.25–$9.25 (US$4.80–$6.10), main course C$12.95–$15.95 (US$8.55–$10.50), kids' menu C$3.95 (US$2.60). AE, MC, V. Open daily 11:30am–10pm. Highchairs, boosters, kids' menu.

Rosie's on Robson WEST COAST   With its dark carpeting, drapes, black-and-white tiled floor, and stage, Rosie's has the feel of a New York–style deli, except that it serves up burgers, pastas, and pancakes. Located right in the entertainment district close to GM Place, BC Place, and the theaters, it's a handy place to grab a meal, and all the show times for sports and theater are posted on a blackboard.

298 Robson St. (at Hamilton St. across from the Vancouver Public Library). ☎ **604/689-4499.** Reservations recommended. Main courses C$8.95–$16.95 (US$5.90–$11.20), kids' menu C$3.95–$5.25 (US$2.60–$3.45). AE, DC, MC, V. Open daily 6:30am–11pm. Highchairs, boosters, kids' menu.

INEXPENSIVE

Bellaggio Cafe (Value) ITALIAN   Kids are very welcome here and breakfast is available all day. The Value Breakfast at C$5.95 (US$3.95) is a particularly good deal. You can also choose from a selection of European crepes, moussaka, or seafood. It's a very warm and friendly Mediterranean-style restaurant overlooking the Vancouver Art Gallery. It has a large sunny patio outside and booth seating inside with a wall devoted to wine, and it offers live piano and violin music after 8:30pm on Fridays and Saturdays.

773 Hornby St. (between Robson and Smithe sts). ☎ **604/408-1281.** Reservations accepted. Main courses C$9.95–$12 (US$6.55–$9.90), children eat for half price on any menu item. AE, MC, V. Open daily 7am–10pm. Highchairs, boosters.

Death by Chocolate DESSERT   If you are in need of a sugar buzz, try the restaurant's signature Death by Chocolate; the Ice Burger—two chocolate ice-cream patties on a sesame seed bun (sponge cake) served with ketchup (raspberry coulis), mayo (whipped cream), and fries (pineapple sticks); or perhaps the Whistler and Blackcomb Twin Peaks—chocolate ice-cream cake with white chocolate sauce, whipped cream, and meringue, with dark chocolate ski poles, of course. Kids can either share or get their own chocolate brownies and ice cream or an ice-cream sundae.

818 Burrard St. (at Robson St.). ☎ **604/688-8234.** Desserts C$3.95–$10.95 (US$2.60–$7.25). V. Open daily 8am–11pm (hours vary according to location). Highchairs. Others locations are 1001 Denman St. (at Nelson St.), Vancouver. ☎ **604/899-2462.** 1598 W. Broadway Ave. (at 1st St. in the West Side's Kitsilano), Vancouver. ☎ **604/730-2462.**

Urban Fare ⋆ BAKERY/CAFE   This ultra-modern supermarket, cafe, and wine bar has become a local hangout for grocery shoppers and diners since opening in August 1999. Even picky eaters can find something they like from the offerings of vegetable lasagna, Asian noodle salads, quiches, pizza, muesli, fresh fruit, and more. The food is cafeteria style—you take a number, place your order, and wait for it to be delivered to your table, fast. The supermarket is also worth a browse. Flowers, pottery, vases, and preserved strawberries are displayed on rough wooden shelves. You can find bread flown in from Paris that day at C$33 (US$21.80) a loaf. Prosciutto and garlic strings hang over the cheese counter and the meat counter sells ostrich meat, certified Angus beef, and prepared veal and salmon. There's even a lobster tank. The spotless, wheelchair-accessible washroom is also a pleasure to visit. There's a diaper-changing table and bottles of hand cream, hair gel, and spray.

177 Davie St. (at Pacific Blvd. in Yaletown). ℂ 604/975-7550. Main courses C$5.95–$11.95 (US$3.95–$7.90). MC, V. Open daily 6am–midnight. Highchairs, boosters.

Introducing Vancouver's Chains

For some reason Vancouver has spawned some unique restaurants that have spread to the east and often to south of the border. The restaurants vary from inexpensive cafes to burger joints to upscale casual restaurants, but all are worth a visit if you are looking for good food at decent prices with a staff that welcomes families.

Boston Pizza   In 1964, a Greek immigrant named Gus Agiortis made his way to Edmonton and opened the first Boston Pizza. The restaurant chain grew in Alberta, then sold and moved its headquarters to Vancouver in the early 1990s. There are now more than 140 locations in Canada and some in the United States. The restaurant makes a great gourmet pizza, the pastas are good, and there is a range of wraps, sandwiches, and meat dishes. On Sundays, kids under 10 eat for C$1.99 (US$1.30) all day. On Tuesdays, adult-sized pasta is C$5.75 (US$3.80).

The Bread Garden *Value*   You'll find dozens of these upscale cafes all over Vancouver either as stand-alone restaurants or sharing space with Chevron gas station's Town Pantry convenience stores. The cafes are frequented by families because of the reasonable prices, quality food, and large patios. Food is baked at the central kitchen each morning and then microwaved when you order. The cafe has a large assortment of pies, pastas, salads, and sandwiches. Kids like the noodles and cheese C$1.49 (US$1) (add C$1.49/ US$1 for a salad and fresh baked roll) and the kids' wrap—a turkey dog with cheddar for C$2.99 (US$2). You can also pick up bread to go at many of the locations and the cinnamon knot is the cafe's decadent signature dish.

De Dutch Pannekoek House *Value*   These old-fashioned–looking restaurants have been in Vancouver since 1975 and give the feeling that you are eating in an old aunt's kitchen. Pannekoeks are delicious Dutch pancakes that come in a range of styles, everything from granola and trail mix to apple and onion. Kids can choose from the chocolate, Fruit Loop, or apple sugar and cinnamon pannekoek. There are also hash browns, French toast, eggs and toast, and peanut butter and jam sandwiches or grilled cheddar and edam. Kids can also order pannekoeks off the main menu and get a half serving—so can adults for that matter. **www.dutchpanne koekhouse.com.**

Keg Steakhouse & Bar   This 83-strong chain with restaurants across Canada and now in Washington, Oregon, and Texas had its beginnings in 1971 in North Vancouver. The original Keg is gone, but the formula is still a good one, and you can pick up a large steak, seafood, or pasta at reasonable prices. The atmosphere is also upbeat and good for families. Staff will give out crayons and the kids' menu includes fish and chips, chicken strips and fries, and a small sirloin steak.

Milestones   If you are tired of eating at low-end family restaurants but still want a kid-friendly environment, Milestones is a nice change of pace. The music is loudish, the crowd young, and the staff fast and friendly. The restaurant has booth seating and serves up a variety of gourmet burgers and pastas, and while there is no written kids' menu, they will serve your kids pasta, macaroni and cheese, chicken fingers, or grilled cheese with either a salad or fries and a pop for C$5 (US$3.30).

The Pantry (Value)   While the value is good at any time, on Wednesdays the restaurant has "family night" when several entrees sell at C$5.99 (US$3.95) for adults and C$2.49 (US$1.65) for kids. The menu has burgers, sandwiches, and wraps, but excels at comfort foods like roast beef and turkey dinners, steaks, veal cutlets, and fish and chips. My kids love the clam chowder. The staff are terrific and give the little ones crayons to color with, and the older ones love the electronic games. **www. thepantry.com.**

White Spot   Kids never seem to tire of seeing their meals arrive in a pirate box with a straw for a mast, stickers, and a gold chocolate coin. The rest of the fare is pretty much burgers and shakes with some wraps and pastas for variety. This chain has been in BC since 1928 and remains much loved for its now famous (and secret) Triple O sauce. Kids get crayons and an activity book and service is generally fast and friendly. This is a popular spot with locals, and if you come at peak lunch and dinner times expect to wait up to 15 minutes or sometimes longer. **www.whitespot.ca.**

Other Chains

McDonald's, Burger King, Wendy's and all the other familiar fast food chains are here in droves, and many have ball rooms and other play areas that can keep kids entertained on rainy days. Two U.S. imports that serve a quality product at good prices follow.

Denny's   Kids eat free from 4 to 10pm every night of the week and the consistently good comfort food and fast and friendly service make this good value for the family. The kids' menu has the usual toasted cheese, chicken nuggets, and pizza, but also has corn dogs and a great smiley-face hotcake dish that little ones love. Open 24 hours.

Red Robin   An upmarket burger joint that has put a lot of thought into its surroundings. Service is friendly and fast and kids will like the crayons and menu as well as all the things the restaurants have managed to cram in, including a 1950s sports car, large model train, carousel horses, and circus pictures. There is a patio in summer.

3 The West End

EXPENSIVE

Fish House ⭐⭐ SEAFOOD   Hotel concierges often point families to this restaurant because, as well as being one of the more elegant in the city, it also welcomes children. It is a lovely old white and green house set in the grounds of Stanley Park. In the evening watch the sun set over English Bay or, during the day, watch the tennis, the pitch'n'putt, or just gaze out to sea. In the warmer weather, the restaurant opens up its two large patios and here kids can be kids. The restaurant is well regarded for its oyster bar and has a good selection of salmon, trout, and other local specialties. The kids' menu, which comes with a drink and a choice of vanilla ice cream, sorbet, or cinnamon biscotti, is well priced and has chowder, cornmeal fried fish and chips, and grilled salmon with maple glaze, among other dishes, served with vegetables or fries. If you eat between 5 and 6pm Sunday to Thursday, staff will take C$15 (US$9.90) off the lowest priced entree on a dinner for two. There's also afternoon tea from 2 to 4pm for C$20 (US$13).

8901 Stanley Park Dr. (in Stanley Park by the pitch'n'putt). © **604/681-7275.** www.fishhousestanleypark .com. Reservations recommended in summer. Main courses C$18.95–$29.95 (US$12.50–$19.75). AE, DC, DISC, MC, V. Open daily 11am–10pm. Highchairs, boosters, kids' menu.

Zin ⭐ *Finds* GLOBAL   You can't miss this bright pink and purple building in front of the Pacific Palisades Hotel on Robson Street, newly opened at the end of 2000. Adults and children of any age should enjoy this rather eclectic experience. There are wild green-checked tiles behind the fireplace, an orange curtain that divides part of the restaurants and the "zap strap" light meant to look like the flash bulb of a camera. In fact, the whole theme of the restaurant is photography. You will find goat cheese fondue, yakisoba from Japan, and dishes from Korea, India, and the Southern United States on the menu, and presumably anywhere else the fancy takes the chef. If Moroccan-spiced tuna or tandoori salmon is too much for your little ones, the restaurant offers a kids' menu with burgers, hot dogs, and all the usuals.

1277 Robson St. (at Jarvis St.). © **604/408-1700.** www.zin-restaurant.com. Reservations accepted. Main courses C$12–$20 (US$7.90–13.20), kids' menu C$4–$6 (US$2.65–$4). AE, DC, MC, V. Open 8am–11pm. Highchairs, boosters, kids' menu.

MODERATE

Capers Community Market BAKERY/CAFE   This organic market has its own cafe with a heated patio open all year. Whether you are into organic food or not, the sandwiches, panini (Italian grilled sandwiches, pronounced pah-*nee*-nee), and wraps are delicious. They have everything from peanut butter and jam to sockeye and herb cream cheese bagel to a vegetarian foccacia sandwich with tzatziki, avocado, and Asiago cheese. There is a great soup and salad bar and you can find take-out pizza made with organic flour, fresh-baked banana bread, and a citrus loaf. There are even recycled postcards at the cash to drop a quick line home.

1675 Robson St. (between Bidwell and Cardero sts.). © **604/687-5288.** C$3–$6 (US$2–$3.95). AE, MC, V. Open daily 8am–10pm (hours vary according to location). Other locations: 2285 W. 4th Ave. (at Vine St. in Kitsilano), Vancouver. © **604/739-6676.** 2496 Marine Dr. (at 25th Ave.), West Vancouver. © **604/925-3316.**

The Grove Inn *Value* NORTH AMERICAN   The local *WestEnder* newspaper bestows its annual award for the best bacon and eggs year after year on this gem, and at C$3.95 (US$2.60) it's also probably the cheapest. There is nothing fancy about this old-fashioned diner, but the food is plentiful and unpretentious. In addition to the all-day breakfast, the Grove also serves a selection of Chinese food, steaks, chickens, and pastas.

124 Denman St. (at Comox St.). © **604/687-0557.** Main courses C$7.25–$10.50 (US$4.80–$6.95). Sandwiches and hamburgers under C$6 (US$4). No credit cards. Open daily 7am–8pm. Highchairs, boosters.

Hon's Wun-Tun House *(★ (Value* CANTONESE   Hon's is a large, bright, and sparkling clean noodle house that started out 25 years ago as a small Chinatown restaurant. The consistently great food, prices, and service have made it a fixture in this city and it has now branched out to other locations. Hon's specializes in Chinese and Japanese noodles (udon and somen) and potstickers, but food choices are extensive and there is a large vegetarian menu. We like the soy sauce chicken and barbecued duck on rice, the potstickers (perennial favorites with the kids), the excellent stir-fried wide egg noodle dish with calamari strips, and congee fried rice and noodles. Food comes with tea and soup. Service is fast and friendly—my 2-year-old kept dropping his spoon to see how fast it would be picked up and he was overjoyed to see that it was within seconds every time. The food preparation and cooking are fascinating and the kids will enjoy watching their meals cooked at the gleaming stainless steel stations clearly labeled wonton, barbecue, potstickers, chef's specialties, and vegetarian.

1339 Robson St. (between Jervis and Broughton sts.). © **604/685-0871.** www.shinnova.com. Reservations recommended. Main courses C$6.50–$10.50 (US$4.30–$6.95). MC, V. Open weekdays 11am–10pm, weekends 11am–11pm. Highchairs, boosters. Other locations: 108 Keefer St., Chinatown © **604/688-0871;** 101-4600 No. 3 Rd., Richmond © **604/273-0871.**

Kenichi Japanese Restaurant *(Value* JAPANESE   At this all-you-can-eat lunch and dinner restaurant, even picky kids will find the cucumber sushi, California rolls, chicken teriyaki, chicken *karaage* (deep-fried chicken), or perhaps the *gyoza* (dumplings) to their liking. If not, most kids love noodles (yakisoba), and if you are having trouble getting them to eat their vegetables, try the tempura. This is a large restaurant that has both booth and table seating, but it does get very busy at the lunch period.

1542 Robson (at Cardero St.). © **604/688-4789.** Reservations recommended. Lunch Sun–Thurs adults C$8.50 (US$5.60), children 5 and over C$5.95 (US$3.95), Fri–Sat adults C$9.95 (US$6.60), children 5 and over C$6.95 (US$5). Dinner Sun–Thurs adults C$13.95 (US$9.20), children 5 and over C$8.95 (US$5.90), Fri–Sat adults C$15.95 (US$10.50), children 5 and over C$9.95 (US$6.60). Children under 5 pay C$1 (US65¢) for each year old they are. MC, V. Open daily 11am–3pm lunch, 5pm–midnight dinner. Highchairs, boosters.

Thai House THAI   This may be the perfect place to introduce the kids to Thai food. While there are no menus especially for kids, the food is similar to Chinese in texture and presentation. The menu's inscription "For those who like it hot…for those who like it mild," pretty well sums it up and you can count the chilies—0 to 3—to regulate the heat factor. The restaurant consistently wins readers' choice awards for its food and the decor is great. There is a waterfall as you walk in, a fish tank, palm trees, and lots of religious icons and Thai ornaments. Service is friendly and the staff will happily suggest dishes, but you can't go wrong with the five-course lunch special for C$6.50 (US$4.30), which includes awesome mango ice cream for dessert. The restaurant has an all-you-can-eat buffet from noon to 2:30pm on weekends for C$8 (US$5.30).

1116 Robson St. (at Thurlow St.). © **604/683-3383.** www.thaihouse.com. Reservations recommended. Main courses C$9.95–$15.95 (US$6.55–$10.55). Open Mon–Fri 11:30am–10pm, Sat–Sun noon–10pm (hours

vary slightly according to location. Highchairs, boosters. Other locations: 1766 W. 7th Ave., Vancouver
© **604/737-0088;** 1103 Denman St., Vancouver © **604/685-8989;** 1119 Hamilton St., Vancouver
© **604/408-7788;** 180 Esplanade, North Vancouver © **604/987-9911;** 4600 Kingsway, at Metrotown,
Burnaby © **604/438-2288;** and 4940 No. 3 Rd., Richmond © **604/278-7373.**

Vina VIETNAMESE   This small and cheerful restaurant, located on Denman
Street in the West End near Stanley Park, is worth a trip particularly if you're sick
of eating out at "family" restaurants. It doesn't have a kids' menu, but the prices
are great, the staff are eager to please, and there is a variety of food including
salad rolls, brochettes (chicken or pork skewers), and chow mein dishes that
would appeal to the fussiest eater. For lunch you can't go wrong with the combo
for C$6.95 (US$4.60). The steamed crepes and shrimp salad rolls are great
accompanied by either steamed rice or vermicelli. Dishes come with both chopsticks and familiar cutlery. Desserts are great and my kids love the fried bananas
and ice cream.

851 Denman St. (at Haro St). © **604/688-3232.** Reservations recommended on weekends. Most entrees
under C$8 (US$5.30) at lunch, main courses at dinner C$7.95–$15.95 (US$5.25–$10.55). AE, MC, V. Open
daily 11am–midnight. Highchairs, boosters. Other location: 2508 Marine Dr., West Vancouver.
© **604/926-6001.**

4 Chinatown & Gastown
MODERATE
Floata Seafood Restaurant CANTONESE   Not the best Chinese restaurant in town, but at 1,000 seats this Hong Kong transplant is most definitely the
biggest. Size means fast seating and service and plenty of room for strollers and
highchairs. Being on the fringes of Chinatown, parking is easy. Mid-week we
found the dim sum selection a bit disappointing, but there was plenty to keep
the kids occupied and happy. There were some unusual dim sum dishes that we
hadn't come across in other restaurants, and the lunch and dinner menus carry
a good selection of beef, seafood, chicken, and hot-pot dishes. Unlike most
Chinese restaurants, the Floata charges for tea C$3.25 (US$2.15) and pop was
a hefty C$2 (US$1.30) a person.

400-180 Keefer St. (at Columbia and Quebec sts.). © **604/602-0368.** www.floata.com. Main course lunch
C$12.80–$18.80 (US$8.45–$12.40), dinner C$13.80–$24 (US$9.10–$15.80). Dim sum C$3–$4.20 per dish.
AE, DC, MC, V. Open daily 7:30am–10pm. Highchairs, boosters. Other location: 1425-4380 No. 3 Rd. (between
Cambie and Alderbridge rds.), Richmond. © **604/270-8889.**

The Old Spaghetti Factory ⟨★ ITALIAN   A Gastown fixture for more than
30 years, the Old Spaghetti Factory is loud and messy. Kids love sitting at one
of the six tables in the 1904 tram car, especially when it rocks and creaks as other
customers get on and off. The ambience of this restaurant is great: there are lots
of stained glass windows, wooden kegs, and things for kids to look at when they
are sick of coloring the menu. The room at the back of the restaurant has the
feel of an old-fashioned library, and the kids can watch the trains in the rail yards
and the Canada Place sails through a large picture window. The menu has every
type of spaghetti and sauce imaginable as well as a good selection of lasagnas and
veal dishes. If your child is picky like mine, ask for sauce on the side. Adult meals
are huge and are accompanied by a salad, sourdough bread, and coffee or tea.
Drinks and spumoni ice cream are included with the kids' meals. The food is
decent and a good value. Staff are fast and accommodating—they quickly
whipped up a fruit salad for my son who was allergic to nuts in the ice cream.

53 Water St. (at Abbott St.). ℂ **604/684-1288.** Reservations for parties of 6 or more only. Main courses C$7–$13.75 (US$4.60–$9.10), kids' menu C$4.95–$6.15 (US$3.25–$4.05). AE, MC, V. Open Mon–Thurs 11:30am–10pm, Fri–Sat 11:30am–11pm, Sun 11:30am–9pm. Highchairs, boosters, kids' menu.

Park Lock Seafood Restaurant CHINESE   Kids will like the colorful aquariums—one with tropical fish, the other filled with lobsters, crayfish, and other fish that will eventually end up on the table. The restaurant looks a little worn but, as the lineups suggest, the dim sum is excellent. Things move quickly so you shouldn't have to wait very long, if at all. If you are ordering off the menu at lunch or at dinner, there is a good selection of all the things you expect to see at a Chinese restaurant, but you will also find vegetarian dishes, birdnests, hot pots, and satays.

544 Main St., 2nd floor (at E. Pender St.). ℂ **604/688-1581.** Reservations recommended. Main courses C$8.50–$15.50 (US$5.60–$10.25), dim sum C$2.90–$3.90 (US$1.90–$2.55) per dish. MC, V. Open Tues–Sun 8am–10pm, Mon 5–10pm. Highchairs, boosters.

INEXPENSIVE

Buddhist Vegetarian Restaurant _Value_ VEGETARIAN CHINESE   It may not be much to look at, but this little Chinatown gem is busy for a reason. It has a huge range of dim sum and other vegetarian wonders at dirt cheap prices. Try any of the dim sum (steamed and deep-fried dumplings, rice-sheet rolls, turnip cakes, and other delights) for C$2.40 (US$1.60) from 11am to 3pm. Aside from dim sum, there are Shanghai-style fried rice cakes, chow mein, hot pots, and vermicelli dishes. Try the sweet sesame balls for dessert.

137 E. Pender St. (between Main and Columbia sts.). ℂ **604/683-8816.** www.members.home.net/ buddhistveg. Reservations recommended. Lunch most items under C$7 (US$4.60), dinner C$4.50–$15 (US$3–$10). AE, V. Open daily 11am–8:30pm.

Sodas Diner BURGERS   Walk off Gastown's Water Street straight into the 1950s with this burger joint. There are crayons at the tables as well as Archie and Jughead comics to keep the kids amused, red booth seating, and all types of burgers, steaks, and hot dogs. There is no printed kids' menu, but staff will rattle off five dishes of the burger, grilled cheese, hot dog, and chicken finger variety for C$4 (US$2.65). Watch for lineups at peak lunch and dinner times.

375 Water St. (at the Landing). ℂ **604/683-7632.** Reservations recommended. Most items under C$10 (US$6.60). AE, MC, V. Open daily 11am–9pm. Highchairs, boosters, kids' menu. Other location: 4497 Dunbar St. (at 29th Ave.), West Side. ℂ **604/222-9922.**

🎱 Sweet Dreams

The Candy Aisle   The sign out front says: "DON'T JUST STAND THERE, BUY SOME CANDY," and why not indeed. This store makes its own cotton candy on-site and you can buy cherry-, grape-, or strawberry-flavored candy lipstick. Girls will love the Barbie Candy necklace that they make first and eat later, and there are ring pops, suckers, and pixie sticks. 2083 W. 4th Ave. (at Arbutus St.), Vancouver. ℂ **604/739-3330.** Open Sunday to Thursday 10am to 7pm, Friday and Saturday 10am to 9pm.

Candy Kitchen   Buy just about anything that comes to mind—jelly beans, liquorice allsorts, it's all here. 1689 Johnston St. (at Granville Island Public Market), Vancouver. ℂ **604/681-7001.** Open daily 9am to 6pm.

Charlie's Chocolate Factory 𝒦𝒦 _Finds_   Much more than a candy store, this is an experience that kids of all ages will love. Charlie is a dapper gent and on special occasions sports a vest, bowler hat, and bow tie. He created a chocolate river after the one in the movie *Willie Wonka and the Chocolate Factory*, made from real chocolate. There is always something exceptional to see—a Cinderella horse and carriage, a set of false teeth made from chocolate, or a chocolate toothbrush. You can see chocolate being made through glass windows and you can also buy chocolate-making supplies. 3746 Canada Way (at Boundary Rd.), Burnaby. © **604/437-8221.** Open daily 9am to 5pm. Closed Sundays.

Chocolate Arts   The Haida Medallion is only one of many distinct designs by this Kitsilano chocolate-maker. The store dries its own BC organic blueberries and cherries and uses local hazelnuts and raspberries. 2037 W. 4th Ave (at Arbutus St.), Vancouver. © **604/739-0475.** Open Monday to Saturday 10am to 6pm, Sunday noon to 5pm.

Olde World Fudge Co.   You can phone ahead and find out when this store is making its fudge, lollipops, or chocolate of the season and they are happy to have you watch, or just drop in and pick up some milk chocolate or perhaps the chocolate swirl fudge. 123 Carrie Cates Crt. (Lonsdale Quay Public Market), North Vancouver. © **604/980-8336.** Open Saturday to Thursday 9:30am to 6:30pm, Friday 9:30am to 8pm.

Purdy's Chocolates   A local chocolate-maker since 1907, Purdy's and its mascot, Philbert the Hedgehog, can be found all over Western Canada in stand-alone stores and malls. The store makes more than 100 different chocolates. www.purdys.com. © **888/478-7397** for the nearest store location.

Rocky Mountain Chocolate Factory   (see also p. 98, "Great Ice Cream"). Killer handmade fudge in a whole bunch of decadent flavors. Try Black Forest, Cappuccino, Rocky Road, or Creme de Menthe. Of course, there are also shelves and shelves of chocolates, and at some locations, candy apples covered in Smarties. www.rockychoc.com. © **800/567-2207** for store locations nearest to you.

Suckers Candy Store   A hard store to pass by when you are visiting the dozens of kid-friendly stores in this market. Suckers has a great selection of lollipops and every other brand of colorful candy you can imagine. 1496 Cartwright St. (at the Kids' Market on Granville Island), Vancouver. © **604/682-4240.** Open daily 10am to 6pm.

Sugar Mountain ⊛ (Finds)   All the candy is imported from England, South Africa, and the States. Kids will love it, adults will feel nostalgic (the Elvis Presley music will help) rediscovering Pez, Tootsie Rolls, Sour Bottle Pop candy, ant and bug candy, Traditional Pear Drops, and chocolate-covered Gummy Bears. 917 Denman St. (at Barclay St.), Vancouver. © **604/689-3341.** Open daily 11am to 9pm.

The Sweet Factory   You can buy everything from cantaloupe- to cappuccino- to margarita-flavored jelly beans. There are also combinations like pineapple salsa, chocolate-covered cherry, and mud pie, or you can opt for the sugar-free beans. 1114-4700 Kingsway (at Eaton Centre Metrotown), Burnaby. © **604/430-9730.** www.jellybelly.com. Open Monday to Friday 10am–9pm, Saturday to Sunday 10am to 6pm.

5 The West Side

MODERATE

Bridges Restaurant *(★)* *(Finds)* WEST COAST   On a sunny summer's day you'd be hard pressed to find a more pleasant way to enjoy a meal than watching the boats sail by from the deck of this Granville Island restaurant. The food comes from the bistro, which is also a pleasant place to eat any time of the year, and while it changes according to the season, the fare is pretty much pizza, salmon, burgers, and fish and chips. There is a kids' menu where you can get the usual chicken fingers and pastas. When the sun is shining the place starts to hop around noon for lunch and gets busy around 6pm for the dinner crowd. There is also the upscale Bridges Dining Room (named because the building is nestled between the Granville and Burrard street bridges) on the second floor, where kids are also welcome, and the pub, where kids are not.

1696 Duranleau St. (at Granville Island across from the public market). © **604/687-4400.** www.bridges restaurant.com. No reservations on the deck. Main courses C$12–$20 (US$8–$13). AE, DC, MC, V. Open daily 11am–11pm. Highchairs, boosters, kids' menu.

Las Margaritas MEXICAN   This Cantina-style restaurant gets busy on the weekends, so aim to get there by noon for lunch or before 6pm for dinner to avoid lineups. In summer, Las Margaritas opens its patio and that can be a pleasant place to sit with children and watch the Kitsilano foot traffic. Food is well priced and servings are ample. The kids' menu offers chicken strips, burritos, and pizza for smaller appetites.

1999 W. 4th Ave. (at Maple St.). © **604/734-7117.** www.lasmargaritas.com. Reservations on weekdays only. Main courses C$7–$14 (US$4.60–$9.25), kids' menu C$3.95 (US$2.60). AE, MC, V. Open daily 11:30am–10pm. Highchairs, boosters, kids' menu.

INEXPENSIVE

Calhouns BAKERY/CAFE   This barn-like Kitsilano cafe is open 24 hours a day, which is particularly handy if you happen to be on a different time zone from the rest of the city. It's a serve-yourself cafeteria-style joint and your selection is heated when you order. There is a good breakfast selection, with everything from waffles and fresh fruit to ham, egg, and cheese muffins to granola. Lunch and dinner selections include lots of vegetarian dishes, burritos, wraps, quiches, and pot pies. There is a suggested kids' menu that includes a generous serving of penne and cheese, fresh fruit salad, and a peanut butter and banana sandwich. When I ordered the sandwich for my 5-year-old, I was handed two slabs of bread and invited to make it myself at no charge. There is a small outdoor patio.

3035 W. Broadway Ave. (at Balaclava St.) © **604/737-7062.** Most items under C$7 (US$4.60), kids' menu C$2.50–$3.50 (US$1.65–$2.30). MC, V. Open daily 24 hours. Highchairs, boosters, kids' menu.

Sophie's Cosmic Cafe *(★★)* *(Value)* NORTH AMERICAN   Sophie's opened in 1990 and most weekends still has lineups for its incredible breakfasts/brunches. It's easily recognizable by the enormous knife and fork on either side of the door. Sophie will tell you she's the Queen of the Garage Sale and you'll find everything from a Darth Vader lamp to a giant fish on a pool table crammed into the space. Three-dimensional arcana seem to leap at you from the walls and will keep the kids busy, as the service can be on the slow side. There is also a huge box of toys in a corner and the place is so busy and noisy, nobody seems to mind little people running from table to toy box. You'll find burgers, chicken kebabs, pizza, sandwiches, and a good selection of vegetarian dishes. There is no kids' menu, but staff are happy to split an order of grilled cheese and ham, pancakes, or a burger, and the adult meals are so huge that they could easily feed an extra child. The Eggs Mexicano is superb, and my husband, the fast food connoisseur, says the hamburger is the best he's had in years.

2095 W. 4th Ave. ✆ **604/732-6810.** Reservations accepted only for parties of 5 or more. Main courses breakfast and lunch C$4–$8.95 (US$2.65–$5.90), dinner C$7.95–$15.95 (US$5.25–$10.55). MC, V. Open daily 8am to 9:30pm. Highchairs, boosters, toys.

Get a Babysitter

Sure you can take the kids, but for a few hours without them you can kick back and enjoy some of Vancouver's greatest eating experiences, our incredible views, and world-class wines. This list is, of course, highly subjective; there are dozens of other fine restaurants in the city.

The Pacific Starlight Dinner Train ✹✹✹ *Moments* WEST COAST   Go back in time to the golden age of train travel in BC Rail's 1930s and 1940s Art Deco train cars. It's a fine-dining experience in a small, but luxurious setting, and on a clear night you'll enjoy some of the world's most breathtaking scenery and killer sunsets. The journey begins with a send-off by a three-piece swing band. The train then winds through the backyards of West Vancouver—Canada's wealthiest suburb—with views of downtown Vancouver, Stanley Park, and the Lions Gate Bridge. There are spectacular views of Howe Sound as the train travels up through Lions Bay and finally stops at Porteau Cove. Passengers can disembark and walk off dinner or dance to swing band music. The three-course menu changes according to season. Departs from North Vancouver's Pemberton Station Wednesday, Friday, Saturday, and Sunday June 27 to September 9; Friday, Saturday, and Sunday May 4 to 20, September 14 to October 14, November 16 to December 16. Departs 6:15pm and arrives back at the station at 10pm. Reservations required. Dress is fine-dining attire, but high heels are not a good idea. ✆ **800/363-3733** or 604/984-5246 or 604/631-3500. www.bcrail.com. Salon seating C$85.95 (US$56.75), dome seating C$109.95 (US$72.55), tips and taxes included. Drinks are extra.

The Beach House ✹✹✹ WEST COAST   Our absolute favorite restaurant when we have friends or relatives in from out of town. The food is always unusual and special, the service top class, and I just can't imagine a better view from this waterfront location. The original house was built in 1919 and has been a bed-and-breakfast and an inn before becoming a restaurant in 1963. The best views are from the lovely heated patio, but the house is designed in three levels, so you have a view from anywhere in the restaurant. Sunsets are extraordinary. Meals are in constant change, but items may include something along the line of a rack of lamb, Pacific salmon, venison, or free range duck. Personally, I would walk over hot coals for the crème brûlée. 150–25 St., West Vancouver. ✆ **604/922-1414.** www.beachhousewestvan.com. Reservations recommended. Main courses lunch C$13 to $16 (US$8.60 to $10.55), dinner C$16 to $29 (US$10.50 to $19.15). AE, DC, MC, V. Open Monday–Thursday 11:30am to 11pm, Friday to Saturday 11am to 11pm, and Sunday 10:30am to 11pm.

Il Giardino *☆☆☆* ITALIAN   The last time we were here, the waiter was so overcome by the beauty of a group of women sitting near us that he broke into an aria. It turned out that when he wasn't waiting tables he was singing in an opera. Just one of the pleasant surprises at this downtown restaurant, which doesn't have a view but does have a fabulous outdoor garden terrace in the summer and, in winter, a cozy villa atmosphere. The menu reflects owner Umberto Menghi's Tuscan roots and has a selection of pastas, an exquisite veal chop, reindeer, lamb, and pheasant. 1382 Hornby St. (at Pacific St.), Vancouver. ℂ **604/669-2422**. Reservations required. Main courses C$13.95 to $29.95 (US$9.20 to $19.75). AE, DC, MC, V. Open Monday to Friday noon to 11pm, Saturday 5:30 to 11pm, closed Sunday.

Joe Fortes Seafood and Chop House *☆☆☆* SEAFOOD   The restaurant, like the bartender and lifeguard it was named after, is a colorful fixture in downtown Vancouver. Styled as an American brasserie, Joe's has a very popular oyster bar, and the restaurant itself is bright and airy with lots of brass and marble and mahogany. Live piano music plays at night and it is always busy. Prices are reasonable, staff is attentive, the wine list is inspired, and the food is terrific. Try the Lifeguard Tower on Ice for a really good selection of local seafood. The roof garden with its garden patio and open fireplace is one of the few places you can smoke, and a favorite for actor Arnold Schwarzenegger, who quipped "I'll be back," and was— again and again. 777 Thurlow St. (at Robson St.), Vancouver. ℂ **604/669-1940**. www.joefortesseafoodrestr.com. Reservations recommended. Main courses lunch C$8.95 to $16.25 (US$5.90 to $10.75), dinner C$18.95 to $56.50 (US$12.50 to $37.30). AE, DC, DISC, MC, V. Open daily Monday to Friday 11:30am to 11pm, Saturday to Sunday 11am to 11pm.

Raincity Grill *☆☆☆* WEST COAST   A small but incredibly popular restaurant, the Raincity Grill overlooks English Bay and has a patio in the summer for lunchtime beach watching. The menu is in constant flux, but in season you can find jumbo Alaskan spot prawns, shrimp risotto, barbecued quail, or perhaps a grilled Fraser Valley loin of veal. The restaurant has won a slew of awards for its wine list and almost every dish is accompanied by a recommended wine by the glass. 1193 Denman St., (near Davie St.), Vancouver. ℂ **604/685-7337**. www.raincitygrill.com. Reservations recommended. Main course lunch C$11 to $17.50 (US$7.25 to $11.55), dinner C$18 to $32 (US$11.90 to $21.10). AE, DC, MC, V. Open Monday to Friday 11:30am to 10pm. Call ahead as they may close earlier in winter months.

6 The East Side

MODERATE

Pink Pearl *☆☆* CHINESE   A Vancouver fixture since 1981, the Pink Pearl consistently gets picked in magazines and newspaper polls as the best Chinese restaurant and the best place for dim sum. It's also our family's favorite for the great variety of food, the bustling, comfortable atmosphere, and the very friendly staff who seem delighted to have messy toddlers, and, because there are 700 seats, you rarely have to wait more than a few minutes. The dim sum carts come around very quickly and change dishes frequently, but if you are there for dinner or choose to order from the menu, there is a great selection of Cantonese and Szechwan dishes and sizzling hot plates. The only real downside to the restaurant is that it's in a pretty seedy area of town.

1132 E. Hastings St. (at Clarke St.). © **604/253-4316.** www.pinkpearl.com. Reservations accepted. C$10.95–$18 (US$7.25–$11.90). Dim sum C$2.95–$3.95 (US$1.95–$2.60) per dish. AE, DC, MC, V. Open daily 9am–10pm. Highchairs, boosters.

INEXPENSIVE

Cafe Deux Soleils (★ (Value) VEGETARIAN   Kids will love this funky little place on "The Drive," an arty, ethnic street in East Vancouver. Food is plentiful and kids can order a peanut butter or grilled cheese sandwich or the obliging staff can make up half an order of anything on the menu for roughly half the price. In fact, you get the feeling that anything you or your kids could do would be just fine. Few tourists get out here, so if you are from out of town you'll be able to soak up some local flavor. And speaking of flavor there is a huge selection of egg dishes, fresh fruit, and French toast in the morning, and soups, wraps, veggie burgers, and pastas during the day—all made in the open kitchen. Little kids will love the stage area that fills with toys during the day and fills with musicians during weekend evenings. There is a small patio on the street in the summer time. This place is hugely popular on weekends, so expect lineups in the morning and lunch hours.

2096 Commercial Dr. (at E. 5th Ave.). © **604/254-1195.** Reservations not accepted. Most items under C$10 (US$6.60), kids' menu C$2.50 (US$1.65). V. Open Mon–Sat 8am–midnight, Sun 8am–4pm. Highchairs, boosters, toys, kids' menu.

Lombardo's Pizzeria (★ PIZZA   This small restaurant was voted best pizza place in the city by the *Vancouver Sun* newspaper in 2000. Tucked away in the Il Mercato mall in East Vancouver, you will find a traditional Sicilian wood-burning oven, the highest quality food made fresh daily, and, perhaps best of all if you are eating with young children, a couple of boxes brimming with toys in the hall. If you don't feel like pizza, there is a selection of salads, pastas, and chicken.

1641 Commercial Dr. (at 1st Ave.). © **604/251-2240.** Reservations recommended. Pizzas (medium) C$11.95–$13.95 (US$7.90–$9.20), (large) C$22.95–$24.95 (US$15.15–$16.45). AE, MC, V. Open Mon–Sat 11am–11pm. Sun and holidays 4–10pm. Highchairs, boosters, toys.

7 The North Shore

MODERATE

Cheshire Cheese Inn BRITISH   If you are hankering for some bangers and mash, steak and kidney pie, or perhaps toad in the hole, this is the place for you. The restaurant looks like a traditional English pub and has a comfortable waiting area with a fireplace and lots of red wainscotting. There is comfortable booth and table seating. Crayons are given to you as you enter and there is a kids' menu for those under 8 with all the standard fare—fish and chips, hamburgers, chicken fingers, and grilled cheese with a drink for C$4.95 (US$3.25). If you've been shopping at the Lonsdale Quay Market or doing a lot of local sightseeing, it's not a bad place to kick back. Get a table at the back so the kids can watch the tugboats.

Lonsdale Quay Market, 2nd floor, North Vancouver. © **604/987-3322.** Reservations recommended. Main courses C$6.95–$12.95 (US$4.60–$8.55). AE, DC, MC, V. Open daily 11am–9pm. Highchairs, boosters. Other locations: 4585 Dunbar St. (at 30th Ave.), West Side © **604/224-2521;** 5645 West Blvd. (at 41st Ave.), Vancouver © **604/261-2834.**

C-Lovers FISH AND CHIPS   If you feel like fish and chips, and who doesn't, C-Lovers has the quality. It's on the pricey side, but if you go before 7pm on Tuesdays or Sundays or for lunch Wednesday to Saturday, you and the kids can eat all the cod and chips you want for a set price of C$8.95 (US$5.90) adults, C$4.95 (US$3.27) kids over 4, and C$2.99 (US$1.97) for the little ones. The price includes bottomless pop as my 8-year-old says—"That rules!" Not included in the all-you-can-eat, but worth paying for anyway, is the restaurant's awesome homemade clam chowder. There are also healthy-looking items like Caesar salad and mushy peas, prawns and oysters, and, if your child refuses to eat anything else, chicken strips and a c-dog. Service is fast, though slightly churlish. And the restaurant does a thriving takeout business.

1660 Pemberton Ave. (at Lonsdale St.), North Vancouver. © **604/980-9993.** Main courses C$7.95–$11.95 (US$5.25–$7.90). MC, V. Open Tues–Sun 3:30–8pm. Highchairs, boosters.

Coveside Restaurant SEAFOOD   Deep Cove is just such a great setting for a restaurant that getting there is much of the fun. This is a very laid-back place with friendly service. The house specialty is fish and chips made with fresh cod or halibut and served with a salad or french fries. The seafood platter is awesome, but fish lovers will also love the restaurant's signature "Famous Fisherman's Chowder"—a bowl crammed with scallops, prawns, mussels, salmon, and halibut. There is a kids' menu with all the usuals, but if they want a change, appetizers include calamari, garlic ribs, potato skins, spring rolls, and zucchini sticks. If you have room, try one of the fruit pies and wander down to the water and the children's park.

4355 Gallant Ave. (Deep Cove), North Vancouver. © **604/929-4877.** MC, V. Main courses C$7.95–$15.95, kids' menu C$4.25–$6.50 (US$2.80–$4.30). Open daily 11am–8pm. Highchairs, boosters, kids' menu.

Troll's ✹✹ FISH AND CHIPS   This is one of our family favorites. The restaurant has a nautical theme with a First Nations flair and is done up in knotty pine and stone with booth table seating. A popular spot since the 1940s, Troll's has large picture windows that look out onto mountains, ocean, and the comings and goings of the huge white BC Ferries from Horseshoe Bay to Bowen Island, the Sunshine Coast, and Nanaimo on Vancouver Island. According to the menu, customers eat more than 125,000 pounds of cod and more than 500,000 pounds of potatoes at this restaurant every year. Troll's makes a mean clam chowder, a delicious fish stew, and some pretty decent burger and pasta dishes. Kids get crayons and a menu to color, and their food includes pop with a plastic mermaid in it and an ice-cream cone. This is a hugely popular spot on weekends and sunny days, so try to get there early or expect a wait. You can walk off your meals at the water park and playground across the road and take the kids for a stroll along the pier.

6408 Bay St. (Horseshoe Bay), West Vancouver. © **604/921-7755.** Reservations for 6 or more only. Sandwiches C$8–$13 (US$5.30–$8.60), main courses C$9–$17 (US$5.95–$11.35), kids' menu C$4–$5.50 (US$2.65–$3.65). AE, MC, V. Open daily 6am–8pm. Highchairs, boosters, kids' menu.

INEXPENSIVE

Hot Dog Jonny's HOT DOGS   You can't miss this upscale weenie joint with the giant hot dog on the sidewalk. Jonny's opened in September 2000 and is a cheerful place with a colorful plastic table-and-chair set for little people and crayons and most kids' favorite food. Jonny's boasts that its product is made with "no preservatives, no artificial flavoring, no liquid smoke or mechanically separated meats." There are almost a dozen different types and on Tuesdays the over 60s and the under 6s get a 20% discount.

1425 Marine Dr. (at 14th Ave.), West Vancouver. ✆ **604/913-DOGS.** C$2–$4.30 (US$1.30–$2.85). Open daily 11:30am–7:30pm. Highchairs, boosters.

Indigo Books, Music & Cafe BAKERY/CAFE   This Toronto transplant opened its first Vancouver store in December 2000 and immediately became a meeting place for the locals. Part of the attraction is you can sit back and sip on your latte or grab a sandwich or wrap, while the kids head for one of the three computer stations and the kids' books section, all in view of the cafe. The twice-daily story time and the two giant checker board tables are also a hit with the older kids.

Lynn Valley Centre, 1199 Lynn Valley Rd. (at Mountain Hwy.), North Vancouver. ✆ **604/904-7970.** Most items under C$6 (US$4). AE, DC, MC, V. Open Mon–Sat 9am–10pm, Sun 9am–8pm. Highchairs.

Nando's CHICKEN   This is an inexpensive, upmarket chicken franchise that does a thriving take-out business but also has a comfortable restaurant setting if you prefer to eat in. The flame-grilled chicken comes in various shapes and sizes, in pita with salad, or shaped into kebabs. The kids' menu is a choice between the kebab or a sandwich and comes with french fries and a bottomless pop. Adults get to choose between four types of sauce ranging in heat from the mild lemon and herb, which kids will like, right up to the extra hot peri-peri. Service is fast, but there is a small kids' seating area with Lego and crayons if they are bored.

1301 Lonsdale St. (at 13th Ave.), North Vancouver. ✆ **604/990-1530.** www.nandos.co.za. Main courses C$5–$11 (US$3.30–$7.25), kids' menu C$5 (US$3.30). MC, V. Open daily 11:30am–9:30pm. Highchairs, boosters, kids' menu.

Tomahawk ⟨★★ ⟨Value NORTH AMERICAN   A fixture since 1926 largely because of its fantastic and enormous breakfasts and ultra-friendly service. The staff is great with kids and it's one of the few places where all my kids love the food. The restaurant has crayons and a kids' menu that includes pancakes and their own miniature bottle of maple syrup, eggs, Yukon-style toast (a really thick slice), and hash browns, French toast, and old-fashioned oatmeal. The restaurant remains family-owned and run and has an incredible collection of hand-crafted artifacts from West Coast First Nations. You certainly can't miss the giant totem poles at the front entrance and inside—past the water fountain with the rubber duckies—there are cedar woven baskets, masks, hatchets, and wood carvings that fill nearly every inch of the building. If you miss breakfast, there is a variety of hamburgers, fish, steaks, and chicken. There is an outdoor patio in the summer that adds much to the size of the restaurant, but this place really hops on the weekend and you can expect to wait up to 20 minutes between 10am and 2pm.

1550 Philip Ave. (turn at Marine Dr.), North Vancouver. ✆ **604/988-2612.** Reservations for groups of 8 or more only. Main courses C$4.70–$18.40 (US$3.10–$12.15). AE, DC, MC, V. Open Sun–Thurs 8am–9pm, Fri–Sat 8am–10pm. Highchairs, boosters, kids' menu.

Great Ice Cream

These ice-cream parlors are located all over Greater Vancouver so if that craving for the sweet stuff hits, one shouldn't be too far away.

Amato Gelato Café   Owned by Mario Loscerbo, this giant factory and retail outlet had humble beginnings at the Granville Island Public Market in 1980. It now does a booming export business with Mario's Gelati and sells huge quantities to local hotels, restaurants, and conventions. You can find anything from green-tea ice cream to purple yam gelato to amaretto and gianduia (chocolate hazelnut). 88 E. 1st Ave. (at Quebec St.), Vancouver. © **604/879-9011.** Open daily Monday to Friday 9am–10pm, weekends 11am–10pm.

Baskin-Robbins   You can't go wrong with this brand's 950 tried-and-true flavors. And, the cakes are always a favorite. © **800/268-4923** for the location closest to you.

Cows   You can't miss this shop with the huge plastic black-and-white cow outside, usually with one or more children on its back. Aside from great ice cream with names such as turtle cow, chocolate monster, and mud puddle, this Prince Edward Island import sells cards, T-shirts, souvenirs, kiddy rompers, and adult boxers—with a cow theme, of course. 1301 Robson St. (at Jervis St.), Vancouver. © **604/682-2622.** Open daily 9am to 11pm summer, 10am–10pm winter.

House of Brussels Chocolates   Try the hedgehog ice cream for true decadence, or just pick up some chocolate for that special sugar buzz. 105-925 W. Georgia St. (at Hornby St.), Vancouver © **604/684-5444;** 750 Terminal Ave. (at Main St. and Clark Dr.), Vancouver © **604/713-8063;** 1669 Johnson St. (at Granville Island), Vancouver © **604/684-9678;** 4416 W. 10th Ave. (at the West Side's Point Grey), Vancouver © **604/228-4265.** Hours vary according to location.

La Casa Gelato *(★★ Finds)*   People come from all over the mainland to this pink and green ice-cream palace. And where else could you find 188 flavors in one room with names such as pear, gorganzola, and blue cheese, wasabi, purple yam, and asparagus? Tasting spoons are available for the asking, which is how we decided against the bright yellow curry flavor. The Toblerone, though, is indeed decadent and the kids recommend the bubblegum and cotton candy. 1033 Venables St., Vancouver. © **604/251-3211.** www.lacasagelato.com. Open daily 10am to 11pm.

Ice Cream Café   Pick up a cotton candy or perhaps the tiger tail or bubble gum and fight the birds for space outside on the Quay. In summer there is entertainment on weekends or just watch the SeaBus and all the other activity in Burrard Inlet. 123 Carrie Cates Court (at Lonsdale Quay), North Vancouver. © **604/987-8796.** Open Saturday to Thursday 9:30am to 6:30pm, Friday 9:30am to 8pm.

Mum's Gelato *(★)*   Small cafe with a little patio and Mediterranean feel where you can grab a coffee, a milkshake, or an excellent homemade gelato. Mum's has 150 rotating flavors. The passion fruit is particularly good; others that deserve mention are the port wine, pear sorbet, and amaretto. Kids will like the outdoor tables that have plastic fruit arranged under the glass. 855 Denman St. (at Barclay St.), Vancouver. © **604/681-1500.** Open daily 7:30am to 10pm. Other location: 2028 Vine St. (at 4th Ave.) Kitsilano, open Tuesday to Sunday noon to 10pm.

Orca's Favorite Ice Cream Café   This is worth it just for the drive. Grab one of the 40 premium flavors and wander down to the water in what must be one of the world's most beautiful places. 4367 Gallant Ave. (in Deep Cove), North Vancouver. © **604/924-2616.** Summer daily 10am to 10pm. Winter daily noon to 6:30pm.

Rocky Mountain Chocolate Factory   Also has great ice cream bought from none other than La Casa Gelato, listed above. If you can't get to the pink East Vancouver factory, this is the next best thing. www.rockychoc. com © **800/567-2207** for store locations nearest to you.

Sara's Old-Fashioned Ice Cream   The name pretty much says it all. Kids will love the bubble gum flavor. You can also get home baked pies, sandwiches, and other desserts. Grab your cones then wander down to Ambleside Beach to swim, fly a kite, or play in the playground. 1393 Marine Dr. (at 14th Ave.), West Vancouver. © **604/925-2401.** Monday to Saturday 8:30am to 6pm, Sunday 9:30 to 6pm.

8 Richmond
MODERATE

Fukuroku Sushi ★★ *Finds* JAPANESE   Kids will love the bedroom-sized playroom at this restaurant. In fact, you can book a table beside the glass window that looks right onto the room and watch the kids while you eat. The playroom is gated and has a climbing structure, toys and, on the day we were there, a television showing Pokémon in its native Japanese. If they tire of the playroom they will be fascinated by the sushi that sails around in a boat around a very large bar. The staff are great with kids and no one seemed to mind the little ones darting back and forth. The food is excellent and the menu has hot pots, sukiyaki, udon noodle soup, and rice bowls, and an extensive vegetarian section. Kids can choose from a hot dog or Japanese pan-fried noodles or the chicken fried rice and jello, which comes with a Japanese toy. Or they can order favorites like *gyoza* (dumplings), *chicken karaage* (deep-fried chicken), and spring rolls, or, for the fun of it, take some sushi from the bar.

4260 No. 3 Rd. (at Cambie Rd.), Richmond. © **604/273-0622.** Reservations recommended. Main courses C$6.95–$12.95 (US$4.60–$8.55), sushi C$2–$5 (US$1.30–$3.30), kids' menu C$4.95 (US$3.27). AE, DC, MC, V. Open daily 11:30am–2am. Highchairs, boosters, kids' menu. Other location: Fukuroku Express, 155-4651 No. 3 Rd. (at the ground floor of Super Store), Richmond. © **604/279-0922.**

6

What Kids Like to See & Do

While Vancouver is no New York or even Toronto when it comes to shopping and entertainment, you'd be hard pressed to find a city better suited to children. There is just so much to do for kids—with our beautiful parks, fabulous natural attractions, nature-based creepy crawlies, and quirky museums, you could easily spend a week or two just visiting attractions.

Don't, of course—little ones don't have the attention span and preteens and teens tend to get bored. Over-scheduling can be an exercise in major frustration and misery for everyone. Spend time in the hotel pool if you have one, and in the many public pools and water parks, if you don't. Visit our beaches and climb our mountains, and pick a few of the attractions that most appeal to your family.

Some just don't work at all. I took my kids, then aged 2 and a half, 5, and 8, to the Museum of Anthropology, thinking that they would like the sweeping views and all the bright colors of the exhibits. And they did, for about 3 minutes, and then they wanted to get hands-on. They found that the sloping stroller- and wheelchair-friendly floors were perfect for running down, and their shouts echoed beautifully off the cavernous rooms in this otherwise library-quiet museum.

I took a second to look at a fabulous carved cedar bear by Bill Reid with a sign saying "this sculpture can be gently touched," and was just in time to catch my 2-year-old trying to scamper up its back. Well, to him, there's a similar model at Science World, where he is allowed to do that.

The moral of this story is that you know your kids' interests and abilities and tolerance level, and sometimes it's worth grabbing a babysitter if one is available, and hitting the museums and art galleries alone. If not, it might be worth waiting until your kids are a bit older.

Keep in mind that most attractions shut Christmas and New Year's Day. Hours change on public holidays and it's always a good idea to phone ahead to avoid disappointment. Also, a lot of the websites carry discounted coupons to the various attractions, so get the kids to run some off before you leave home. Also check the front of the Vancouver Yellow Pages. The Cityscene magazine section has many of the attractions listed here, and there is a large section of two-for-one coupons a little further in the Pages that may make your trip a bit cheaper. The regular telephone book also gives comprehensive maps to find the various attractions.

SUGGESTED ITINERARIES

For Preschoolers

Day 1 Be on the doorstep of the Vancouver Aquarium in Stanley Park when it opens (9:30am in summer, 10am the rest of the year). The crowds will be smaller and small children can get a good look up close at the displays, climb the rocks, and have room to play. Have a sandwich or maybe some grilled fish at the Upstream Cafe, and watch the Beluga whales while you eat. Or grab a hot dog or fish and chips at one of the food concessions outside in the park. Put young children in a stroller, load up on snacks and drinks, take along a sweater or jacket and maybe a raincoat, and walk the 10.5 kilometer (6.5 mile) Stanley Park Seawall. If it's great weather make a stop at the water park at Lumbermen's Arch on the east side of the park.

Day 2 Take a mini-ferry to the Granville Island Public Market. Walk down Anderson Street, under the Granville Bridge, and stop in at the Granville Island Sport Fishing, Model Ship, and Model Train Museum. Kids will be so taken with the model train display, you'll be able to have a close look at some of the other exhibits. Cross the road and go to the Kids' Market at 1496 Cartwright Street. Have a snack there or walk back to the public market and eat there. Then, if it's hot, cool off at the Waterpark or just let the kids play in the playground or on the tug boat by the pond, or run on the grass. In summer you can take the Downtown Vancouver Historic Railway from the corner of Anderson and West 2nd Avenue at the entrance to Granville Island, along False Creek, and make your way back downtown by ferry or bus.

Day 3 Take the SeaBus to Lonsdale Quay in North Vancouver. Let the kids chase the seagulls on the boardwalk outside the public market. Have a look at the tugboats tied up alongside the market, and at the fish inside the public market. If you haven't brought your own, pick up some lunch to go from the food fair and hop on a no. 212 or no. 215 bus to Maplewood Farm. Take the bus back to the market and let the kids have a play in the second-floor ballroom before heading back downtown on the SeaBus. If it's a clear day and you feel you still need a lay of the land, head to the Lookout! At Harbour Centre Tower for 360° views of Vancouver.

For Ages 6 to 8

Day 1 Pack some swimwear, some water, and a snack and rent some bikes (see chapter 7, "For the Active Family," p. 143), and take the kids to the Stanley Park Seawall. Give yourself lots of time for stops along the way—to see the Nine O'Clock Gun, Siwash Rock, the Brockton Point Lighthouse, and at least one beach, as well as to stare at starfish and drink in the different views as you travel. Have fish and chips or a hot dog for lunch at Second Beach and let the kids play in the playground near the vintage fire engine. In summer, spend the afternoon at the outdoor pool. Bike back along Lost Lagoon and visit the Vancouver Aquarium.

Day 2 Same as day 2 for preschoolers, but in summer, take the Downtown Vancouver Historic Railway to the last stop at Quebec Street and 1st Avenue and visit Science World. In cooler months, either take a mini-ferry to Vanier Park or walk up Anderson Street and turn right along the Foreshore

Walk just before West 2nd Avenue. Follow it along to Vanier Park, watch the kites soar, and visit the Maritime Museum. You can take either a mini-ferry back downtown or a bus along Cornwall Avenue.

Day 3 Take the SeaBus to Lonsdale Quay explore the public market and take the no. 236 bus to Grouse Mountain. Take the SkyRide to the top and either have a picnic lunch or enjoy lunch in the cafe, at the restaurant, or at the Bar 98 Bistro, which has a kids' menu. Take in the 30-minute movie *Born to Fly* at Theatre in the Sky. In winter, there is an outdoor ice rink near the SkyRide terminal, and, of course, there is skiing, snowboarding, and snowshoeing. In summer, wander through the chain-saw carvings, take in a logging show, and, if the family is interested in First Nations culture, book in at the hiwus feasthouse, an authentic native longhouse that serves up dishes and a spectacular show. For a more direct route back, take the no. 247 bus over the Lions Gate Bridge to downtown Vancouver.

For Ages 8 to 10

Day 1 Same as Day 1 for 6- to 8-year-olds, but rollerblades may be the preferred mode of transportation.

Day 2 Same as Day 2 for 6- to 8-year-olds, but instead of visiting the Maritime Museum, head for the H.R. MacMillan Space Centre and the Vancouver Museum.

Day 3 Same as Day 3 for 6- to 8-year-olds, but on the way back down from Grouse Mountain, take the no. 232, no. 236, or no. 247 bus to the Capilano Suspension Bridge.

For Preteens

Day 1 Same as Day 1 for 8- to 10-year-olds. Head to Denman and Robson streets and pick one of the dozens of restaurants and cafes for dinner. On long summer evenings, finish the day with either a performance of Shakespeare's Bard on the Beach at Vanier Park, Theatre under the Stars at Malkin Bowl, or a sports event at either General Motors Place or BC Place Stadium.

Day 2 Same as Day 3 for 8- to 10-year-olds. Head to Gastown or Chinatown for dinner and make your way back to Canada Place and see a show at the CN IMAX.

Day 3 Head to Granville Island on the mini-ferry. Take in the public market, the waterslides, and the artisans. Take the ferry over to Vanier Park and drop in at the Vancouver Museum and H.R. MacMillan Space Centre. Or, if that leaves the kids cold, give them a choice—Playland in the warmer months, or perhaps the BC Sports Museum or the Police Museum, if you'd prefer to stick to the downtown core. After dinner, grab the plastic and take advantage of the late-night shopping along Robson Street.

1 The Top 10 Attractions

I agonized over picking the top 10 attractions, because it is so subjective and largely depends on the age of the child. Also, because many families, like mine, have multiple children, you can't just pick out the attractions based on one age group—you have to please them all, and the adults too. The following 10 are attractions that my kids love, that we go to more than once, and that are good for a wide range of age levels. I hope they will also give your family some diverse views of our city, a little history, a smattering of education, some magical picture opportunities, and lasting memories that you can take home with you from Vancouver.

Stanley Park *(★(★(★*   **All ages.** If you only have time to do one thing when you visit Vancouver, let it be Stanley Park. When I first came to Canada in the early 1980s, Stanley Park had a zoo, a free section of the park filled with polar bears, snakes, penguins, seals, and monkeys, spread out near the entrance to the Vancouver Aquarium. With the exception of the sea life inside the Aquarium and the wildlife that inhabits the rest of the park, all the zoo animals have long since left, but just about everything else in this park remains the same. It's a natural wonder waiting to be walked around, trekked through, and uncovered, a 1,000-acre rain forest in the middle of a city.

It's one of the largest urban parks in North America—New York's Central Park is 843 acres—surrounded by water except for the edge that connects it to the West End. It's filled with flower gardens, walking trails, lagoons, beaches, towering western red cedar, hemlock, and fir trees, incredible views, coyotes, bald eagles, raccoons, squirrels, trumpeter swans, brant geese, ducks, and skunks. On the human-made side, it has the Vancouver Aquarium, the Children's Farmyard, a miniature train, restaurants, snack bars, cricket greens, an outdoor swimming pool, and a water park.

The Seawall, the walk-bike-rollerblade path that runs around the perimeter of the park, is a brisk 2-hour jaunt, but it's much better to take your time and stop and see Deadman's Island, the Nine O'Clock Gun, Prospect Point, the Brockton Point Lighthouse, the *Girl in a Wet Suit* statue, and Siwash Rock. Or for a shorter walk, take a stroll around Lost Lagoon at the Georgia Street entrance to the park, and visit the Nature House by the bus loop. In the center of Lost Lagoon you'll see a fountain spouting columns of water that reflect multicolored lights at the base of the fountain. The pattern constantly changes, except in midwinter when the whole fountain freezes into a white sculpture. If you prefer a quieter spot, try Beaver Lake in the middle of the park off Pipeline Road.

The best time to visit Stanley Park on a hot summer's day is early in the morning or later in the day. You'll find it far less crowded.

Where to Eat   There are snack bars selling a variety of junk food (in other words, a big hit with the kids) at the Children's Farmyard, the Cricket Clubhouse, Lost Lagoon, Lumbermen's Arch, and Second Beach. Stanley Park also has four restaurants: the upmarket Fish House Restaurant and the Ferguson Point Tea House, the Prospect Point Cafe, and the Stanley Park Pavilion.

There is pay parking in effect throughout the park, and you can enter the park either from Georgia Street or Beach Avenue. If you are traveling by bus, catch the no. 19 Stanley Park bus to the Georgia Street entrance. The nos. 3 and 8 buses drop passengers near the park at the corner of Robson and Denman streets. From mid-June until mid-September, you can take the free Stanley Park Shuttle. The bus starts at the Children's Miniature Railway and there are 14 stops around the park. You can get on and off whenever you want. The bus runs every 15 minutes between 10am to 6:30pm daily.

What Kids Like to See & Do

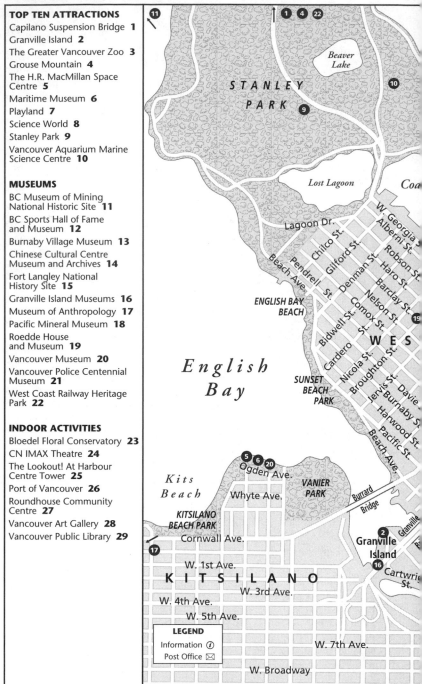

Burrard

Inlet

...arbour

Canada
Place

24

Seabus
Terminal

Canadian
National
S.S. Pier

Centennial
Pier

29

W. Hastings St.

W. Pender St.

Melville St.

18

W. Cordova St.

GASTOWN

Railway St.

Bute St.

Dunsmuir St.

25

Water St.

Powell St. **JAPAN**

7

Thurlow St.

28

(i)

Victory
Sq.

E. Cordova St. **TOWN**

26

**LSON
RK**

Burrard St.

Robson
Sq.

W. Georgia St.

Abbott St.

Carrall St.

21

E. Hastings St.

Hornby St.

Granville St.

Robson St.

Post
✉ Office

CHINATOWN

Howe St.

Seymour St.

Richards St.

Homer St.

■ Bus
Depot

14

Dunlevy Ave.

Helmcken St.

Hamilton St.

Cambie St.

Beatty St.

29

Gore Ave.

Davie St.

12

Stadium

Drake St.

Main St.

Pacific Blvd.

8

VIA/Amtrak Station

27

Cambie

St. Bridge

Québec St.

Terminal Ave.

13

False

W. 1st Ave.

15

3

W. 3rd Ave.

Great Northern

M O U N T

W. 5th Ave.

Way

P L E A S A N T

W. 7th Ave.

0   1/2 Mi

F A I R V I E W

0   .5 Km

(N)

23

Stanley Park

Ferguson Point **16**
Girl in a Wet Suit statue **9**
Hollow Tree/Geographic Tree **14**
Hummingbird Trail/Malkin Bowl **3**
Japanese Monument **5**
Mallard Trail/Brockton Oval **7**
Nature Centre **1**
Nine O'Clock Gun **12**
Ravine Trail/Beaver Lake **11**
Second Beach **17**
Siwash Rock **13**
Third Beach **15**
Totem Poles **8**
Vancouver Aquarium **6**
Vancouver Children's Zoo/Variety Kids Farmyard **4**
Vancouver Rowing Club **2**
Variety Kids Water Park **10**

Legend

Pedestrian/Cycle Route
Cycle Route
Cycle/Roller Route
Seawall Pedestrian Walk
Railway

Burrard Inlet

Coal Harbour

Brockton Point

DEADMAN'S ISLAND

Cricket Pitch

Brockton Oval

Prospect Point

Seawall Promenade

Avison Trail

Reservoir Trail

Hanson Trail

Ravine Trail

Tunnel Road

Pipeline Road

Beaver Lake

Thompson Trail

Lake Trail

Tatlow Walk

Cathedral

Lost Lagoon

Lees Trail

Lovers Walk

Picnic Area

Pitch and Putt Golf Course

Pool

English Bay

Georgia St.

Robson St.

Chilco St.

Lagoon Dr.

Denman St.

1/4 mi
.25 km

Stanley Park Facts

- The 400-hectare (1,000 acre) peninsula now known as Stanley Park was originally set aside as a military reserve in 1859 to ward off a potential invasion by aggressive American troops. It was named Stanley Park in 1889, by Lord Stanley, Governor General of Canada.

- Lost Lagoon was named by Pauline Johnson, a West End resident and poet. Before the construction of the causeway that leads to Lions Gate Bridge, Coal Harbour would fill up the tidal flat to the west, almost reaching English Bay. At low tide the tidal waters would slip, inspiring Johnson to write "Ode to the Lost Lagoon."

- Every night at 9pm the boom of the cannon rumbles out over Hallelujah Point. Cast in England in 1816, the Nine O'Clock Gun has sounded every evening since 1894, except for a short period during World War II when it was conscripted into service. Some say it started as a fishing curfew signal, others just a noisy timepiece, but originally the gun was there to help ships in the harbor set their chronometers.

- Deadman's Island, now a naval reserve, was named because it was once a native burial ground, and later used by white settlers for the same purpose following a smallpox epidemic that broke out between 1888 and 1892.

- The squirrels of Stanley Park are not native sons and daughters; eight pairs were given to Vancouver by the City of New York in 1909. Now the park is riddled with the critters. Be sure to bring peanuts (especially if you are from New York).

- Hallelujah Point is named after the Salvation Army revivals that used to take place there every Sunday around the turn of the 20th century. Reportedly, the cries of "Hallelujah" could be heard all the way across the water in downtown Vancouver.

- Of the more than 700,000 passengers who board Stanley Park's miniature railroad each year, roughly half are adults.

- Look for the National Geographic Tree located near its much more famous and more photographed cousin, the hollow tree. The National Geographic Tree is a huge red cedar, almost 30 meters (98 ft.) around, that the National Geographic Society believes is the largest of its kind in the world. You can find it just along the trail to Third Beach.

- Vancouverites love Stanley Park so much that according to the annual survey by the *Georgia Strait*, a free weekly newspaper, we repeatedly choose it as the best place in town to take a romantic stroll, watch the rain fall, experience bliss, have sex, break up, make up, and take visitors. Readers also voted Stanley Park the best local tourist attraction, the second-best place to be in an earthquake, and the third-best place to get married.

Fun Fact

The Giant Pacific Octopus is the world's biggest octopus and lives off the shores of British Columbia. It can weigh more than 70 kilograms (154 lbs) and stretch 7 meters (23 ft.) from the tip of one of its eight arms to another. It has more than 200 suckers, some as big as a lemon, and some researchers think it's as smart as a house cat. It can squeeze through a hole not much bigger than a toonie.

Vancouver Aquarium Marine Science Centre ⟨★⟩⟨★⟩⟨★⟩   **All ages.** Even though Bjossa the orca whale, the aquarium's biggest draw, left for San Diego's Sea World in April 2001, there is still plenty to delight any age at this fabulous marine attraction. We've been members for years, and while repetitive visits aren't as appealing to a 9-year-old, my 6- and 3-year-olds never tire of this wonderful underwater wonderland. Staff have gone out of their way to make this as hands-on for children as possible; they can climb rock-like surfaces to peer into fish tanks and get right up close to wonderfully colored fish, sharks, and the giant octopus, and they can even feel like a frog and have tadpoles sit on their head in one clever display. In fact, more than 24,000 creatures live here. In the usually quiet mornings, my kids and I head for the Strait of Georgia ⟨★⟩ display, which gives you the sensation that you are scuba diving among these local fish and you can almost touch a sturgeon, wolf eel, rockfish, salmon, or the thousands of flashing silvery herring as they float past. The Amazon Gallery ⟨★⟩ is also pretty special, and the first thing we do is hunt for the sloth in the trees, to see if we can catch it awake. There are three now, so it's somewhat easier. There are nasty-looking crocodiles, an anaconda snake, turtles, tropical birds, piranhas, and a prehistoric-looking fish called an arapaima.

The BC Salmon Stream Project in Stanley Park runs from the Aquarium down to the Seawall at Coal Harbour on the southeastern edge of Stanley Park by the Rowing Club to its headquarters at the Aquarium. The idea is to let you get right up close to watch salmon return from the wild to spawn—there aren't a lot of places you can do this, especially one that's basically in the middle of a city. The project only opened in October 2000, but over the prior 2 years staff released more than 30,000 specially imprinted salmon fry into Coal Harbour along with a special scent that will guide the spawning salmon back. The plan is that they'll find their way home over thousands of kilometers, and wind up in the salmon pool display inside the aquarium.

If the kids are tiring, take them down to look at the beluga whales from below. There is a great Arctic exhibit here, and the kids can run around and push buttons to hear the sounds that whales, seals, bowheads, and walrus make in the wild. They can also see the stellar sea lions and harbor seals through the floor-to-ceiling window. Take along some money for the gift shop, because it has a great selection of unusual toys for kids, and it's where I do a lot of Christmas shopping—you can pick up interesting souvenirs, soapstone carvings, and prints.

If you are visiting in the summer, this place gets quite crazy by about 11am. The best times to visit are first thing in the morning or early in the evening during the week. Expect to spend between 2 to 3 hours here.

Where to Eat   The Upstream Cafe overlooks the Beluga whale tank and serves lattes, pop, pizza, wraps, and sandwiches. From June through September, the aquarium opens a barbecue, which is particularly handy if you've worked up an appetite watching all those fish. Take Georgia Street west to Stanley Park and follow the signs.

Stanley Park. © 604/659-3552. www.vanaqua.org. C$13.85 (US$9.15) adults, C$11.70 (US$7.70) children 13–18, C$9.15 (US$6.05) children 4–12, C$45.95 (US$30.35) family rate, children under 4 free. Open daily 9:30am–7pm late June through early Sept; daily 10am–5:30pm Sept through June.

⸤Fun Fact **Save the Whales**

Vancouver is the birthplace of Greenpeace, which was formed in 1970 to oppose nuclear testing in the Pacific Ocean. Guess it didn't save our whale.

Science World ⭐⭐⭐   **Ages 2 to 12.** Give yourself at least 3 hours for this attraction. You just can't help but learn something at this giant golf-ball look-alike building. Kids love it, all the way up from crawling age—there's just so much movement and color and things to do. There is a great area called Kid-space ⭐ designed for kids 6 and younger (although my 9-year-old can spend time here happily also). It has a spaceship, a wooden structure where kids can build a house with foam bricks and a pulley, Velcro fabric to make your own alien, huge Lego blocks, a Water Table where kids can change the flow of the water, and the Graviram, where kids can build a path using Velcro tubing and watch balls move through it. There is a comfortable nursing room complete with a one-way mirror where you can also keep an eye on your older kids, and it has a gorgeous view of False Creek, the downtown, and the North Shore mountains from a huge picture window.

Little ones can also spend a lot of time in the Search Gallery. Here they can climb through a lodge made by a beaver, climb inside a giant tree trunk, sit on a tree frog, put a human body back together, stare at a tarantula, or sit in the comfortable lounging area and read a book.

Exhibits change fairly frequently in other parts of Science World, but there are some great experiments for young scientists to carry out in the Main Gallery. You can lose your shadow on a wall, play chopsticks with your feet on a giant piano keyboard, control a cyclone, and try out lots of interactive computer games and plain old-fashioned brain teasers. By early 2002 this permanent exhibit will be upgraded into the Science Arcade with more physical experiments and hands-on displays to explore.

At press time Science World was in the middle of renovating its Science Theatre to complement a new exhibit called Our World. The plan is to talk about issues of sustainability, water, transportation, and food by using a game called Quest, much like SimCity, directed to kids aged 6 and up. All the seats in the theater will be wired with key pads and people can interact directly with the game—slide through a garbage dump, find out what really goes into those Big Macs, or make a group of robotic musicians sing and dance by using different types of solar, energy, thermal, and wind power.

The daily shows are definitely worth making time for. The young staff make a point of getting the kids involved and demonstrate everything from electricity to bubbles on the first-floor stage. There is usually an explosion or a flash of some kind, or a demonstration like the one where they had about a dozen kids stand on plank over a bunch of balloons to demonstrate elasticity.

Older children will still enjoy a movie at the Alcan Omnimax Theatre's five-story wrap-around dome screen. Evening screenings are Sunday and Wednesday at 7:30pm. The absolutely best time to see Science World is on a sunny day and first thing in the morning.

Where to eat: There is a White Spot Express with decent burgers and other junk food, a McDonald's, and a Burger King across the road, or bring a picnic and eat out on the patio overlooking False Creek.

1455 Quebec St. (at Terminal St.), Vancouver. © **604/443-7440.** For shows and times at the Alcan Omnimax © **604/443-7443.** www.scienceworld.bc.ca. C$19.75 (US$13) adults with a ticket to the Alcan Omnimax or C$14.75 (US$9.75) without. C$14.25 (US$9.40) children aged 4–18 with a ticket to the Alcan Omnimax or C$9.25 (US$6.10) without. Free for children 3 and under. Open Mon–Fri 10am–5pm; Sat, Sun, and public holidays 10am–6pm. From Vancouver: take Georgia St., across the Georgia Street Viaduct to Quebec St.

The H.R. MacMillan Space Centre ✮✮✮ Ages 4 and up.

Kids from about 4 and up will really enjoy the Space Centre (which is actually our revamped planetarium—people who haven't been here for years are shocked when they come here because it has changed so much and has so much to offer). After our first visit, we bought a one-year membership based solely on the Virtual Voyages simulator ✮. It's worth the price of admission alone. You can save the world from a comet one minute, dive down for an undersea exploration in a submarine the next, or fight pirates on the high seas the next. Kids have to be 1 meter (3 ft.) tall and need to be belted in as the simulator gets rocking, and you can watch it from outside first to get a sense of the movement. There are terrific interactive exhibits in the Cosmic Courtyard exhibit gallery where you can explore the universe at your own pace, travel the solar system, view a huge model of a J2 rocket engine, or touch a moon rock. Kids can use a very easy computer program to morph themselves into aliens, or try to fly a space shuttle, and another called Mission to Mars has them setting up, staffing, budgeting, and stocking their own space mission.

There are super interactive shows for kids upstairs at the H.R. MacMillan Planetarium, and they'll tell you what age they are designed for when you buy your tickets. We saw a particularly good one called "Where in the Universe is Carmen San Diego," based on the television show and computer game, with a live actor to get the kids involved. There are shows with children's entertainers like Fred Penner and Sharon, Lois, and Bram. And, for older children of about 12 and up there are evening laser shows with names like U2 and Pink Floyd. Back on the ground floor at the GroundStation Canada Theatre, enthusiastic young staffers with obvious acting ability do shows about living in space, including such mystifying details as how astronauts pee with no gravity. Another, called Rocket Lab, gives the science behind rockets in easy-to-understand language, including watching one made from a 2-liter pop bottle and rubbing alcohol launch at the end. Staff make a point of getting the kids involved, and they just can't help but learn something educational while they're having fun.

Where to Eat There is nothing on site at the Space Centre and at the nearby Vancouver Museum, although I'm told this is something that they are looking into for 2002. There is a concession at Kitsilano Beach at Cornwall Avenue and Arbutus Street, and a number of interesting food places and cafes along Cornwall Avenue between Cypress and Maple streets.

1100 Chestnut St. (at Ogden St.). © **604/738-7827.** www.hrmacmillanspacecentre.com. C$12.75 (US$8.40) adults, C$9.75 (US$6.45) seniors and students, C$8.75 (US$5.75) children 5–10, C$5.25 (US$3.45) children under 5 with the simulator or free without it. C$40 (US$26.40) family pass (maximum 2 adults, 3 children) Open July 1–Sept Labour Day daily 10am–5pm. Sept–June Tues–Sun 10am–5pm. You can also buy a combo that gives you admittance to the Space Centre and the **Vancouver Museum,** which is in the same building. From Vancouver, take Burrard St. and cross the Burrard Street Bridge, continue along Cornwall Ave., turn right at Ogden St. There is free parking on your right.

Fun Fact

You can't miss the giant crab outside the entrance to the Vancouver Museum and the H.R. MacMillan Space Centre—it sits in the pond and generally keeps watch over the resident ducks. The crab was looked on by the Indians as the guardian of the harbor and is also the sign of the zodiac for the period beginning July 1st—Canada's birthday.

Grouse Mountain ⭐⭐⭐   **All ages.** North Vancouver's Grouse Mountain may just be the world's biggest billboard. Locals ski down it, tourists stare up at it, and the lights on the Cut are highly visible from all over Greater Vancouver. Take the Skyride gondola from the base of the mountain and while it sucks you up to the top 1,100 meters (3,700 ft.) above sea level in 8 minutes flat, enjoy the perfect aerial view of the city of Vancouver, the Cleveland Dam, and the rest of the sprawling Lower Mainland.

Most people who live on the North Shore and ski learned how at Grouse Mountain. It acts as a feeder to its upmarket cousins at Whistler/Blackcomb, Sun Peaks, and Baker. In winter, people trek up the mountain day and night for skiing, snowboarding, ice skating on the outdoor pond, and snowshoeing. There's a small snow park for children, ice skating on the outdoor pond, and sleigh rides that are included in the price of the Skyride ticket.

In the last 2 years, the privately run Grouse Mountain has poured more than C$10 million into renovating its restaurants and improving services. It's now positioning itself as a true year-round resort, and not just another ski hill. There is a mini IMAX-like theater called Theatre in the Sky that runs *Born to Fly,* a 30-minute movie about Southwestern BC from an eagle's perspective, every hour on the hour. In summer there are helicopter rides, interpretive hiking trails that lead you past giant 5 meters (16 ft.) high chain-saw sculptures, and logging sports shows. A few years ago, the hiwus feasthouse opened to the public in the summer. It's a longhouse that seats 110 people on handmade chief-style bench seating. It's as authentic as they could make it and the show—dancers in traditional garb sing and beat drums around a fire pit—is supported with a very 1990s video presentation. It also serves a five-course meal of Coast Salish foods such as bannock bread, alderwood salmon, and wild berry tart, but be aware that these are very small courses.

The other thing about Grouse Mountain is that while you feel that you are on top of the world, it's a mere 20-minute drive from downtown Vancouver. For those who are fit, you can climb the 2.9 kilometer (1.8 mile) almost vertical Grouse Grind up and catch a C$5 (US$3.30) ride on the SkyRide back down.

Where to Eat   There are a number of places to eat, from the upmarket Observatory, which is gaining good reviews, to Lupin's Cafe and the Bar 98 Bistro, which has drop-dead views and a kids' menu.

6400 Nancy Greene Way, North Vancouver. © **604/984-0661** www.grousemtn.com C$17.95 (US$11.20) adults, C$11.95 (US$7.90) children 13–18, C$6.95 (US$4.60) children 7–12, children under 7 free. Departs every 15 minutes daily 9am–10pm. From Vancouver take W. Georgia St. over the Lions Gate Bridge, turn right at Marine Dr., then take the first left onto Capilano Rd. and continue to Grouse Mountain. By bus: no. 232.

Fun Fact

The Lions Gate Bridge crosses the First Narrows waterway to connect Vancouver with the North Shore. It was completed in 1938 and modeled after San Francisco's Golden Gate Bridge. Lions Gate is the name of the body of water at the mouth of Burrard Inlet over which the bridge crosses. The passage derives its name from the Lions—the mountain peaks that overlook the water on the North Shore.

Capilano Suspension Bridge *(★(★*   **All ages.** Okay, let's get this out of the way first: I'm terrified of heights and didn't want to look like a coward in front of my kids so I've been putting off a trip to the Capilano Suspension Bridge since before they were born. Anyway, in the interests of research I packed up the family and we headed off to this matchstick structure that dangles 69 meters (230 ft.) above Capilano River. On closer inspection it is pretty sturdy-looking, and I figured if it hadn't fallen down under the weight of 800,000 people a year swinging over it, I should survive. Just to put this in perspective, and I'm cribbing from the kids' fact sheet that they gave me, the bridge stands about chest height on the Statue of Liberty and its 135 meter (450 ft.) length is equivalent to two Boeing 747s flying wing tip to wing tip through the canyon with room to spare.

The 3-year-old wasn't quite sure about all of it, although he was clutching my sweating palm, but the older kids loved the sensation of having only a few planks between them and the churling waters below. It also sways, and I do mean sways, particularly when a lot of other people are bouncing on it.

At the other side of the bridge there's still an old-growth West Coast rain forest. There are some well thought-out displays and kids can take the card that they received on the way in and get it stamped at various spots. There are beautiful nature trails that wind their way around ponds teeming with wiggling trout, waterfalls, and old-growth trees. On the way back I got a certificate that says "I made it across the Capilano Suspension Bridge" (everybody does, though mine is on the fridge).

Back on the other side, where you came in, if you haven't already you can wander through the Interpretative Centre and watch native carvers at work on totem poles, masks, and bowls. The gardens are quite beautiful, and smaller children will like running up the stone stairs behind the waterwheel. There's also a lookout over an outcrop from where you can get some decent pictures of the bridge. The attraction gets kind of crazy in the summer time and the busiest time is on the weekends between 10am and 2pm. So try to avoid that and come early and in the first part of the week.

Where to Eat   There is a cafe in the gift shop building, and in the summer, the Loggers' Grill serves up chicken, beef, salmon, and veggie burgers. The Bridge House Restaurant across the street is a full-service restaurant.

3735 Capilano Rd., North Vancouver. ℂ 604/985-7474. www.capbridge.com. C$11.95 (US$7.90) adults, C$7.50 (US$4.95) students, C$3.50 (US$2.30) children 6–12, children under 6 free. Open daily summer 8:30am–dusk, winter 9am–5pm. From Vancouver take W. Georgia St. over the Lions Gate Bridge, take North Vancouver exit, then the first left onto Capilano Rd., keep going past the Trans-Canada Hwy., and you will see the Capilano Suspension Bridge on your left. By bus: no. 246 from W. Georgia St. to the stop at the corner of Ridgewood Dr. and Capilano Rd. and walk 1 block north on Capilano Rd. About a 20-min. ride.

⌜Fun Fact

More on the Capilano Suspension Bridge: the two steel cables that hold up the bridge can support 90,000 kilograms (180 tons) or roughly 1,333 average people. It is held up by concrete blocks weighing 13,000 kilograms (13 tons) anchored at each end of the bridge. That's equivalent to four elephants on each side.

Granville Island ⟨★★★⟩   **All ages.** The name of this site was originally Industrial Island, which will give you a clue to its origins, but fortunately it didn't stick for long. Not really an island, the area around Granville Island was originally a mudflat and what's now the island was a sandbar. Around 1915, the government came up with the brilliant idea of putting sea mud from False Creek's bed between 700,000 meters of the island's wooden walls and voila! a 35-acre human-made island, quite unlike anything you've seen before.

Granville Island is a place that offers up everything to everybody. It's in the city, but not really; it's connected by boardwalks and walks along the water. It has a Waterpark (see chapter 7, "For the Active Family," p. 154), the Kids' Market, a shopping and playing oasis for little people, and playgrounds. It has a public market (see chapter 10, "Shopping for the Whole Family," p. 185), interesting and unique shops, three theaters, floating homes, restaurants, and places where you can watch a kayak being built, or a violin maker plying his trade. It's also bustling and full of life all year around (see chapter 8, "Neighborhood Walks," p. 167 for a full walking tour). For more information about Granville Island or a free map, contact the Information Centre, 1398 Cartwright St. (ℂ 604/666-5784; www.granvilleisland.com).

Where to Eat   There is a cornucopia of choices. There are fresh goods from the public market and a vast array of restaurants and food stands all over. Take your pick.

Granville Island is at the south side of False Creek right beneath the Granville Street Bridge and accessible by car, bus, or foot from W. 4th Ave. Take the W. 4th Ave. exit off Granville Street Bridge when driving from downtown Vancouver. Parking is horrendous, but if you can find it you can park free for 3 hours (7am–7pm) or pay C$1.50 (US$1) per hour in one of four parking garages. By bus: The no. 50 bus runs down Granville St. from downtown and stops at the Granville Island entrance (at Lamey's Mill Rd. at Anderson St.) every 15 minutes including Sun and holidays. 5-minute mini-ferry rides from the Aquatic Centre in the West End, the south end of Hornby St. downtown, Stamps Landing to the east of Granville Island, Vanier Park to the west, the Plaza of Nations, Yaletown, Science World, to the north of the public market, and to the northwest. Granville Island Ferries, 1804 Boatlift Lane ℂ 604/684-7781; Aquabus Limited, 1617 Foreshore Walk ℂ 604/689-5858. Retail stores open daily 10am–6pm. Public market open daily 9am–6pm.

Fun Fact **Mild, Milder, Mildest**

Vancouver is known among Canadian cities for its mild climate, and Granville Island's is milder still. As a result of the combination of urban convection (whereby the city generates its own heat) and being on the water—where, thanks to the Japan current, the temperature consistently stays above 5° Celsius (41°F)—the island seldom suffers a frosty morning.

Vancouver Maritime Museum ⊛ *Value*   **Ages 2 and up.** You can't miss the triangular glass and wood structure, built to house the historic *St. Roch*. A visit here is a great deal price wise, and you can easily spend a few hours as there are lots of hands-on things to keep the kids occupied. In fact, it will be hard to get little ones out of the Children's Maritime Discovery Centre, with its drawers full of sea gear, toys, and maritime treasures to touch and marvel at, displays that move when you push buttons, a pirate ship and a box of pirate clothes, and a replica tugboat wheelhouse complete with the sounds of the sea, bells, whistles, and vessel traffic that makes it feel authentic. There are dozens of model ships and many were built at the museum, by its own resident model ship-builder. Kids can view Vancouver's active port life through high-powered telescopes, load a container ship, or conduct an undersea exploration at computer stations and pilot an undersea robot through the depths of the ocean.

Just behind the reception area, there is a 15-minute video, which probably won't interest the kids, but make sure you take the tour of the *St. Roch*. It's quite fascinating, even for little ones, to see life as it was in 1944 and be one of the crew. Kids get to climb up to the top on a ladder, take a turn at the wheel, and check out the cabins with bunks not much bigger than a crib, see the captain's quarters, and where an Inuit family once lived. They can even ring the ship's bell (this wears thin after the tenth kid has tried it). In case you opt to skip the video, the *St. Roch* was the first ship to sail the Northwest Passage across the top of Canada from west to east, and the first ship to cross in both directions. It was built in 1928 for the Royal Canadian Mounted Police and used as a patrol and supply ship in the western Arctic for more than 20 years. On the way out, wander down to the Heritage Harbour on the water at Vanier Park, and check out the historic and classic boats moored down at the edge and see what's happening at the small boat building and repair workshop. This is also where you can catch a mini-ferry.

Where to Eat   There is nothing on site either here at the Maritime Museum or at the nearby Space Centre and Vancouver Museum. There is a concession at Kitsilano Beach at Cornwall Avenue and Arbutus Street, and a number of interesting food places and cafes along Cornwall Avenue between Cypress and Maple streets.

1905 Ogden Ave. (at Chestnut St.). ⓒ 604/257-8300. www.vmm.bc.ca. C$7 (US$4.60) adults, C$4 (US$2.65) children 6–19, C$16 (US$10.55) family, free for children 5 and under. Open summer daily 10am–5pm; winter Sept–mid-May Tues–Sat 10am–5pm, Sun noon–5pm. From Vancouver take Burrard St. across Burrard Street Bridge, continue west along Cornwall Ave., turn right at either Chestnut or Cypress sts., and drive north to the water. There is pay parking in front of the museum.

The Greater Vancouver Zoo ⊛   **All ages.** This isn't the world's greatest or the world's biggest zoo, but the kids won't care, and they can still see close to 200 species and more than 900 animals, many of which are on the endangered list or face extinction in the wild. It's 48 kilometers (30 miles) from Vancouver, about a 45-minute drive, which is just before Abbotsford in the Fraser Valley. The zoo is set on 49 hectares (120 acres). Give yourself at least 3 hours, not including lunch, to see it properly. Start with the little red train—it's noisy, the kids will love it, and it will give you a lay of the land to plan your walk. Since it's narrated, it will also arm you with a bunch of information and answers to questions like: "Why do people hunt the white rhino for its horn, Dad?" (Answer: "Because it's an aphrodisiac, son.") And, "Mom, what's an Aoudad?" (Answer: "Why, it's a type of sheep that lives in the Sahara Desert, dear.")

Make sure you introduce yourself to Tina and Tumpe, the zoo's two elephants that are just on the right of the entrance. Tina is an Asian elephant now over 30 and Tumpe is from Africa. The zoo has also finished a walkway that takes you nose to nose with its 4.5-meter (15 ft.) giraffe. And there are zebras, wolves, lynx, wild boar, an overly friendly ostrich, wallabies, pink flamingos, and an exhibit that features two massive Siberian tigers, lions, jaguars, and cougars near the miniature train. One of the better times to visit is at 1:30pm for the tiger feeding where you can see them pound down beef, horsemeat, or maybe turkey—it's dead—and again at 3:30pm when the two hippos, Gertrude and Harvey, munch on lettuce, watermelons, or perhaps a juicy pumpkin. Don't mess with these guys—the male weighs in at 2,925 kilograms (6,500 lbs) and hippos are said to be the most dangerous animals in the world. And while they might look sluggish they can get up to 35kmph (21 mph) over short distances.

Summer is probably the most pleasant time to visit, but last time we went it was at the end of April, and there were a bunch of baby animals: a small joey that kept leaping in and out of its mother's pouch, six playful lion cubs, and a bunch of ducklings and chickens. Don't miss the capybara, which looks like someone has messed with your pet guinea pig in a weird scientific experiment. It's the largest rodent in the world and makes the common rat look pretty tame.

You can take a free narrated bus tour through the 17 acres that house the North America Wild exhibit at the northeast end of the zoo; the tour takes about 15 or 20 minutes. (This is closed between December and the end of February to let the bears hibernate.) Here you can get close to black bears, a wolf pack, and an elk and bison herd. A tram runs from spring through to the fall and provides a shuttle service, dropping you off at different points of the zoo; it costs C$2 (US$1.30) per person or C50¢ (US33¢) per stop. But probably the best way to see the zoo is to walk it, bike it, rollerblade it, or, as I saw one family doing, throw the kids into one of those large plastic wagons and pull it.

A new exhibit opening in the summer of 2001 is Grizzly Bear Habitat and sounds worth another visit. It will be filled with native trees, shrubs, and plants, a swimming pond, and a bear den complete with a camera to watch Shadow the Grizzly Bear at work, at play, and at snooze. For kids who can't get enough of the animals, the zoo runs a 5-day adventure day camp for 8- to 12-year-olds through July and August. And there's a gift shop so you can take home a stuffed version of what you've just seen.

Where to Eat   The Safari Grill sells hot dogs, hamburgers, and all the usual junk fare, and you can eat in there or take it outside in a covered area by the playground. But if it's a nice day, bring your own picnic lunch and have it on the lawns by the gazebo. It's in the middle of the park and has a large gazebo, duck ponds, and lovely gardens with rhododendrons and azaleas throughout. There is also the Starbright Coffee concession stand and another one that sells mini donuts.

5048 264 St., Aldergrove. © **604/856-6825.** www.greatervancouverzoo.com. C$12 (US$7.90) adults, C$9 (US$5.95) children 3–15, family rate for 2 adults and 2 children C$40 (US$26.40) and additional children are C$6.50 (US$4.30) each. Children under 2 free. Train rides C$2 (US$1.30). Open 365 days a year 9am–dusk. Parking is C$3 (US$2) per day; strollers and wheelchairs can be rented. Take the Trans-Canada Hwy. (Hwy. 1) east past Surrey and Langley and then take the Aldergrove exit on 264th St. and travel south for 2 blocks.

Playland ⊛   **Ages 9 and up.** There's nothing much that says Vancouver about this particular attraction—in fact it's pretty much a dump, but kids don't care about any of that. They will love the rides, the carnival-type stalls, the candy floss, and mini donuts. For parents with older kids, it might just be the perfect place to drop them for a few hours and have a leisurely meal at a non-family-type restaurant or visit an art gallery or museum. For kids who like 'coasters there is the 1958 wooden rollercoaster that is unofficially ranked third in North America and is a hit for people who follow these things (and yes there really is a club called the American Coaster Enthusiasts, which has 5,000 members). There is the Corkscrew, and the name pretty much gives it away, the Wild Mouse ride (bumper cars on a roller coaster), and the wild Wasserbahn, a log ride over roaring water where you get wet. Then there are park favorites, the Tilt-a-Whirl, the Octopus, a kind-of ferris wheel that flips you upside down, the Pirate ship, which slides at a nauseating angle, and, for kids with real guts (or no brains), the Hellevator—a gruesome, torturous-looking device that sucks you up a sky-scraper-sized 60-meter (200 ft.) tower, flings you back down again at 75kmph (47 mph), picks...anyway you get the idea. There is also the Hell's Gate, another evil-looking blue and orange thing that flips you up and over several times at a huge height and at a dizzying speed. Others that will appeal to daredevils are the Revelation, a 16-story windmill that turns at 100kmph (60 mph) an hour—the selling factor for daredevils is that it has the same G-force of that of a fighter pilot—and the Drop Zone, a kind of skydiving free fall in a swing. Both these rides cost an extra C$19.95 (US$13) for a 3-minute thrill.

Personally, I was happy that at least one of my kids (the 6-year-old) was the right age to accompany on really cool rides at Kids' Playce for kids under 8. Actually she was a lot braver and wanted to go on the Hellevator, but luckily you had to be taller than 68 centimeters (52 in.). Kids' Playce is a large section for kids of about 2 to 8. There is a small version of the swing ride, a small roller-coaster called Dragon Coaster, the scrambler, Paddle Wheelers, elephants, bumper cars, a play area with lots of plastic and climbing things, and a glass wall maze (so you can fish them out if they panic). Little ones will love the petting zoo, where they can get right up to an assortment of healthy-looking llamas, goats, donkeys, chickens, pigs, and rabbits. And, older ones will like the 12-meter (40 ft.) climbing wall and the mini golf, batting cages for budding base-ballers, PlayStation, 3-on-3 basketball, and games arcade.

In the past, the Pacific National Exhibition, which takes place at Playland, has run for 3 weeks from mid-August and the admission and times change. Although the fair has run since 1910, it looks like 2002 could be its last year.

The best time to visit to avoid the crowds is at 11am when it opens, and early in the week, Monday to Wednesday.

Where to Eat   There is a sit-down White Spot Express restaurant with kids' packs, decent hamburgers, and coffee, and a bunch of concession stands scattered about.

Hastings Park, E. Hastings St. (entrance is between Renfrew and Cassiar sts.), East Vancouver. © 604/255-5161. www.pne.bc.ca. C$22.95 (US$15.15) general passport; C$9.95 (US$6.55) limited passport for children under 122cm (48 in.) tall and for an adult accompanying paid child. Children under 3 free. Admission price includes unlimited access to 25 rides. The Drop Zone, the Revelation, games, and the batting cages not included in the admission price. Open weekends and public holidays only mid-Apr–mid-June and Sept 11am–7pm. Open daily from mid-June–mid-Aug 11am–9pm. Take Hastings St. east, continue to Renfrew St. until you see the main gate. There is pay parking across the road.

2 Museums & Local History

BC Museum of Mining National Historic Site ⭐ Ages 4 and up. While the word "museum" often suggests otherwise, the mine is a fun day trip for the kids. It's 52 kilometers (32 miles) from Vancouver on the way to Whistler, and the drive out there is spectacular—you get to take in some of the best parts of Howe Sound, along the Sea-to-Sky Highway (Hwy. 99). You can't miss the museum, which is actually a former copper mine, because it has a 235-ton Super Truck, once used in open pit copper mining, sitting out front. Sign up for the tour at the Gift Store, which runs between 1 and 1½ hours, and the big hit for kids will be the 30-minute train tour that takes them, wearing hard hats and traveling through tracks once used regularly, through an underground mine shaft. Staff dress as miners and point out things like where the dynamite was stored, and you can experience a hard rock mine and what miners had to do to open up a mine shaft 100 or so years back. Suddenly those math books don't look so bad, eh, kids? The tunnel itself is 360 meters (1,200 ft.) long and was used with the old mill buildings for high-grade ore. The tour also includes some gold panning, museum displays of the history of Britannia and mining, and live demonstrations of mining equipment.

Chatterbox Gifts has a terrific selection of minerals and fossils, and kids can pick out their own polished rocks by the bag for under C$6 (US$4).

Hwy. 99, Britannia Beach. © 604/688-8735. www.bcmuseumofmining.org. C$9.50 (US$6.25) adults, C$7.50 (US$4.95) children 6–15. Children under 5 free. Open daily early May–mid-Oct 9am–4:30pm. Winter days and hours subject to change, so phone in advance.

BC Sports Hall of Fame and Museum ⭐ Ages 8 and up. The largest sports museum in Canada, this is definitely worth a visit even if you are only vaguely interested in hockey, football, tennis, baseball—well, any sport at all. You can ask for a tape recorder at the front desk and take your own self-guided tour, or just wander at leisure through the various exhibits. The tour starts in the 1860s at the time-tunnel entrance. My kids (all under 9 at the time) were quite interested in the Rick Hansen and Terry Fox galleries and the Hall of Champions, but weren't too excited about the history and we whipped through this and the First Nations Gallery at record speed. We didn't seem to slow down much through the sports sections, which are neatly divided up into decades. It's a great colorful maze to wander through and it finished up at the 1990s—that's where it really started to get the kids' attention. First, there's the Star Dome Theatre, which shows the highlights of the 1994 NHL when the Vancouver Canucks made it into the finals (this is indeed a bit of history), the 1994 BC Lions game, and the Commonwealth Games, obviously a good year. But what's really fun is that the theater looks out onto BC Place Stadium through a large picture window. When they tire of this, the prize at the end is the Participation Gallery. There is a climbing wall and a slap-happy game to test reactions by hitting

colored buttons as they light up. There's also a hockey table game, a running track where you can time your speed over 14 meters (46 ft.), and a throwing cage where you can check your speed throwing or kicking a variety of round things (soccer, football, tennis balls). If they are older, you can leave kids here while you go through the museum at a more leisurely pace, or just drop them here at the beginning. There's plenty of street meter parking on Robson and it's right near Stadium Station and West Georgia Street buses.

777 Pacific Blvd. (at the corner of Robson and Beatty sts. at Gate A at BC Place Stadium), Vancouver. © 604/ 687-5520. C$6 (US$4) adults, C$4 (US$2.65) children. Open daily 10am–5pm.

Fun Fact

Rick Hansen won 19 international wheelchair races, wheeled 40,000 kilo-meters (24,880 miles) through 34 countries on four continents, and returned May 22, 1987, two years, two months, and two days after leav-ing Vancouver. He raised C$23 million for spinal cord research, rehabilita-tion awareness programs, and wheelchair sports.

Burnaby Village Museum   **All ages.** Little ones will love the vintage carousel that flings them around at a pretty fast pace, but kids of all ages should like wan-dering through this recreated township. In 1891 an interurban tram line was built between New Westminster and Vancouver and passed through what is now called Burnaby. People moved here and it became a municipality. The 4 hectare (10 acre) open-air village is designed to represent a typical Burnaby tram-stop community around 1925. It has costumed interpreters to guide you through the grounds, and at the various homes and shops to give you an idea of what life was like over 75 years ago. The village has 30 full-scale buildings, including a won-derful Chinese herbalist who can talk to you about your ailments and recom-mend some interesting-looking cures, a drug store, a barber shop, a post office, and a general store. You can watch a silent movie, tour Seaforth School, the one-room schoolhouse that was moved from the north side of Burnaby Lake and had 20 students in 1922, wander through a village church, and watch a blacksmith at work on some horseshoes. The gardens are beautiful and you can stroll through them and over a creek to visit the farmhouse at the back of the prop-erty. It's a great spot to visit at Christmas, as the village goes all out from the end of November to early January with crafts and entertainers, Christmas carolers, stories, and puppet shows. In summer, you can ride in an old-fashioned trike race or play hopscotch. Afterwards grab some lunch or an ice cream at the old-fashioned ice-cream parlor.

6501 Deer Lake Ave., Burnaby. © 604/293-6501. www.burnabyparksrec.org. C$6.60 (US$4.35) adults, C$4.55 (US$3) students and children 13–18, C$3.95 (US$2.60) children 6–12, children under 6 free. Carousel rides C$1 (US66¢).

Fort Langley National History Site   **All ages.** You'll find the oldest build-ing on BC's mainland at this settlement, which was established by the Hudson's Bay Company in 1827 and is the birthplace of British Columbia. You can get a glimmer of what life was like in the early 1800s fur-trading days from costumed guides who use stories, reenactments, and demonstrations to bring this trading post to life. Visitors can pan for gold, watch a blacksmith at work, and watch weaving demonstrations. The nearby village is worth exploring as it has a mix of shops, cafes, restaurants, antiques, and art galleries.

23433 Mavis Ave., Fort Langley (50km/31 miles and about 40 minutes east of Vancouver on Hwy. 1). ℂ 604/513-4777. http://parkscan.harbour.com/fl/servicee.htm. C$4 (US$2.65) adults, C$2 (US$1.30) children 6–16, C$10 (US$6.60) family rate, children under 6 free. Open daily 10am–5pm March through October. From Vancouver: take the Trans-Canada Hwy. (Hwy. 1) east to the 232nd St. north exit, follow 232nd St. to the stop sign on Glover Rd., turn right and follow Glover Rd. into the village of Fort Langley, at Mavis St., just before the tracks, turn right. You'll see the fort at the end of the street.

Granville Island Museums 🖈 **Ages 4 and up.** This is the dream of John Keith-King, a former Vancouver architect and developer who has a passion for ships, fishing, and trains and has combined all three into a fascinating museum in about 11,000 square meters (12,000 sq. ft.) of space. While the idea of a Sports Fishing Museum, fly fishing, antique reels, Rufas Gibb's lures, plugs, and trophy fish might put your kids to sleep, and the tugs, steams, and coastal working boats in the Model Ships Museum might not hold their interest for too long, I bet you'll have a hard time getting them away from the Model Train Museum. Here you'll find the largest international collection of model and toy trains on public display in the world. There is one of those wonderful marketing disasters—a 1957 pink Lionel train set, brought out to entice girls to play with trains (it bombed) and the blue one for boys didn't take off either. (But if you have one at home, dust it off—they are worth between US$7,000 and US$12,000 now.) There is a train stamp collection, and a railroad china and silver collection. But the 24 meter (80 ft.) long model train display is a three-dimensional work of art, or to quote one visitor I overheard: "Amazing, amazing, amazing!" Modeled after the Fraser and Kettle valleys, it is built at waist height so kids can get up close, with almost 300 meters (1,000 ft.) of train track and five lines on four levels, featuring the Royal Hudson, BC Electric Inter-Urban, and CN and CP freight trains. There are trestle bridges; oceans, mountain passes, and tunnels; and 6,000 handmade western old-growth red cedar, Douglas fir, and hemlock trees made to scale. The biggest, an old-growth red cedar, is 7.5 centimeters (3 in.) (45m or 150 ft. if it were real). The model took eight people working full time a year to build, and it is made from 2 kilometers (3 miles) of Johnson & Johnson orthopedic bandages, which knit it all together. Get the kids to find a beaver, mountain goats, a rock climber, a floatplane, a bear, and an eagle. If you didn't see "the big boys room" on the way in, on the ground floor near the boardwalk, be sure to check it out on the way out. You'll find the Northern, a live steam train with a 6 meter (20 ft.) long, 1 meter (3 ft.) high 484 engine. There is also a gift shop, which sells rare old rods and model ship-building kits, and a coffee shop on the boardwalk.

1502 Duranleau St. (at Anderson St.) in the Maritime Market at Granville Island, Vancouver. ℂ 604/683-1939. www.sportfishingmuseum.bc.ca; www.modelshipsmuseum.bc.ca; www.modeltrainsmuseum.bc.ca; www.museumstore.bc.ca/store. C$6.50 (US$4.30) adults, C$5 (US$3.30) seniors and students, C$3.50 (US$2.30) children 4–12, C$42 (US$27.70) family rate up to a maximum of 5. Children under 4 free. Open daily 10am–5:30pm.

Museum of Anthropology **Ages 12 and up.** This award-winning concrete and glass building designed by Arthur Erickson to reflect the post-and-beam structures of northwest coast First Nations opened in 1976. Dramatic floor-to-ceiling windows provide gigantic totem poles with a spectacular backdrop of the North Shore mountains and English Bay, and outside there are two Haida longhouses, which is also probably the safest area for young children.

In the Great Hall, you can also see work by the Haida and Nisga'a featured prominently. In fact, the museum is probably best known for its collections from the aboriginal people of BC and is built on Musqueam ancestral land. The museum is filled with beautiful artwork, masks, and sculptures, all of which won't do much for kids under about 10, although the Visible Gallery has drawers filled with spears, native ornaments, utensils, toys, and games that little fingers can pull out and look at. There are two interactive computers and a terrific jewelry display by Haida artist Robert Davidson.

The Koerner Ceramics Gallery on the west side of the museum is easy to miss, and it houses a collection of European ceramics unique to North America.

The gift shop sells native jewelry, prints, and carvings as well as books on art, culture, history, and First Nations.

6393 NW Marine Dr., Vancouver. ✆ **604/822-5087.** www.moa.ubc.ca. C$7 (US$4.60) adults, C$4 (US$2.65) children, C$20 (US$13.20) 2 adults and up to 4 children, children under 6 free. Free 5–9pm Tues. Open mid-May–Sept Wed–Mon 10am–5pm, Tues 10am–9pm; Oct–mid-May Wed–Sun 11am–5pm, Tues 10am–8pm. Take Burrard St. and the Burrard Street Bridge and turn right on W. 4th Ave., which turns into Point Grey Rd., and then into N.W. Marine Dr.; follow this up to UBC and the museum is on your right.

Fun Fact

Haida artist Bill Reid, who crafted the fabulous *Raven and the First Men*, on display at the Museum of Anthropology, also created *The Spirit of Haida Gwaii*, a huge jade canoe sculpture on display at the International Terminal of the Vancouver International Airport. You can also see his stunning bronze killer whale outside the Vancouver Aquarium.

Pacific Mineral Museum   **Ages 5 to 12.** Kids from about 5 to 12 should be pretty fascinated by some of the finds of this newish museum. There are three galleries, and each one tells a different story about minerals and how they fit into our lives—not just around our necks, on our fingers, and in our earlobes. There are beautiful opals, emeralds, gold, silver, and jade in the vault. Staff won't tell you how much the gems are worth, but have a look at the Treasure Display and try to guess which one is worth the most—the huge and sparkly yellow gem, one small and one big black mineral crystal, two big gold nuggets, an Alexandria coin, a couple of sapphires, and a crystal. Bet you picked the gem, right? Wrong, it's the cheapest of the lot. The most valuable is the large black crystal. It's made from a common copper ore, but this particular one has worked itself into very large, well-formed crystals. Kids can touch a dinosaur bone and pull out drawers in the vault filled with fossils and stones, adults can read about meteorites that crashed into the back of people's cars, and everyone can check out the drawers full of diamonds and the ammonite fossil that looks like mother of pearl but covers fossils, minerals, and gems all in the one specimen. The exhibits change frequently.

848 W. Hastings St. (at Hornby St.). ✆ **604/689-8700.** Open daily mid-May–mid-Sept Mon–Fri 10am–5pm and Sat–Sun 10 am–6pm; mid-Sept–mid-May Tues–Fri 10am–5pm, Sat–Sun 10am–6pm. C$4 (US$2.65) adults, C$3 (US$2) students and seniors, children under 5 free.

Roedde House and Museum   **Ages 6 and up.** This is a beautifully restored Queen Anne–style house that forms part of the Barclay Heritage Square in the West End, a short hop from Robson Street. This particular house was built in 1893. It has a gazebo out on the front lawn with a large magnolia tree. The house, which originally belonged to Gustav Roedde, Vancouver's first book-binder, is now a museum and has guided tours, afternoon teas, and recitals. There are nine historic houses dating from 1890 to 1908 in the block bounded by Haro, Broughton, Barclay, and Nicola streets, each kept pretty much in their original settings. Every Christmas Roedde House holds a special teddy bear Christmas for children up to about the age of 12 on Sundays in December. There are dozens of teddy bears in the house, and kids are encouraged to bring their own and listen to carolers and storytellers.

1415 Barclay St. (at Broughton St.). © **604/684-7040.** www.roeddehouse.org. C$4 (US$2.65) adults, and free for children under 12. You need to book a guided tour in advance. Tours 2–4pm Tues–Fri only. From Granville St., walk down Robson St. and turn left at Broughton St. (about 6 blocks). By bus: no. 5 Robson bus; disembark at Broughton St.

Vancouver Museum *★* **All ages.** Shaped like a giant white spaceship, the building houses both the Vancouver Museum and the H.R. MacMillan Space Centre and is quite easy to find. But if you're still in doubt, the giant metal crab at the front will clue you in. My kids groan if I mention the word "museum," but this one has a lot to interest even very young children. (My favorite argument: "Hey, was Indiana Jones boring?") The temporary exhibits are super and always have a lot of hands-on stuff for kids to do—arts, games, computers, and scheduled live shows and entertainers. The staff is constantly on the lookout to help, and whenever my kids start to get restless, staff members tend to pop up with age-appropriate toys—a box of wooden trains, blocks, and boats for the 3-year-old, or a computer game for the 9-year-old. If they are busy, you just have to ask and they seem to have endless things on hand. My kids spent ages trying to write their names in Egyptian hieroglyphics, and were pretty interested in how a 10-year-old male mummy named Panechates, who lived somewhere between the 1st and 3rd centuries AD, was made. Kids also seem to gravitate to the In-Gallery activities, which include early Vancouver toys, Whatsits (a guessing game about how children lived in 1901), and early Vancouver school activities. The exploration and settlement of Vancouver includes three re-created rooms from an Edwardian Home from around 1898 to 1914. Kids can also climb aboard an old tram and see how a century-old house was furnished, before television and microwaves—egad, whatever did they do? There's also a great view of English Bay through a floor-to-ceiling picture window and pictures of how the same view looked 70 years ago.

1100 Chestnut St. (at Ogden St.). © **604/736-4431.** C$8 (US$5.30) adults, C$5.50 children 5–18, C$25 (US$16.50) 1-day pass for a group of 5, children 4 and under free. Fri–Wed 10am–5pm, Thurs 10am–9pm. From downtown, take Burrard St. across the Burrard Street Bridge, continue along Cornwall Ave., turn right at Ogden St., and follow it to Chestnut St. There is free parking on your right.

(**Fun Fact**

It's not really a space ship. The 1981 building that houses the Vancouver Museum and the H.R. MacMillan Space Centre is actually a distinctive dome shape similar to that of a woven basket hat made by Northwest First Nations People.

West Coast Railway Heritage Park   All ages. Anyone into trains—and is there a kid who isn't?—will love exploring these vintage railway cars. There are about 60, including the Great Northern No. 182, a fully restored CPR No. 4069, the Canadian Pacific Railway Business Car, and an assortment of steam, diesel, and electric locomotives. If you fancy, you can also take a seat in the observation lounge and be a railway baron—it's a kind of '90s (that's 1890s) business car, and you won't find any fax or data hookups here. When the kids tire of belting through the train aisles and climbing through a caboose or a snow-plow, put them into motion on the miniature railway that circles the park. There is a playground, a snack bar, and a gift shop. You can drive here in less than an hour, or make a day trip of it by taking the Royal Hudson steam train from the North Vancouver station or catch the *M.V. Britannia* boat at the north foot of Denman Street in downtown Vancouver.

39645 Government Rd., Squamish. © **604/898-9336.** www.wcra.org. C$6 (US$4) adults, C$5 (US$3.30) seniors and students, C$18 (US$11.85) families, children under 6 free. Open daily 10am–5pm. Train rides are C$2 (US$1.30). Take Georgia St. west over the Lions Gate Bridge and left into West Vancouver; take the first right at Taylor Way and onto the Trans-Canada Hwy., until Horseshoe Bay; follow signs to Hwy. 99 (the Sea to Sky Hwy.); take Hwy. 99 to Squamish; once at Squamish, turn west at Industrial Way and follow signs to the park.

✏ For Kids Who Like to Ride the Rails & Sail ⍟⍟⍟

The Royal Hudson   The scenery is so breathtakingly beautiful that you'll soon be whistling, too. And while the kids probably won't care about the seascapes, the snowcapped peaks, rock cliffs, waterfalls, forests, and human-made mansions along the way, they will love this noisy locomotive, the tunnels, and the sensation of rumbling over giant trestle bridges. The train travels up to Squamish, and then, after a 2-hour break, travels back again. But if, like my kids, the 2-hour ride up to Squamish on the train is enough train for one day, then let the *M.V. Britannia* bring you back. The kids will enjoy the novelty—well, for a little while—and you can drink in the views of Howe Sound from the water.

You can upgrade your seat to the Parlour Class, which includes a meal, or to the Dome Car, which gives you panoramic views, but for small children, the train and boat round trip is excellent value. The ticket price also includes a stop at the West Coast Railway Heritage Park. The train and boat combination ranges from C$21 (US$13.85) for children under 12 up to C$70 (US$46.20) for adults, while the train only is more reasonable at C$12.75 (US$8.40) for children under 12 and C$48 (US$31.70) for adults. Teens get their own price in between. For Parlour Class you're looking at C$75 (US$49.50) for adults; kids' prices range from C$57.50 to $75 (US$37.95 to $49.50). Dome Car is a whopping C$90 (US$59.40) for adults; it's C$75 to $90 (US$49.50 to $59.40) for kids. The train departs the BC Rail station at 10am, arrives at Squamish at noon, and departs at 2pm so it arrives back in North Vancouver at 4pm. The boat departs Squamish at 1:30pm and arrives at 4:30pm at Harbour Cruises at the north foot of Denman Street in downtown Vancouver. Call BC Rail Passenger Services, 1311 W. 1st St. (© **800/663-8238** or 604/984-5246) if you need more information. The Royal Hudson operates Wednesday to Sunday from the end of May through end of September.

3 Animals & Other Creatures

Capilano Salmon Hatchery   All ages. From July to August, fresh-from-the-sea salmon struggle up human-made fish ladders to help them get past the rapids to spawn. BC's first fish farm, this hatchery shows the life cycle of salmon. Trails lead through forests of Douglas fir and cedar to the Cleveland Dam and Capilano Lake, which supply much of Vancouver's drinking water. Observe one of the great life-cycle stories in nature. The self-guided free tour offers information panels describing the life cycles of the salmon. From July to December you can watch the juvenile Pacific salmon in the ponds and see the returning adults jump up a fish ladder, which is a series of steps. The hatchery produces three million salmon each year, and houses display aquariums, adult holding ponds, and the fry-filled juvenile rearing area.

4500 Capilano Park Rd., North Vancouver. © 604/666-1790. Open Nov–Mar daily 8am–4pm; Apr–Oct open until dusk. Free. From Vancouver: Take Georgia St. west over the Lions Gate Bridge and go east on Marine Dr., take the first exit to the left at Capilano Rd., follow the signs. By bus: Take the SeaBus to Lonsdale Quay and transfer to bus no. 236.

Children's Farmyard ⍟   **Ages 2 to 8.** Another Stanley Park treasure, this is a petting zoo with goats, ducks, pigs, rabbits, shetland ponies, sheep, a llama that you can pet, and a reptile house full of snakes and spiders that you probably wouldn't want to. There is also a farm tractor that seems to be a big draw for kids.

Stanley Park. © 604/257-8530. Open mid-May–mid-Sept daily 11am–4pm; Oct–Mar Sat–Sun 11am–4pm. C$3 (US$2) adults, C$2.25 (US$1.50) children 13–18, C$1.50 (US$1), children 3–12, family members are charged at the C$1.50 (US$1) child rate. A family combo is C$3 (US$2) per member and lets kids ride the miniature rails.

Lost Lagoon Nature House   Ages 2 to 8. Find out about the Lost Lagoon bird sanctuary at this Stanley Park Nature House, which has a bunch of information and educational materials on the park's flora and fauna. The Nature House offers seasonal walking tours and is a good way to see the park's swans, ducks, and Canada geese, among other things. The rushes and small islands in the lake make a natural nesting place for the various species that live here, and the best time to visit is in April and May for the ducklings, and in late May and early June for the signets and the wood ducks. Lost Lagoon also has resident herons, raccoons, and bald eagles, and the carp that live here grow up to 2 meters (6 ft.) long. In fact in the 1950s and 1960s the Nature House was called the Boat House and you could rent a row boat and a rod and go fishing in the lagoon. Every Saturday at 11am the Nature House has a drop-in hour with stories and crafts for children aged 3 to 6. There are always different topics and your young ones could learn about anything from how to make a robin's nest, make paper, or build a bird feeder. The cost is C$5 (US$3.30).

At the southeast corner of Lost Lagoon, by the bus terminal at Chilco and Alberni sts., Stanley Park. © 604/257-8544. Open summer weekends 11am–3pm, weekdays 3–7pm, closed Tues; winter Fri–Sun 11am–3pm; spring Fri–Sun 11am–5pm.

Lynn Valley Ecology Centre   Ages 3 to 12. Set in a 600-acre park amid stands of 100-year-old Douglas firs, this is a fun way to see a bit of the area and give kids an idea of the local animals and bugs that live here. You will probably spend about 1 hour here as there are lots of hands-on displays, a puppet theater area with native animals and fish, lots of pull-out drawers to keep hands busy, and a slide show of local fauna and flora that even very small kids can operate themselves in the Kids Exploratorium. Kids can choose from a long list of videos from the National Film Board that has everything from animated shorts to films on Canadian wildlife and wild animals that live in Vancouver (actually we saw *The Grinch* in the center's small theater, but our last visit was at Christmas), and all the films have suggested ages on them. There are some interesting sections on the history of the area, lots of stuffed animals and birds (I mean real raccoons, northern flickers, towhees, and the like, not the Beanie Babies kind, though you can pick up a stuffed bear at the gift shop). One display shows the effects of a fire on an old-growth rain forest. Ask for a free map of the 250-hectare (617 acre) Lynn Canyon Park and don't forget to stop at the free Lynn Canyon Suspension Bridge just below the center (see "10 Things That Are Free (or Almost)," later in this chapter).

Lynn Canyon Park, 3663 Park Rd., North Vancouver. ℂ **604/981-3103.** Admission by donation (suggested donation is $1 per person). Open Mon–Fri 10am–5pm year-round. Open Sat–Sun 10am–5pm Apr–Sept and noon–4pm Oct–Mar. Take the Trans-Canada Hwy. east into North Vancouver, take the Lynn Valley Rd. exit, turn right on Lynn Valley Rd., drive for about 2 km (just over a mile) turn right on Peters Rd., and continue along to the Lynn Canyon Park.

Maplewood Farm   Ages 2 to 6. Children under about 6 love this small 5-acre farm. It has more than 200 domestic animals and birds, including horses, goats, cows, pigs, sheep, chickens, and ducks, and lovely shady walks that cross over bridges, a creek, and a large duck pond. Pick up some of the birdseed and you'll make a few feathered friends. There is a hot house you can wander through and a bird aviary; kids can walk right into the bunny cage to pat and feed them carrots; and on the weekends there are milking demonstrations and pony rides on Sundays. There is a small museum tucked away behind the picnic tables with some of the history of the area. It also has a covered picnic area and hosts many a kid's birthday party. Just outside the farm, at the other side of the car park, is a small playground with swings, a slide, a jungle gym, and a train.

405 Seymour River Place, North Vancouver. ℂ **604/929-5610.** www.maplewoodfarm.bc.ca. C$2.15 (US$1.40) adults, C$1.60 (US$1.05) children 19 months–16, C$6.95 (US$4.60) family of 4, children 18 months and under free. Open Tues–Sun 10am–4pm. Take the Second Narrows Bridge to North Vancouver, stay in the right lane and take the first exit to Dollarton Hwy., turn left onto Seymour River Place from highway. Maplewood Farm is on your left. Park here or if it's full and in the summer or a weekend, you can park in the school across the road.

Richmond Nature Park   All ages. For a suburb that has grown exponentially over the last decade, with hotels and shopping malls, and the Vancouver International Airport, it's a pleasant surprise to find 90 hectares (223 acres) of preserved bog land, smack in the middle of Richmond. The nature park houses a variety of birds, squirrels, raccoons, coyotes, migrating waterfowl, and songbirds, and if you stop in at the Nature House you can rent a backpack for the family to take on your walk. It's a clever idea that gets the kids involved and comes with several different themes—rainy-day fun, birdwatcher, mini beast safari, and the bog explorer self-guided tour. The self-guided backpack tour takes about 1 to 1½ hours, and is designed for kids aged 5 to 10. Depending on the pack you'll find them crammed with an assortment of things such as guide books about the birds and insects that live here to magnifiers, bug boxes, bug viewers, bug catchers, bird callers, and binoculars. The Bog Explorer kit is a hit with junior scientists as it comes with an assortment of magnifiers and bug boxes, and a pH test—to test the acidity of sphagnum. Sphagnum is the "boss moss" in the park.

The park has free guided tours every Sunday between 2 and 3pm, which introduce you to the bog and point out some of the inhabitants: chickadees, finches, warblers, grosbeaks, and robins. There are also chipmunks, frogs, foxes, and deer that live in the park, but you'd have to make a lot less noise than my brood to see them. The walk along springy mulch and wood chip paths is stroller friendly as long as there hasn't been a lot of rain, and you can check weather conditions at the board at the entrance. The four trails are well sign-posted, and you can walk around with little ones in about 45 minutes. You can take a boardwalk to the duck pond, behind the Nature House. Get a trail guide from the Nature House, which also has puzzles, games, live animals, and a gift shop inside. One display shows you various animals that you can search for: a banana slug, rough skin newt, northwestern salamander, northern alligator lizard, red-sided garter snake, and northwestern garter snake. There is a picnic area and playground.

11851 Westminster Hwy. (between Shell and No. 5 rds.), Richmond. © 604/273-7015. www.geog.ubc.ca/richmond. The park is open daily from dawn to dusk. Admission to the Nature House is by donation. The Nature House opens daily 9am–5pm.

4 Indoor Activities

Ceramics Studios   All ages. Check out the paint-your-own ceramics studios that are popping up around the city. You start by picking some ready-made pottery from the shelf—pieces range from about C$8 (US$5.30) for a small figurine to well over C$100 (US$66) for a large vase or planter. A mug, one of the more popular items would cost around C$15 (US$9.90). The price includes the paints, the fire, and glazing. And there are cups and plates and bowls and watering cans, and pretty much anything you can think of in between. (Keep in mind that it takes 2 to 4 days to get the piece back.) Personally, I wouldn't let my toddler loose in here, but apparently small handprints and footprints are big for newborns on up, and for little ones and kids of about 10 and up there are stencils and stamps. Because little kids tend to whip right through their masterpieces, it can get pretty costly and some places, like **Crankpots,** keep a bunch of crayons, coloring books, and finger paints on hand to distract little ones while the big ones do their thing. Most stores open 7 days a week, but it's a good idea to confirm hours before you go.

Bella Ceramica, 1053 Marine Dr., North Vancouver (© **604/985-6113**); 1531 Marine Dr., West Vancouver (© **604/925-3115**). Hours vary at both locations, but the stores open daily. **Crankpots,** 202-1184 Denman St. (at Davie St.), Vancouver (© **604/731-2286**, January to September open 12 to 8pm Monday to Saturday, 12 to 6pm on Sunday, extended hours October to December. **Paint and Fire Cafe,** 3436 W. Broadway Ave. (between Collingwood and Waterloo sts.), Vancouver (© **604/739-8868**), closed Mondays. **Wee Workshop Wonders** (© **604/451-1437**) does things a little differently. It has more than 700 pre-cut wood (mainly pine and cedar) things on hand—everything from a fridge magnet to a coat rack or a napkin holder for kids to paint and assemble. At press time it was planning to move from its Metrotown location, but the phone number will stay the same. For kids who like woodworking, the **Revy Home Centre,** 2727 E. 12th Ave., (at Renfrew St.), East Vancouver (© **604/253-2822**), holds free workshops 10am to 2pm on the last Saturday of every month.

Bloedel Floral Conservatory   Ages 2 and up. The conservatory, with its triodetic dome, noisy parrots, tropical feel, and large koi fish, is a treat for small children. In fact there are more than 100 different kinds of free-flying exotic birds to search for, colorful koi fish at your feet, and rocks to jump on, and plants from deep jungle to cacti under this 52-hectare (130-acre) garden under glass. We like to go during the week when it's quieter as my kids like to tear around the covered walkways and around the lighted fountains and count fish and birds, and they like to do this 10 or more times. This tropical rain forest opened in 1969, and remains the second largest in North America—there is one larger in St. Louis. Another bonus is that the conservatory sits on top of Little Mountain, the highest spot in Vancouver at 152 meters (500 ft.), and overlooks the landscaped gardens of Queen Elizabeth Park and spectacular views of the city and North Shore mountains. There is also a gift shop.

Queen Elizabeth Park, 33rd Ave. & Cambie St., Vancouver. ℂ **604/257-8570.** C$3.75 (US$2.45) adults, C$2.85 (US$1.90) children 13–18, C$1.85 (US$1.20) children 6–12, children 5 and under free. Family pays child rate. Open summer Mon–Fri 9am–8pm, Sat–Sun 10am–9pm; winter Mon–Fri 10am–5:30pm. Take Georgia St. east over the Cambie Street Bridge, turn left at 33rd Ave. and you'll see the entrance to the park on your right. By bus: no. 15 from Burrard St.

Bowling   Ages 5 and up. My kids seem to get invited to a stream of birthday parties at bowling alleys for kids turning 5 to 7, and it's not a bad activity, especially on a rainy day. There are several lanes around Greater Vancouver, some with specially equipped bumpers so that the ball doesn't keep rolling into the gutter. Some also have snack bars and video arcades. Well, you can't bowl all day. **Commodore Lanes,** 838 Granville St. (ℂ **604/681-1531**), has 12 adult-sized lanes. **Park Royal Bowling Lanes,** 1080 South Park Royal (just past Park Royal Shopping Centre on Marine Drive), West Vancouver (ℂ **604/925-0005**), has 36 lanes; 16 are for children 10 and under. It also has a games arcade and snack bar. **Varsity Ridge 5 Pin Bowling Centre,** 2120 W. 15th Ave. (at Arbutus St.), Vancouver (ℂ **604/738-5412**), doesn't have bumpers but it does offer glow-in-the-dark bowling—they turn the lights off and get out the disco balls, loudish music, and flashing lights (eek! the 1970s!). There are 15 lanes, but mostly only 7 are used for glow bowling. Sessions are usually an hour long, and while you can book a party, you can also drop in Fridays from 6:30pm to midnight, Saturdays from noon to 6:45pm, and Sundays from 1 to 6:45pm. **The Zone Bowling Centre,** 14200 Entertainment Blvd. (at Steveston Hwy. and No. 6 Rd.), Richmond (ℂ **604/271-2695**), has 28 10-pin lanes and 12 5-pin lanes with bumpers for children, plus a video arcade. It is close to **Watermania** and other distractions.

CN IMAX Theatre   Ages 4 and up. This 5-story theater—it's actually 15 meters (50 ft.) high by 21 meters (70 ft.) wide—shows a variety of IMAX films that cover wildlife themes and adventures. Reservations are recommended.

201-999 Canada Place (north end of Canada Place near the Waterfront SkyTrain Station and SeaBus Terminal). ℂ **800/582-4629** or 604/682-4629. www.imax.com/vancouver. One film: C$10 (US$6.60) adults, C$8 (US$5.30) children 4–12. Double feature rates are C$14.50 (US$9.60) adults, C$12.50 (US$8.25) children 4–12. Children under 4 free. Open summer daily noon–10pm; winter weekdays noon–3:30pm and 7–10pm.

The Lookout! At Harbour Centre Tower   All ages. While it's pretty puny compared to other towers (ranks 15th in the World Federation of Great Towers), it's still an acceptable 174 meters (581 ft.) and is the tallest building in BC. It's also pretty expensive for a family, but if the weather is great and you can't get to either Grouse or Cypress mountains, it will give you a quick 360-degree look at Vancouver. You can see the University of British Columbia and the Gulf Islands to the south; Vancouver Island, the harbor, Lions Gate Bridge, and Stanley Park to the west; the North Shore and the SeaBus to the north; and Burnaby and Mount Baker to the east. Kids will like the floor-to-ceiling glass elevator that sucks them up to the observation deck. The Lookout offers 35-minute guided tours year-round to visitors at no extra charge, or you can grab a drink and a muffin at the coffee bar while you soak in the view. There is a restaurant—Top of Vancouver Revolving Restaurant—but it is expensive and not at all kid-friendly. The admission price is good for the day, so if you find it clouded over or hazy, try again later.

555 W.Hastings St. (across from Waterfront/SeaBus Station). © 604/689-0421. www.lookout.bc.ca. C$9 (US$6) adults, C$6 (US$4) students, children under 6 free. Open late spring and summer 8:30am–10pm; winter 9am–9pm. The Lookout is open 365 days of the year, but as we found out the hard way, it opens at 10am on New Year's Day and some other public holidays.

⸜Fun Fact

Something to think about while you're enjoying the view: BC is seven times the size of New York State and two and a half times as large as Japan, and equal to the combined size of France, Germany, Austria, and Belgium.

Port of Vancouver   **Ages 6 and up.** Get right down to the docks of North America's third busiest port (after Louisiana and Texas), and visit the public viewing center and get an up-close look at how a container terminal operates. The observation deck is open all year from 9am to 4pm Monday to Friday, but from early June until the end of August the port holds two free 1-hour drop-in tours at 10am and 2pm on Wednesdays. The tour starts with an 8-minute film starring the Port's mascot, Salty the Seagull, and puts things like export and import and containers into perspective (one ship holds enough lumber to make 2,000 homes); the kids also get stickers and coloring material. After the tour wander up to the observation deck via the covered walkway where you can walk over the action at the Vanterm Container Terminal and onto the deck where kids can play the interactive "Port at a Glance" video game, or play a computer game to see who can load a ship to the limit in the shortest possible time. Check out the top and side loaders whizzing by and the huge orange and green cranes. There is a telescope to view the action in the harbor—which incidentally is the second busiest airport in BC. The best time to come is when there is a ship in at Vanterm, which happens about four times a week and you can check the *Vancouver Sun*'s business section to find out which day.

1300 Stewart St., Vancouver. © 604/665-9177. Take Hastings St. east and turn left at Victoria Dr., turn left again at Stewart St. and the Public Viewing Centre is clearly marked on your right. Parking is free.

The Roundhouse Community Centre ⭐ ⸜Finds   **Ages 2 and up, 8 and up for games room.** Built in 1914, this building was refurbished for Expo 86 and then was turned into a community center largely to serve the new residents of Pacific Place and the north False Creek area. But it has much to offer visitors from outside the area. For one thing, C$12 (US$8) will buy your family an annual membership. This membership gets you into the games room that has among other things, table tennis, hockey game tables, and free Nintendo. It also gives you access to the gym, which has various programs that include basketball, volleyball, and badminton, and, especially for rainy days, offers up a solution to older children who insist "I'm bored." There is also the Roundhouse Cafe where you can pick up soup and a sandwich or a coffee, while the kids are occupied. At the front of the building nearest Davie Street, you'll see the 1888 red-brick roundhouse, which is now home to Engine 374, a former Canadian Pacific Railways steam train. The train was the first to cross Canada in 1887 and ran until 1945. Then, I guess nobody knew what to do with it, so it sat rusting at Kitsilano Beach for 30 years, before being brought here and restored for Expo 86. Now it stays here in its splendor and kids love to climb up on it and sit in it. There are also train paraphernalia here for aficionados. Admission is free, but volunteers run it and opening hours are sketchy. It's usually open daily in the summer from 11am to 3pm and in the winter on Friday, Saturday, and Sunday at the same time.

181 Roundhouse Mews (corner of Pacific Blvd. and Davie St., in Yaletown), Vancouver. © **604/713-1800.** Open Mon–Fri 9am–10pm, Sat–Sun 9am–5pm.

Vancouver Art Gallery   **Ages 12 and up.** Built at the turn of the 20th century, the art gallery building served as Vancouver's courthouse up until 1979. It's been completely renovated, but still has the original marble imported from Alaska, Tennessee, and Vermont, and oak woodwork throughout. There are four floors, but getting to the second is the most impressive—you go up a double marble staircase underneath the rotunda. You'll find works by the Group of Seven here, including some stunning local scenes by Frederick Horsman Varley, and a much larger exhibition of West Coast artist Emily Carr on the third floor. Local painters such as Jack Shadbolt and Gordon Smith are given prominent display areas on the second floor, as is a particularly disturbing painting of a naked man crouching in a cell by Vancouver artist Attila Richard Lukas in the contemporary section. The third floor, with its quirky multimedia displays, will most likely hold the interest of older children.

You need to leave coats and packs at the coat check, but it's free. The gallery also has a great gift shop with toys and prints of familiar icons such as Curious George, Babar, jungle fish, and a scene from *Lord of the Rings*, which will appeal to kids. You might want to drop in here first and pick up something for the kids to keep them occupied while you browse the gallery.

750 Hornby St. (at Robson St.). © **604/662-4700** or 604/662-4719 for a recording. www.vanartgallery.bc.ca. C$10 (US$6.40) adults, C$6 (US$4) students, children 12 and under free, C$30 (US$20) for a family with a maximum of 5. Open daily 10am–5:30pm, until 9pm on Thurs. Thurs evening open by donation (suggested donation C$5/US$3.30).

⌒Fun Fact

Try to time your visit to the **Vancouver Art Gallery** for the third Sunday of the month between noon and 5pm. Here you'll find that the art gallery opens up its space to kids for art-making performances, demonstrations, and hands-on crafts such as painting a flower pot or perhaps a T-shirt with their own hands. While activities are designed with school-aged kids in mind, younger ones should find plenty to keep them entertained also.

Vancouver Public Library (★   **All ages.** This Coliseum knock-off isn't just a good place to get out of the rain, the Vancouver Public Library really is fun, and for a whole range of ages. The architecture was controversial at the time, but I really like it, love the feeling of spaciousness, the walkways around the floors, and the whole quirkiness of it. If you are an Arnold Schwarzenegger fan you may have already seen the library make a cameo appearance in the movie *The Sixth Day*. We can easily spend a few hours in the kids' section downstairs, which is good for kids up to about 10 or 12. There is a toddlers' play area for kids under 3, which is gated and filled with wonderful huge colorful blocks, a giant caterpillar, and toys. Adults can curl up with a book in the room next door and keep an eye on the little ones. There is a preschoolers' and parents' lounge with a huge colorful dinosaur and a floor-to-ceiling window with a waterfall and bright blue kid-sized chairs to cuddle up in, and there's a little playhouse nearby. There are seven computers with Hoyle board games and other CD-ROM products (two for preschoolers, one for 6- to 9-year-olds, and one for 9- to 12-year-olds. My 8-year-old and his friend immediately grabbed a bunch of comics, draped over some bean bags, and camped out in the kids' lounge. There is also an Explorations Gallery where there are more books, games, puzzles, and software, and over by the stairs there are jigsaws and other puzzles, and of course everywhere there are rows and rows of books. On my last visit, the children's art gallery was filled with beautiful paintings from local kids in grades 3 and 4, and a round brightly lit room had the original covers of well-known BC story illustrators such as Celia King, and a painting by Ann Blades of *Back to the Cabin*. For older kids, from about grade 6 and up, drop them at the teen section as you walk into the entrance of the library. And afterwards reward everyone at one of the restaurants or coffee shops outside the front door of the library.

Library Square, 350 W. Georgia St. (between Hamilton and Homer sts.). ℂ 604/331-4000 or the children's library ℂ 604/331-3603. Open Mon–Thurs 10am–8pm, Fri–Sat 10am–5pm, and Sun Oct–Apr 1–5pm.

5 Where to Play

Adventure Zone   **Ages 3 to 8.** Find your way to the Granville Island Kids' Market and take the rainbow bridge on the second floor to this multilevel plastic playground. There is a 6 meter (20 ft.) spiral slide, web climber, tunnel maze, club house, and ball pit.

Granville Island Kids' Market, 1496 Cartwright St. ℂ **604/608-6699.** C$5 (US$3.30) gives kids in-and-out privileges all day. Kids under 3 need an adult with them, but adults are free.

Gator Pit   **Ages 2 to 8.** This four-level indoor playground also comes with a separate area and ball pit for kids 3 and under. That's a good thing, because it gets hectic, especially on a wet weekend or around 3pm when school gets out. We've now had a total of four birthday parties here, so I'm far more intimate with this plastic parent purgatory than I want to be. But the kids love it, it's noisy, and the staff are young and are good with the kids. For an extra C$4 (US$2.65) you can drop off kids over 4 and leave them for up to 2 hours while you shop, eat, or just pace around in the Park Royal Shopping Centre. You are given a pager and the kids get a special electric wristband that beeps if they try to get out.

Park Royal Shopping Centre, south, at Taylor Way and Marine Dr., West Vancouver. ℂ **604/925-9576.** C$6.50 (US$4.30) over 4, C$3.99 (US$2.65) under 3. Parents free.

Laser Tag   Ages 6 and up. Another birthday favorite for boys from about age 6 and up. This is where kids and adults don computerized colored vests and go around shooting lasers at each other in the dark. You get points for shooting an opponent, and lose points if you get shot. It's very dark in these places, with black lights, fog, strobe lights, loud music, and neon painting that glows all in a kind of multilevel maze. If you are planning to drop in, make sure you call in advance as they get pretty crazy especially on the weekends. Prices are around C$6.50 to $7 (US$4.30 to $4.60) for a 15-minute game.

Laserdome, 141 W. 16th St. (at Lonsdale Ave.), North Vancouver ℂ 604/985-6033. **Planet Lazer Extreme Lazer Tag,** 108-100 Braid St., New Westminster ℂ 604/525-8255. **Planet Laser,** 7391 Elmbridge Way, Richmond ℂ 604/821-0770, and 20104 Logan Ave., Langley ℂ 604/514-2282.

North Shore Fun & Fitness   Ages 6 and up. A nine-hole mini-golf with a jungle theme, two batting cages for baseball and softball, and an indoor golf simulator with 54 golf courses to choose from—these should keep kids busy on a wet day. The golf appeals most to children of about 9 and up, while kids as young as 6 try out their skills at the batting cage. It's best to phone and make a reservation.

1172 W. 14th St. (at Pemberton St.), North Vancouver. ℂ 604/983-0909. Batting cages C$16 (US$10.55) for 30 minutes before 5pm on weekdays or C$20 (US$13.20) evenings and weekends. Golf special is C$8 (US$5.30) for 30 minutes before 5pm on weekdays or C$10 (US$6.60) evenings and weekends.

Playdium   Ages 10 and up. A giant colorful and noisy video arcade that kids love with five sections to choose from—the sports zone, speed zone, virtual reality zone, action sports zone, and extreme sports zone. It's 3,700 square meters (40,000 sq. ft.) of floor space that has a line of eight Indy 500 cars set on a dais. They actually move and are hooked up to race the screen or race one or all of the others. There's a boat section with a wave runner on virtual water, a Harley-Davidson, a water skiing area, virtual skateboarding, snowboarding, or hand-gliding, and a martial arts zone where the blood runs green or blue to be less gory…If you need to entice the kids out, Playdium is housed in the sprawling Metrotown complex, right nearby to the Silver City Theatres, the Rainforest Cafe, and dozens of shops. If you have a bored or overly active toddler, the Jellybean Park Play Care (ℂ **604/431-8870**) babysits kids from 18 months to 5 years. There is a restaurant with the standard pizza and hot dog fare but the twist here is that you order online through Hanna, Playdium's interactive Virtual Hostess.

4600-4800 Kingsway, Burnaby. ℂ 604/433-7529. www.playdium.com. C$5 (US$3.30) = 20 credits; C$10 (US$6.60) = 45 credits and so on. A ride averages between 4 to 6 credits each and the virtual IMAX ride costs 14 credits (children must be taller than 122cm/48 in.). Open Sun–Thurs 10am–midnight, Fri–Sat 10am–2am. Take Hwy. 1, Willingdon South exit, turn left on Kingsway; from downtown, take Kingsway east between McKay and Nelson. Free parking. By SkyTrain: Metrotown stop.

✐ 10 Things That Are Free (or Almost)

Well, the **kite** will cost you, but the flying is free, and the best spots to hit are Vanier Park, on Vancouver's West Side, or Ambleside Beach in West Vancouver. (See shops that sell kites in chapter 10 "Shopping for the Whole Family.")

Granville Island   For a real holiday take the mini-ferry (see below) and head out to Granville Island. If it's sunny, hit the Water Park and the playground, wander the boardwalks, check out the artisans, listen to the buskers, chase the pigeons, or just relax on the grassy area around the pond and search for turtles. At any time of year, the Kids' Market, with its unusual clothes, off-beat toys, play area, and video arcade, will entrance the kids, and all ages will love the incredible model train at the Granville Island Museum.

Lynn Canyon Suspension Bridge ★★ *Moments*   My kids actually prefer this one to the more famous Capilano Suspension Bridge a few miles away. It's free, for a start, and they say that this bridge, which hangs about 20 stories above Lynn Creek, is more scary than the other—anyway it hasn't fallen down yet. Ironically, when the bridge was first built in 1912, it was constructed as a private money-making venture and visitors were charged a dime to cross. The river here is also wilder than the Capilano, and the bridge—while only about half as long as the other suspension bridge—is about 3 meters (10 ft.) higher. Once you cross the bridge a 10-minute walk downstream brings you to the 30 Foot Pool. Or choose another path and 15 minutes downstream is a wooden footbridge that crosses the creek at Twin Falls. (This fixed-deck bridge is a good alternative if you'd rather not cross the suspension bridge.) Look for old-growth stumps from the late 1800s—some of these trees were over 90 meters (295 ft.) high and 11 meters (36 ft.) in circumference. Watch for black bears in the summer, the giant banana slug and chickadees, steller's jay, varied thrush, the pileated woodpecker, and the rare wild orchid. While some of the trails may look harmless and the waters placid, the boards at the entrance list the deaths of people over the years who have either fallen or drowned. The park is open from 7am to dusk.

Mini-Ferries   Aquabus (© **604/689-5858**) and the **Granville Island Ferry** (© **604/684-7781**) operate a privately run, scheduled ferry service. Especially on a sunny day, there is no better way to get around Vancouver than by buzzing back and forth between Granville Island, downtown, the West End, Science World, Vanier Park, Stamps Landing, or Yaletown. Depending on the distance, the fares range from C$2–$5 (US$1.30–$3.30) for adults, and C$1–$3 (US66¢–$2) for children over 4.

Public Markets   There are three on the water, and you can see them all by taking a combination of the mini-ferries (above), and SkyTrain and the SeaBus (below). **Granville Island Public Market** (see chapter 7, "For the Active Family") and **Lonsdale Quay** in North Vancouver will take you roughly the same time to reach, while **Westminster Quay** in New Westminster will be more of an adventure. All three have great places to eat, entertainment, and ice cream.

SeaBus *Finds*   This is the greatest, fastest, and cheapest cruise of Burrard Inlet available. It takes all of 12 minutes and goes from the downtown Waterfront Station to Lonsdale Quay in North Vancouver. Depending on the time of day, an adult fare costs between C$1.75 and $2.50 (US$1.15–$1.65) to take a catamaran ferry there and back (if you do it under 90 minutes—if not, double that fare). Get up close to large ocean liners, see floatplanes and helicopters in this busy port, take in the North Shore mountains and a sea view of Stanley Park, and don't forget your camera.

To avoid the work crowd, ride between 9:30am and 3pm or after 6pm in the evening. ☎ **604/986-1501.**

SkyTrain Take this driverless, magnetic-rail train to Westminster Quay. You'll whiz past Science World and stop at 20 stations along the way in this 35-minute trip from downtown Vancouver, and go through the neighborhoods of Surrey, Burnaby, and New Westminster. These sleek red, white, and blue trains travel at 30kmph (50 mph), and feel like a mini roller coaster in some parts. The fare is the same in the evenings and weekends as the SeaBus, but goes up to C$3.50 (US$2.30) during weekdays. Probably the best deal is the **DayPass,** which is good on all public transit: C$7 (US$4.60) adults, C$5 (US$3.30) children 5 to 13, children under 5 free. As with the SeaBus, avoid the rush hour and the crowds. ☎ **604/521-0400.**

Stanley Park Shuttle Bus (Finds) Of course there's no need to mention again that Stanley Park is free, free, free. But if you are pushed for time, it's raining, or your little ones will not walk, then you can get around the park by bus for free also. In the summer months from mid-June until mid-September, the Vancouver Parks Board operates the Stanley Park Shuttle, a free bus service through Stanley Park. The run starts at the Children's Miniature Railway and there are 14 stops around the park. You can get on and off whenever you want. The bus runs every 15 minutes between 10am and 6:30pm daily. ☎ **604/257-8400.**

Vancouver Public Library It's fun to wander around the outside and check out this strange Roman Coliseum architecture, and it's fun to grab some pizza and a drink at the food court in the middle. You have to be a little quieter, but the walkways around the business, history, and other sections of the library are definitely worth a look, and the Children's Library with its cascading waterfalls, art, toys, and books is just a sheer joy to spend a few hours with the kids.

6 For Kids with Special Interests

Canadian Museum of Flight   All ages. Kids, or, for that matter, anyone who likes planes, will love this Museum of Flight. You'll find a bunch of vintage aircraft including a DeHavilland Vampire, a Handley Page, and one of the world's two remaining Bowlus gliders. On a nice day the museum opens up its Canadian Forces 104 jet and kids can sit inside it. They can also go inside the Beach Expediter (Beach 18), and another hit is the Millennium Kids Room, which has computers with programs that let the kids interact with plane engines—turn a prop and see how the cylinders work, or see how a jet tunnel works. There's Morse code and kids will probably want to spend 1 to 1½ hours here. There's also a bunch of aviation photos, artifacts, and memorabilia to interest parents.

Langley Airport, 5333-216th St., Langley. ☎ **604/532-0035.** www.canadianflight.org/index01.htm. C$5 (US$3.30) adults, C$4 (US$2.65) children, family rate for 2 adults and up to 4 children C$12 (US$8), 6 and under free. Open daily 10am–4pm.

Chinese Cultural Centre Museum and Archives   Ages 10 and up. If you're wandering around Chinatown, step into the museum and have a look at the changing photographs and exhibits that describe Chinatown's past from the

1858 Gold Rush to today. The museum is also home to the Chinese Canadian Military Museum. It's the first museum and archives dedicated to Chinese Canadian history and culture. You'll find exhibits, guided tours, talks, workshops as well as exhibitions on Chinese Canadian history, and contemporary and traditional arts and crafts. Permanent collections focus on early Chinese pioneers and World War II veterans.

555 Columbia St. (at Pender St.), Chinatown. ℂ 604/658-8865. C$3 adults, C$2.50 seniors, students, and children. Admission is by donation on Tues. Open Tues–Sun 11am–5pm.

Military Museums   There are several museums scattered around the Greater Vancouver area that may interest military buffs. They tend to open from Tuesday to Friday, and hours change so call first. You can expect to see World War II memorabilia, uniforms, firearms, and photographs. The **British Columbia Regiment** (DCO), 620 Beatty St., in downtown Vancouver (ℂ **604/666-4396**), has a museum, but it also has two huge tanks and two cannons bookending the building, which kids can view any time. Others: **Fifteenth Field Artillery Regiment,** 2025 W. 11th Ave., Vancouver (ℂ **604/666-4876**); **Museum of the Royal Westminster Regiment,** 530 Queens Ave., New Westminster (ℂ **604/666-4374**); **Twelfth Service Battalion,** 5500 No. 4 Rd., Richmond (ℂ **604/666-1086**); **Twelfth Medical Company,** 4050 W. 4th Ave., Vancouver (ℂ **604/666-4354**).

Museum of Archaeology and Ethnology   **Ages 10 and up.** This is a smallish museum and it concentrates on the archaeology and anthropology of BC. You'll find totem poles, and a stratagraphic profile, which gives a cross section of an archaeology site at Namu on the central coast. There is also an exhibit about Barkerville, a historic BC town, which goes into its Chinese history.

Simon Fraser University, 8888 University Dr., Burnaby (on Burnaby Mountain). ℂ **604/291-3325.** Open Mon–Fri 10am–noon and 1–4pm, but best to call first. Located at the northeast corner of the academic quadrangle on the university's campus. Admission by donation.

Trev Deeley Motorcycle Museum   **Ages 10 and up.** Motorcycle enthusiasts love ogling the collection of over 250 bikes and 51 different makes from limited-edition Indians to restored Harleys.

13500 Verdun Place, Richmond. ℂ **604/273-5421.** Free. Open Mon–Fri 10am–4pm.

Vancouver Police Centennial Museum ⍟   **Ages 10 and up.** For kids who like cops and robbers, are budding scientists, or are history buffs, this 1886 heritage building should be on their list. When you walk in the front door, on display is a Vancouver Police Keystone Kop car and, further along, a display of matchbox police cars from around the world. Who says cops don't have a sense of humor? There are a bunch of historical photos, badges, stories about police dogs and horses, a display of counterfeit money, and another of lie detectors and drunkometers. And, if junior thinks crime pays, there's a forlorn-looking wax effigy locked up in a holding cell.

Not surprisingly, over a hundred or so years, the police have pretty much come across every kind of weapon that has ever been thought up, and older kids will be fascinated by the display of just under 200 prohibited weapons. Some look like they came off the set of a *Mad Max* movie, not from the streets outside the building.

The museum is in the old Coroner's Court, complete with the morgue that was fully operating up until 1980. This is also the morgue where Errol Flynn, the Australian film star, was autopsied after dropping dead in the arms of a 17-year-old girl. Some of this stuff is pretty gory—you'll see the warning signs at the back—but most kids will love the re-created murder scene. Fortunately, it's not a real one, but kids can still investigate along with the displays, and see how police lift prints and act at a crime scene that's not on television. Kids can also check out the "coolers" in the morgue here, and walk through into the old lab. The wax morgue attendant and body on the slab are pretty creepy, but the Coroner's Forensic Exhibit, complete with body parts labeled with everything from "hemorrhage of brain stem" to "a gunshot wound to the larynx," gives you a sharp jolt of realism.

There is a gift shop if you want to take home souvenirs, and, depending upon your family's age and level of interest, you could spend up to 2 hours here. The museum is on the outskirts of Gastown and Chinatown, but it's also in the Downtown East Side so take extra care when walking around this area.

240 E. Cordova St. (between Main and Gore sts.). ℭ **604/665-3346**. www.city.vancouver.bc.ca/police/museum. C$5 (US$3.30) adults, C$3 (US$2) children 7–13, children under 7 free. Open Mon–Fri 9am–3pm, and Apr 30–Sept 1 also open Sat 10am–3pm.

The X-Tour

This is a city tour for film buffs. As the third-largest movie-making city in the world (after Los Angeles and New York), Vancouver is Hollywood North, and it seems, we have endless buildings, apartment buildings, and other locations to prove it. There are several tours, but the one that would appeal most to families is the 3-hour Vancouver Film and TV location X-Tour. While it's been a few years since *The X-Files* was actually shot in Vancouver, it seems interest is still strong in the show. The tour, which includes a limousine pick-up and drop-off at your hotel, includes a tour of the Pendrell Suites (you already know it—it doubles as a Boston brownstone for *The X-Files*, *Romeo Must Die*, and dozens of others), and into the former television home of *X-Files* Agent Dana Scully—she was abducted here—as well as Trish in *Romeo Must Die*, and where Jet Li does his kung fu in the meditation garden. Oh, and keep an eye out for those *X-Files* aliens. The tour takes in Gastown, Chinatown, and downtown Vancouver, and guides point out where movies such as *Legends of the Fall* or television series like *The X-Files*, *Stargate*, *Highlander*, and *Dark Angel* were shot. And if you're only just beginning to get stars in your eyes, you can arrange accommodation at the Pendrell Suites, where Hollywood stars such as Daryl Hannah (*Roxanne*), James McAffrey (*Viper*), and Wilford Brimley (*Cocoon*) stayed and worked.

Or skip the limo tour and go straight to the home/workplace of the stars: Tour of the Pendrell Suites, 1419 Pendrell St. (at Broughton St.) in the West End. The cost is C$29 (US$19) for adults, C$19 (US$12.55) for children 3 to 11, and C$98 (US$65) for a family of up to 5 people. The full tour costs C$145 (US$96) for 1 to 3 people, C$125 (US$83) for 4 to 6 people, C$90 (US$59) for 7 to 9 people. For information, call ℭ **800/250-7211** or 604/609-2770; www.pendrellsuites.com and www.x-tour.com.

7 City Tours

ON WHEELS

Early Motion Tours   Run by a real character of a guy, Early Motion Tours has offered personalized tours in a 1930 Model A Ford Phaeton convertible in good weather, and in a 1947 Ford sedan when it's not, since 1985. The car holds up to four passengers, five if there are little kids, and reservations are a good idea in the summer. The average tour lasts about an hour, and is charged out at limo rates of around C$100 (US$66) an hour. He'll pick you up at your hotel, but you can usually find him and his car outside the Pan Pacific Hotel at Canada Place.

1-1380 Thurlow St., Vancouver. ✆ 604/687-5088.

Gray Line of Vancouver   This tour line offers two good tours for families. The first, the Grand City Tour, is a fully guided and narrated 3½-hour tour of the city, which is offered year-round and stops at all the top tourism attractions—Stanley Park, Gastown, Chinatown, Queen Elizabeth Park, and so on. The other is a more flexible option, and has four double-decker buses doing a loop and making 20 stops at points such as the Vancouver Aquarium, Robson Street, Gastown, Science World, Granville Island, and the H.R. MacMillan Space Centre. The buses pass each stop every 30 minutes. It does not include the cost of the attractions, but a ticket is valid for 2 days and they need not be consecutive. The double-decker bus operates between April and early October.

255 E. 1st Ave. ✆ 604/879-3363. www.grayline.ca/vancouver. Grand City Tour C$42 (US$27.70) adults, C$30 (US$19.80) children 6–12, children 5 and under free. Double-decker tours C$25 (US$16.50) adults, C$14 (US$9.25) children aged 6–12.

Landsea Tours   This tour agency offers a variety of city tours, including a daily 4-hour tour of Vancouver city highlights that includes Gastown, Chinatown, Granville Island, and Stanley Park, and a 5-hour tour of the North Shore, which includes Cleveland Dam, Grouse Mountain, and Capilano Suspension Bridge.

875 Terminal Ave. ✆ 877/669-2277 or 604/255-7272. www.vancouvertours.com. City Highlights Tour C$42 (US$28) adults, C$25 (US$16.50) children. North Shore Tour C$71 (US$47) adults, C$40 (US$27) children.

Vancouver Trolley Company   This looks like a combination between bus and tram and runs along downtown, Chinatown, the West End, and Stanley Park. Passengers can get off at any of the 23 stops to explore and catch another trolley when they feel so inclined. You can take the entire tour in 2 hours or get off the trolley when the urge to stop, visit an attraction, or eat moves you.

4012 Myrtle St., Burnaby. ✆ 888/451-5581 or 604/801-5515. www.vancouvertrolley.com. C$24 (US$14.50) adults, C$12 (US$6.60) children 4–12.

West Coast City and Nature Sightseeing   Several minicoach tours are offered, including the 5½-hour Native Culture Tour that stops at Grouse Mountain, the Capilano Suspension Bridge, the Capilano Salmon Hatchery, the Stanley Park Totem poles, English Bay, and Spanish Banks and the Museum of Anthropology, among other sites. The best for families is the 4½-hour Vancouver City Tour with stops including the Stanley Park Totem Poles, Prospect Point, Queen Elizabeth Park, and The Lookout! At Harbour Centre Tower.

4012 Myrtle St., Burnaby. ✆ 604/451-1600. www.vancouversightseeing.com. Native Culture Tour C$69 (US$45.55) adults, C$44 (US$29) children 4–12. Vancouver City Tour C$44 (US$29) adults, C$27 (US$17.80) children 4–12; includes admittance to the Lookout observation deck. Both tours: children under 4 free.

BY HORSE

Stanley Park Horse-Drawn Tours   Take an old-fashioned horse-drawn carriage through Stanley Park for a change of pace. The tour lasts an hour. It highlights Deadman's Island, Vancouver Harbour, Lions Gate Bridge, a coastal red cedar forest and includes stops at the totem poles, the *Girl in a Wet Suit* statue, the SS *Empress of Japan* figurehead, and the Rose Garden. Tours depart every 20 to 30 minutes from the Coal Harbour parking lot beside the information booth on Park Drive, east of the Rowing Club. March 15 to end of October. Carriages available for rent over the Christmas period. No reservations required. You can buy a carriage ride and a ticket to the Aquarium and receive C$2 (US$1.30) off.

© **604/681-5115.** www.stanleyparktours.com. C$18.65 (US$12.30) adults, C$16.80 (US$11.10) seniors and students, C$11.20 (US$7.40) children 3–12, C$55.95 (US$36.90) families (4 passengers total). Children 2 and under are free if not occupying a seat.

For the Active Family

1 Parks, Gardens & Other Green Spaces

In the Greater Vancouver area, our regional parks cover 11,400 hectares in 22 green spaces from Bowen Island to Abbotsford. They're where you can see sensitive habitats, awesome views, huge trees, roaring creeks, and towering mountains. Of course, there is Stanley Park in the middle of the city, which someone once described as "half savage, half domestic," and lots of worthy parks and gardens scattered around Vancouver that are definitely worthy of a closer look.

For more information about our parks or for a map, contact the **Greater Vancouver Regional District Parks Department,** 4330 Kingsway, Burnaby, BC V5H 4G8 (© **604/432-6350;** www.gvrd.bc.ca).

Bear Creek Park   This Surrey park, about a 45-minute drive from Vancouver, is definitely off the beaten track, but it really is an all-round great family day out. The big hit for kids is Eddie the Engine, a covered miniature train that runs all year, takes about 8 minutes, and travels through the woods in the park. There is a huge playground filled with swings and slides, tunnels, teeter totters, and nets, plus a separate playground for toddlers. In the summer, the water-spray park is a hit for little ones. You'll also find the 5-acre Bear Creek Gardens and a salmon habitat stream. In the summer, older kids will like the large outdoor Bear Creek Pool, and there is a sports field with a running track, climbing wall, skateboard park, and roller hockey. You'll also find public washrooms open year-round near the train, and an undercover picnic area.

13750 88th Ave. (at King George Hwy.), Surrey. Take Hwy. 1 to 152nd St., south to 88th Ave., west to 137th St., then left into the Surrey Arts Centre parking lot. © **604/501-5050.**

Cleveland Dam   This is always on my sunny-weather list when we have visitors staying with us, and sometimes just the kids and I take a picnic out here in the summer, or stop by and grab one of the over-priced ice creams from the cart and walk along the dam. The Cleveland Dam with the Lions (mountain peaks) in the background must be one of the most beautiful places for a picture, and it's worth a stop if you're on the way to Grouse Mountain or visiting the Capilano Suspension Bridge. Walk across the dam and watch 100 million gallons of our drinking water rush down these steep canyon walls each day. The dam spans 195 meters (640 ft.) across the canyon water. Just before you get to the dam, there are stairs that lead to another viewing level below. You'll often find people practicing Tai Chi here.

Take W. Georgia St. over the Lions Gate Bridge, turn right at Marine Dr., then take the first left onto Capilano Rd.; the dam is on your left, about 1km (.6 miles) past the Capilano Salmon Hatchery.

Dr. Sun Yat-sen Classical Chinese Garden   These tranquil gardens, hidden behind high white walls, offer a respite in the middle of bustling Chinatown. The best times to visit are in the spring when the rhododendrons and the azaleas are in full bloom and in the fall when the maples and the burning bush are changing colors. If your kids are bored get them to look for a tree shaped like a dragon, a seahorse in the rocks, and the live turtles and brightly colored koi fish in the pond. Get them to guess what the white lines are that make the peony leaves in the tiles at the entrance (recycled tea cups), the brown-brick–like lines in the tiles at the back of the gardens (broken flower pots). If it's raining, look for the banana tree in the small courtyard. The rain cascading down like a beaded curtain makes a musical sound when it hits the leaves of the banana plant. The classical garden was built in the Suzhou province of northern China around 1492 and moved to Vancouver for Expo 86. It's the only full-sized classical garden of its kind outside China. If you're hankering to learn more, there are eight daily tours in the summer that run on the hour and last between 30 and 45 minutes. Try the free orchid tea on your way in.

578 Carrall St. (at Pender St.), Chinatown. ℭ **604/689-7133.** C$7.50 (US$4.95) adults, C$5 (US$3.30) children and students, free for children under 5. C$18 (US$11.85) family rate. Open daily 9:30am–7pm summer; 10am–6pm spring; 10am–4:30pm winter.

Hastings Park   Most people know this as the grounds for Playland, the Hastings Park Racecourse at Exhibition Park, the Pacific Coliseum, and the Pacific National Exhibition (PNE). The PNE has held its 3-week fair here every year since 1910, but the City of Vancouver and the Parks Board and a bunch of local residents have been arguing over relocating the PNE for years, and it looks like 2002 may be the last one at Hastings Park. In the meantime, the park has undergone a lot of greening. It is 65 hectares (162 acres), which makes it the second largest park in Vancouver, and is bounded by Hastings Street, Renfrew Street, McGill Street, and Cassiar Street in East Vancouver. Amongst all the grass, the ponds, and thousands of newly planted native trees and shrubs is a huge new cement skateboard park.

Take Hastings St. east. There is a pay parking lot on the corner of Hastings and Renfrew sts.

John Lawson Park   This West Vancouver park has a huge children's playground, with a large pirate ship that kids can climb in and over, a rope net, a steering wheel, and a slide. There are swings and a train, and a big rope spider web for older kids to climb. There is a rocky beach with logs and driftwood, a wading pool for toddlers open in the summer, and a pier. It's a super place where we often spend a lot of time on warm days. It does get pretty crazy though, so you need to keep a watch on little ones. The walkways are good for rollerblading or triking; there is a covered picnic area, lots of grass, public toilets, and it's close to Marine Drive and all the shops and restaurants. From May to the end of September from Wednesday to Sunday, if you time your trip just after 10am or around 3:30pm, you can see the Royal Hudson chugging past. At around 5pm, the cruise ships leave Canada Place and Ballantyne Pier and head to Alaska so they sail right by. At other times, you can just relax and watch the yachts. It's also a pretty walk down to Ambleside Beach, which has another playground, sandy beach, and concessions.

On Bellevue Ave. (at 17th St.), West Vancouver. Take W. Georgia St. over the Lions Gate Bridge, turn left at Marine Dr., continue until 17th Ave. and turn left. There is a parking lot at the bottom of 17th St.

Park and Tilford Gardens _Finds_   If you are visiting North Vancouver, stop in at this gem of a spot hidden behind a small North Vancouver shopping mall. This is a great spot to grab a coffee or some lunch at the nearby Bread Garden or White Spot, and wander through these privately owned theme gardens. It was originally commissioned by Park and Tilford Distillers as a beautification project. We go there all the time, after grocery shopping, or before or after watching a movie at the next-door theater. The gardens are always in a state of flux. You'll find various groups of flowers and flowering plants: native, herbs, roses, rhododendrons, and two annual gardens. There is the oriental garden at the back, where a wooden bridge crosses over a pond and leads to a pagoda where the kids can play. The gardens are a little under 3 acres and filled with surprises. The gardens are also on our Christmas itinerary every year as they are magically transformed through December by more than 50,000 lights.

440-333 Brooksbank Ave. (between Keith and Main sts.), North Vancouver. © **604/984-8200.** Free. Open daily dawn to dusk. Take Hastings St. east until Cassiar St.; take the turnoff for the Trans-Canada Hwy. (Hwy. 1) to North Vancouver, cross the Second Narrows Bridge, and take the Mountain Hwy. exit; turn left at Mountain Hwy., take the next right at Keith Rd., and left again at Brooksbank Ave. The park and Tilford Shopping Centre are on your right.

Portside Park   This is a great spot to bring kids on a sunny day and dogs any time. There is a sandy beach, lots of logs, a playground, lots of grassy areas, incredible views of the North Shore and the Burrard Inlet, and you can clearly see Canada Place to the west, often with a huge white cruise ship hugging its side. Everything around the park seems busy. The Port of Vancouver is the third largest in Canada, the rail yards are busy, and you can walk to the warehouses and historical buildings of Gastown that you can see to the south of the park. While the water may look tempting, don't let the kids near it—it's filthy.

Foot of Main St., which you reach by crossing over the Alexander St. overpass and braving the big stone lions that guard it.

Queen Elizabeth Park   On a sunny day, you might feel as though you are attending a wedding, as this is one of the hottest spots to get your wedding photos taken, and so popular that the photographers are only allowed a few minutes each and then moved along to make way for visitors and more wedding parties. Little Mountain, as it is known because its summit is just over 150 meters (500 ft.), began life as a volcano, and just 100 years ago it was a rock quarry. Now where there was once a pit is a sunken garden, and Queen Elizabeth Park is 52 hectares (130 acres) of landscaped gardens, duck pond, experimental rose garden, disc golf, tennis, pitch'n'putt golf, and the Bloedel Conservatory. In the mornings, the plaza between the car park and the conservatory is filled with people practicing Tai Chi, and as you walk through the plaza make sure you stop at the sculpture *Knife Edge-Two Pieces* by Henry Moore. And just below the conservatory is a much-photographed life-size bronze sculpture by American artist Seward Johnson, called *Photo Session.*

Take Georgia St. east over the Cambie Street Bridge and continue along Cambie until 33rd Ave.; turn left and you'll see the entrance to the park on your right. By bus: no. 15 from Burrard St.

Stanley Park *(★(★(★*   Columnist Allan Fotheringham once described Stanley Park as a "1000-acre therapeutic couch." While the park is perhaps known more for its 400 hectares (1,000 acres) of rain forest, its magnificent seawall, and beaches, Stanley Park also is the home of some beautiful gardens. In the spring there is a fabulous display of rhododendrons, azaleas, and magnolias just near the pitch'n'putt golf course, and in the summer, the perennial and rose beds and the arbor draped with roses and clematis are sensory experiences. In fact, there are more than 3,000 different types of roses grown in Stanley Park (see chapter 6, "What Kids Like to See & Do," p. 103.)

North end of Georgia St., Vancouver. © **604/299-9000** ext. 4100. The Ted and Mary Greig Rhododendron Garden and Rose Garden are open daily from dawn until dusk. There is also a formal garden just in front of the Stanley Park Pavilion.

University of British Columbia Botanical Garden   The Botanical Garden is set in more than 28 hectares (65 acres) with plants from around the world. A proper tour of the gardens takes about an hour. Kids tend to gravitate to the Food Garden, which has raised beds and is filled with vegetables in the summer. This is also where you'll find the espaliered fruit trees—those are the ones that are trained into different shapes and grow along a wall. In the fall the gardens host a weekend-long apple festival when you can taste apples, pick up your own apple tree, and listen to buskers. The gardens are divided into different sections, the largest being the 12.1-hectare (30-acre) David Lam Asian Garden, which holds the largest collection of woody Asian plants in North America, and where you'll also find 400 species of rhododendrons. The E.H. Lohbruner Alpine Garden is the largest alpine garden in North America. It is made from volcanic rock and limestone and laid out in pathways so you can walk through Africa, South America, Australia, and other regions of the world. The garden was established in the 1960s. There is a shop at the entrance that sells a variety of plants, books, and garden accessories.

6804 SW Marine Dr. (at 16th Ave.). © **604/822-4208.** C$4.75 (US$3.15) adults, C$2.50 (US$1.65) students, C$2 (US$1) children 6–12, children under 6 free. Free admission in winter. Adults can buy a ticket that gives them entrance into both the Nitobe Memorial Garden and the UBC Botanical Garden for C$6 (US$4). Open summer daily 10am–6pm; winter Mon–Fri 10am–2:30pm.

VanDusen Botanical Garden   Situated in Shaughnessy, one of Vancouver's wealthiest residential suburbs, this is a gorgeous garden that offers a complete family experience. The gardens are 22 hectares (55 acres) and filled with roses and fuchsia, rolling lawns, bridges, ponds, and woodlands. A big hit with kids is the Elizabethan hedge maze, one of only three in North America. In the spring, a treat for adults is the gorgeous Rhododendron Walk. There is a children's garden with topiary trees in the shape of animals, a gazebo, and bark mulch paths that lead off the main paths. The gardens will supply older children with the material for a self-guided pond tour, which takes them by lakes, over a floating bridge, turtle watching, and to a waterfall. The tour takes between 1½ and 2 hours. The garden regularly hosts "kid-friendly family adventures" for kids from about 7 to 12. In the past these have included learning about forest ecosystems, growing plants from seed, and potting your own sunflower. Parking is free, and there is a gift shop and upmarket restaurant on the site. This is another one of our must-do Christmas stops. Around late November, the gardens are transformed into a beautiful wonderland illuminated by thousands of bright twinkling lights, entertainers, a Santa's workshop, and Mrs. Claus's festive kitchen with hot chocolate and gingerbread cookies.

5251 Oak St. (at W. 37th Ave.), Vancouver. © **604/878-9274.** wwwcity.vancouver.bc.ca/parks/parks&gardens/vandusen. C$6.50 (US$4.30) adults, C$5 ($3.30) youth 13–18, C$3.25 children 6–12, C$15 (US$9.90) family rate, children under 6 free. Open daily 10am–6pm or 9pm, depending on the season. Take Granville St., cross the Granville Street Bridge, continue south, and then turn left on W. 37th Ave.

Vanier Park   This is the absolutely best kite-flying park in Vancouver, and you can either watch some of the professionals do their thing or try out your own kite. Vanier Park is right on the water, and you can look out to English Bay and Stanley Park. It's close to Kitsilano Beach and the Kitsilano outdoor pool, and it's a short walk or ferry ride to Granville Island. You'll find the H.R.

MacMillan Space Centre, the Vancouver Museum, and the Maritime Museum here, and in the spring the park is filled with kids for the Children's Festival. In the summer months, you can spend a very pleasant evening at the Shakespearean festival, Bard on the Beach.

Take Burrard St. and the Burrard Street Bridge; continue along Cornwall Ave.; take the first right on Chestnut St. and continue to Vanier Park at the end of the street. By bus: nos. 2 or 22. By ferry: Granville Island, Hornby St., Yaletown, Stamps Landing, and Science World stops.

2 Lakes

As you already know, Vancouver is a city with abundant creeks, ocean, and rainfall, but there is also a handful of lakes in fairly close proximity to the city, and they make a fun day out for a family.

Beaver Lake   This is a small lake—2.3 kilometers (1.5 miles) around in the middle of Stanley Park between the Stanley Park Causeway and Pipeline Road. It's rather swampy, but it's a quieter part of the park and you can often catch a blue heron on the shoreline, bald eagles in the trees, carp in the lake, and other park wildlife in the rushes and forest surrounding the lake.

Take W. Georgia St. to Stanley Park and Pipeline Rd.; go past the Miniature Railway; the lake is on your left.

Deer Lake   In the summer, you can rent a canoe, sailboat, or rowboat (see "Outdoor Activities," below) and really explore the lake from the inside. There is a beach at the lake's east end, lots of birds to watch, a playground, hiking trails, and marshlands and meadows to explore. If you're looking for a bit more excitement, the area is also home to the **Burnaby Heritage Village and Carousel.**

At Sperling Ave. and Canada Way, Burnaby. Take the Trans-Canada Hwy. (Hwy. 1) to the Kensington South turnoff; turn west on Canada Way and follow the signs to Deer Lake Park.

Rice Lake   After less than a 30-minute drive from downtown Vancouver, you will really feel that you're in the middle of the wilderness when you reach Rice Lake. This small freshwater lake has resident ducks and is filled with trout— you'll see fisher people on the dock trying their luck. There is a network of trails and boardwalks around the perimeter of the lake, and they are both stroller and wheelchair accessible. The 2-kilometer (1.2 mile) Rice Lake Loop Trail around the lake takes about an hour and is a good one for even quite small children, and in summer the lake warms up enough to swim in.

Take Trans-Canada Hwy. (Hwy. 1) to exit 22 in North Vancouver; follow Lillooet Rd. north past Capilano College and the cemetery, and onto the gravel road that will take you to the Rice Lake parking lot and information area.

⌒ *Fact*

If you are still in doubt that you really are in the wilderness as you hike through Rice Lake, stop and read the memorial plaque located near the entrance to Rice Lake and the Rice Lake Loop Trail. A map points out the spot where Trans-Canada Airlines Flight 3, flying from Lethbridge, Alberta, to Vancouver, crashed in April 1947. It took nearly half a century to locate the remains of the plane that was finally discovered in September 1994 just west of Mount Elsay.

Trout Lake   In summer there is a lifeguard and swimming is allowed from the south end of the lake, and kids can swim out to a permanently fixed floating board. Bring digging tools for the little ones as there is a sandy beach with logs, but you can leave your fishing lines at home—there are no trout in this lake. There is a children's playground nearby and public washrooms open year-round. The lake has a fabulous backdrop of the North Shore mountains, and it's a fairly short walk around the lake through the willow trees, with lots of places to stop and look at the ducks right up close in their natural habitat. If you are going in the rainy season, it can get awfully muddy, so dress appropriately (or just throw in a change of clothes).

John Hendry Park, between Victoria Dr., Nanaimo St., 21st Ave., and Grandview Hwy. There is parking at the Grandview Hwy. entrance and at 21st and 16th aves.

3 Suggested Bike Trips

Barnston Island   This is a super trip for young children, because you get to the tiny island in the Fraser River by taking a free ferry over on a barge. The trip takes about 5 minutes and then you hop on your bikes and enjoy an easy ride along the flat road while you watch the farms and animals whiz by (actually they'll be standing still, but you know what I mean). Stop and take a look at the tug boat and other logging activity in the river. The ride takes about an hour if you take your time.

Take the Trans-Canada Hwy. (Hwy. 1) over the Port Mann Bridge and exit at 176th St.; continue north to 104th Ave. and turn right. You'll see the ferry straight ahead.

Seymour Demonstration Forest   Part of Vancouver's watershed since 1928, the SDF only opened to visitors in 1987. The area is a bit of a forest-management success story—okay it's a tree farm, as most of the massive western red cedar, hemlock, Douglas fir, amabilis fir, and Sitka spruce are younger than 75 years old. There are 50 kilometers (31 miles) of paved and gravel logging roads and trails, some along the Seymour River, but the big draw for bikers, hikers, and inline skaters is the 22-kilometer (14 mile) round trip to the Seymour Dam. There are swimming holes up here, so pack a swimsuit, a towel, and some food, and don't forget water. Bikes are permitted on the paved road to Seymour Dam only on weekends, holidays, and evenings.

© 604/987-1273. Open daily summer 7am–9pm; winter 8am–5pm. No dogs or cars allowed. Take Trans-Canada Hwy. (Hwy. 1) to exit 22 in North Vancouver and follow Lillooet Rd. north past Capilano College and the cemetery, and onto the gravel road that will take you to the Rice Lake parking lot and information area.

Stanley Park Seawall and beyond   Remember that if you are traveling by any kind of wheels you must go counterclockwise around the park to go with the flow and avoid any accidents. Watch out for walkers. Give yourself plenty of time to take in all the stops of interest along the way: the Nine O'Clock Gun, Prospect Point, the Brockton Point Lighthouse, the *Girl in a Wet Suit* statue, and Siwash Rock. Also search for starfish and blue herons fishing by the shoreline. If you find that the 10.5-kilometer (6.5 mile) seawall is just getting you warmed up, then continue on from English Bay to UBC. This 15-kilometer (9.4 mile) ride takes you along English Bay, down to the Plaza of Nations, past Science World, Granville Island, the H.R. MacMillan Space Centre, the Kitsilano Pool, the Jericho Sailing Centre, and the Spanish Banks, and up a pretty steep hill with killer views to the university. You can stop at the beaches along the way, drop into the Museum of Anthropology and the Nitrobe Gardens, or just ride around the peaceful campus. The good news is that there is a long hill back the way you came, or via 10th Avenue shopping and residential neighborhoods, for a change of scenery.

Bike & Rollerblade Rentals

Most bike rental shops have an assortment of mountain bikes, tandems (double bikes), hybrid cruisers (city bikes), children's bikes, children's trailers, in-line skates, jogging strollers, helmets, bike locks, and protective gear. Bike helmets are mandatory for everyone. Bike rental shops are open daily, usually from 9am to dusk. Depending on the type of bike, prices range from C$3.50 to $5.60 (US$2.30 to $3.70) an hour, and from C$9 to $18 (US$5.95 to $12) for half a day.

Bayshore Bicycle & Rollerblade Skate Rentals, 745 Denman St. (between Robson and Alberni sts.) © **604/688-2453;** and at the Westin Bayshore Hotel, 1601 Bayshore Dr. © **604/682-3377.**

Bikes N'Blades, 718 Denman St. (between Robson and Alberni sts.) © **604/602-9899.**

Pacific Palisades Hotel, 1277 Robson St. (at Jervis St.) © **604/891-5189.** Opens at 6am.

Spokes Bicycle Rentals, 1798 W. Georgia St. (at Denman St.) © **604/688-5141.** Offers two guided tours suitable for children. The Stanley Park Seawall takes 1½ hours and costs C$29.95 (US$19.75) for adults, C$24.95 (US$16.45) for kids; and the Granville Island tour takes 3½ hours and costs C$59 (US$38.95) for adults, C$49 (US$32.35) for kids. The shop has a coffee shop to rest up when you get back.

4 Outdoor Activities

BOATING (LAKE)

Silent Waters at Deer Lake, 5400 Sperling Ave., Burnaby (© **604/667-2628**), rents canoes, kayaks, and paddle and row boats for exploring Deer Lake in Burnaby. Paddle boats can fit five, canoes can fit three, or two adults and two small children in the middle. C$14 (US$9.25) for an hour (includes taxes and lifejackets). Open weekends only from Easter until June 30 and then daily through to the September Labour Day weekend.

BOATING (OCEAN)

Deep Cove Canoe and Kayak Rentals (at the foot of Gallant St.) in Deep Cove, North Vancouver (© **604/929-2268**), rents canoes and kayaks for paddling along Indian Arm, a beautiful 30-kilometer (19 mile) fjord about 30 minutes from downtown Vancouver. C$26 (US$17) an hour, with a 2-hour minimum. The company also gives lessons for people over the age of 8, tours of the area, and guided trips. **Ecomarine Ocean Kayak Centre,** 1668 Duranleau St., Granville Island (© **604/689-7575**), rents a double kayak or a three-hold kayak (meaning you can put a child in the center hatch) for C$36 (US$23.75) for 2 hours. In July and August the Centre also runs kayak lessons for kids as young as 8, where they learn the rudiments of getting in, getting out, staying in, and making them go. A 3-hour lesson is C$39 (US$25.75).

SAILING

Cooper Boating Centre, 1620 Duranleau St., Granville Island (© **604/683-6837**), has a sailing school that offers courses for those just beginning to certified skipper and navigator training for age 16 and up. It also rents a wide range of sailboats by the hour or by the day.

SPEED BOATS

Granville Island Boat Rentals (© **604/644-3256**) at Dock A, next to Bridges Restaurant and Pub, rents motor boats for a day cruise up Indian Arm or out to Bowen Island. You can take out the 15-foot 40hp boat on the weekends for C$22.50 (US$14.85) an hour, on weekdays for C$17.50 (US11.55) an hour, or you can take it out for an 8-hour day for C$119 (US$78.55). The 17-foot 40hp boat is C$32.75 (US$21.60) an hour on the weekends, C$27.50 (US$18.15) on weekdays, or C$159 (US$105) for an 8-hour day. Insurance is C$4 to $7 (US$2.65 to $4.60) extra.

Sewell's Marina, 6695 Nelson Ave., Horseshoe Bay (© **604/921-3474**; www.sewellsmarina.com), rents a 15-foot 40hp boat for C$30.75 (US$20.30) for the first hour, and C$24 (US$15.85) an hour after that; and the 17-foot 40hp boat rents for C$39.75 (US$26.25) for the first hour and C$31 (US$20.45) an hour after that. Sewell's also does fishing charters, ecotours, and guided tours.

FISHING

Close to the downtown core, fishing charters are available on Granville Island from **Bonnie Lee Charters,** 1676 Duranleau St. (© **604/290-7447**), and **Granville Island Charter Centre Ltd.,** 1808 Boatlift Lane (© **604/683-1447**). Enthusiasts can head up to Howe Sound and hunt for Chinook or Coho, snapper, lingcod, and halibut, depending on the season. Of course, you can also grab some rods and bait and head up to the Capilano River or Rice Lake in North Vancouver, or Ambleside in West Vancouver, or try some bar fishing for salmon, steelhead, and white sturgeon on the Fraser River. To fish you need a nonresident saltwater or freshwater license, which can be bought at tackle shops. **Ruddick's Fly Shop,** 1654 Duranleau St., Granville Island (© **604/681-3747**), specializes in fly fishing, and sells licenses and equipment. Fly fishing seems to appeal to kids of about 12 and up. Kids under 16 don't need a license, but parents do. Licenses for freshwater fishing are C$8.55 (US$5.65) for 1 day or C$18.20 (US$12) for 8 days, and C$32.10 (US$21.20) for a BC resident for 1 year. Saltwater fishing licenses are free for kids (but they still need one), and cost adults C$5.60 (US$3.70) for 1 day, C$11.75 (US$7.75) for 3 days, C$17.10 (US$11.30) for 5 days, and C$22.45 (US$14.85) for a BC resident for 1 year. Pick up a regulation book (yes, book), while you are there.

GOLF

There are five public 18-hole courses around Vancouver and golf truly is a year-round sport. However, if you have a young family, you'll most likely be heading to one of the pitch'n'putt courses listed below. For real enthusiasts, the **British Columbia Golf Association,** 7382 Winston St., Burnaby (© **888/833-2242**; www.bcga.org), offers 12 children and youth clinics a year, as well as a Spring Master Golf Clinic.

HORSE RIDING

Maynard's Southlands, 3249 W. 54th Ave., Vancouver (✆ **604/266-6398**), offers pony rides on the weekends for C$10 (US$6.60) for 10 minutes. **Langley 204 Equestrian Centre,** 543 204th St., Langley (✆ **604/533-7978**), offers year-round trail rides for C$30 (US$19.80) for a 1-hour trail ride and C$45 (US$29.70) for 2 hours. Children must be 9 years or older and you must book in advance. The rides go through the 1,400-acre Campbell Valley Regional Park.

ICE SKATING

There are community center ice rinks all through Vancouver, though most close in the summer. In Vancouver, the **West End Community Centre,** 870 Denman St. (✆ **604/257-8333**), is one of the closest to downtown, now that the Robson Square rink has closed, but for an adventure take the SkyRide up to **Grouse Mountain** and skate outdoors at the 743-meter square (8,000 sq. ft.) pond just in front of the Peak Chalet. The rink is free with a SkyRide purchase and skates are C$5 (US$3.30) to rent. If you want to skate in the summer months, the **Ice Sports Centre,** 6501 Sprott St., Burnaby (✆ **604/291-0626**), is open year-round, has eight rinks, and is the Vancouver Canucks' official practice facility.

KITE FLYING

The best parks to fly a kite and get great views of the city and mountains are **Vanier Park** on Vancouver's West Side and **Ambleside Beach Park** in West Vancouver.

PITCH'N'PUTT

Stanley Park (✆ **604/681-8847**) has an 18-hole par 3 golf course, surrounded by the Rhododendron Garden, towering trees, and ocean views. Holes range from 40 to 100 yards. Public tee times are year-round from dawn to dusk, 7 days a week. The cost is C$9 (US$5.95) for adults, C$6.75 (US$4.45) for children under 18. At **Queen Elizabeth Park** (✆ **604/874-8336**) there is an 18-hole course built in 1965 just near the tennis courts and a short walk from the Bloedel Conservatory. Daily public tee times are February through November from dawn until dusk, and the cost is C$9 (US$5.95) for adults, C$6.75 (US$4.45) for children under 18. **Rupert Park Pitch & Putt** in East Vancouver (✆ **604/257-8364**) is the only course of the three that has a pond to make it a bit more challenging. The cost is C$8.25 (US$5.45) for adults, C$5 (US$3.30) for children under 18. The **Murdo Frazer Golf Course,** 2700 Pemberton St., North Vancouver (✆ **604/980-8410**), also has a 9-hole par 3 pitch'n'putt. It is in a forest setting and open daily from mid-April through October from 10am until dusk, and from 9am until dusk during July and August. The cost is C$4.50 (US$3) for adults, C$3 (US$2) for children under 17.

ROCK CLIMBING

If I were young and single with a buff body and looking for love, I'd forget the bars and nightclubs and spend my nights at these indoor climbing centers. Even though I'm not, it's still a great place to take the family, and kids of about 5 and up can have a blast scaling these climbing structures. There are more than 743 square meters (8,000 sq. ft.) of climbing structures at **Cliffhanger Indoor Rock Climbing,** 106 W. 1st Ave. (✆ **604/874-2400;** www.cliffhangerclimbing.com). The facility has great views of downtown and the North Shore and is open from noon to 10:30pm on weekends, and noon to 9:30pm during the week. On Saturdays there is a special kids' drop-in from 10am to noon, and also on public holidays from 1 to 3pm. The cost is C$20 (US$13.20) for 2 hours and includes equipment and instruction. **The Edge Climbing Centre,** 2-1485 Welch St., North Vancouver (© **604/984-9080;** www.edgeclimbing.com), is open Monday to Friday from 1 to 11pm and noon until 9pm on weekends. It has 1,400 square meters (15,000 sq. ft.) of climbing structures. The Edge runs a 2-hour climbing session on Monday, Wednesday, and Friday from 4 to 6pm and again on weekends between 1 and 3pm. The cost is C$18.70 (US$12.35) and you need to book 48 hours in advance.

For those looking for more of a challenge, the **Stawamus Chief,** a sheer granite rock face near Squamish, has put BC on the world rock-climbing map since it was first scaled in 1958. It's worth a trip just to watch other adventurers try one of the 200 different ways to scale this 650-meter (2,132 ft.) high face.

SCUBA DIVING

Vancouver boasts some of the best diving spots around. Some of the hot spots are Lighthouse Park and Whytecliffe Park in West Vancouver, West Cates Park in North Vancouver, and Porteau Cove, which is located roughly half-way between West Vancouver and Squamish on the Sea to Sky Highway and has a sunken steam tug and a World War II minesweeper to explore in its waters. **Rowand's Reef Scuba Shop,** 1512 Duranleau St., Granville Island (© **604/ 669-3483;** www.rowandsreef.com), has courses in everything from wreck diving to underwater photography. Offers 2-week courses for kids aged 10 and up. Courses start at C$259 (US$171). Rowand's also rent tanks, wet suits, and snorkels. **The Diving Locker,** 2745 W. 4th Ave. (© **604/736-2681**), runs a camp in the summer for kids aged 10 and over, which is a 5-day course that includes time in the pool, classroom study, and a visit to the dive site, and a trip out to the Vancouver Aquarium. It also includes reading and homework. The cost is C$199.95 (US$132) for classroom and pool, or to upgrade to a weekend of ocean diving, it's another C$160 (US$106), which includes Saturday at Whytecliffe Park and Sunday at the Sunshine Coast.

TENNIS

Vancouver has more than 180 free public tennis courts. The outdoor courts are open all year and are run on a first-come, first-served basis, with a 30-minute maximum time limit if someone is waiting. **Stanley Park** has 17 free courts near the Beach Avenue entrance, and 6 are available to rent by the hour in summer. There are another 3 courts just below South Lagoon Drive near the Lost Lagoon Nature House, also free with the same rules. To make tennis reservations call © **604/605-8224,** summer only. **Queen Elizabeth Park** (at 33rd Ave. and Cambie St.) has 17 free courts, and at **Kitsilano Beach** there are 6 free courts for public use. **Bayshore Bicycle and Rollerblade Rentals,** 745 Denman St. (© **604/688-2453**), rents tennis rackets for C$10 (U$6.60) a day.

5 Winter Wonderland

Sure you can join the rich folk and visiting royalty and head up to the slopes of Whistler/Blackcomb, but if you don't have the bucks or the time, there are three really good family ski hills right near Vancouver. In fact, one of Vancouver's favorite urban myths is that you can spend the day sailing in the harbor and head up to the slopes at night for a little night skiing. I've never met anyone this enthusiastic.

The season changes depending on the year, but basically runs from mid-November to mid-April. To check out the white stuff while you're in Vancouver, and take your pick of skiing, snowboarding, snowshoeing, tobogganing, and tubing, head to Lions Gate Bridge and the North Shore and choose between Grouse Mountain to the north, Cypress Mountain to the east, or Cypress Bowl to the west. You'll find plenty of winter sports running between November and April.

Tips **Snow Phone**

Phone before you leave home. The Snow Phone hotline: For **Grouse Mountain** ⓒ 604/986-6262; for **Blackcomb/Whistler** ⓒ 604/664-5614; for **Cypress Mountain** ⓒ 604/419-7669; and for **Seymour Mountain** ⓒ 604/718-7771.

Cypress Mountain   This West Vancouver mountain about 30 minutes from downtown Vancouver has got just about anything involving snow you could think to do, and it offers up some sensational views as you go. The mountain has 23 downhill runs for varying abilities and 16 kilometers (10 miles) of groomed cross-country trails, 5 kilometers (3 miles) of which are lit for night skiing. It's said that if you can walk, you can snowshoe, and the sport is growing in popularity: 10 kilometers (6.2 miles) of self-guided snowshoe trails are open from dawn until dusk, then the tours kick in. A favorite is the 4-hour Hollyburn Lodge Snowshoe Fondue Tour, starting at 6:30pm. Wearing a head-lamp, you snowshoe for 1½ hours over easy terrain. When you reach the lodge you warm up with hot apple cider, followed by a cheese fondue, and finish off with a chocolate fondue—and port for the adults. The cost is C$69 (US$45.55) and includes rentals, food, tour guide, and trail fee. To go it without a tour for the day, including trail fee and rental, is C$20 (US$13.20) for adults, C$15 (US$9.90) for children 13 to 18, C$11 (US$7.25) for children 6 to 12. Poles are C$3.50 (US$2.30) each.

Smaller children might want to head straight for the SnowPlay area where they can toboggan and kids over 122 centimeters (48 in.) tall can slide down shoots in a snow tube. No need to waste valuable sliding time climbing back up the hill—they can catch the tube tow. It costs C$11 (US$7.25) per person for the tube park, and C$5 (US$3.30) to rent a toboggan. The mountain also runs a drop-in ski camp for kids between 3 and 5 years old from 9:30am to 3:30pm: C$9 (US$5.95) an hour buys you basically babysitting, a lesson, and the rope and lift tow. Hourly skiing or snowboarding lessons for children 6 to 12 cost C$12 (US$7.90). If you come up short, you can rent a full range of clothing including ski jackets, pants, hats, and boots.

Cypress Bowl Rd., Cypress Provincial Park, West Vancouver. ⓒ 604/926-5612; www.cypressmountain.com. Take W. Georgia St. over the Lions Gate Bridge; turn left at Marine Dr.; take the first right at Taylor Way; follow the signs to the Trans-Canada Hwy. (Hwy. 1), and head west to exit 8 onto Cypress Bowl Rd.; follow this for 13km (8 miles) for cross-country, snowshoeing, and SnowPlay/Tubing or for 15km (9.3 miles) for downhill. By bus: West Vancouver Blue buses nos. 250 or 252 on W. Georgia St. to the Park Royal Shopping Centre and board the Cypress Shuttle bus. The shuttle also departs from Lonsdale Quay.

Grouse Mountain   This is the closest to Vancouver of the three ski hills, but not by very much, and when you factor in the price of the SkyRide gondola, Grouse Mountain is also a bit more expensive. But it does have a whole bunch of winter sports activities geared to families, and some extras that are included in the price of your ticket. There is a mini IMAX-like theater called Theatre in the Sky that runs *Born to Fly*, a 30-minute movie about southwestern BC from an eagle's perspective, every hour on the hour. There are a number of places to eat, all with fabulous views, and of course there is day and night skiing, snowboarding, snowshoeing, ice skating, and sleigh rides. The last two are included in the price of the SkyRide ticket. Once up on top you'll find 24 ski runs, 3 kilometers (2 miles) of beginner and 2.3 kilometers (1.5 miles) of advanced cross-country ski trails, 4 chairs, 2 beginner tows, 2 T-bars, and a 90-meter (300 ft.) half-pipe for snowboards. It also has equipment rentals and a kids ski school. Drop-in lessons for children 7 to 12 are C$25 (US$16.50) for 1½ hours.

6400 Nancy Greene Way, North Vancouver. ℂ 604/984-0661; www.grousemtn.com. SkyRide C$17.95 (US$11.20) adults, C$11.95 (US$7.90) children 13–18, C$6.95 (US$4.60) children 7–12, children under 7 free. Departs every 15 minutes daily 9am–10pm. Take W. Georgia St. over the Lions Gate Bridge, turn right at Marine Dr., then take the first left onto Capilano Rd. and continue to Grouse Mountain. By bus: no. 232.

Mount Seymour   This is the favorite mountain for local preschool and kindergarten classes. Just 30 minutes from downtown Vancouver, Mount Seymour has built the Enquist Snow Tube Park, located on the east side of Parking Lot 2 at the base area, for tubing and tobogganing. Kids must be over 122 centimeters (48 in.) tall to tube in specially designed tubes and the mountain has five lanes with a 50-meter (164 ft.) vertical drop. There is a customized tow lift to bring the kids and their tube back to the top and the park is fully supervised. The cost for two hours is C$11 (US$7.25), C$50 (US$33) for the family rate to a maximum of five people. It's open during the season on Fridays, Saturdays, and holidays from 10am to 8pm, and on Sunday to Thursday from 10am to 6pm. The tobogganing is open daily from 10am to 4pm and costs C$3 (US$2). Children between 4 and 6 can sign up for four tiny tots lessons at C$84 (US$55.45), which includes ski rental and a free lift ticket for parents on Fridays. Children 7 to 12 can get four lessons for C$145 (US$95.70), with ski rental C$213 (US$141).

1700 Mt. Seymour Rd., North Vancouver. ℂ 604/986-2261; www.mountseymour.com. Take the Second Narrows Bridge to exit 22 onto Mount Seymour Pkwy.; follow the signs to the Provincial Park; turn left at Mount Seymour Rd. (at the Mohawk station), and it's 15 minutes up the road. By bus: no. 215.

6 Hiking

You can find hiking trails for all levels of ages and abilities—everything from a gentle stroll along the beach to the Grouse Grind in North Vancouver—scattered throughout Greater Vancouver. Trail maps are available from **International Travel Maps and Books,** 552 Seymour St., Vancouver (ℂ **604/687-3320**), and from the **Greater Vancouver Regional Parks District,** 4330 Kingsway, Burnaby, BC V5H 4G8 (ℂ **604/432-6350**; www.gvrd.bc.ca). For more information on the parks in the District of North Vancouver (ℂ **604/990-3800**), the Parks District puts out a very good booklet called "North Vancouver Trails" with detailed maps of dozens of walks including different sections of the Baden Powell Trail. For information on West Vancouver parks call ℂ **604/925-7200.** Make sure you dress appropriately with proper hiking boots and warm clothing, and take snacks and water along for the hike.

Baden Powell Trail   If you'd really like to hike the North Shore, head to Deep Cove and take this 42-kilometer (26 mile) trail that runs from Deep Cove at the eastern tip of North Vancouver to Horseshoe Bay in West Vancouver. Along the way you'll see rocky bluffs with views of Burnaby Mountain, ravines running with snow-fed streams, and lots of majestic trees. The trail has orange markers to help you keep on track. Can't say we've ever done the whole trail, but we do sections of it all the time around the Lynn Valley and Upper Lonsdale areas. The Baden Powell Trail starts between Cates Park on the Dollarton Highway to the east and Panorama Park to the southwest. If you decide to do the whole thing, give yourself a long day.

Bridgman Park   Located at Keith Road and Mountain Highway just over the Second Narrows Bridge in North Vancouver, this is a terrific park for kids. It has a huge playground to reward them with after you've hiked along Lynn Creek. If you follow the trail north you go under the highway and head to the Boy Scout Camp; it's a longer walk and you can cross a footbridge over the river. If you head south instead, it's a pretty short walk, but the kids can stop and play on the rocks by the creek, and there are picnic and grassy areas to play on. There's also a jogging trail and exercise circuit with a bunch of spots to stop to try out various torturous-looking equipment for adults and kids over 12. You can also take a detour and cross over to the Park and Tilford Shopping Centre for a coffee or a bite to eat, or a movie for that matter. There are also clean public washrooms. Watch out for the bikes and dogs—it's usually pretty full of both.

Take the Trans-Canada Hwy. (Hwy. 1) over the Second Narrows Bridge to the Mountain Hwy. exit; turn left at Mountain Hwy., left again at Keith Rd., and Brigman Park is on your right.

Caulfield Cove *(Finds*   One of our favorite hikes, this kid-friendly walk is shorter than 2 kilometers (1.2 miles) and takes you along a twisting coastal trail in what must be one of the most beautiful spots in Greater Vancouver. In the summer, bring swimsuits, towels, and a picnic. If you start at Marine Drive you'll see the trail marked Caulfield Cove Trail. Follow it down the stone steps as it winds along the ocean shore. A trail leads down onto a small sandy beach, perfect for a picnic, or go farther along and sit on the rocks and watch the sailboats in English Bay with Lions Gate Bridge and Stanley Park in the distance. As you walk farther along, you can also catch a glimpse of some of the beachfront houses of the wealthy. There are little bridges to cross and rocks to scale, perfect climbing for older kids, though you'll need to keep a careful eye on the younger ones. We've done this easily with a 2-and-a-half-year-old, but there are anxious moments when he tries to follow the bigger kids onto the rocks that hang over the ocean. Raw granite runs into the lapping ocean, it's a gentle climb down to the water, and the flat rocks are great for sun bathing or picture taking of ducks paddling and killer city views way in the background. Walk along the little English-country–like Pilot House Lane to Government Dock. There is another great little rocky beach, full of shells, with driftwood and logs for climbing, beach combing, and hunting for crabs. Keep walking in the same direction and you come to St. Francis In the Woods, a lovely little church surrounded by more little lanes and mansions with beautiful gardens. In fact, it's worth the walk just to come and look at some of these gardens. You can take the same way back or wander through the lanes and back to Marine Drive.

Take W. Georgia St. over the Lions Gate Bridge; turn left at Marine Dr., then follow it to Piccadilly St.. It's hard to find and there's not a lot of parking. If you can, park along Marine Dr., Pilot House Rd., and near the church.

Cypress Falls Park   A rain-forest park with two awesome waterfalls, and a 2-kilometer (1.2 mile) trail that leads to the rushing waters and an old-growth forest. It's a really lovely, peaceful area, especially on a hot summer's day. We took our 2-and-a-half-year-old and it wasn't a good idea. The paths are pretty rough, some are quite steep, and there are lots of rock and rotting wood stairs and sheer drops from the lower paths into an unforgiving canyon below. That said, it is a beautiful hike for older kids. About 10 minutes into the walk you hit a waterfall; there is also a lookout, which is quite safe, so you can look down at the waterfall. If you keep going, you cross a rickety old wooden bridge over a flowing stream (this was also a nightmare with a 2-year-old) and climb up a pretty steep path and find yourself in an old growth forest surrounded by hemlocks, cedars, and Douglas firs that are a couple of hundred years old. If you ignore the bridge and continue to climb up another steep path, you find yourself faced with a sign that says something along the lines of "British Properties Ltd. Proceed at own risk." I gave up at this point, but apparently if you keep going there is another spectacular waterfall, and another treacherously steep cliff.

Take W. Georgia St. over the Lions Gate Bridge; turn left at Marine Dr.; turn right at Taylor Way and follow it to the Trans-Canada Hwy. (Hwy. 1), which you take west to Woodgreen Dr. (exit 4); turn right onto Woodgreen Dr.; then drive to Woodgreen Pl. and look for the park at the end by the tennis courts.

Grouse Grind 🕿 **604/984-0661** or the Grind information line 🕿 **604/451-6107.** This is not for the unfit or the very young. But if you have older children with lots of energy and who are used to hiking, the Grouse Grind is pretty well guaranteed to wear you all out. Think of it as a 2.9-kilometer (1.8 mile) Stair-Master, and when you're done, instead of being in one place, you'll be 2,300 kilometers (3,700 miles) above sea level. It's also quite trendy, and people often do "the Grind" regularly. You need hiking boots and water. For those in very good shape, it takes about an hour; an average time would be 1½ to 2 hours, and the world record for doing the Grind is under 27 minutes. Don't hike down—pay the C$5 (US$3.30) and ride the gondola to the bottom.

Take W. Georgia St. over the Lions Gate Bridge; turn right at Marine Dr.; then take the first left onto Capilano Rd. and continue to Grouse Mountain. The Grind starts near the entrance by the parking lot.

Lighthouse Park Once you walk the easy trail down to the 1912 Point Atkinson lighthouse, which is one of the last working lighthouses on the coast, you will be rewarded with fabulous views of the Burrard Inlet and the Strait of Georgia, huge rocky outcroppings, seaside cliffs, and a walk through a virgin rain forest and one of the last stands of unlogged forest with the biggest Douglas fir trees in the Greater Vancouver area. If you are with very small children, stick to the stroller-friendly route down the old road. There are great trails that lead back to the car park, but, as we discovered the hard way, they are not stroller friendly. There are nearly 13 kilometers (8 miles) of hiking trails running through this 75 hectare (184 acre) park.

Take W. Georgia St. over the Lions Gate Bridge; turn left at Marine Dr. and continue along past Dundarave and Caulfield; turn left at Beacon Lane and you'll see the car park. By bus: no. 250 from Park Royal Shopping Centre.

Pacific Spirit Park 🕿 **604/224-5739.** Still known to most of us locals as the University Endowment Lands, this massive 800 hectare (2,000 acre) urban wilderness on the West Side of Vancouver became a park just over a decade ago. Located right by the University of British Columbia, it has 53 kilometers (32 miles) of trails, beaches, marshes, rain forest, and a bog, which is easily accessible from Camosun Street and 19th Avenue. This park houses squirrels, owls, tree frogs, coyotes, raccoons, and all the other usual urban wildlife, as well as **Wreck**

Beach, Canada's largest nude beach. You can pick up a map from the Interpretive Centre on 16th Avenue, and also arrange a tour with a park staffer if you book in advance, and kids can sign up for the Something's Up programs. Watch out for bikes, dogs, and horses. The park is bordered by 16th Avenue, Camosun Street, and Southwest Marine Drive.

Seaview Walk   This is another one of our favorites, mainly because of its gentle sloping trail, which is actually an old railway route and perfect for young children, and for its killer view of Fisherman's Cove roughly halfway through the walk. The walk is actually part of the Trans-Canada Trail, but this particular stretch is only 2.5 kilometers (1.5 miles) long and can be hiked, biked, or traveled by stroller. While there are no railway tracks in existence now, you can see where they blasted out the rock, and what is left makes great climbing and will keep the older kids interested and the adults on their toes. The reward: a drop-dead view of Fisherman's Cove and all the fishing boats, and the tiny Eagle Island, and a pretty view of the back of Cypress Bowl—it all feels a bit like you've hit the Riviera on a sunny day. The path meanders around people's houses and you can get a close-up look at some pretty wild cliff-hugging architecture and a good look into the backyards and decks of some of West Van's well-to-do. There are hundreds of the beautiful arbutus trees that grow up and down the Pacific West Coast, and you end up almost under the huge trestle bridge at the end of the walk.

Take W. Georgia St. over the Lions Gate Bridge; turn left at Marine Dr. and continue along this fabulously scenic road to the Gleneagles Golf Club. Park in the car park across from the golf club and you'll see the trail start at the eastern end of the car park. For a speedy trip back, turn right on Marine Dr. and take the Trans-Canada Hwy. (Hwy. 1) back to Vancouver.

The Seymour Demonstration Forest   Hiking just doesn't get any better than this. There are about 40 kilometers (25 miles) of trails that snake their way through this forest, some that are very challenging and others that are easier and shorter and make quite an adventure for young children. Our favorite is to take the Homestead Trail to the Fisherman's Trail, and back up the Twin Bridges Trail. The round trip is about 5 kilometers (3 miles) and takes us about 2½ to 3 hours; it's not particularly easy, but definitely worth it. The Homestead Trail is actually a very steep old logging road, and while we have gone down this with a stroller, I wouldn't recommend it with a child in it. The rain forest changes as you descend and when you get to the Fisherman's Trail you make a gradual ascent up along the Seymour River. Along the way are the remnants of a housing settlement from the beginning of the 1920s, an old cave that you can walk through and explore, and a gentle trail that follows along the river. When you get to the junction of Twin Bridges, you'll see a beautiful old bridge and a swimming area—in fact, there are several swimming holes along the river. The walk back to the car park is fairly steep and can get a bit tedious, plus with the "are we there yets" and passing a rifle range and the shots in the background it can be a bit unnerving. If you want a shorter walk, this is the same car park for **Rice Lake,** which has the very easy and pretty 2-kilometer (1.2 mile) Rice Lake Loop Trail. Jump in the car, and you'll be back downtown in less than half an hour.

Take exit 22 off the Trans-Canada Hwy. (Hwy. 1) in North Vancouver and follow Lillooet Rd. north past Capilano College and the cemetery, and onto the gravel road that will take you to the Rice Lake parking lot and information area.

7 Organized Tours

BY WATER

Burrard Water Taxi   This company's main line of business is shunting the captains and crews of the freighters anchored in the Burrard Inlet to and from their ships. While the company does not offer scheduled tours, you can arrange your own guided ones through the inner harbor.

2255 Commissioner St., Vancouver. © **604/293-1160.** C$145 (US$96) for a maximum of 12 people and you must get yourself to the water taxi. For pickup and delivery, add C$40 (US$26.40).

Canadian Outback Adventure Company   Offers rafting tours from the end of April through September of the Lower Cheakamus River, about 1¼ hours outside Vancouver. Tours are suitable for kids of about 5 and up, they say, and take about 3 hours and include a snack and a meal. The company also offers horseback riding in the Squamish Valley.

100-657 Marine Dr., West Vancouver. © **604/921-7250;** www.canadianoutback.com. C$129 (US$85) adults, C$79 (US$52.15) children.

Harbour Cruises   Has several cruises (including the Royal Hudson train-and-boat combo in chapter 6, "What Kids Like to See & Do," p. 122), but the most suitable for children is the 75-minute narrated tour of Burrard Inlet aboard the MPV *Constitution*, an authentic 19th-century sternwheeler with a smokestack. The tour runs three times a day between mid-May and the end of September at 11:30am, 1pm, and 2:30pm.

#1 North Foot of Denman St., Vancouver. © **800/663-1500** or 604/687-9558; www.boatcruises.com. C$18 (US$12) adults, C$15 (US$10) children 12–17, C$6 ($3.30) children 5–11, children 4 and under free.

Paddle Wheeler Adventures   The company offers a 3-hour lunch cruise of the Fraser River on the 19th-century vessel SS *Native* on Wednesdays and Fridays. On Thursdays, Saturdays, and Sundays, a 7-hour trip to Fort Langley includes live entertainment on board and admittance to the historic fort.

139-810 Quayside Dr., New Westminster. © **604/525-4465;** www.vancouverpaddlewheeler.com. Fraser River Tour: Wed and Fri; C$35.95 (US$23.70) adults, C$31.95 (US$21.10) seniors and students, C$11.95 (US$7.90) children 6–12, children under 6 free. Fort Langley Tour: Thurs, Sat, and Sun; C$59.95 (US$39.55) adults, C$53.95 (US$35.60) seniors and students, C$24.95 (US$16.45) children 6–12, children under 6 free.

BY AIR

Glacier Air Tours and Pacific Spirit Tours   Vancouver is the only major city that has glaciers within 1 hour of downtown. Depending on your level of enthusiasm, helicopter pilots will swoop into small alpine valleys to check things out or land gently on a glacier. A 30-minute tour that takes you over the Tantalus Mountain Range and lands you on the prehistoric Seratus Glacier costs C$149 (US$98) for adults, and C$129 (US$85) for children. There is a two-passenger minimum.

Squamish Airport, Squamish. © **800/265-0088** or 604/898-9016; www.glacierair.com.

Vancouver Helicopter   Daily tours of different variations depart from the Vancouver Harbour Heliport near Canada Place Pier. The West Coast Spectacular is a 20-minute tour of the city that takes off from either downtown or the airport and spins you along False Creek, gives you an aerial view of the whole city and downtown core, heads across Stanley Park over to the North Shore, up along Howe Sound and over the Lions peaks. There is a three-person minimum and the price of C$120 (US$79) applies to anyone over the age of 2. The 30-

minute Greater Vancouver Scenic Tour is C$170 (US$112), and the 45-minute North Shore Discovery Tour, which also takes in Squamish and the Stawamus Chief, Shannon Falls, and a glacier, is C$240 (US$158). The helicopters operate all year, weather permitting, and depending on the helicopter can take up to five people. Vancouver Helicopters also runs tours that take off and land on Grouse Mountain for C$65 (US$43) for 8 minutes, and C$95 (US$63) for 15 minutes. 5911 Airport Rd. S., Richmond. © **604/270-1484.**

8 City Beaches

Ambleside   This West Vancouver beach, just over the Lions Gate Bridge, gives you a different angle on the city of Vancouver, Stanley Park, and Burrard Inlet. It has a sandy beach and a large park, and it's minutes from Marine Drive's restaurants, cafes, and ice cream, plus there is a seawall that you can follow up to **John Lawson Park,** another beach and playground close by. Ambleside is also a great place to fly a kite, and to watch the cruise ships slide out from Canada Place on the way to Alaska. Take W. Georgia St. over the Lions Gate Bridge; turn left at Marine Dr. and left again at 13th Ave., just past the Park Royal Shopping Centre.

Cates Park   Just outside Deep Cove in North Vancouver, Cates Park is such a lovely area for kids that it seems all of the preschool and elementary schools in North Vancouver congregate here at the end of the school year. So it may just be a good place to avoid in June. It has both sandy and rocky beaches, a large park with lots of shade, a concession stand, and a really lovely walk that takes you to Little Cates Park, another playground, tennis courts, the remains of a fort, and amazing views of the Indian Arm fjord. Take the Trans-Canada Hwy. (Hwy. 1) over the Second Narrows Bridge; take the first exit and drive east to Mount Seymour Pkwy. You'll find Cates Park just before Deep Cove, on your right.

Dundarave   Another West Vancouver beach with one of my favorite restaurants—the Beach House, which has a fabulous outdoor patio if you're hungry. You can also go next door to the hamburger shack and sit on the beach. There is a wading pool for little ones, a park, a playground, and a decent-sized sandy beach. It also has a very quaint little village to explore, with lots of shops, restaurants, and cafes. At Christmas time, the beach and park become a showcase for dozens of Christmas trees decorated by the various businesses in the area, and a nativity scene. Same directions as for Ambleside, except Dundarave is further along Marine Dr. at 25th Ave.

English Bay   You can't get much closer to the city than this beach. Close to Stanley Park, the Second Beach pool, and minutes from dozens of restaurants, cafes, and ice cream should you feel the urge. Stay into the evening and you'll be rewarded with killer sunsets. Corner of Denman and Davie sts.

Jericho Beach   This beach has a little something for everyone. A great sandy beach, drop-dead views of the city, a park, a pond, and trails through the marshy park. A great place to lug a hibachi in the summer and join the locals for dinner. Take Burrard St. across the Burrard Street Bridge; continue along Cornwall Ave., which becomes Point Grey Rd., and up to 4th Ave.; turn right onto NW Marine Dr., and the first beach, between Wallace and Trimble, is Jericho.

Kitsilano Beach   Known as Kits Beach to the locals, this is the beach for the body beautiful, where the young and gorgeous hang out to check each other out, play volleyball, and be seen. But don't let that put you off. It's okay for the less-than-perfect too. It's also very pretty and fun to explore at low tide, and it's close to shops and restaurants and a playground.

Take Burrard St. across the Burrard Street Bridge; continue along Cornwall Ave. There is a car park at Cornwall Ave. and Arbutus St.

Spanish Banks   When the tide is out you can walk for miles, with the views of Vancouver and the North Shore mountains in the distance. It feels like you can reach out and touch those boats, and sometimes you can if they get too close to the sandbar. There's a park and a grassy area to fly a kite or play ball.

See directions for Jericho Beach. Spanish Banks is just a little further along NW Marine Dr., past Locarno Beach.

Wreck Beach   This is Canada's largest nude beach and sure to gross your kids out, but I include it here because it's famous/infamous beach that everyone knows about. It's a beautiful secluded spot, reached by hundreds of stairs, and is just by the University of British Columbia. You get to the beach by taking Trail 6 on the UBC campus near Gate 6. It's very private, and also has a reputation for having a bit of a drug culture.

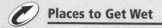

Places to Get Wet

Granville Island Waterpark   Billed as the largest free water park in North America, this park has two waterslides, geyser jets, curtain sprays, and water canyons. Little ones have their own water playground next to the rest area. Open from May to September. Call the False Creek Community Centre for more information at ℭ 604/257-8195.

Kitsilano Pool   Yew St. and Cornwall Ave. ℭ 604/731-0011. A huge outdoor pool, it attracts a lot of serious swimmers who work out here. But it's also a lot of fun for families in the summer and has a gradual entry that is good for smaller children. A bonus is the killer views, and it's right next to Kits Beach and a large grassy area. Open from Victoria Day (third Monday in May) through Labour Day in September. Will extend the season if the weather is good.

Lumberman's Arch Water Park   Located at the east side of Stanley Park, just below the Vancouver Aquarium, this is a great water park on the Seawall and a kid magnet on hot sunny days. It also has killer views of the harbor and North Shore mountains, and a concession stand.

Second Beach   ℭ 604/257-8371. Right in Stanley Park, this is a huge outdoor pool that hugs the ocean in one of the best spots in the city. Great as a destination on its own, or as a stopover while you're doing the Seawall. There is a concession stand and playground next door, and, of course, a beach. Open from Victoria Day (third Monday in May) through Labour Day in September. Will extend the season if the weather is good.

Splashdown Water Park   4799 Nulelum Way, Tsawwassen. ℭ 604/943-2251; www.splashdownpark.ca/gi_loc.html. About 3 minutes from the Tsawwassen ferry terminal, this water park has 13 huge waterslides, a giant hot tub, a pool, inner tubes, volleyball, and a large picnic area. It costs C$19.95 (US$13.15) for adults, C$13.95 (US$9.20) for children 4 or up to 122 centimeters (48 in.) tall, C$64.95 (US$42.85) for a family of 4, C$11.95

(US$7.90) for spectators only, and children under 3 are free. It's open from June 23 to August 19 10am to 8pm, from August 20 to September 3 10am to 7pm, and from May 28 to June 22 weekends only 11am to 5pm. To get there, take Highway 17 south and turn right on 52nd Street just before the Tsawwassen Ferry Terminal, then turn left onto Nulelum Way. By bus, take the no. 404, no. 601, or no. 640.

Trans-Canada Waterslides   53790 Popkum Rd. (off Hwy. 1), Bridal Falls. *C* **888/883-8852** or 604/794-7455; www.waterslides.chwk.com. Heated waterslides include the Black Hole and the Rapids River Ride. There are also slides for little ones, a playground, a giant hot tub, and mini-golf. It's open daily 10am to 8pm from mid-June to September and costs C$15 (US$9.90) for adults, C$12 (US$7.90) for children 4 to 12, twilight price C$10 (US$6.60).

Vancouver Aquatic Centre   1050 Beach Ave. (at the north side of Burrard Street Bridge). *C* **604/665-3424.** This pool has a 50-meter (164 ft.) indoor pool, diving tank, special pool for tots, dry sauna, whirlpool, and weight room. It's also home to many of Vancouver's competitive swim clubs and Olympic-standard divers. Admission is C$4 (US$2) for adults, C$3 (US$2) for youth 13 to 18, C$2 (US$1.30) for children 6 to 12, and includes access to the sauna and weight room. Call for public swim times.

WaterMania Aquatic Centre   14300 Entertainment Blvd. (at Steveston Hwy. and No. 6 Rd.), Richmond. *C* **604/448-5353;** www.city.richmond. bc.ca/pools. When the kids are looking for more water action, try out this water paradise in Richmond. There is a wave pool, a 50-meter (164 ft.) pool with diving boards, an exercise room, whirlpools, a sauna, and two 3-story waterslides. And, if they get sick of the water, there are theaters, lots of food, bowling, and ice skating. Admission is C$5.25 (US$3.45) for adults, C$4.25 (US$2.80) for youth 13 to 18, C$3.75 (US$2.45) for children 2 to 12; children under 2 are free. Open Monday to Saturday 6am to 10pm, Sunday 10am to 10pm. The waterslides are open Monday to Friday 3:30pm to 9pm and weekends noon to 9pm.

8

Neighborhood Walks

Walking is really the best way to get the feel and flavor of an area, and Vancouver is made up of some unique areas that make exploring easy for families with children of all ages. I've purposely made these walks short, so they can be done fairly quickly in under 2 hours, or, if you have little kids, they can take up most of the day. The tours are all stroller accessible, and you are almost always near a bus route if short legs have a tough time making it back. For older kids, or if you are on bikes, these tours can easily be extended or joined together.

WALKING TOUR 1   GASTOWN

Originally the center of Vancouver, Gastown is a delightful mishmash of upscale furniture stores and Cowichan sweaters, art galleries, and tacky T-shirts, minutes from the downtown core. Gastown is actually 6 blocks running between Water and Hastings streets and Cambie and Columbia streets. Vendors hawk their wares on the street and buskers entertain summer and weekend visitors.

To really get into the mood, take a free 90-minute tour of the area with a costumed historian between mid-June and the end of August. These tours leave from Maple Tree Square at 2pm daily and are suitable for kids of about 12 and up. For more information contact the **Gastown Business Improvement Society (© 604/683-5650)**.

The majority of Vancouver is quite safe to wander around, but you do need to keep an eye out for panhandlers, drug addicts, and the generally downtrodden who sometimes venture into Gastown from the area to the east of Columbia Street.

Start:	Tourism Vancouver InfoCentre.
Finish:	Blood Alley.
Time:	Under 2 hours.

Begin your tour by the water at:

❶ Tourism Vancouver InfoCentre
The Tourism Vancouver InfoCentre at 200 Burrard St., at the foot of Burrard by Canada Place. Use this opportunity to pick up brochures or arrange tours. It's a great location to start your walk, being just minutes from Gastown.

Leave the InfoCentre and turn right on:

❷ Canada Place
Cross the road and stop at the fountain with the flags of Canada's provinces and territories. If you've had no other chance to get to know Vancouver, this stop will give you solid bearings. You are most likely already quite familiar with the enormous white "sails" of Canada Place from countless photo-

graphs, maps, and tourist brochures of the city. Now, take a self-guided tour around the promenade. It's a beautiful spot with the noise of the buzzing sea planes overhead—you can watch them take off and skim the water on landing. There are lots of boats to see, of course, and helicopters and the busy rail yards to the east. The prow at the front of the pier is also a fabulous viewpoint.

The **CN IMAX Theatre** is at the north end of Canada Place and offers up films about everything from Mount Everest to wolves on a three-story high screen. You may want to time your visit to hit one of these 45-minute films, which run daily from noon to 9:30pm.

⌐ Fun Fact

Canada Place is, of course, built to look like a ship in full sail and its five teflon-coated fiberglass "sails" are suspended by cables from 10 steel masts that soar 30 meters (98 ft.) above the top of the surrounding building. When it was finished in 1985 it was the largest fabric tension structure in the world. Underneath the sails are the World Trade Centre, the Pan Pacific Hotel, the Vancouver Trade and Convention Centre, a cruise ship terminal, and the CN IMAX Theatre.

When you come back out on Canada Place turn left and you'll be at the foot of Howe Street. Take the stairs (see note) to the west of the SkyTrain that lead up to:

❸ Granville Square
At 200 Granville St. stands the 142-meter (466 ft.) tower of Granville Square. This building was the start of an ambitious C$1 billion waterfront complex in the early 70s. The locals revolted against all the coming high-rises and managed to get the development plans cancelled.

Walk under the weird-looking wooden structure and down another flight of stairs that lead to **Waterfront Station** and the former Canadian Pacific Rail's Vancouver passenger-rail terminal. This is now home to the SkyTrain, the West Coast Express, and the SeaBus.

⌐ Note

If you have a wheelchair or a stroller, just walk straight up Howe Street and turn left at 601 W. Cordova St., and you are at the front entrance of the station.

You've already seen some killer views, but why not take a closer look? Depending on the time of day, the SeaBus runs every 15 to 30 minutes and is a 12-minute crossing across Burrard Inlet to **Lonsdale Quay** in North Vancouver. It's also the cheapest harbor tour you will ever find, and the public market on the other side is definitely worth a visit.

Back outside the rail terminal at Cordova Street, turn left, and head east down Water Street. Immediately on your left is:

❹ The Landing
A beautifully restored old building, The Landing also has useful things in it, such as a currency exchange, a newspaper and magazine store, designer clothes stores, and another upmarket restaurant called **Raintree**.

TAKE A BREAK
If lunch is in order, kids will thank you if you stop in a Sodas Diner at The Landing, 375 Water St., a 1950s-style burger joint. If a coffee is more in line you can watch the Steam Clock do its thing from the patio or inside counter at the **Starbucks** on the corner of Water and Cambie streets.

It also has yet another drop-dead view of the North Shore mountains and Burrard Inlet from its floor-to-ceiling arched picture window.

Now you are in the heart of Gastown, and you can follow the cobblestones and the gas lights to the **Steam Clock**—another well-photographed spot in Vancouver that never fails to appeal to tourists and kids.

After you cross Cambie Street, you'll see the Courtyard on your left at 131 Water St. It now houses the Calico Cat and Kites on Clouds, among others, but when **Gaslight Square** was built in 1974, its bay windows and brick facade and awnings were designed to fit in with its older neighbors, mostly 1920s warehouses.

At the corner of Water and Abbott streets, you'll see:

❺ Dominion Hotel

Now a historical landmark, the Dominion Hotel was built in 1899. The hotel has been completely restored and now provides inexpensive accommodation.

Just before you come to the intersection of Water and Carrall streets, you'll see:

❻ Gaoler's Mews

Once the residence and site of Constable Jonathan Miller's police station, the first telegraph office, and fire station, 12 Water St. is now a pretty courtyard with offices, a restaurant, and a coffee shop. You'll also see the glass blocks built into the sidewalks. That's because the basement of the building extends out onto the sidewalk and the glass blocks provide the light. Walk down the stairs to the London School of Hairdressing and you can look up through them to the sidewalk above.

At the intersection of Water and Carrall streets, you'll see:

❼ Maple Tree Square

This is the place where Vancouver quite literally began. You'll also see a statue of Gastown's namesake, Gassy Jack Deighton, a former steamboat captain who talked or "gassed" a lot. Deighton's claim to fame, the story goes, was that he managed to float a barrel of whiskey ashore and persuaded lumberjacks to build Gastown's first saloon in exchange for some of the contents. It was built in 24 hours. In 1870, the village of Gastown, as it was known, officially became Granville.

Half-a-block south of the square is:

❽ Blood Alley

The Alley is so named because of the row of butcher shops that once worked here.

Finish at:

❾ Hastings Street

Just walk up Carrall Street to Hastings Street and several buses, including nos. 4, 7, 10, 16, and 20, can take you back downtown. If you feel like shopping, you'll see the bright orange signage of the **Army & Navy Department Store.** The building was erected in the early 1890s, and the first tenants were the city's first synagogue, the Knights of Pythias, the Vancouver Electric Railway and Light Company, and a subscription Reading Room. Now you can hunt for designer bargains and all sorts of curios you haven't seen since your childhood at this recently renovated store.

If you are still in the mood to walk, just continue up Carrall Street 3 blocks to Chinatown.

Walking Tour: Gastown & Chinatown

Legend

"Take a Break" stop 🍵

Photo Opportunity 📷

GASTOWN
Tourism Vancouver InfoCentre **1** [start]
Canada Place **2**
Granville Square **3**
The Landing **4**
Dominion Hotel **5**
Gaoler's Mews **6**
Maple Tree Square **7**
Blood Alley **8**
Hastings Street **9** [finish]

CHINATOWN
Dr. Sun Yat-sen Classical Chinese Garden **10** [start]
Chinese Cultural Centre **11**
Pender Street **12**
Keefer Street **13**
Chinese Cultural Museum & Archives **14**
International Village **15** [finish]

⌒Fun Fact The Sound of Steam

Many of Vancouver's hospitals and other institutions draw their heat from the city's underground heat system. Because the steam needs an outlet, you'll see concrete planters around the city in unusual places hiding the vents. When Gastown went through its revitalization in the 1970s, the city planner decided that, rather than putting another ugly concrete blob on the sidewalk, Gastown should have a steam clock. After being told it was impossible by horologists (clock makers) around North America, he went to Vancouver's Raymond L. Saunders. Being fairly new to the trade, Saunders didn't know it couldn't be done and was able to build the world's first steam-powered clock in 1977. Unfortunately, the noise made by the 90 pounds of pressure required to power the steam clock could be heard all the way to the West End. So, if you don't recognize the Westminster Chimes when you listen to the Steam Clock, it's because Saunders lowered the pressure and, consequently, the sound—so it changed the tune. Tourists liked it so much that the Gastown Business Improvement Society decided to keep it that way. The clock weighs over 2 tons.

WALKING TOUR 2 CHINATOWN

Some years ago two friends of ours went to Chinatown in search of dinner. They were pretty unimpressed with a tank full of what looked like half-dead rock cod. When one mentioned this to the storekeeper, he threw up his hands and yelled "not dead, not dead." He then retrieved a net, scooped out the fish, and threw it onto the floor, where it flapped its way across the store very much alive. Our friends quickly bought the fish and say it was delicious.

Vancouver's Chinatown is an exotic experience and once you walk into its territory it's like being transported to Hong Kong. My kids are fascinated by the duck and pig carcasses that hang in the butchers' windows, the unusual sweet cakes in the bakeries, and the live bullfrogs in buckets on the street. If nothing else, it's a good lesson in the production of food.

And speaking of food, restaurants are plentiful and you can find one for every budget. There are quite a few bakeries along Pender and Keefer streets with tables and chairs at the back. Many serve dim sum for around C$2 (US$1.30) a plate.

On a Friday, Saturday, or Sunday night between June and September, drop into Chinatown's **night market** between 6:30 and 11pm. You will find fortune tellers, fresh food, and more of the exotic on the 200-block of Keefer Street and 500-block of Main Street.

It's fun to wander about by yourself, but if you're strapped for time, or want more information than you can get wandering around, you can book a tour through the **Chinese Cultural Centre,** 50 E. Pender St. (© **604/687-7993**). Tours take you through the history of Chinatown, its heritage buildings, shops, and temples, and last 90 minutes. Tours operate from June to September daily at 10am and 2:30pm and cost C$5 (US$3.30) for adults, C$4 (US$2.65) for children.

There are several main roads that lead to Chinatown, including Hastings, Main, and Pender streets. You can drive, but don't if you can avoid it. It's busy, traffic crawls along the street, people dart in and out of the traffic, and cars dive for parking spaces. Chinatown is only a 10- to 15-minute walk from downtown Vancouver and easily accessible by several buses that travel down Granville and Hastings streets (get off at Carrall Street), the no. 4 or no. 7 bus from Granville and then down Pender Street, or the Stadium SkyTrain station on Beatty Street near the International Village.

While Chinatown is a pretty small area overall, there is just so much to see and explore that you'll want to give yourself about 2 hours to do it, longer if you plan to eat.

Start: Dr. Sun Yat-sen Classical Chinese Garden.
Finish: International Village.
Time: About 2 hours.

Start your walk in the tranquil:

⑩ Dr. Sun Yat-sen Classical Chinese Garden

The **Dr. Sun Yat-sen Classical Chinese Garden,** 578 Carrall St. between Pender and Keefer streets, is a beautiful garden filled with ponds and sculptures, natural rock formations, and plants. It is the first authentic, full-scale garden built outside China and built to resemble a private garden for very wealthy Chinese. The garden is open from 9:30am to 7pm in the summer, 10am to 6pm in the spring, and 10am to 4:30pm in the winter. The garden holds an Enchanted Evening Series at 7:30pm every Friday night in the summer and you can explore it by lantern light and listen to Asian music in the main hall. If you're in a time crunch, drop in to **Dr. Sun Yat-sen Park**, which is the city-run garden next door. It's not authentic—it uses Mexican lava rock, for example —but it's quite lovely. It's also free and you can sit at the Chinese Pagoda and wander around the pond.

Next to the gardens at 50 E. Pender St. is the:
⓫ Chinese Cultural Centre
You can't miss the China Gate at the entrance—it first stood in front of the China Pavilion during Expo 86. The center runs tours in the summer (see above) and offers classes in Chinese language, arts, and martial arts.

Take a slight detour and turn left onto:
⓬ Pender Street
On the south side of the street you'll come to **Shanghai Alley,** once a thriving settlement and the original site of Chinatown in the 1880s. You can't miss the **Sam Kee Building** next door at 8 W. Pender St., now the home of Jack Chow Insurance. As the signs tend to scream at you, the building has made both the Guinness Book of Records and Ripley's Believe It or Not for being the world's thinnest building. It has a ground-floor width of just 1.5 meters (just under 5 ft.). There is a staircase that runs under the building and once housed communal baths,

toilets, and barbers and led to a tunnel that ran under Carrall Street.

Double back on your path an head for 1 E. Pender St. for the **Chinese Times Building.** Built in 1902 by the Wing Sang Company. The *Chinese Times* published between 1914 and 1994. The structure has a "cheater floor" or an "invisible" mezzanine above the first floor. The idea was to avoid paying tax on one of the floors.

Continue east on Pender Street and you'll pass the **Wing Sang Building** at 67 E. Pender St., built in 1889 and the oldest building in Chinatown. **Market Alley** at the back of the building once produced opium, which was legal in Canada until 1909.

Keep walking along Pender Street and you'll find an array of trading stores and restaurants. **N&S Trading Co.** at 120 Pender St. sells everything from flip flops, jade, and Chinese tea sets to paints, Chinese dominoes, and Chinese happy coats. Across the road, **Bamboo Village** sells beautiful birdcages, dim sum steamers, chairs, sideboards, and baskets.

TAKE A BREAK
You can grab a pork bun, a sweet cake, or another Chinese delicacy to go, or sit down and have some Chinese tea and dim sum at the back of the **New Town Bakery & Restaurant** at 158 E. Pender St. For vegetarian tastes, try the **Buddhist Vegetarian Restaurant** across the road at 137 E. Pender St.

Fun Fact
The Sam Kee Company was one of the wealthiest businesses in the early 1900s and owned by a merchant by the name of Chang Toy. Originally Chang Toy owned a standard 9-meter (30 ft.) lot at the West Pender site, but most of it was appropriated by the City of Vancouver in 1912 in order to widen the street. Legend has it that a neighbor was waiting to purchase the remaining 1.8 meters (6 ft.) very cheaply. In revenge, Chang Toy had this building constructed.

Continue east on Pender past Main Street (this is one of the blocks of the **night market**) and you'll find the crowds get busier and a little pushier, which can be a bit disconcerting with small children. There is plenty to keep the kids occupied here though, with foreign-looking seafood and unusual vegetables spilling out onto the street.

Turn right at Gore Street past more butchers and fish shops and turn right again at:

⓭ Keefer Street

The **Kiu Shun Trading Co.** is at 261 Keefer St. and you can find a herbalist working there 6 days a week. He will make a diagnosis, give consultations, and write prescriptions for various herbs and Chinese medicines in the store. Twenty percent of customers are non-Chinese.

Across the road in the **Sun Wah Centre** at 268 Keefer St., a flea market runs daily from 10am to 6pm. Pick up a snack at **Maxim's** at 257 Keefer St. Kids love the sweet cakes, and it's a popular place to buy your wedding cake.

Stop in for a tea tasting at the **Tea Shop** at the corner of Keefer and Main streets. The purple-coated Chinese ladies recommend the Sphere Jasmine tea from China or the 338 Tung Ting Oolong Tea from Taiwan.

> **TAKE A BREAK**
> If it's lunchtime and you haven't eaten already, go for dim sum at the **Park Lock Seafood Restaurant,** second floor, 544 Main St. (at Keefer St.).

Continue down Keefer Street. If you turn right on Columbia Street, you'll see the:

⓮ Chinese Cultural Museum & Archives

This building is the keeper of Chinatown's fascinating history and backs onto the Dr. Sun Yat-sen Classical Chinese Garden and the start of the tour. Back on Keefer Street, you'll pass the **Chinatown Plaza,** a large bazaar with a small Chinese food fair, lots of stalls with Chinese clothes, toys, and music—feel free to haggle, it's expected —and on the third floor is the enormous **Floata Restaurant.**

At the end of Keefer Street, you'll reach Abbott Street and the:

⓯ International Village

The actual address is 88 W. Pender St., and this newish center, still very much a work in progress at the time of writing, will be full of retail shops and already has a great food court on the second floor with a mixture of Chinese, Japanese, Thai, Indian, Vietnamese, Mexican, awesome desserts, and Sammi's, a shop that serves dozens of variations of Chinese bubble tea, including green apple and taro milkshake. On the third floor there are a dozen stadium-style movie theaters and a video arcade. International Village is also very near to the Stadium SkyTrain station if you want a fast ride back to downtown, or you can take the no. 2, no. 15, or no. 17 bus.

WALKING TOURS 3 & 4 DOWNTOWN ✕ 2

I've suggested two walking tours of downtown Vancouver that may appeal to your family. Neither is very long in distance and they can be started at any point; it really depends on the ages and interests of your children. The walks can also easily be lengthened by adding Gastown or Chinatown or just joining the two downtown tours together.

The first tour takes you through the entertainment district and into Yaletown, the second down through the trendy stores of Robson, one of North America's busiest streets, and into the West End. Of course, you could do Stanley Park here too, but it's so special it's worth a trip of its own.

WALKING TOUR 3 DOWNTOWN #1

Start:	Vancouver Art Gallery.
Finish:	The Roundhouse Community Centre.
Time:	2 hours.

Start at:

❶ Vancouver Art Gallery

750 Hornby St. (at Robson Street). Depending on your group's age and level of interest, you might stop in to check out an impressive collection of Emily Carr and Group of Seven painters. Your kids will probably be thankful if you just hit the gift shop. Turn left on Robson Street and you'll see Chapters on one side and the new and improved Eatons department store on the other.

TAKE A BREAK

Okay, I know you've just started out on your walk, but **Chapters** is just such a cool place for any age, you've got to either stop at the resident **Starbucks** and grab a latte to go, or lounge around on its purple overstuffed furniture with a newspaper or book. There is also a great kids' section with a castle.

Continuing on Robson Street, you'll cross:

❷ Granville Street

This street was the happening place in the 1950s. It fell upon hard times, and in the 1970s, city planners decided to turn it into a pedestrian-only mall. That didn't work, or rather, it's still a work in progress, managing to attract more adult-only stores and street people than trendy nightclubs and restaurants and good wholesome entertainment.

Cross Seymour Street, then just before Homer Street you'll see on the left the:

❸ Westin Grand

This hotel was built to look like a grand piano, by Moshe Safdie, the same architect who built the now closed Ford Centre for the Performing Arts next door, and the **Vancouver Public Library,** which really is meant to look like the Roman Coliseum. The main entrance to the library is on Georgia Street, but you can also enter from Robson Street. There's a food court in the atrium, or if you're after more literary pursuits, there is a truly great kids' section in the library, with computer games, a toddlers' play area, games, and, yes, books, one floor down.

Come back onto Robson Street and retrace your steps half a block and turn southwest onto Homer Street. This will take you down into:

❹ Yaletown

You've entered Vancouver's former warehouse district.

Continue down Homer Street, cross Smithe Street, and turn left on Nelson Street until you hit Mainland Street. You're now in the heart of Yaletown. This is where the warehouses really take advantage of their sloping sites. The fronts of buildings with office space are located uphill. Downhill are the loading bays. Most of the warehouses were built between 1909 and 1913 and are four to six stories high with internal elevators.

Walking Tours: Downtown #1 & Downtown #2

Coal Harbour

Legend
"Take a Break" stop
Information
Photo Opportunity
Beach

Sunset Beach Park

DOWNTOWN #1
Vancouver Art Gallery **1** [start]
Granville Street (Pedestrian Mall) **2**
Westin Grand **3**
Yaletown **4**
Roundhouse Community Centre [finish] **5**
DOWNTOWN #2
Fairmont Hotel Vancouver [start] **6**
Robson Street **7**
Barclay Heritage Square **8**
Roedde House **9**
English Bay **10** [finish]

start here

finish here

Granville Island

Granville Bridge

Cambie St. Bridge

False Creek

False Creek Park

Continue down Mainland Street and turn left at Davie Street. Cross Pacific Boulevard and you'll see the:

❺ Roundhouse Community Centre

The red brick building closest to Davie Street is now the permanent home to Engine 374, a CPR steam train and the first train to cross Canada to Vancouver in 1887. It's usually open on weekends from 11am to 3pm in the winter and daily 11am to 3pm in the summer, and kids can climb up on it and explore.

From here, you can catch a no. 1 or no. 2 bus on Pacific Boulevard back downtown.

TAKE A BREAK
Stop in at the **Yaletown Brewing Company** at the corner of Mainland and Helmcken streets. It's a beautiful building with lots of exposed brick, wide plank floors, and beautiful paintings by local artist Tiko Kerr. The brew kettles are at the back of the bar (it's been voted the best brew pub in Canada 2 years running). There is a lovely outdoor patio on the bricks on the old loading dock, and inside the restaurant you can watch the chefs make pizza at the open kitchen or simply people watch from the windows.

WALKING TOUR 4 DOWNTOWN #2

Start:	Fairmont Hotel Vancouver.
Finish:	English Bay Beach.
Time:	2 hours.

Start at:

❻ Fairmont Hotel Vancouver

Start in the lobby of **Fairmont Hotel Vancouver** at 900 W. Georgia St. (between Burrard and Hornby streets). This lovely old building is smack in the middle of downtown and easily recognizable by its green copper roof and gargoyles. Take the Burrard Street exit and turn left. You'll come to **Vancouver Television** (VTV) at the corner of Burrard and Robson streets. VTV airs its live breakfast show Monday to Friday from 6 to 9am from the street. Next door on Robson Street is the **Planet Hollywood** restaurant and **Virgin Megastore** at what must be the busiest corner in Canada. Oh, and when the kids tell you that they have to buy tapes and CDs at Virgin because they are such a great deal—it's true. Vancouver has the cheapest music of about any city in North America, and most other industrialized countries, and visitors often fill up their suitcases here.

Head northwest along:

❼ Robson Street

Clothes-conscious kids and teenagers will be dazzled. There is designer shop after designer shop sporting brand names such as Armani, Club Monaco, United Colors of Benetton, Roots, Guess, and French Connection. At

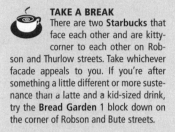

TAKE A BREAK
There are two **Starbucks** that face each other and are kitty-corner to each other on Robson and Thurlow streets. Take whichever facade appeals to you. If you're after something a little different or more sustenance than a latte and a kid-sized drink, try the **Bread Garden** 1 block down on the corner of Robson and Bute streets.

this point, you'll be leaving the downtown core and heading into the West End, one of the densest, and in my humble opinion, most interesting residential areas on the planet.

Window shop your way down Robson Street until you come to Broughton Street and then turn left toward:

❽ Barclay Heritage Square

You're leaving behind the designer duds and restaurants, but instead you'll find a glimpse of life in the West End around the turn of the century. Walk past the beautiful old heritage houses painted in reds and blues and mud yellows and turn right at Barclay Street. You are now at **Barclay Heritage Square,** which is bounded by Haro, Broughton, Barclay, and Nicola streets. There are nine historic houses dating from 1890 and kept pretty much in their original settings.

(Fact

Roedde House architect Francis M. Rattenbury also designed the Parliament Buildings, the Empress Hotel, the Crystal Gardens in Victoria, and a number of banks and courthouses in BC. However, he remains infamous not for his architecture, but for his murder in 1935 by his former mistress Alma Pakenham and her young lover, George Stoner. Alma was acquitted and committed suicide, and Stoner was sentenced to life imprisonment but later released.

---

⑨ Roedde House

Roedde House (1415 Barclay St.), on the corner, is a beautifully restored Queen Anne–style house that was built in 1893. It has a gazebo and a lovely garden with a large magnolia tree in the front. The house, which originally belonged to Gustav Roedde, Vancouver's first book-binder, is now a museum and has guided tours, afternoon teas, and recitals.

You can walk around the square and get a better look at the houses here; there's also a small children's playground at the back of the square near Nicola Street. The house with the sweeping verandah back on Barclay Street is **Barclay Manor,** another Queen Anne–style house built in the 1890s and now used for seniors' events.

Wander down Barclay Street and turn left at Denman Street:

⑩ English Bay

It doesn't seem to matter what time of day or night you are down here—

TAKE A BREAK
Stop in for ice cream at **Mondo Gelato** at 1094 Denman St. (near Comox Street). Its gelato—regular, soy, or yogurt—is a work of art, filled with fresh berries and nuts and chocolate, and the staff are generous with tasting spoons. (The zuppa inglese is to die for.) For larger meals, try **Nats New York Pizzeria** at 1080 Denman St. or **Delany's**, a great local cafe across the street at the corner of Denman and Pendrell streets.

Denman Street is always alive. Walk down toward English Bay and you'll pass half a dozen restaurants, cinemas, and colorful shops.

Join the crowds at **English Bay** and let the kids play or sunbathe at the beach. From here, you can catch the no. 6 bus back downtown via Davie Street.

Off-Leash Walks for Kids with Dogs

The pro-dog people and the anti-doggy do people seem to be constantly at each other's throats regarding what's appropriate in today's doggy society. In other words, regulations change rapidly so it's a good idea to check beforehand if you're not sure. Some parks allow dogs off the leash only in the morning and/or early evenings, others only in the off-season, and others not at all. There are many more, but these are interesting spots to explore and most afford great views of different parts of Vancouver. For more information: in Vancouver call ② **604/257-8400,** in West Vancouver ② **604/925-7204,** and in North Vancouver ② **604/985-7761.**

Dogs are so important in West Vancouver that they have their own section of beach at Ambleside and a parallel fenced runway on the seawall. Take the Lions Gate Bridge to the North Shore and turn left into West Vancouver. Turn left again at the first set of traffic lights at Taylor Way and park at the back of the Park Royal Shopping Centre.

Baden Powell Trail, a 42-kilometer (26 mile) trail that runs from Deep Cove at the eastern point of North Vancouver to Horseshoe Bay in West Vancouver, is terrific for dogs. Of course, you can just pick a small section along the way. From Deep Cove, the trail starts between Cates Park on the Dollarton Highway and Panorama Park.

At **John Henry Park and Trout Lake** in East Vancouver you can let Fido run and swim between 6am and 10pm, but only at the north end of the park. Take Hastings Street east from downtown Vancouver and turn south at Victoria Drive. You can access the park from 15th to 19th avenues.

Lighthouse Park is another park in West Vancouver, but this time with lots of rocky outcrops, forest trails, ocean, fabulous views, and a working lighthouse. Take the Lions Gate Bridge, turn left onto Marine Drive, and continue down this windy road until you reach the turnoff to the park, which is just past Caulfield Cove.

North Vancouver's **Mosquito Park** doesn't have a view, but it has a playground at the entrance and an easy and gentle uphill walk along a creek. Take the Lions Gate Bridge and turn right onto Marine Drive and then left at Fell Avenue. The park starts at the intersection of Fell Avenue, 16th Street, and Larson Road.

Portside Park is a nice grassy inner city park with a sandy beach and a dirty ocean that might be okay for Fido to play in, but don't let the children near it. At the foot of Main Street, the park is accessible by crossing over the Alexander Street overpass.

Spanish Banks is a fabulous beach where dogs are allowed off-leash just west of the concession stand. They are also allowed in nearby **Locarno Park**. From downtown Vancouver take the Granville Bridge and at 4th Avenue exit to the west. Continue along 4th Avenue until it turns into Northwest Marine Drive, and you'll see Spanish Banks just past Locarno Beach.

Don't forget to bring a kite to **Vanier Park**. This is also the home of the **Vancouver Museum**, the **Maritime Museum**, and the **H.R. MacMillan Planetarium**. Take Burrard Street from downtown Vancouver, over the Burrard Street Bridge and onto Cornwall Avenue, turn right on Chestnut Street, and continue down to the park.

WALKING TOUR 5 GRANVILLE ISLAND

My favorite time to visit Granville Island is around 9am. Although the people who work in the market have likely been there for hours, it feels as though the island is just waking up and you can really experience the smell of freshly baked bread. The retail shops don't open until 10am, and it's a great time to grab a latte and check out the boats from the cafe, or wander the boardwalk and chase the pigeons if you're under the age of 6. Even if the weather is lousy, or if you are visiting in the off-season, the kids won't be disappointed. Oh, and another nice thing about wandering this piece of earth with little ones is that there are public washrooms located all over Granville Island.

Start: Granville Island Public Market.
Finish: Granville Island Public Market.
Time: From 2 hours to all day.

Start at:

❶ Granville Island Public Market

Begin at the Granville Island Public Market at the west end of Johnston Street. It's open 7 days a week, 9am to 6pm, except in January when it is closed Mondays for maintenance. Wander through the stalls and get yourself acquainted with the layout, and maybe start thinking about where you'll have lunch on your return.

Stroll along the:

❷ Boardwalk

Follow False Creek past the **Aquabus Ferry** dock and just beyond the **Arts Club Theatre.** You'll find more shops and studios at the **Creekhouse,** as well as the **Ocean Art Works** site, featuring First Nations work. Keep walking along Johnston Street and you'll see **Ocean Cement,** a not-so-subtle reminder of the island's industrial heritage. About halfway down Johnston Street is the **Emily Carr Institute of Art and Design.** You can watch the student artists work away here or visit the free **Charles H. Scott Gallery.**

Next to the college and Pier 32 is:

❸ Sea Village

This is Canada's first legal floating subdivision. There are a dozen floating homes, some quite luxurious.

Beside Sea Village is the:

❹ Granville Island Hotel

The **Granville Island Hotel** is the upmarket accommodation at the east end of the island and if you follow the boardwalk around you'll come to the **Mound,** a grassy parkland that's used for performances or just to bask in the sun. Stop and get your bearings from this elevation above False Creek.

As you leave the Mound, you'll be walking southwest along:

❺ Cartwright Street

The first building is **Performance Works,** a developmental space for actors, musicians, and dancers. You will pass **Arts Umbrella,** an arts organization devoted to kids, then on your left you'll see the tennis courts, the **False Creek Community Centre,** and the **False Creek Racing Canoe Club**—the home of the False Creek Women's Dragon Boating Team.

TAKE A BREAK
Now the kids can get their first major reward. Walk down beside the community center and you'll come to the **Waterpark** and a large kids' playground. The Waterpark, which is open from May through September, has two waterslides and a separate area for toddlers, and gets awfully busy on a summer's day. If they'll sit still long enough, this is a good place for a drink and a snack.

𝘍 Fun Fact

A century and a half ago, False Creek was a rich tidal basin covering four times the area it does today. The area was heavily populated with beaver, muskrat, ducks, trout, and sturgeon. The native village of Snauq (pronounced Sn-owg) fished using traps off the great sand bar now known as Granville Island.

Walking Tour: Granville Island

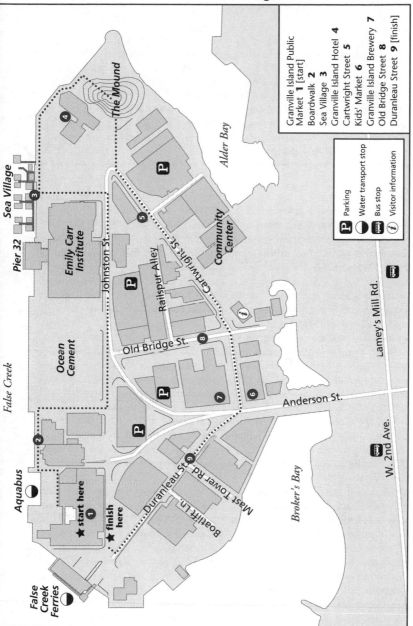

Granville Island Public
Market **1** [start]
Boardwalk **2**
Sea Village **3**
Granville Island Hotel **4**
Cartwright Street **5**
Kids' Market **6**
Granville Island Brewery **7**
Old Bridge Street **8**
Duranleau Street **9** [finish]

P Parking
◗ Water transport stop
▣ Bus stop
(*i*) Visitor information

⌒ Fun Fact

In the early part of the twentieth century, False Creek was an industrial sewer. Sawmills and machine shops dumped their toxic waste into the water. Chemical leaks were common. By 1970, there was no sea life to be seen in the murky, dirty waters surrounding Granville Island. All that's changed. Granville Island has a healthy variety of flora and fauna. Sightings include harbor seals, otters, and beavers; a great blue heron; bald eagles, loons, and cormorants; and the mynah, brought from China around the turn of the century, and the only place on North America where it can be found.

---

❻ Kids' Market

Even if it's sunny, be sure to stop in at the **Kids' Market,** a shopping and playing oasis for little people. If you've brought Fido, at the front of the market is **Doggylicious Deli**—a canine cafe in an old trolley car. Behind the trolley car is a kid-sized door entrance to the market (there's another one for big people, too). In the summer and on holidays, you can find entertainers and face painters on the lawn at the back of the Kids' Market, by the pond. Look for the family of turtles that lives here. There's also a tug boat that the kids can play on permanently moored behind the **Crystal Ark,** a gemstone store with its own indoor cave where kids can dig for polished stones.

❼ Granville Island Brewery

Depending on the age and level of enthusiasm at this point, you can take a shortcut back to the public market by way of Old Bridge Street, which is a little to the east of the Kids' Market (if you're confused, turn right when you come out the front door). Adults may want to make a quick stop at the **Granville Island Brewery** for a taste test, one of the province's first craft breweries. There are tours available and a retail shop.

❽ Old Bridge Street

If you are opting for the shortcut along Old Bridge Street, stop and watch the glass blowers craft hot glass

into jars and bottles at the **New-Small Sterling Glass Studio,** 1440 Old Bridge St. (*②* **604/681-6730**). Turn right at Railspur Alley and you'll see a row of glass-fronted studios with a dozen artists making jewelry or working with textiles or clay in the window. You'll also find **Micon Industries** at the end of the Alley, one of the original businesses on the island and still making drill bits for the mining industry the same way they did in 1930. Keep heading north along Old Bridge Street, and you'll come to Johnston Street where you can turn left and head back to the market.

❾ Duranleau Street

If little people can handle more, when you step outside the Kids' Market cross back under the Granville Bridge to Duranleau Street and the waterfront. Drop in to the **Maritime Market** and see the incredible model train display at the **Granville Island Museum Company,** a pretty amazing place that showcases sport fishing and model ships and trains. Stroll down the waterfront and you can see kayak shops, seafood restaurants, river rafting, and other tour companies.

Be sure to visit the **Lobster Man,** on Mast Tower Road to the left of Duranleau Street. With its huge tanks of live shellfish, Atlantic lobsters, and dung crabs, it's like a giant aquarium for kids. The **Net Loft** is also on Duranleau Street and worth a visit, particularly if you are hankering for a trendy hat, First Nations jewelry, or perhaps some souvenirs. Walk out the front and you are back on Johnston Street and at the Granville Public Market.

If Granville Island has only whetted your appetite, then there are several things you can do from here, all in walking distance. Walk back up Anderson Street, under the Granville Bridge, and you'll come to a tram stop at 2nd Avenue. The **Downtown Vancouver Historic Railway** operates two trams from here to Quebec and 1st avenues, right near **Science World.** Ride it back or take a mini-ferry back to Granville Island, or continue downtown via the Main Street SkyTrain station.

If you're feeling like a longer walk, walk up Anderson Street as above, but turn right along the Foreshore Walk just before West 2nd Avenue. Follow this west and you'll come out at **Vanier Park,** one of the city's finest kite-flying areas, and near the **H.R. MacMillan Space Centre,** the **Vancouver Museum,** and the **Maritime**

Museum. You can catch a mini-ferry here or keep walking along the water —you'll pass a children's playground, a basketball court, and sand volleyball, and end up at **Kits Beach,** one of Vancouver's trendiest summer spots for the body beautiful (but it's still fun if you're less than perfect).

You can take a bus downtown at this point along Cornwall Avenue, or continue up Arbutus Street to West 4th Avenue, a trendy shopping area with dozens of clothing shops, restaurants, and **Capers,** a local organic supermarket. The no. 4 or no. 7 bus will take you back downtown.

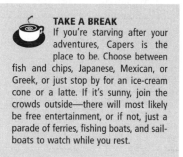

TAKE A BREAK
If you're starving after your adventures, Capers is the place to be. Choose between fish and chips, Japanese, Mexican, or Greek, or just stop by for an ice-cream cone or a latte. If it's sunny, join the crowds outside—there will most likely be free entertainment, or if not, just a parade of ferries, fishing boats, and sailboats to watch while you rest.

Fun Fact

The most expensive boat docked on Granville Island is *Amnesia*, worth C$3,000,000.

WALKING TOUR 6 **EDGEMONT VILLAGE**

Not many people know about this area, which is a pity because it's a super place to bring young children. It is a lovely little village in North Vancouver with a toy shop and a book store especially for kids, a bakery, a great duck pond in a forest setting where kids can climb trees and bridges and dip their feet in the creek's mountain cool water, and tennis courts where the family can play for free. If you are planning to visit **Grouse Mountain,** the **Capilano Suspension Bridge,** or the **Capilano Salmon Hatchery,** the village is right on your way and a perfect place to stop for coffee or a pop.

If you're driving from downtown Vancouver, take Georgia Street west through Stanley Park and over the Lions Gate Bridge and take the exit to North Vancouver. Turn left at Capilano Road, which is the first set of traffic lights off the bridge, and watch your speed limit—it's 50kmph (30 mph)—as the information center on the right is a favorite hangout for traffic police. Keep heading north past the Upper Levels Highway, turn right at Ridgewood Drive, right again at Edgemont Boulevard, and you are in the heart of the village. Park where you can.

Start:	Delany's coffee shop.
Finish:	Delany's coffee shop.
Time:	30 minutes for adults, up to a few hours with kids.

Start at:

❶ Delany's

Delany's ✸ at 3089 Edgemont Blvd. (✆ **604/985-3385**) is part of a really excellent local chain of three coffee shops that has a West Coast feel, a large outdoor patio, floor-to-ceiling windows, tables, or stool seating. It has a patio on the street that seems to be well used all year around, and as it's a meeting place for locals, it always seems to be packed.

Walk down Highland Boulevard past the Capilano Library and turn left at Crescent View Drive. Walk two house lengths and turn right after no. 2905. This is one entrance to the:

❷ Murdo Frazer Park

This park is named after a local reeve who served in the early 1960s and died while in office (although it's not clear from the sign whether he died while actually serving in office, or while at the office).

Go down the 98 stairs (see note) straight in front of you and follow the path over the little wooden bridge to the **duck pond.** This is a great place for a picnic or to just stop for a snack. Bring a bag of food for the ducks also, and kids and ducks will have a great time. On sunny days, you can see the turtles sunning themselves on the rocks.

Take the same path to:

❸ Children's Playground

Follow the same path past a fast-flowing creek in the spring, which turns into a more gentle run in the summer. Children can stop and dip little toes in the water or skip rocks. There are lots of ferns and old fir trees and it has the feel of an ancient forest. Keep walking along the path and you will come to the **tennis courts.** There are seven of them and two large green practice walls. Turn right at the end of the tennis courts and follow Elizabeth Way up past the **children's playground,** which has swings and slides and a jungle gym, and turn right at Paisley Road. The mountains are straight ahead and you follow this street until you get to Ridgewood Drive. Turn right by the creek, continue up to Edgemont Boulevard, and you're back at the village.

Accessible by Wheel

If you have a person in your party in a wheelchair or a child in a stroller and cannot manage the stairs to the park, you can go to another entrance. As you come up Capilano Road, turn right at Ridgeway as if you were going into the village, but turn right at Paisley Road, two streets before Edgemont Boulevard. Follow the road down until you come to Elizabeth Way and then turn left. You'll see the playground on your left and you enter the park by the tennis courts and follow the trail until you reach the duck pond.

TAKE A BREAK
Edgemont Village has about 70 shops including a **Starbucks** coffee shop with a kids' table and Lego blocks. There is a **Rocky Mountain Chocolate Factory,** where you can often watch staff making caramel apples with Smarties or Irish creme fudge or perhaps chocolate marshmallow pops in the front window. They also sell awesome gelato.

The entire walk takes just under half an hour for an adult and a couple of hours with little ones.

Now that you're back at **Delany's** reward yourself with a coffee. The coffee shop also has excellent grilled panini sandwiches, homemade soups, Rocky Road bars, and delicious lemon squares. Grab a latte and treat the kids to a cocoa for C95¢ (US65¢) or a Jones Soda.

For extra fun try:
❹ BC Playthings
Kids of about 8 and under will thank you if you cross the street and drop in to tiny **BC Playthings,** a toy store that sells everything from paints and construction paper to large puppet people and sturdy wooden jigsaws for toddlers. Walk another block and you'll find the equally fine **Kids Books,** another wonderful store with a huge selection of books, cassettes, crafts, and puppets for babies up to late teens.

TAKE A BREAK
Continue walking along Edgemont Village, then turn right at the traffic lights. Here you'll find the **Bakehouse,** hidden at 1050 W. Queens Rd., with wonderful breads and pies of all sizes and shapes to take out or eat in. In the winter there is a roaring fire and in the summer you can sit outside at the small patio.

❺ Columbus Farm Market
At the corner of Edgemont Village and West Queens Road is the **Columbus Farm Market,** where people come from miles away to buy mainly local produce at good prices. Note that they don't take credit cards.

9

Entertainment for the Whole Family

Let's get this out of the way first. Vancouver is not New York or even Toronto. Especially since the demise of the Ford Centre for the Performing Arts, we rarely stage large musicals, nor do we have Broadway-type shows that run for years. What we do have are some great venues and professional theater, dance, and music groups to fill them.

In a way, Vancouver is an ideal place to introduce your children to the arts and spectator sports. It's more grassroots, often more about doing than watching, usually held in a casual, non-threatening setting. Go to the opera or the ballet and you'll find ball gowns standing next to jeans and sneakers, no one is turned away, and well-behaved kids are welcomed.

The theater season tends to run from September to April, while festivals and events rooted in the community fill the warmer months. Many arts companies recognize that the future rests on today's children, so many productions are aimed at children or at least tend to have universal appeal.

FINDING OUT WHAT'S ON

There are two local parent monthlies that have calendars of upcoming events and entertainment options. Both have websites and are available free from public libraries, recreational centers, malls, and just about anywhere kids hang out. Look for *West-Coast Families* magazine (www.westcoastfamilies.com) and *BC Parent* newsmagazine (www.bcparent.com). The annual *Kids' Guide* put out by *Where* magazine is an excellent resource and you can either pick it up free at tourist information centers, hotels, and border crossings when you are in Vancouver or call © **604/736-5586** or email info@wherevancouver.com for a free copy before you leave home. The *Vancouver Sun* (www.vancouversun.com), the city's largest daily newspaper, publishes "Queue," a full entertainment section every Thursday, and the *Georgia Straight* (www.straight.com), a free weekly magazine that comes out every Thursday with up-to-date listings can be found at most of the same places as the parenting magazines. *Vancouver Magazine* is a monthly fashion and city magazine at www.vanmag.com. There is a variety of websites that have travel, entertainment, and attractions information. Some of the better ones are www.vancouver-bc.com, www.mybc.com, and www.vancouvertoday.com.

There's also the hotline for the **Alliance for Arts and Culture,** 100-938 Howe St. (between Smithe and Nelson sts.), Vancouver, at © **604/684-2787** or www.allianceforarts.com. It's a great source for music, theater, films, dance, and performing arts, including where and how to get tickets. You can also drop into the arts information center Monday to Friday 9am to 5pm and gather brochures, posters, and other information about what's going on in the local arts community.

GETTING TICKETS

TicketMaster   TicketMaster appears to have the same monopoly on venues as in most Canadian cities, along with service charges and a handling fee. You can sometimes save a couple of dollars by going straight to the venue's box office. (Vancouver Ticket Centre) 1304 Hornby St. (at Drake Street), Vancouver. ℂ **604/280-3311.** www. ticketmaster.ca.

Tips Calling All Bargain Hunters

While you can't buy half-price tickets the day of a show as you can in many other North American cities (although I'm told it's something the city is looking into), there are "pay what you can" matinees and dress rehearsals that are either free or very inexpensive in a production's preview week. Because they are rarely advertised, it does take time to hunt them down. Phone the **Arts Hotline** at ℂ **604/684-2787** and also phone the various companies if you see a production that has yet to premier.

---

1 The Big Venues

The Chan Centre for the Performing Arts   Bing Thom, a local architect, designed this 1,400-seat theater, which is said to have the city's best acoustics. The theater showcases the work of UBC's School of Music and Department of Theatre and Film as well as ceremonies, festivals, and a winter concert series. For architectural buffs, tours are held at 1pm every Thursday and are free of charge. 6265 Crescent Rd. (at the UBC campus). ℂ **604/822-9197.** www.chancentre.com. Walking tours ℂ **604/822-1815.**

The Orpheum Theatre   Home of the Vancouver Symphony Orchestra since 1977, the Orpheum originally opened in 1927 as a vaudeville house. The theater's ornate interior is filled with crystal chandeliers, gilded arches, and domes, and also hosts a variety of pop, classical, choral, and chamber recitals. 801 Granville St. (at Smithe and Seymour sts.). ℂ **604/665-3050.** www.city.vancouver.bc.ca/theatres.

The Queen Elizabeth Complex   This theater complex houses the Queen Elizabeth Theatre and the Vancouver Playhouse. The 668-seat Playhouse opened in 1962, 3 years after the Queen Elizabeth Theatre, and hosts the Vancouver Playhouse Theatre Company, Friends of Chamber Music, and the Vancouver Recital Society, plus chamber music performances and recitals. The Queen Elizabeth Theatre hosts major national and touring musical and theater productions. It is also the home of Ballet British Columbia and the Vancouver Opera and has more than 2,700 seats. Check out the Mezzanine Art Gallery, which changes every month with a new exhibit by new or emerging local artists. 600 Hamilton St. (at Dunsmuir St.). ℂ **604/665-3050.** www.city.vancouver.bc.ca/theatres.

2 The Not-So-Big Venues

While lacking in size and financial clout, the city of Vancouver also has a number of smaller venues worth a mention.

Arts Club Theatre   This theater at the Granville Island Stage holds year-round productions ranging from musicals and comedies to new works and classics. There is also the Revue Stage next door, home to Vancouver TheatreSports, and the relatively newly acquired and renovated 1931 Art Deco Stanley Theatre. 1585 Johnston St. (Granville Island) and the Stanley Theatre, 2750 Granville St. (at 12th Ave.). ✆ 604/687-1644. www.artsclub.com.

The Firehall Arts Centre   This was a functioning firehall until 1975 when the firefighters moved out of Vancouver's Firehouse No. 1, and the arts moved in. More than 300 theatrical and dance performances that reflect Canada's cultural mosaic are held here each year. 280 E. Cordova St. (at Gore St.). ✆ **604/689-0926**, www.firehall.org.

Vancouver East Cultural Centre *(Value*   A former church built in 1909, the "Cultch," as it is known by locals, puts on some of the more interesting dance, music, and avant-garde theatrical productions, performances by international musical groups, festivals, and cultural events. It also runs a series of six children's performances for 5- to 11-year-olds on Saturday afternoons from September to May, sells a youth pass for C$2 (US$1.30) for 14- to 19-year-olds to any show, and hands the programming over to a group of 14- to 19-year-olds who program dance, music, and theater in the second week of May. 1895 Venables St. (at Victoria St.), East Vancouver. ✆ **604/251-1363**. www.vecc.bc.ca.

3 Seasonal Events

Reel to Real Film Festival   **Ages 8 and up.** This international film festival is geared entirely to kids aged 8 and up. It also has filmmaking activities for kids to do when they're not actually watching the movies. Held first Wednesday in March. Tickets C$5 (US$3.30). Tinseltown Cinemas, 88 W. Pender St. (at Abbott St.). ✆ **604/224-6162**. www.eciad.bc.ca/r2r.

Spring Break Theatre Festival *(Finds*   **Ages 4 and up**. Here is a chance to see work from local professional theater companies that is usually only seen in the schools. The festival runs 2 to 3 shows a day in March at Green Thumb Theatre, Hooked on Books, Axis Theatre, and other local companies. Main performances at Granville Island. ✆ **604/738-7013**. All tickets C$7.50 (US$4.95). Also at Shadbolt Centre for the Arts, 6450 Deer Lake Ave. (at Canada Way), Burnaby ✆ **604/291-6864**, and the Surrey Arts Centre, 13750 88th Ave. (at King George Ave.), Surrey ✆ **604/501-5566**.

Vancouver International Children's Festival *(Finds*   **Ages 2 to teens.** See the best children's performers from all over the world, and browse through 20-plus educational and activity tents, dance, music and storytelling workshops, and crafts to make and take. Starts last Monday in May and runs for 1 week. The festival is busiest on the weekends, but the last Friday also gets quite packed with school visits. Vanier Park (Ogden Ave. at Chestnut St.). ✆ **604/708-5655**. www.vancouverchildrensfestival.com. All tickets C$5 (US$3.30) to the festival and can be bought at the site. Performance prices C$6.25–$13.90 (US$4.15–$9.15). You can buy advance tickets to performances through TicketMaster ✆ **604/280-4444** (which also gives you free admittance to the site) or order online at www.ticketmaster.ca. The weekend before the festival there are free performances 11:30am–4pm at Granville Island on the stage behind the public market.

Haywood Bandstand   All ages. A mix of professional and community-based live music aimed at all age groups performed at the bandstand, representing a cross section of Vancouver's ethnic communities. Held every Sunday weather permitting from 2 to 4pm from the May long weekend to September Labour Day. Haywood Park (across from English Bay at Bidwell St. and Beach Ave.). © 604/257-8400. Free.

Bard on the Beach Shakespeare Festival *(Finds* **Ages 8 and up.** Even if you're not a fan of Shakespeare, you have to love the location. Held in a 520-seat open-ended tent you have fabulous sea, mountain, and city views. Plays run 2 to 3 hours and some are obviously more suitable for children than others. In the past productions have included *Anthony and Cleopatra, The Taming of the Shrew,* and *Romeo and Juliet.* Dress warmly and bring a blanket and a cushion to sit on. Runs from mid-June until late September. Vanier Park (Ogden Ave. at Chestnut St.). © 604/737-0625. www.bardonthebeach.org. All tickets C$23–$25 (US$15.20–$16.50).

Dance at Dusk at Ceperley Park   All ages. Take free lessons in Scottish country dancing, international folk dancing, ballroom dancing, and West African dance, which run Monday to Thursday 7 to 9:30pm, weather permitting, from mid-June to mid-August. Second Beach, Stanley Park. © 604/257-8400. Free.

Kitsilano Showboat   All ages. Take in everything from square dancing to martial arts and Hawaiian dancing in an open-air theater at the beach. Runs from late June to late August, weather permitting, Monday, Wednesday, and Friday nights 7:30 to 9:30pm. 2300 Cornwall Ave. (at Kitsilano Park). © 604/734-7332 or 604/733-7297. Free.

Vancouver International Jazz Festival   All ages. This 10-day festival in late June features more than 1,500 musicians from Canada and around the world performing at 40 venues around the city and playing all sorts of jazz as well as blues, funk, and Latin fusion. Look for the huge outdoor stage at David Lam Park off Pacific Boulevard in Yaletown and next to the Roundhouse Community Centre, which holds more indoor stages. There is also a kids' zone called Kid.calm, with face painting, board games, and other activities where kids can make their own musical instruments or just burn off steam at the adjacent playground. Other locations include Gastown's Water Street, the Dr. Sun Yat-sen Classical Garden, and Lonsdale Quay in North Vancouver. © 604/872-5200. Prices range from free to C$50 (US$33) for events at the Orpheum Theatre.

Vancouver Folk Music Festival   All ages. Enjoy folk music performances from around the world and a festive market atmosphere held on a weekend in mid-July. Jericho Beach Park (off Point Grey Road). © 604/602-9798. www.festival.bc.ca. Tickets (Sat or Sun) C$50 (US$33) adults, C$25 (US$16.50) youth 13–18, C$6 (US$3.30) children 3–12.

Vancouver Storytelling Festival   All ages. While the majority of the festival is aimed at an adult audience, this festival does include some children's programming, and it usually sells out. Events take place at various venues during the first weekend in November. For information call © 604/876-2272. Ticket prices for the children's programming are around C$5 (US$3.30).

Theatre Under the Stars   Ages 4 and up. Dress warmly, because it chills off quickly, and toss in a few blankets to sit on and wear. Also toss in dinner or at least an after-dinner snack. Most plays are family-friendly and *Annie Get Your Gun, Oklahoma, West Side Story,* and *Little Orphan Annie* are just a few of the past productions. Runs from mid-July to mid-August. Malkin Bowl, behind the Pavilion at Stanley Park. © 604/687-0174. Tickets C$22 (US$14.50) adults, C$16 (US$10.55) children.

4 Dance

Vancouver is a major Canadian dance city with 18 professional dance companies and 40 independent choreographers. You can pretty much find a group for any taste—from traditional Japanese and Chinese dance, to Brazilian heritage, to modern and classical ballet. Look for Ache Brasil Music & Dance, EDAM Performing Arts, Karen Jamieson Dance, Kokoro Dance Company, and others performing at local theaters and festivals throughout the year. For fans of modern dance, the **Dancing on the Edge Festival** (✆ **604/689-0691**) presents 60 to 80 original pieces over 10 days in July. Most programs are suitable for young fans of dance, but some have nudity and are a bit risqué, so call ahead to check.

Ballet British Columbia   Vancouver's classical ballet company stages productions at the Queen Elizabeth Theatre. In the past, productions have included *Swan Lake, Beauty and the Beast, The Nutcracker,* and *Gizelle.* As well as original choreography by Ballet BC, look for productions by visiting companies such as the American Ballet Theatre, the Royal Winnipeg Ballet, and the Moscow Classical Ballet. These productions are full-length ballets, so suitability largely depends on the child. In general most productions would be suitable for about 9 and up. Queen Elizabeth Theatre, 600 Hamilton St. ✆ 604/732-5003. www.balletbc.com. Tickets C$20–$46 (US$13–$30).

The Dance Centre   Find out information on Vancouver's dance companies. 400-873 Beatty St. ✆ 604/606-6405. www.vkool.com/dancentre.

5 Children's Theater Companies

Most of these professional companies tour a large part of the year, and when at home, perform mostly at elementary schools around the Lower Mainland. You can catch them at the March **Spring Break Theatre Festival** at Granville Island and sometimes at children's series concerts around Vancouver.

Axis Theatre   Ages 5 to 14. This Vancouver touring company has 25 years of experience in producing original physical theater for all ages. 203-1398 Cartwright St. ✆ 604/669-0631. www.axistheatre.com.

Carousel Theatre   Ages 7 and up. When at home, this local company stages most of its productions at the Waterfront Theatre on Granville Island. 1411 Cartwright St., Granville Island. ✆ 604/669-3410.

Green Thumb Theatre   Ages 5 to 17. This theater company produces original Canadian scripts for children, exploring everything from racism and bullying to illiteracy to abuse. 1885 Venables St. ✆ 604/254-4055. www.greenthumb.bc.ca.

Hooked on Books   Ages 4 to 9. Based on the belief that reading stimulates the imagination, this company presents plays based on children's books, but mixes up the plot with the actors' quirky humor. Often they'll finish on a cliffhanger to encourage kids to go out and read the actual book. 2965 W. 29th Ave. ✆ 604/736-2492. www.hookedonbooks.net.

Vancouver TheatreSports League   Ages 10 and up. This 20-year-old Vancouver institution plays at the New Revue Stage on Granville Island from Wednesday to Saturday. The late shows are definitely raunchy, but the weekday 7:30pm shows and the weekend 8pm shows are a lot of fun for older kids and it's a great way to see comedy improv—no scripts, no rehearsals, just quick thinking and spoofs based on audience suggestions. TheatreSports office at 104-1177 W. Broadway Ave. ✆ 604/738-7013. www.vtsl.com. Wed–Thurs C$12.50 (US$8.25) adults, C$9.50 (US$6.25) children; Fri–Sat C$14.50 (US$9.55) adults, C$11.50 (US$7.60) children.

Fun Fact

Track down a movie or TV star through the **BC Film Commission,** BC Business Info Centre, main floor, 601 W. Cordova St. (at the SeaBus Terminal) (℃ **604/660-2732;** www.bcfilmcommission.com). You can always tell that a movie or TV series is being shot if you see big white trailers parked head to toe along a block or two of city streets. Or you can pick up the BC Film Commission's Film List of projects in production.

---

6 Films

There are all the usual theater chains showing the latest in box office hits—Capital 6, Cineplex Odeon, Famous Players—but there are also giant screen theaters and others specializing in foreign films, independent films, and second runs. Adult prices for evening shows at the regular cinemas tend to be from C$9.75 to $10.50 (US$6.45 to $6.95) for adults and C$5.50 (US$3.65) for children. For real film buffs (but for only those aged over 18), the **Vancouver International Film Festival** (℃ **604/685-0260;** www.viff.org) holds its annual festival in September/October with 250 new works from filmmakers from 40 countries.

BIG SCREEN THEATERS

The screens in these theaters are five stories high, and the size and the sound tend to pack a double sensory wallop for sensitive kids. Shows that have screened in this format include *Everest, Olympic Glory, The Mysteries of Egypt,* and great nature shows.

CN IMAX Theatre   201-999 Canada Place (at SeaBus Terminal and Waterfront SkyTrain Station). ℃ **800/582-4629** or 604/682-4629. Tickets C$10 (US$6.60) adults, C$8.50 (US$5.60) 4–12, double feature C$14.50 (US$9.55) adults, C$12.50 (US$8.25) 4–12, kids under 4 free.

OMNIMAX Theatre   During the day you must also buy an admission to Science World. 1455 Quebec St. (at Science World). ℃ **604/443-7443.** C$19.75 (US$13.05) adults, C$14.25 (US$9.40) children. Evenings for OMNIMAX only C$14.75 (US$9.75) adults, C$9.25 (US$6.10) children, kids under 4 free.

REPERTORY THEATERS

These are usually independently run theaters that show second-run movies, many of which are double features for the same price. Tickets are usually around C$5 (US$3.30) adults, C$3.50 (US$2.30) children.

Denman Place Discount Cinema   Single features are C$4 (US$2.65) adults C$2 (US$1.30) for children. 124-1030 Denman St., West End. ℃ **604/683-2201.**

Hollywood Theatre   On Mondays everyone pays C$3.50 (US$2.30) for two feature films. 3123 W. Broadway Ave. (at Balaclava St.). ℃ **604/738-3211.**

Ridge Theatre   This cinema features a soundproofed, glassed-in baby room with 8 seats so you can still watch the movie with a fussy baby without disturbing the rest of the audience. 3131 Arbutus St. (at 16th Ave.). ℃ **604/738-6311.**

FOREIGN FILMS

Fifth Avenue   Evening tickets are C$10.50 (US$6.85) for adults, C$6 (US$4) seniors and children any show, any time. 2110 Burrard St. (at W. 5th Ave.). ℃ **604/734-7469.**

Pacific Cinemathèque   Annual membership fee of C$6 (US$4) payable at door; first admission half price. Call for details. 1131 Howe St. (between Helmcken and Davie sts.). ℂ 604/688-3456. www.cinematheque.bc.ca.

Vancouver East Cinema   On Tuesdays everyone pays C$2.50 (US$1.65). 2290 Commercial Dr. (at 7th Ave.), East Side. ℂ 604/251-1313.

Fun Fact   **10 Movies Shot in Vancouver**

As the third largest movie-making city in the world (after Los Angeles and New York), Vancouver is Hollywood North. Unfortunately, Vancouver is rarely Vancouver in these movies, and some of the movies are just plain bad, some have major league stars, while others are very recognizable at the box office.

3000 Miles to Graceland, 2001. Starring Kevin Costner, Kurt Russell, and Courteney Cox.

The Sixth Day, 2000. Starring Arnold Schwarzenegger and a cameo by the Vancouver Public Library.

MVP: Most Valuable Primate, 2000. An ice-hockey movie with a chimp, starring Jamie Renee Smith and Kevin Morrow and set in Nelson, BC, and Vancouver's General Motors Place Stadium.

Double Jeopardy, 1999. Starring Tommy Lee Jones, Ashley Judd, and Bruce Greenwood and spectacular coastal scenery.

The Sweet Hereafter, 1997. Starring Ian Holm, Bruce Greenwood, and Sarah Polley and directed by Atom Egoyan.

Titanic, 1997. Written and directed by James Cameron. Starring Leonardo DiCaprio and Kate Winslet.

Little Women, 1994. Directed by Gillian Armstrong of Australia and starring Winona Ryder, Claire Danes, and Susan Sarandon. Mostly filmed in Victoria.

Bird on a Wire, 1990. Starring Mel Gibson, Goldie Hawn, and some great shots of the Amazon section at the Vancouver Aquarium.

The Accused, 1988. Oscar-winning performance by Jodie Foster.

McCabe and Mrs. Miller, 1971. Starring Warren Beatty and Julie Christie and directed by Robert Altman.

---

7 Music

Cafe Champlain   On the last Friday of every month from September to May, the community center at Champlain Heights Community School puts on a night of blues, folk, or perhaps individual local talent for families. There is also a play area for restless little ones. Champlain Heights Community School, 6955 Frontenac St. (at 49th Ave.). ℂ 604/257-8315.

Canadian Music Centre   The center maintains a circulating library of 16,000 titles as well as information on Canadian composers and their works. Recordings, reference works, and composers' supplies are available for sale. The library services are free. 837 Davie St. ℂ 604/734-4622. www.musiccentre.ca. Open Mon–Fri 9am–5pm.

The Rogue Folk Club   This local club puts on over 50 concerts a year of Celtic, folk, and roots music. It's open to all ages and the audience is encouraged to dance and interact with the performers. The Wise Hall, 1882 Adanac St. © 604/736-3022. www.roguefolk.bc.ca.

Vancouver Opera   While some operas are definitely not kid-friendly, productions such as *The Magic Flute, The Marriage of Figaro,* or *The Barber of Seville* are suitable for kids aged 10 and up. 845 Cambie St. © 604/683-0222. Tickets C$18–$100 (US$11.90–$66).

(*Tips*   **The Arts for Less**

Look for last-minute deals on good seats sold 1 hour before the performance for C$25 (US$16.50).

Vancouver Symphony Orchestra   The VSO is the largest arts organization west of Ontario, and the third largest symphony orchestra in Canada. The orchestra presents over 140 concerts annually at the Orpheum Theatre and they include a really wonderful Kids Koncerts series that runs between October and June for kids aged 4 to 12. These performances run an hour and a quarter, and my kids still talk about the finale that played the theme from *The Simpsons* television series. 601 Smithe St. © 604/876-3434 or 604/684-9100. www.vancouver symphony.ca. Cost for Kids Koncerts C$23.75 (US$15.70) adults, C$17 (US$11.20) 13 and under.

8 Story Hours

Most public libraries offer a free range of story times from story times with rhymes and songs for babies to story times for toddlers, and story times for preschoolers with songs and activities. While these don't usually run in the summer, the library system offers an annual Summer Reading Club program for children 6 to 12. Kids collect stickers each week, and get bookmarks and coupons to various attractions. At the end they get to choose a book to keep. The main library, the **Vancouver Public Library,** is at 350 W. Georgia St. Call for times and locations of branches around Vancouver (© 604/331-3600; www.vpl.vancouver.bc.ca). Besides the libraries, free regular story readings are held at **Chapters** (788 Robson St. at Howe St. © 604/682-4066) at 3pm Sunday to Friday for kids. On Saturdays the store also holds free children's crazy crafts at 3pm. There are also free readings at **Indigo Books, Music & Cafe** (Lynn Valley Centre, 1199 Lynn Valley Rd. at Mountain Hwy., North Vancouver. © 604/904-7970). Story time is at 11am daily. Older kids will love the checkerboard tables and puck-sized pieces for playing checkers next to the cafe.

9 Spectator Sports

BC Lions Football Club   The Lions are Vancouver's darlings after winning the Grey Cup in 2000. The team is part of the Canadian Football League and plays July to November. While kids don't get a break in the ticket prices, the club has a deal where it sells Cub Zone seats for C$20 (US$13.20). Kids under about 8 can sit in a special section, and while it's not a babysitting service, kids are in full view of their parents, able to run around, get visits from a clown, can be taken to the washroom, and are generally watched over by a group of volunteers. BC Place Stadium, 777 Pacific Blvd. (at Robson St.). ℂ **604/589-ROAR**. www.bclions.com. Tickets C$20–$60 (US$13–$40).

Vancouver Canadians Vancouver's Triple-A baseball team play April to September. Nat Bailey Stadium, 4601 Ontario St. (between Cambie and Main sts). ℂ **604/ 872-5232**. www.canadiansbaseball.com. Tickets C$7–$10.50 (US$4.60–$6.95).

Vancouver Canucks Part of the National Hockey League, the Canucks play from September to May. General Motors Place, 800 Griffiths Way (at Expo Blvd.). ℂ **604/ 899-4625**. www.orcabay.com. Tickets C$31–$120 (US$21–$80).

⌒ Tips

General Motors Place (ℂ **604/899-7440**) offers tours of the facilities that get you behind the scenes of the arena and into the dressing rooms of the **Vancouver Canucks** hockey team and the NBA's former **Vancouver Grizzlies** and into the hospitality suites of those with the big bucks. Tours operate every Wednesday and Friday from 10:30am to 1:30pm. The arena is at 800 Griffiths Way, with tickets sold at Gate 6 on Abbott Street at Pacific Boulevard. There is a family rate for two adults and two children of C$25 (US$16.50); otherwise it's C$9 (US$6) for adults, C$4 (US$2.65) for children, and kids under 5 are free.

Vancouver Giants Vancouver's Western Hockey League is part of the Canadian Hockey League, and a lot cheaper than the professionals if you're hankering to see a game. The Giants played their first season in 2001 and you can catch them at the Pacific Coliseum, at Exhibition Park, East Vancouver, from September to May. ℂ **604/444-2687**. www.vancouvergiants.com. Tickets C$11.50–$15.50 (US$8–$10) a game.

Vancouver Whitecaps This is the professional soccer club formerly called the Vancouver 86ers. Swanguard Stadium, Central Park, Boundary and Kingsway, Burnaby. ℂ **604/930-2255**. www.whitecaps.com. Tickets C$10 (US$6.60), reserved seating C$15–$20 (US$10–$13) adults, C$9–$14 (US$6–$9) children.

Western Lacrosse Association The season runs from May to September at six different venues around Greater Vancouver. 4041B Remi Place, Burnaby. ℂ **604/421-9755**. www.theboxrocks.com.

⌒ Fun Fact

BC Place Stadium was built in 1983 and is the world's largest air-supported domed stadium. It has a circumference of 760 meters (2,500 ft.) and a 60-meter (197 ft.) height and covers 10 hectares (25 acres). It has been dubbed the giant pincushion because of the air-venting system that keeps the dome stable. The roof is constructed of teflon-coated fiberglass.

---

10 Tea Parties

You don't need to be a member of the Royal Family to enjoy the experience of high tea.

Fairmont Hotel Vancouver   This grand old hotel serves traditional afternoon tea service with scones and small finger sandwiches in the lobby lounge. Unfortunately that means you also have to be over 18 to partake. The Griffin Restaurant also serves high tea in a more kid-friendly setting. 900 W. Georgia St. (at Burrard St.). © 604/684-3131. Adults C$21.50 (US$14), children C$10.75 (US$7). Daily 2–4pm.

The Secret Garden Tea Company   This tea service includes scones, pastries, finger sandwiches, and chocolates. There is also a children's service for kids aged up to about 12 for C$12.95 (US$8.55) that offers smaller portions and treats to appeal more to kids, such as peanut butter teddy bears and banana pin-wheel sandwiches. A couple of times a month, the restaurant holds a special high tea with a live harpist. This is C$20.95 (US$13.85) and usually has a theme such as Mother's Day, Easter, or Christmas and the foods are fancier than the daily tea. 5559 West Blvd. (between 39th and 40th aves.). © 604/261-3070. Regular prices are full tea C$20 (US$13), half tea C$12 (US$8). Mon–Fri noon–4:30pm; Sat–Sun noon, 2pm, and 4pm sittings.

The Teahouse in Stanley Park   This restaurant has a truly awesome setting with drop-dead views of English Bay. It might be a bit much for really young children, but older kids might enjoy the afternoon tea and a selection of fancy finger sandwiches, scones, and tea cakes served on a three-tiered serving platter with tea served in dainty porcelain cups. Stanley Park. © 604/669-3281. C$17.95 (US$11.85). Mon–Fri 2:30–4pm, Sat–Sun noon, 2pm, and 4pm sittings. Enter Stanley Park from W. Georgia St. and follow the signs to the Tea House.

Tearoom T   Enjoy an English-style tea, scones, and cookies served on fine china. Kids may prefer the herbal fruit teas. Kids can also just order dessert—apple turnovers and various cakes and bars. 1568 W. Broadway Ave. (between Granville and Fir sts.). © 604/730-8390. Open Mon–Sat 9:30am–7pm, 11am–6pm Sun. Traditional tea is served 2–5pm.

10

Shopping for the Whole Family

If you have a 9- to 13-year-old you are no doubt aware that for the last few years marketers have been swooning over this target group, the group they call "the tweens." In Canada alone, this group of kids is said to have billions of dollars a year to spend on anything their little heart desires, and that means clothes, toys, music, snowboards, and whatever else strikes their fancy.

Vancouver, like any decent North American city, has accommodated the tweens' desires in its shops. Here you will find a plethora of toy stores, clothing stores, bookstores, arts and crafts suppliers, and sporting goods stores. The main shopping districts are outlined below, as are malls, upscale designer boutiques, department stores, and the much less expensive consignment stores that are scattered around the city. There is the Kids' Market at Granville Island, a funky two-story building with a child-sized entrance crammed full of retail stores, a video arcade and an adventure zone, and a restaurant. I've included a few venues for adults, too, with suggestions for fashion, art, and souvenirs.

STORE HOURS Most stores in downtown Vancouver and in the malls are open Monday to Wednesday 10am to 6pm, Thursday and Friday 10am to 9pm, Saturday 10am to 6pm, and Sunday and public holidays noon to 5pm.

TAX The provincial sales tax (PST) in British Columbia is 7% and the federal goods and services tax (GST) is another whopping 7% on top of any purchase price. While it's a bit complicated as to what applies to what, generally GST applies to everything except groceries, and PST does not apply to children's clothing and shoes for kids under the age of 15.

1 The Shopping Scene

SHOPPING DISTRICTS
ROBSON STREET

If Vancouver became a happening city after Expo 86, Robson became the happening street. No doubt about it, this is the destination for expanding upscale retailers. Here you'll find Armani Exchange, Banana Republic, The Gap and Gap Kids, Virgin Megastore, and Planet Hollywood. While Robson Street runs from BC Place Stadium to Stanley Park, the three blocks catching all the attention—1000, 1100, and 1200—run from Burrard to Jervis streets. Particularly in the summer, stores stay open quite late. Pre-teens, tweens, and teens will love this street.

THE DOWNTOWN CORE

The intersection of West Georgia Street and Granville Street is dominated by The Bay and Eatons, Canada's two major department stores. They also sit on top of the underground malls of the Pacific Centre and Vancouver Centre. Entrances to the Royal Centre Mall are further down the street at the Hyatt Regency Hotel at the intersection of Georgia and Burrard streets. Here you'll find designer clothing, sportswear, and jewelry, all out of the rain.

WATER STREET

Right in the heart of Gastown, you can pick up everything from tacky souvenir ashtrays to collectible Barbie dolls and stunning First Nations art and jewelry. Check out The Landing near the SeaBus Terminal, a 1905 heritage warehouse renovated to house upscale retailers and a mix of expensive and funky restaurants, and then wander down through the cobblestones and wrought-iron lamps of Water Street. This area has things for all ages.

YALETOWN

Bordered by Homer, Mainland, Davie, and Nelson streets, Yaletown is a small slice of city that's been compared to SoHo in New York. It's an area that has transformed warehouses into luxury lofts, converted loading docks into fashionable eating terraces, and turned wholesale operations into a Mecca for the fashion conscious. It's where you can shop for both clothes and lunch at a place like the Boy's Co. General Store, pick up an apple and brie sandwich on fig and anise bread, or buy a Versace shirt.

GRANVILLE ISLAND

Just under the Granville Bridge, and not really an island, you will find a wonderful public market, a lively arts and crafts community, and the Kids' Market, which has everything your child could want, from clothes to books to kites, a climbing area, and a video arcade. You can buy a fresh salmon at the market, get a live lobster from the Lobster Man, or chase pigeons on the pier. When the kids tire of shopping, head to the waterpark and waterslide near the Kids' Market.

SOUTH GRANVILLE

The 10-block stretch of Granville Street from 6th Avenue up to 16th Avenue has really changed in the past few years. It's always been close to the moneyed area of Shaughnessy and you'll find some of the city's most expensive boutiques here. You'll also find an enormous Chapters bookstore, the upscale Cactus Restaurant, and many art galleries.

KITSILANO

The main shopping areas are West Broadway and West 4th avenues from Broadway to Alma streets. Both areas have a really fine mix of upmarket clothing stores, home furnishings, specialty bookstores, and restaurants. A bonus for 4th Avenue is that it's close to both Granville Island and the Kitsilano Beach and playground.

ASIA WEST

Here you can step into an area just like Hong Kong on Richmond's No. 3 Road. Between Capstan and Alderbridge you'll find the Aberdeen Centre, Yaohan Centre, President Plaza, and Parker Place, catering to Vancouver's Asian community. These malls not only include some great retail shopping, but also have specialty Asian supermarkets, theaters, bowling centers, herbalists, and restaurants.

SHOPPING CENTERS

Metrotown Shopping & Entertainment Complex This is a sprawling, confusing series of buildings made up of three complexes—Station Square, Metrotown, and Metropolis—but once you get in there it has 500-odd places to shop and play for kids and adults. Great for rainy days. There is Playdium, a sort of giant video arcade where you can easily spend hours, the Rainforest Cafe for sustenance and entertainment, Chapters books, Toys'R'Us, the SilverCity cinemas, and much, much more. Strollers and wheelchairs are free, or if you prefer to drop little ones somewhere, the Jellybean Park Play Care (*©* **604/431-8870**) takes kids from 18 months to 5 years for 1 to 3 hours and charges C$6 (US$4) an hour. The playcare has a ball playpen, toys, learning materials, and a playhouse. 4600-4800 Kingsway, Burnaby. *©* **604/438-3610.** SkyTrain: Metrotown.

Oakridge Centre Positioned as a high-fashion mall, you will find 160 shops, which include well-known brand names such as Roots, Harry Rosen, and Gap Kids, as well as Jax, Kookai, MaxMara, and Gymboree. The mall offers free strollers and has a great play area in the middle about the size of a retail store. Babies to kids of about 7 can tear around on bright carpet over bumps and curves while parents can sit around the edges and watch. There are also pay rides. 650 W. 41st Ave. (at Cambie St.). *©* **604/261-2511.**

Pacific Centre This huge mall spans 3 blocks and has more than 140 stores including anchors Holt Renfrew and Eatons as well as Eddie Bauer, The Gap, Harry Rosen, Banana Republic, and many more. The mall has three baby changing rooms. 550-700 W. Georgia St. *©* **604/688-7236.** www.cadillacfairview.com.

Park Royal Shopping Centre Wander among well over 200 shops spread over two malls on each side of Marine Drive, just west of the Lions Gate Bridge and about a 10-minute drive from downtown. There's the Disney Store, The Gap, Banana Republic, and Future Shop, but younger kids will love you if you stop at the Gator Pit play area in the south mall. Guest services has strollers for children and wheelchairs at no cost. Taylor Way and Marine Dr., West Vancouver. *©* **604/925-9576.** www.shopparkroyal.com.

Sinclair Centre While nothing stands out as being particularly kid-friendly at this mall, except perhaps the food fair, you'll find some of Vancouver's oldest buildings now restored into trendy stores like Leone and Dorothy Grant, and art galleries. 757 W. Hastings St. *©* **604/659-1009.**

Between Capstan and Alderbridge on Richmond's No. 3 Road are a number of Asian shopping malls with predominantly Asian goods and restaurants. **Aberdeen Centre,** 4151 Hazelbridge Way, Richmond (*©* **604/270-1234;** www.aberdeencentre.com), is one of the largest specialty malls in North America. It includes a theater, bowling alley, boutiques, herbalist, teahouse, and Japanese and Chinese restaurants. At **President Plaza,** 8181 Cambie Rd., Richmond (*©* **604/270-8677;** www.pplaza.com), you'll find a top Chinese seafood restaurant, T&T Supermarket, a food fair, and specialty shops, as well as the Radisson President Hotel. **Yaohan Centre,** 3700 No. 3 Rd., Richmond (*©* **604/231-0601**), has 80-odd stores including a food fair.

2 Shopping A to Z

ARTS & CRAFTS

Beadworks   Pick up your bead tray at the entrance and proceed into the store to gather beads and accessories from this huge store dedicated to beading. Find beads in any color and any size, even semi-precious stones. You can also cheat and buy ready-made accessories. 5-1666 Johnston St. (at the Net Loft), Granville Island. ✆ 604/682-2323.

Grand Prix Hobbies & Crafts   A good selection of arts and crafts supplies, as well as models and trains. 3038 W. Broadway Ave. (near McDonald St.). ✆ 604/733-7114.

Lewiscraft   Frames, baskets, paints, wool, and all sorts of crafts are available here to make just about anything. Outlets in Capilano Mall ✆ 604/980-6744, Richmond Centre ✆ 604/270-8004, Metrotown ✆ 604/439-2054, Lougheed Mall ✆ 604/420-4054, Guildford Town Centre ✆ 604/582-7082, Coquitlam Centre ✆ 604/941-0422, and Seven Oaks ✆ 604/855-1969.

Urban Source   This is an arts and crafts shop with a difference, aimed at kids 3 to 14. Urban Source gets its materials—springs, foam, stickers, wood, fabrics and leather scraps—from local businesses that would otherwise throw them away. Some traditional supplies, but the recycled materials, especially dye cuts and pre-cut colored shapes, are perfect for little ones. 3126 Main St. (between 15th and 16th aves.). East Vancouver. ✆ 604/875-1611. Closed Sundays.

BALLOONS

Balloon Action   Balloons, cards, calendars, gifts, and lootbags. You can also order a singing telegram or perhaps a clown or magician for fun. Denman Place Mall, 123-1030 Denman St. (at Nelson St.). ✆ 604/684-7555.

Balloon Shop   Choose from any size, shape, color, or configuration. Buy one, buy a thousand and one. The shop does bouquets and singing telegrams, too. 2407 Burrard St. (at 8th Ave.). ✆ 604/684-0959.

The Flying Rhino   This store is big on birthdays, if you happen to be in town for one. Get your balloons and novelties, plus all sorts of party items, including streamers and paper plates, palm trees, martini accessories, weird sunglasses, and that belly button light you always wanted. 3696 W. 8th Ave. (at Alma St.). ✆ 604/738-7447.

BOOKS

Banyen Books & Sound   A bookstore created to give a feeling of light, space, and time, it encourages customers to sit and read or just browse. Banyen has now been around for 30 years and the store and its website sell more than 27,000 books, CDs, tapes, and videos to do with personal growth and spiritual awareness. 2671 W. Broadway Ave. (between Trafalgar and Stephens sts.). ✆ 800/663-8442 or 604/732-7912. www.banyen.com.

Blackberry Books   This neighborhood bookstore opened in 1979, with a staff who really love books and share their opinions through informal written reviews. It's a great environment where classical music plays as you browse. They also specialize in mail orders, gift wrapping, and special orders. 1663 Duranleau St. (at Granville Island). ✆ 604/685-4113.

Book Warehouse   A chain of local discount bookstores, the Book Warehouse has carved out a niche with remainders and overstock books. Prices are good, as is the selection, and you can often find obscure titles on the shelves. 1181 Davie St. (at Bute St.) ℭ 604/685-5711; 632 W. Broadway Ave. (between Ash and Heather sts.) ℭ 604/872-5711; 2388 W. 4th Ave. (at Balsam St.) ℭ 604/734-5711; and 4444 W. 10th Ave. (at Sasamat St.) ℭ 604/221-5744.

Chapters   A Canadian chain, Chapters inspired fear in other bookstores when it opened in 1997. But its more than 110,000 books, its environment, and Starbucks coffee shop are a boon for customers, as are its wonderful kids' sections and play areas, the padded bench seating around its floor-to-ceiling windows, and its daily opening hours from 10am to 11pm. 788 Robson St. (at Howe St.) ℭ 604/682-4066; 2505 Granville St. (at Broadway Ave.) ℭ 604/731-7822.

Comic Shop   This kitsilano institution has long been the first stop for spotty youths in search of the latest in comics, science fantasy and fiction. Gaming paraphenalia as well. 2089 W. 4th Ave. (at Arbutus). ℭ 604/738-8122.

Duthie Books   At one time, Duthie's was a local chain of nine bookstores. Competition and financial troubles have reduced the store to its Kitsilano location only. It's still a great place to hunt down local authors or out-of-print books. 2239 W. 4th Ave. (at Yew St.) ℭ 604/732-5344. www.duthiebooks.com.

Humpty Dumpty Books & Music   On the ground floor of the Kids' Market, this store caters to children from infant to about age 7. 1496 Cartwright St. (Granville Island). ℭ 604/683-7009.

Indigo Books, Music & Cafe   Another nationwide Canadian chain, Indigo recently purchased a controlling share of Chapters. Book-selling wars aside, Indigo is a great addition to the North Shore and my kids are always asking to go here—to a bookstore, go figure! You'll find a huge book collection, a great kids' section complete with computer games, and a cafe with checkerboard tables and puck-sized game pieces. Lynn Valley Centre, 1199 Lynn Valley Rd. (at Mountain Hwy.), North Vancouver. ℭ 604/904-7970.

Kidsbooks   Here is an incredible selection of books, puppets, games, and ideas for presents for infants to teenagers. It also has great music and story tapes and unusual card games for keeping kids busy on long car trips, as well as puppets, dolls, cards, crafts, and a decent French section. Special orders and gift wrapping. 3083 W. Broadway Ave. (at Balaclava St.). ℭ 604/738-5335.

Kidsbooks in Edgemont Village   This microcosm of the Kidsbooks main store is situated 5 minutes from the major attractions of Capilano Canyon and Groose Mountain, making it a useful destination for soothing end-of-the-day cranky kids. 3040 Edgemont Blvd., North Vancouver. ℭ 604/986-6190.

Smithbooks   This Canadian mall chain owned by Chapters and, by extension, Indigo offers the Avid Reader card, so for C$15 (US$9.90) a year you can get 10% off all your purchases. Bentall Centre, 595 Burrard St. ℭ 604/689-8231.

Sophia Books   Vancouver's local foreign language bookstore carries children'z books in French, German, Spanish, Italian, and Japanese, as well as Japanese "manga" books, graphic novels, and french children's videos. Open 7 days a week. 492 W. Hastings St. (at Richards St.) ℭ 604/684-0484.

Travel Bug   This store has a large section of books about Vancouver as well as travel guidebooks to about every other place in the universe. You can also pick up maps, luggage, a money belt, or a Swiss Army knife. 2667 W. Broadway Ave. (at Trafalgar St.). ℭ 604/737-1122.

UBC Bookstore   Located on the university campus by the bus loop, this store has an extensive kids' section with everything from fiction and activity books to the sciences and reference material. 6200 University Blvd. (University of British Columbia campus). ℂ 800/661-3889 or 604/822-2665. www.bookstore.ubc.ca.

Wanderlust Travellers Store   This store offers thousands of guidebooks and maps as well as luggage, backpacks, and everything from electrical adapters and money belts to mosquito repellent designed especially for kids. 1929 W. 4th Ave. (at Cypress St.). ℂ 604/739-2182.

CLOTHES–KIDS
N E W

Aunt Em's   Find lots of trendy designer clothes, also snazzy hats, scarves, gloves, and tights. Infants to 10 years. 1496 Cartwright St., Kids' Market, Granville Island. ℂ 604/682-2116.

Bobbit's   This Kitsilano store sells everything from raingear to toys for newborns, nursing pillows, baby slings, designer diaper bags, breast pumps and rentals, crib linen, picture frames, and gifts. Look for Robeez non-slip leather slippers, which are made in Vancouver and are great for babies and new walkers. 2935 W. 4th Ave. (between MacDonald and Bayswater sts.) ℂ 604/738-0333.

The Everything Wet Store   It doesn't matter what time of the year you are in Vancouver—pick up your rain and/or swim wear and sand toys here. 1496 Cartwright St., Kids' Market, Granville Island. ℂ 604/685-5445.

Gap Kids   Choose from good quality but expensive gear for kids from infants on up. 1125 Robson St. (at Thurlow St.). ℂ 604/683-0906.

Lil'Putian's Fashions for Kids   This store specializes in brand names like OshKosh for kids to 3 years, and is also moving into toys for all ages. 2029 W. 4th Ave. (at Arbutus St.). ℂ 604/738-2483.

Please Mum   Clothes from this local designer tend to be on the pricey side, but my kids love them and they tend to last through all three kids with wear left. The store's end-of-season sales tend to go for a long time and are especially good value. From infants to about age 10. 2951 W. Broadway Ave. (at Bayswater St.) ℂ 604/732-4574; Oakridge Shopping Centre, 405-650 W. 41st St. (at Cambie St.) ℂ 604/261-5440.

Popi Childrenswear   This store carries cheerful and reasonably priced clothing for children from infants to about age 10. Pacific Shopping Centre, 701 W. Georgia St. ℂ 604/688-9194.

Roots Canada   This is the Canadian company's flagship store on Robson Street. You'll find Canadian-made casual clothing, leather jackets, bags, a kids' line for infants on up, and those red caps worn by Canadian Olympic athletes. 1001 Robson St. (at Burrard St.) ℂ 604/683-4305; Oakridge Centre, 255-650 W. 41st St. (at Cambie St.) ℂ 604/266-6229.

Under the Monkey Tree   All the clothes in this store are made by a local designer. Clothes are aimed at kids aged 2 to 10 and usually have a jungle theme—at least, they do when the designer can find the material. 1496 Cartwright St., Kids' Market, Granville Island. ℂ 604/685-7226.

Vincenta Haute Couture Pour Bébé   This is fast becoming the store to shop for those with money or buying for special occasions. It carries clothing and accessories from babies to 16-year-olds with brand names that include Kenzo, Elle, and Diesel. Oakridge Centre, 650 W. 41st Ave. (at Cambie St.) © 604/261-6345; Park Royal Shopping Centre South (Taylor Way and Marine Dr.), West Vancouver © 604/913-1868.

USED

You can pick up lots of the above designer goods and many other labels often in pristine condition at a fraction of the price, as well as toys, strollers, and furniture at consignment stores that are scattered around the Lower Mainland. Try the ones in Vancouver below.

Happy Kids   Here you can find clothing for infants and children up to about age 10, as well as kids' furniture, equipment, and toys. 3635 W. 4th Ave. (at Alma St.). © 604/730-5507.

MacGillicuddy's for Little People   This high-end store opened in 1985 and specializes in European lines and quality clothes, toys, equipment, and books for babies and children up to about age 16. 4881 Mackenzie St. (at 33rd St.). © 604/ 263-5313.

Nippers Tog 'N Toy   This shop sells designer label clothes for children up to age 10. It also carries a good line of maternity clothes in good condition as well as children's equipment. 3712 W. 10th Ave. (at Alma St.). © 604/222-4035. Closed Sun & Mon.

Tiggy-Winkle's   Find lots of brand-name, quality clothing and equipment for infants and children up to age 16. 3776 Oak St. (at 22nd Ave.). © 604/731-8647.

Wee Ones Reruns   This shop carries clothes for kids aged up to 14 as well as cribs, car seats, videos, toys, and books. 614 Kingsway (at Fraser St.). © 604/708-0956. Closed Sun & Mon.

CLOTHES–FASHION

Vancouver may be laid back, but you can still find fashion from Paris, London, Milan, and Rome. Find some of the best fashion stores on Robson Street, in Yaletown, around the Sinclair Centre on West Hastings Street, and in the South Granville area between 6th and 16th avenues.

There are also numerous international designer outlets. **Armani Exchange,** 1070 Robson St. (between Burrard and Thurlow sts.) © **604/488-1668; Chanel Boutique,** 900 W. Hastings St. (at Hornby St.) © **604/682-0522; Salvatore Ferragamo,** 918 Robson St. (at Hornby St.) © **604/669-4495; Gianni Versace Boutique,** Sinclair Centre, 757 W. Hastings St. (between Granville and Seymour sts.) © **604/683-1131; Polo/Ralph Lauren,** The Landing, 375 Water St. (at Cordova St.) © **604/682-7656;** and **Plaza Escada,** Sinclair Centre, 757 W. Hastings St. (between Granville and Seymour sts.) © **604/688-8558.**

Some local stores of note include:

Dorothy Grant   First Nation designer Dorothy Grant exhibits her unique Haida motif designs on coats, vests, jackets, caps, and accessories. You can also pick up Haida art and jewelry. Sinclair Centre, 250-757 W. Hastings St. © 604/681-0201.

Leone   Here you will find Versace, Donna Karan, Armani, Prada, and many others in a very elegant setting. Valet parking is provided, which should also tip you off to the prices. Sinclair Centre, 250-757 W. Hastings St. © 604/683-1133.

The Underground and Beauty Bar   Clothing for about age 14 and up, also makeup, makeovers, and wigs. This is the favorite of one of my young nieces for funky clothes. 848 Granville St. (between Robson and Smithe sts.). © 604/681-8732.

COMICS

ABC Book & Comic Emporium   The name pretty much says it all. Find comic books, pocket books, hard covers, and magazines. 1247 Granville St. (at Davie St.). ℂ 604/682-3019.

The Comicshop   There is material here for ages 5 and up, but the store is most popular with teens. A dungeon and games room are downstairs and are well used by kids from 8 and up who can play Warhammer or Pirate of the Seven Seas. 2089 W. 4th Ave. (at Arbutus St.). ℂ 604/738-8122.

Golden Age Collectibles   Check out new and some high-end vintage comic books for serious collectors. This store also sells sports cards, posters, postcards, action figures, and games. 830 Granville St. (at Robson St.). ℂ 604/683-2819.

DEPARTMENT STORES

Army & Navy   Located in the not-so-nice part of town, this local department store recently got a new paint job and reinvented itself as a happening place where you can find anything at a great price. And, so you can. 27 W. Hastings St. (2 blocks from Main St.). ℂ 604/682-6644.

The Bay   Another Canadian institution with stores throughout the Lower Mainland, The Bay has tried to differentiate itself with the unfortunate tagline "Shopping Is Good." Granville and Georgia sts. ℂ 604/681-6211.

Eatons   This is a Canadian dynasty that fell to ruin until it was bought by Sears Canada. A number of once closed locations have reopened, including the flagship store at Georgia and Granville. The store is more upmarket than before and features designer clothing and live in-store mannequins. 701 Granville St. ℂ 604/685-7112.

Sears Canada   The Canadian chain has tried to position itself as more upmarket than Zellers and not as upmarket as Eaton's. Has a good kids' section at reasonable prices. Several locations outside Vancouver.

Wal-Mart   The entry of this American outfit into Canada left smaller retailers quaking, but its good quality and low-priced children's clothing and toys are a great benefit to shoppers. Its service still leaves other department stores for dead. Several locations throughout Vancouver.

Zellers   A chain of discount department stores across Canada, Zellers dropped its advertising tagline "Where the Lowest Price Is the Law," shortly after Wal-Mart entered Canada. Similar to Wal-Mart, but without the breadth of products or the service. Several locations throughout Vancouver.

DOLLS & DOLLHOUSES

Calico Cat   In the heart of Gastown, this store sells collector dolls as well as Ty products, handmade teddies, candles, and figurines. 121-131 Water St. (between Cambie and Abbott sts.). ℂ 604/685-5643.

Enchanted Dolls   The collectible porcelain dolls, handmade dolls, and limited editions are designed more for adults, but there are plenty of teddies that would please young children. 4531 Hastings St. (at Willingdon St.), Burnaby. ℂ 604/298-9299.

Marty's Antiques and Giftware   This Steveston store has a large selection of dollhouses, plus furniture and accessories. 100-3580 Moncton St., Richmond. ℂ 604/271-5637.

Ross' Miniature Treasure House This store does it all—wholesale, imports, and retail, all from this location. Find dollhouses, dolls, crafts, and hobby supplies. Ross' is also the Canadian distributors for Dee's Delights, Aztec Imports, and Handley House, all American dollhouse miniature suppliers. 823 W. 1st St., North Vancouver. ℂ **604/980-2715.** www.rossminiatures.com.

FIRST NATIONS

You may well want to take home some of BC's native art and you can find everything from inexpensive souvenir totem poles to beautiful paintings worth thousands of dollars. Look for paintings and prints, ceremonial masks, bowls, sculptures, carvings, Cowichan sweaters, and beaded items by Pacific Northwest tribes, including the Haida, Coast Salish, and Kwakwaka'wakw. Look for beautifully designed gold and silver jewelry designed with motifs of bear, killer whale, raven, wolf, and others, drawn from local myths and made in 14-karat or 18-karat rings, pendants, and earrings.

Coastal Peoples Fine Arts Gallery An extensive collection of art from the Northwest Coast, Plains, and Inuit peoples. Beautiful jewelry, masks, and sculptures. 1024 Mainland St., Yaletown. ℂ **604/685-9298.** www.coastalpeoples.com

Hill's Native Art The store has one of the largest collections of Northwest Coast art and crafts—also genuine Cowichan sweaters, moccasins, totem poles, button blankets, clothing, books, and carved silver jewelry. 165 Water St., Gastown. ℂ **604/685-4249.** www.hillsnativeart.com.

Leona Lattimer Gallery Close to Granville Island, this beautiful store carries a large selection of Northwest Coast paintings, traditional boxes, masks, panel carvings, large and small totem poles, and unusual gifts. 1590 W. 2nd Ave. (at Fir St.). ℂ **604/732-4556.**

The Raven and the Bear This shop has a huge variety of First Nations art from carvings to limited edition prints, souvenir items, and jewelry. 1528 Duranleau St., Granville Island. ℂ **604/669-3990.**

Wickaninnish Gallery Discover fabulous native-carved 14k gold rings, leather vests, and everything from a sterling silver soul catcher with matching earrings to beautiful wooden bowls. 14-1666 Johnston St. (Net Loft at Granville Island). ℂ **604/681-1057.**

HAIRCUTS

The cuts for kids tend to be on the pricey side, but are great if your kids need to be entertained for the time it takes to get their hair cut.

The Hairloft Restless little ones get to sit on a zebra with a bucket seat while watching a video. Upstairs at the Kids' Market, 1496 Cartwright St., Granville Island. ℂ **604/ 684-6177.** From infants up to adults C$18–$23 (US$11.90–$15.20).

Kids Kutz Kids can choose the race car, boat, or motorcycle seat when getting their hair cut and watch videos while they sit. Lonsdale Quay, second floor, North Vancouver. ℂ **604/990-4900.** From infants to adults C$15–$23 (US$9.90–$15.20).

2 Cute 4 U You can shop for clothes and trendy shoes while your kids get their hair cut and watch a video. 1785 Bellevue Ave., West Vancouver. ℂ **604/926-4365.** From infants up C$16–$29 (US$10.55–$19.15).

KITES

Kites and Puppets   Get an octopus Mylar kite for a 2-year-old for C$7.50 (US$4.95) or a two-string stunt kite for a 14-year-old that starts at C$62 (US$41). The kids will have them doing acrobatics in no time. Then there are delta kites with happy faces and shaped like birds that start at C$20 (US$13.20) recommended for 2 and up, and even a Winnie the Pooh kite with a line for C$22.50 (US$14.85). For kids who prefer puppets, the store sells them for infants as well as ventriloquists. 1496 Cartwright St., Kids' Market, Granville Island. © 604/685-9877.

Kites on Clouds   Choose from a plethora of colored kites and windsocks— black shark, orca whales, and Canadian maple leafs. A boat kite has a note that it really does fly. The Courtyard, 131 Water St., Gastown. © 604/669-5677.

MAPS

ABC Maps and Laminates   This store sells everything from city maps of Vancouver to maps of BC and maps of the world. You can also get them laminated for your wall. 454 W. Broadway Ave. (at Cambie St.). © 604/874-2616.

World Wide Books & Maps   A local company, this store carries 150 titles published through its fellow company International Travel Maps and carries more than 9,000 titles in the store. You can pick up a detailed map of the North Shore hiking trails or a map of Baja for your next trip. It also carries special-interest guides to BC, travel books, maps, and charts. 552 Seymour St. (at Pender St.) © 604/687-3320; 345 W. Broadway Ave. (at Cambie St.) © 604/879-3621.

MUSEUM STORES

If you are looking for local arts and crafts, jewelry, books, and unique gifts, sometimes the best sources are the stores at the various museums. Here are some of the larger gift stores:

Museum of Anthropology   Choose from expensive original art, gold and silver hand-carved jewelry, carved boxes, and masks. On the less expensive side, there are prints, sweatshirts, scarves, books, music, and cards. 6393 N.W. Marine Dr. (University of British Columbia). © 604/822-5087. Open 11am–5pm. Closed Mon.

Vancouver Art Gallery   This gallery shop carries sterling silver jewelry made by BC artists, clocks, watches, ties, and reading glasses. It also has a large poster section, postcards, address books, and a children's section that has puzzles and games and books on European artists like Van Gogh. 750 Hornby St. (at Robson St.). © 604/662-4706.

Vancouver Museum   This is the first place the kids head to when they enter this great building with the dome hat. Find First Nations art and jewelry, books, games, and lots of unusual kids stuff. 1100 Chestnut St., Vanier Park. © 604/736-4431. www.vanmuseum.bc.ca.

MUSIC

Sam the Record Man   Four floors of tapes and CDs and one floor of videos will keep the family browsing. 568 Seymour St. (at Dunsmuir St.). © 604/684-3722.

Virgin Megastore   Three floors house more than 125,000 music titles, books, magazines, 140 listening stations, three Sony PlayStations, two Sega Dreamcasts, and the Virgin Cafe. 788 Burrard St. (at Robson St.). © 604/669-2289. www.virginmega.com.

PERFORMING ARTS

Act 1 Theatrical Makeup & Dance Supplies   If you always wanted to be Snow White, Batman, or Poison Ivy, you can fulfil your fantasy at this store. The North Vancouver location has more costumes oriented to kids. 606 Robson St. (at Seymour St.) ℂ 604/687-0737; 1061 Marine Drive, North Vancouver ℂ 604/985-4316.

Dance Etc: the alternative dance store   Find costumes for ballet, tap, jazz, lyrical, breakdancing, and hip hop. This store also sells street shoes, colorful underwear, and workout wear for about 12 and up. Arbutus Village Shopping Centre, 4255 Arbutus St. (near King Edward Ave.). ℂ 604/731-1362.

Dunbar Costume Rental   You'll find everything from cavemen to *Star Trek* and everything in between, for toddlers up to adults. 8836 Selkirk St. (at 72nd Ave.). ℂ 604/263-9011.

Just Imagine...Fun Clothing Inc.   This dress-up store stocks dance wear and shoes for kids aged 3 and up. 4253 Dunbar St. (at King Edward Ave.), Vancouver. ℂ 604/222-3523.

Miranda Mills and More Madness Costume Rentals   Mainly oriented toward adults, this store has a small selection of kids' costumes and kids will love the accessories—everything from feather boas and a bolt through the head to instant devil kits and fairy wands. 2813 W. Broadway Ave. (at MacDonald St.), Vancouver. ℂ 604/734-8865.

SCIENCE STUFF

Exsciting Worlds   This uniquely named store sells things related to science and nature for everyone from newborns to adults. Find microscopes, magnet kits, and chemistry sets. 2432 Marine Drive (at 24th Ave.), West Vancouver. ℂ 604/925-3563.

Science World   If your kids are budding scientists, head to Science World and find out answers, or at least intelligent responses, to almost everything they want to know. The gift store also has a lot of games and educational projects to take home. 1455 Quebec St. (at Terminal Ave.). ℂ 604/268-6363.

Vancouver Aquarium   For science with a marine bent, the Aquarium has a great gift store with well-priced toys, books, jigsaws, and projects. Most years I pick up unusual Christmas presents and stocking stuffers for my kids and out-of-town friends and family. Stanley Park, off Georgia Street and follow the signs. ℂ 604/659-3474.

SHOES–KIDS

Kiddie Kobbler Shoes   Because they specialize in fitting children's shoes for infants up to about age 12, you get really good-quality runners, hiking boots, sandals, and more. They're expensive, but at least you know they are good for their growing feet. Park Royal Shopping Centre, 2024 Parkroyal South (at Taylor Way), West Vancouver. ℂ 604/926-1616.

Pandas   Another store that specializes in kids' shoes from infants to about 12. Shoes are not cheap, but they do last and are good fits, especially for first-time walkers. Oakridge Shopping Centre, 650 W. 41st Ave. (at Cambie St.) ℂ 604/266-0025; Capilano Mall, 935 Marine Dr. (at Hamilton St.), North Vancouver ℂ 604/986-4450.

SOUVENIRS, T-SHIRTS, ETC.

You can pick up a huge selection of souvenirs—everything from designer T-shirts to cups and ashtrays, Canadian-made clothes, and First Nations art and jewelry—at an incredible range in price all over Vancouver. Some of the best spots are Gastown, Robson Street, the public markets, department stores, and the museum shops.

El Sol Imports   This store is on the tacky side, but carries lots of postcards, calendars, cheap books on Vancouver, toys, glasses with pictures of Vancouver, maps, and even a Beautiful BC jigsaw puzzle. 160 Water St. (Gastown). ℂ 604/685-3575.

Oh Yes! Vancouver   Browse for clothes for babies, children, and adults with original designs on good-quality cotton. You can also pick up mugs, baseball caps, maple syrup, smoked salmon, and other upmarket souvenirs. Pacific Centre, 500-700 W. Georgia St. ℂ 604/681-3184; 1167 Robson St. (between Bute and Thurlow sts.) ℂ 604/687-3187; 375 Water St. (in Gastown) ℂ 604/689-3109; 1496 Cartwright St. (Granville Island Kids' Market) ℂ 604/689-3193.

Suraj Fashion and Gifts   This is one of my favorite touristy places, mainly because you can bargain. I immediately got 10% off when I bought two T-shirts and figure if I can hone my skills I could do much better. They have a huge range of kids' and adults' clothing at good prices, as well as hockey jerseys, moccasins, sew-on emblems of BC, and a huge range of inexpensive gifts such as toy beavers and Mounties, plus boxes of smoked salmon and maple syrup cream cookies. 339 Water St. (Gastown). ℂ 604/682-2524.

SPORTS CONSIGNMENT STORES

Cheapskates   This shop sells golf gear and bicycle parts, also new bike helmets for kids aged 3 to 7 and adult sizes. 3228 Dunbar St. (at 16th Ave.) ℂ 604/734-1191; 3644 W. 16th Ave. (at Dunbar St.). ℂ 604/222-1125.

Ride On   This store stocks kids' racing bikes and just about every sort of bike you can imagine from BMX to road bikes. In winter, it's snowboards. 2255 W. Broadway Ave. (at Vine St.). ℂ 604/738-7734. www.rideon.com.

Sports Junkies Consignors   In the summer, the store stocks bikes, roller-blades, and baseball and soccer equipment, and, at the first sign of winter, changes to skis and snowboards. Lots of clothing for all sports. 600 W. 6th Ave. (at Ash St.). ℂ 604/879 0666.

SPORTS GEAR

I asked my teenage nephew if money was no object where would he go, and he said he'd head to West 4th Avenue and Burrard Street in Kitsilano for its boarding, skating, and surfing clothes and equipment. Look for the **Boardroom**, 1745 W. 4th Ave. (at Burrard St.) (ℂ 604/734-SNOW); **Pacific Boarder**, 1793 W. 4th Ave. (ℂ 604/734-7245); **Thriller**, 1710 W. 4th Ave. (ℂ 604/736-5651); and **West Beach Snowboard Canada**, 1766 W. 4th Ave. (ℂ 604/731-6449). Downtown try **Level Board and Fashion**, 1025 Robson St. (ℂ 604/605-0774) or 25 Alexander St. in Gastown (ℂ 604/681-9098).

If Kitsilano is for snow and surfing, then the 2 blocks east of Cambie Street on West Broadway dubbed "Gore-Tex Alley" are an outdoors delight. Try **Altus Mountain Gear**, 137 W. Broadway Ave. (ℂ 604/876-5255); **A.J. Brooks Outdoor Outfitters**, 147 W. Broadway Ave. (ℂ 604/874-1117); **The Backpackers Shop**, 183 W. Broadway Ave. (ℂ 604/879-4711); **Great Outdoors**

Equipment Ltd., 222 W. Broadway Ave. (© **604/872-8872**); and **Eco Outdoor Sports,** 202 W. Broadway Ave. (© **604/875-6767**). Close by, try the **Taiga Works Wilderness Equipment Factory,** 390 W. 8th Ave. (© **604/875-6644**). Still on the West Side, there is the **Helly Hansen Store,** 2025 W. 4th Ave. (© **604/730-5576**), known for outfitting arctic and ocean expeditions, and **Coast Mountain Sports,** 2201 W. 4th Ave. (© **604/731-6181**), which carries expensive outdoor gear and trendy clothes from manufacturers such as Patagonia and Sierra Designs. Downtown, try **Athletes World/Nike Shop,** 777 Dunsmuir St. (at Granville St.) (© **604/688-1668**); **Comor-go Play Outside,** 1090 W. Georgia St. (at Thurlow St.) (© **604/899-2111**) and 1918 Fir St. (at 3rd Ave.) (© **604/731-2163**); **Fila Boutique,** 1053 Robson St. (between Burrard and Thurlow sts.) (© **604/683-3452**); **Nike Shop,** 1107 Robson St. (at Thurlow St.) (© **604/668-9672**); **Planet Superstar,** 1088 Robson St. (at Thurlow St.) (© **604/668-9696**); and **Sport Mart Discount Superstores,** 735 Thurlow St. (at Alberni St.) (© **604/683-2433**) and 495 W. 8th Ave. (at Cambie St.) (© **604/873 6737**).

Mountain Equipment Co-op   The longest serving outfitter in the area, this is a West Coast institution where we buy the kids' and our own raingear, hiking boots, and backpacks. Because lifetime memberships are only C$5 (US$3.30), so can you. Whether you are planning to climb Everest or just like to walk to the supermarket, this store has got great quality hiking equipment, climbing equipment, bike parts, and canoes. Best of all, you can try your new clothes out on the climbing wall. 130 W. Broadway Ave. © **604/872-7858.**

STROLLERS, CRIBS & KIDS' FURNITURE

Ikea   This Swedish store has just about everything you can think of, from full kitchens and flooring to glasses and sofas. The kids' section is quite good, with innovative bunk beds with slides, tunnels, tents, and bedding. The store supplies free strollers and there is a controlled, but unsupervised play area and a movie theater that's free for kids 94 centimeters to 122 centimeters (37 in. to 48 in.) tall and toilet trained (about age 3 to 5) while you're shopping in the store. 3200 Sweden Way (at Bridgeport Rd.), Richmond. © **604/276-8278.**

Kids Furniture World   Just across from Ikea, this store has good-quality children's furniture including beds, chairs, and mattresses. 12680 Bridgeport Rd. (at Sweden Way), Richmond. © **604/278-7654.**

Soothers Kids Boutique   On the pricey side, this store has a good selection of strollers, furniture, and toys. Capilano Mall, 935 Marine Dr. (at Hamilton St.), North Vancouver. © **604/980-7229;** Brentwood Mall, 4567 Lougheed Hwy. (at Willingdon Ave.), Burnaby © **604/205-0030.**

TOYS & GAMES

If you're not really sure what you are looking for—might be a toy, might be a kite, might be new swimming gear—head to the Kids' Market on Granville Island. A kind of shopping center designed for kids, it has a tram out front with **Woofles Doggilicious Deli** (for pets) (© **604/689-DOGS**), a small kid-sized door next to the entrance, and everything from candies to a video arcade. For toys check out **All Aboard** (© **604/684-1633**), a store devoted to Thomas the Tank Engine, complete with a train table they can try there. **Clownin' Around International College** (© **604/682-0244;** www.clowninaround.net) has magic and juggling supplies for kids to professional magicians, birthday party entertainers, and a party room for up to 30 adults and kids. **The Granville Island Toy Company** (© **888/844-0076** or 604/684-0076) has everything from Brio and puzzles to black Wizard Capes and pink dance gear. **Kaboodles Toy Store** (© **604/684-0066**) carries a good selection of Playmobil, Groovy Girls, trains, Beanie Babies, and Lego. **Knotty Toys** (© **604/683-7854**) makes beautiful wooden xylophones, tambourines, drums, Radio Flyer wagons, and more. **Stay Tooned** (© **604/689-8695**) has all sorts of cartoons—Disney toys, hockey sticks, and pucks.

BC Playthings   A tiny store nestled in Edgemont Village, this store is geared to kids up to about 8. It has everything from paints to large puppet people and sturdy wooden jigsaws for toddlers to digging stuff for the beach. 3070 Edgemont Blvd. (at Highland), North Vancouver. © 604/986-4111. www.bcplaythings.com. Closed Sun and public holidays.

The Game Shop   A Gastown fixture for close to 30 years, the Game Shop has a musty, somewhat tacky atmosphere kids will love. There are limited edition Ken and Barbie and *Star Trek* dolls, Beanie Baby collectibles, and all sorts of board games in large and handy travel sizes. Here you will find that Houdini magic set you always wanted as a kid and fantasy gaming for teens, and you can check your love rating on the machine on the way out. 157 Water St. © 604/685-5825.

Moose Vancouver   This store used to be called the Moose is Loose and it's hard to get kids away from the dozens and dozens of wind-up toys snorting, barking, and braying all over the store. There's a wall of fridge magnets as well as a glow-in-the-dark area. 1195 Robson St. (near Thurlow St.). © 604/609-9945.

Splash Toy Shop   Find toys for babies up to pre-teens, mainly non–brand-name toys—everything from arts and crafts and games to puzzles and books to hobby horses and kites. 4243 Dunbar St. (at 26th and 27th sts.), Vancouver © 604/228-8697; 140-3580 Moncton St. (in Steveston Village), Richmond © 604/228-8697.

The Toy Box   This is a large Kitsilano store with a good cross section of quality toys from Brio and water play to books and costumes. 3002 W. Broadway Ave. (at Carnarvon St.). © 604/738-4322.

Toys'R'Us   This is more like the A to Z of toys and the mother of all toy stores. What kid can't sing the jingle? 1154 W. Broadway Ave. (between Oak and Granville sts.). © 604/733-8697.

11

Easy Side Trips from Vancouver

While there is plenty to do in Vancouver to keep you busy, you may want to explore some more of BC. There are some wonderful trips that are close enough to Vancouver to allow you to leave in the morning and return that night, or if you have the time, spend a night or two and really get to know the area. Whistler is a family favorite, but try some of these other destinations for something off the beaten tourist track.

1 Ladner

45 kilometers (28 miles) S of Vancouver.

Ladner is on the estuary of the Fraser River about 40 minutes from downtown Vancouver. It is surrounded by sloughs, with a fairly large farming community on one side, a fishing community on the other, and a quaint little village more or less squeezed in between. You could easily spend a full day walking, biking, picnicking, and visiting some of the attractions, or just pop out there for a drive and an ice-cream cone.

Ladner is one of three communities (the others are Tsawwassen and North Delta) that make up the large area of Delta south of the city of Vancouver. It's about 20 minutes from the Vancouver International Airport and on the way to the Swartz Bay ferry terminal that takes you to Victoria and the Gulf Islands and where you will also find **Splashdown Water Park** on Highway 17, just north of the terminal.

For more information contact **Tourism Delta,** 1210 Morris Crescent, Delta, BC V4L 2E1 (© **604/943-5187;** www.tourismdelta.bc.ca).

GETTING THERE
By Car
Take Granville Street from downtown Vancouver to 70th Avenue. Turn left and then right again on the Oak Street Bridge. You will now be on Highway 99. Take the first exit to Ladner south of the George Massey Tunnel and you will immediately find yourself surrounded by farmhouses and open land.

By Bus
From Granville Street, in downtown Vancouver, the no. 602, no. 603, and no. 604 operate in the weekday peak hours. No. 601 operates from Granville Street every 30 minutes 7 days a week. The trip can take 40 minutes to 1 hour, depending on the number of stops.

Easy Side Trips from Vancouver

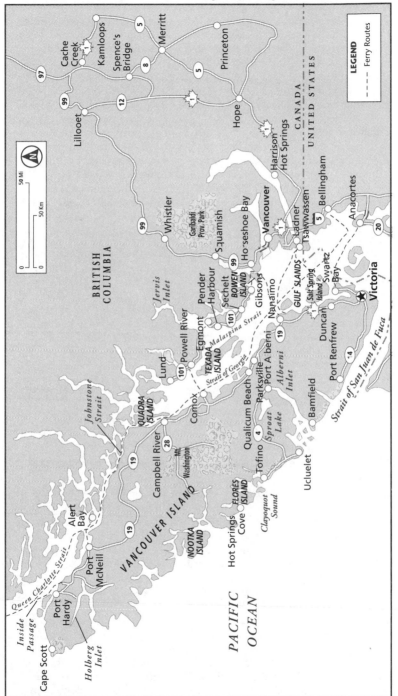

199

WHERE TO EAT

There are several family-style restaurants in the village that serve up pizza, steaks, pasta, or fish and chips, but my suggestion would be to bring or buy sandwiches in the village and head out to the **Ladner Harbour Park** (5100 River Rd.). It's dubbed the "bunny park" by locals because of the dozens of rabbits lazing around in the sun. (In winter, rabbits are scarce, but you'll be able to spot the bald eagles in the trees.)

There are easy trails, ducks in the marsh, a kids' playground, picnic tables, and a barbecue area. **Swenson Walk** is clearly marked to the left of the park's entrance. It takes you along to the Ladner Slough to see all the colorful fishing boats. Keep going and you hit more sloughs, lots of waterfowl, woodpeckers, and robins, and if you keep walking there is a lookout tower in the marshes.

In case of rain or ennui you could try **Uncle Herbert's Fish and Chips,** 4866 Delta St. (near Bridge St.) (© **604/946-8222**), with its themed rooms, wartime tunes, and English mushy peas, or **Sara's Old-Fashioned Ice Cream,** 4857 Elliot St. (© **604/940-4850**).

THINGS TO SEE & DO

Burns Bog   This is the largest undeveloped urban land area in Canada, with some 160 species of birds and mammals including bears, coyotes, beavers, and the threatened sandhill crane, the oldest known bird. Burns Bog is huge—more than eight times the size of Stanley Park—but only a small portion called the Delta Nature Reserve is available to the public. It feels a little like you've left earth for another planet. It's bikable, but if you choose to go on foot, there are four trails into the bog, the longest under 2 kilometers (1.2 miles).

Administration offices at 202-11961 88th Ave., Ladner. © **604/572-0373**. Open daily dawn to dusk. Free. On Hwy. 91, cross the Alex Fraser Bridge and take the first exit at River Rd.; turn right at the second light (east) onto Nordel Way, then east again on Nordel Court so you're almost back under the Alex Fraser Bridge; you'll see the Great Pacific Forum Sports Complex and park at the east end next to the building, and you'll see signs to the Delta Nature Reserve.

Delta Museum and Archives   It's hard to miss the totem poles out front of this quaint 1912 building, which once housed the courts and jail. It now keeps the community's fishing and farming history.

4858 Delta St. (at Bridge St.), Ladner. © **604/946-9322**. Tues–Sat 10am–3:30pm and Sun 2–4pm. Admission by donation.

Reifel Migratory Bird Sanctuary   This is a very pretty drive or bike ride of 10 kilometers (6 miles) from the village through farmland and across a single-lane wooden bridge to Westham Island. On the way, check out Canoe Pass Village's mega-houseboats, complete with kayak davits. Stop for some strawberries, raspberries, and blueberries in summer, and at other times of the year, see the great blue herons fishing by the side of the road. In winter, you'll see thousands of migrating birds at the Sanctuary (many in the car park and in no hurry to move for pesky cars). The bird population fluctuates, but depending on the time of year you may well spot a snowy owl, a bald eagle, or perhaps snow geese, chickadees, and towhees amongst the 850 acres of trails, wetlands, and dykes. Shore birds start arriving in mid-August, followed by mallard and pintail ducks. In September and October, the numbers increase and reach a peak in early November. Most of these birds remain until the end of March. May is the best time to see the ducklings and goslings. The trails are stroller-friendly and you can pick up a bag of birdseed for C50¢ (US33¢) and in the winter, at least, the birds will swarm you.

5191 Robertson Rd., Westham Island (at the mouth of the Fraser River). © **604/946-6980**. Open daily 9am–4pm. C$4 (US$2.65) adults, C$2 (US$1.30) children.

2 Harrison Hot Springs

125 kilometers (78 miles) E of Vancouver

Harrison Hot Springs is an easy hour-and-a-half drive along the Trans-Canada Highway. It's a lovely spot in the Fraser Valley to take your family. Harrison Lake is the largest lake in the Lower Mainland and has water access to the Pacific Ocean via the Harrison River and Fraser River. While Harrison Lake has been a resort since 1886, in many ways it is still delightfully underdeveloped, with a very small-town feel and shops, restaurants, and facilities in easy walking distance from each other and the lake.

It is perfect in the summer, as the lagoon provides a warm spot for swimming or boating and the beach is ideal for sunbathing and digging. In July, the **Harrison Festival of the Arts** is a 10-day festival of world music, dance, theater, and visual arts with over 200 international, national, and local performers, artists, and guests (© 604/796-3664; harrfest@uniserve.com). And, as the summer winds down, there is the **World Championship Sand Sculpture Competition,** in which individuals and teams compete for prize money on a Sunday afternoon in early September. Admission to the sand sculpture park during the competition is C$5 (US$3.30) for adults, C$1 (US66¢) for kids under 13 (© **604/796-3425**).

Harrison Hot Springs is also a great winter getaway. The public pool is open year-round and fueled by the nearby hot springs. If you want to stay over, there are good deals and packages to be had at the Harrison Hot Springs Resort Hotel. In late November nearby **Harrison River** is a draw for up to 1,500 bald eagles and is a short drive away, and **Hemlock Mountain** offers skiing and snowboarding.

For more information: **Harrison Hot Springs Information Centre,** 499 Hot Springs Rd., Box 255, Harrison Hot Springs, BC V0M 1K0 (© **604/796-3525**).

GETTING THERE
By Car
Take the Trans-Canada Highway (Hwy. 1), which bypasses the large districts and towns of Langley, Aldergrove, Abbotsford, and Chilliwack. After Chilliwack, take Highway 9 to the north and follow it past Agassiz to Harrison Hot Springs. Turn off Highway 9, 6.5 kilometers (4 miles) past the junction of highways 9 and 7.

By Bus
The **Super Shuttle** (© **604/594-3333**) provides daily bus service from the Vancouver International Airport to Harrison Hot Springs. The cost one way is C$48 (US$32) for adults, C$24 (US$16) for children 6 to 12, and children 5 and under are free.

⎛ **Fun Fact**

The mineral-rich hot springs at Harrison were originally used by the Salish Coast Indians, who revered them as a "healing place" and traveled by canoe to benefit from their rejuvenating waters. Today, it is believed that the waters bring relief to sufferers of rheumatism and arthritis. The hot springs are reported to promote the elimination of impurities through the skin, bowels, and kidneys.

WHERE TO STAY

Executive Hotel This hotel has an atrium-style lobby with a fountain and is close to restaurants and shops. There is no pool, but the lake and public pool are within a couple of blocks and some rooms have a water view. The kids will like the game room, which has a pool table, table tennis, air hockey, and board games. The suites are actually large rooms, and only one unit has a kitchen.

P.O. Box 70, 190 Lillooet Ave. (across from the Harrison Hot Springs Mall), Harrison Hot Springs, BC V0M 1K0. ℂ **888/265-1155** or 604/796-5555. Fax 604/796-3731. 88 units. C$140 (US$92) May 1–Sept 30 double, C$110 (US$73) Oct 1–Apr 30. Kitchen suite C$180 (US$119) Mar 1–Oct 31; C$150 (US$99) Nov 1–Feb 28. Children under 18 stay free in parents' room. Playpens free. Rollaways C$10 (US$6.60). AE, DISC, MC, V. Free parking. Pets C$10 (US$6.60). **Amenities:** Restaurant; Jacuzzi; sauna; steam room; exercise room; games room; concierge; limited room service; babysitting; coin-op washers and dryers; nonsmoking rooms. *In room:* A/C, TV w/ pay movies, fax, dataport, fridge, coffeemaker, hairdryer.

Harrison Hot Springs Resort 🌟🌟 The outdoor pools are a kid's dream, especially when lit up at night with hundreds of fairy lights. In fact the hotel has 2,400 square meters (8,000 sq. ft.) of natural mineral hot spring pools, open all year. The pools have a temperature range of 29°C to 40°C (85°F to 104°F). The two indoor pools are open 22 hours a day and the three outdoor pools from 8am to 10pm. The indoor rooms and the spa were completely remodeled and updated in the spring of 2001.

Largely filled by conferences and conventions in the winter months, the hotel has been working hard to make itself attractive to families in the summer and at Christmas, Easter, and spring break. Both restaurants offer an artist's corner with paper and markers, a games/play area, and balloons and a sucker on departure. There are coloring books and crayons for the kids with room service, and sandwiches especially for kids at the coffee shop. Buckets and other digging toys are available for kids to cart to the beach and there's a pretty hiking trail at the back of the property accessed by a wooden bridge over the Miarna River, which, at about half a kilometer, is an ideal distance for small children.

Accommodation is made up of guest rooms (some that adjoin), cottages, and suites with various views, some of the lake, some of the pool, some of the garden. It's best to check with the hotel or its website to see which configuration and price best suit your family.

There is a large game room that has video games, table tennis, and floor shuffleboard that will keep the kids entertained for an hour or two at night or on a rainy day. Older ones might enjoy the complimentary afternoon tea, cakes, and cookies served daily at 4pm.

If you stay here, you'll be in good company. According to the PR bumf, guests over the years include the King and Queen of Siam, Clark Gable, John Wayne, Sydney Poitier, and Sylvester Stallone.

100 Esplanade, Harrison Hot Springs, BC V0M 1K0. ℂ **800/663-2266** or 604/796-2244. Fax 604/796-3682. www.harrisonresort.com. 323 units. C$179–$279 (US$118–$184) July–Sept; C$159–$259 (US$105–$171) Oct–June double. 1- and 2-bedroom suites C$179–$619 (US$118–$409). AE, DC, MC, V. Pets in cottages only. **Amenities:** Restaurant (Fraser Valley cuisine); cafe (children's menu in both restaurants); coffee shop; bar; 2 indoor and 3 outdoor natural mineral hot spring pools; full spa; massage therapy; exercise room; 2 tennis courts; water sports equipment rentals; bike rentals; children's program, children's waterpark & playground; game room & video arcade; concierge; babysitting; same-day laundry/dry cleaning; nonsmoking rooms. *In room:* AC, TV w/ pay movies & Nintendo, fax, dataport, minibar, coffeemaker, hairdryer, iron.

WHERE TO EAT

There are several restaurants in the vicinity, although a couple we tried were overpriced and pretty awful. Our friends, also with youngish children, recommend the Japanese restaurant and sushi bar **Kitami,** 380 Hot Springs Rd. (✆ **604/796-2728**), and there is a **Baskin-Robbins Ice Cream Parlour** on the Esplanade (✆ **604/796-5563**), open on weekends from 10am to 6pm.

The Copper Room FRASER VALLEY   This is an upmarket restaurant and the signature restaurant for the Harrison Hot Springs Resort. It is also probably the best in the area, is built in a beautiful setting, and wants to appeal particularly to the family market in summer. A recent touch is to let kids decorate their own ice-cream sundaes in the kitchen. There is a treasure trove of toys presented for the child to select after the meal is finished and a balloon and sucker given when they leave. The band plays kids' songs early in the evening, and children are encouraged to dance. What stood out for us was the awesome Sunday buffet. It was one of the best we'd had and even our picky kids were able to go back for seconds and thirds, before they cleaned up the dessert table. The prices on the kids' menu are C$1 (US66¢) per year of age for children 1 to 5; C$8.95 (US$5.90) for children 6 to 12. For the awesome weekend buffet, kids 12 and under pay C$1 (US66¢) per year of age.

100 Esplanade, Harrison Hot Springs, BC V0M 1K0. ✆ **800/663-2266** or 604/796-2244. www.harrison resort.com. Reservations recommended. Main courses C$19–$32 (US$13–$21). AE, DC, MC, V. Open daily 6pm–10pm. Highchairs, boosters, kids' menu.

THINGS TO SEE & DO
There are several attractions in the vicinity. **Dinotown** (take exit 135 into Bridal) has rides, live shows, golf, hiking, and a bunch of dinosaur characters for kids. It's open mid-June to September and costs C$11.50 (US$7.60) adults and children, with kids under 3 free. Nearby, **Trans Canada Waterslides,** 53790 Popkum Rd. (off Hwy. 1), Bridal Falls (✆ **888/883-8852** or 604/794-7455; www.waterslides.chwk.com), opens daily from 10am to 8pm from mid-June to September and has everything from mini-golf to a volleyball court and a video arcade and children's playground. Admission is C$15 (US$9.90) for adults, C$12 (US$7.90) for children 4 to 12, and there is a twilight price of C$10 (US$6.60).

In the late summer and early fall, kids might like to try their hand at **rock hounding,** which is best in the low water of the Fraser River between Agassiz and Hope. Here gravel bars are exposed and yield over 600 varieties of rocks, including jade.

In winter, the **Harrison River** is home to five different species of salmon, and many of them return between late November and early December. This is also the best time to view the bald eagles that come to the river to feed on the fish. This is, of course, also the time of year to take advantage of cross-country and downhill skiing and snowboarding at the nearby **Hemlock Valley Ski & Recreation Area.** The mountain offers 19 runs and 4 lifts and is 65 kilometers (23 miles) north of Harrison Mills.

In the spring the **Minter Gardens,** 52892 Bunker Rd. (near Hwy. 9, just north of Hwy. 1—take exit 135 off Hwy. 1) (✆ **800/661-3919** or 604/794-7191; www.minter.org), is not really a big hit with kids, but there are enough little winding walks, a maze, and aviaries to keep them happy while you check out at least a couple of the 11 theme gardens and a bonsai or two. It's open April to mid-October, daily from 9am to 5pm in April, May, and October, from 9am to 6pm in June and from 9am to 7pm in July, and August. Admission is C$12 (US$7.90) for adults, C$6.50 (US$4.30) for kids 6 to 18, and kids 5 and under are free.

And, year-round, drop into the **Harrison Hot Springs Public Pool,** right in front of the lake at Harrison Hot Springs Road and Esplanade Avenue (© **604/796-2244**). It's open daily from 9am to 9pm. The price is C$7 (US$4.60) for adults, C$5 (US$3.30) for children, and children 4 and under are free.

3 The Sunshine Coast

While actually part of the mainland, the Sunshine Coast is only accessible by water or air. It's a great ferry ride from West Vancouver or, if you're traveling to Vancouver Island, a short hop from Powell River.

The trip from Vancouver takes about 1½ hours, which includes the 40-minute ferry ride from Horseshoe Bay. It's an extremely easy day trip, but you also might want to stay over and explore the 80 kilometers (50 miles) of coast thoroughly. Especially if you like water, there are dozens of inlets and islands, some great kayaking and canoeing, sailing, and both salt- and fresh-water fishing for trout, spring, and coho salmon, rockfish, and cod. Scuba divers can hunt for giant pacific octopus at Skookumchuck and Tzoonie Narrows, and there is a mass of trails for hiking, biking, and horse riding.

In many ways, the Sunshine Coast is extremely underdeveloped. You won't find any of the big chain hotels, but there are lots of small motels and several resorts that are quite reasonably priced and great for families.

For more information online, see **www.bigpacific.com,** which has extensive information about the Sunshine Coast (© **604/885-5913**). There is also the free **Sunshine Coast Guide,** which has maps and directories and tourism information. Pick it up free on the Coast or write to **Community Projects,** 101-1524 56th St., Tsawwassen, BC V4L 2A8 (© **800/867-5141**), or you can request a copy through www.bigpacific.com. You can also write to the **Sechelt & District Chamber of Commerce Visitor Information Centre,** Trail Bay Mall, Box 360, Sechelt, BC V0N 3A0 (© **877/633-2963** or 604/885-0662; fax 604/885-0691; www.secheltchamber.bc.ca); **Gibsons & District Chamber of Commerce Business & Visitor Information Centre,** Sunnycrest Mall, Gibsons, BC V0N 1V0 (© **604/886-2325;** fax 604/886-2379; www.gibsons chamber.com); and the **Pender Harbour & District Chamber of Commerce and Information Centre,** Madeira Park, BC (© **604/883-2561**), which is only staffed in July and August.

GETTING THERE
By Car & Ferry
From Vancouver: If you're coming from downtown Vancouver, take West Georgia Street over the Lions Gate Bridge, turn left on Marine Drive, turn right on Taylor Way, and follow the signs to the Trans-Canada Highway (Highway 1) and on to the Horseshoe Bay Ferry Terminal. The ferry lane to Langdale on the Sunshine Coast is on the far right.

If there is a long lineup for the Nanaimo ferry leading up to the terminal, be sure to let the traffic flagperson know that you are traveling to the Sunshine Coast. You can go straight down to the terminal and the separate Langdale toll booth.

The first ferry leaves Horseshoe Bay at 7:20am and then about every 2 hours up until 9:15pm. To return to Horseshoe Bay from Langdale, the first ferry leaves at 6:20am and the last at 8:20pm. More ferries are added to the schedule on long weekends and in the summer roughly every 2 hours starting at 7:20am, with the last boat at 9:15pm. For up-to-date ferry schedules call © **888/223-3779** or go to www.bcferries.com. You must buy a return fare at Horseshoe Bay. In the peak summer season—June 28 to September 9—the price is C$8 (US$5.30) for adults, C$4 (US$2.65) for children 5 to 11, plus C$27.75 (US$18.30) for a standard-sized car or van. In the shoulder season (check the website for dates), the cost is C$7.75 (US$5.10) for adults, C$4 (US$2.65) for children 5 to 11, and the vehicle rates vary slightly depending on the time of year from C$22.75 to $25.25 (US$15 to $16.65). Children under 5 are free. There are no reservations on this route, and in the summer, and especially on long weekends, the ferries get quite busy, so give yourself plenty of time or you may miss the sailing. Seats are comfortable on the ferry and offer up panoramic views of Howe Sound and islands such as Galiano and Texada along the way. There is an onboard restaurant, a play area for small children, a gift shop, and a games arcade.

From Vancouver Island: Take a 75-minute ferry ride from Comox on the Island to Powell River on the Mainland. From Powell River you need to drive about 30 kilometers (18.5 miles) southeast to Saltery Bay and catch a ferry to Earls Cove, which is at the top end of the Sunshine Coast and takes about 50 minutes. The first ferry departs Saltery Bay at 5:45am every day except Sunday, when it departs at 7:30am, then roughly every 2 hours until 9:15pm. If you are leaving Earls Cove, the first ferry departs at 6:30am except on Sunday, when it departs at 8:25am. Then it leaves every 2 hours or so until 10:10pm. The fare for the ferry from Earls Cove to Saltery Bay is included in the fare you paid to get from Horseshoe Bay to Langdale, but the return will cost you the same amount again. The one-way fare from Comox to Powell River is C$7.25 (US$4.80) for adults, C$3.75 (US$ 2.50) for children 5 to 11, and children under 5 are free. In the summer, the vehicle fare increases to C$25 (US$16.50), the adult fare increases to C$7.50 (US$4.95), and the child's fare remains the same.

Once you are on the Sunshine Coast, there is one main road—Highway 101—that takes you from one end of the coast to the other. If you have arrived at the Earls Cove terminal, head south.

If you are catching the ferry from Vancouver to Langdale, turn left on Highway 101 when you leave the terminal. Gibsons Landing is 4 kilometers (2.5 miles) along the highway. You can either turn left and take the scenic route through Gibsons Landing (Lower Gibsons) or continue straight ahead and take the highway to Roberts Creek and beyond. The maps of the coast make the distances look huge, but Roberts Creek is only 14 kilometers (9 miles) from the terminal or about a 10-minute drive, Davis Bay is 24 kilometers (15 miles), Sechelt is 27 kilometers (17 miles), Pender Harbour is 64 kilometers (40 miles), and Earls Cove is 81 kilometers (50 miles). The road is windy, especially from Sechelt to Earls Cove, and snakes through small towns and coves, but you can easily drive from one end to the other in under 2 hours.

By Bus

Malaspina Coach Lines (© **604/885-2217**) on the Sunshine Coast offers service from the Vancouver International Airport all the way to Powell River with stops at Gibsons, Sechelt, and Pender Harbour along the way. The bus also picks up at the Pacific Central Station bus terminal (at the corner of Terminal and Main streets in Vancouver). The one-way fare from the airport is C$40 (US$26) for adults and C$20 (US$13) for children 5 to 11, and children under 5 are free. From the bus terminal, the cost is C$30 (US$20) for adults, C$15 (US$10) for children 5 to 11, and children under 5 are free. Buses depart the Vancouver International Airport at 7:30am and 5:30pm daily and leave from the bus depot at 8:15am and 6:15pm. Schedules change and it's always best to call first.

If you are taking the **TransLink** bus to Horseshoe Bay and making the crossing as a foot passenger, contact the local transit bus service, operated by the **Sunshine Coast Regional District,** 5477 Wharf Rd., Sechelt (© **604/885-3234;** www.scrd.bc.ca), for a schedule. The fares are C$1.50 (US$1) for adults, and C$1 (US66¢) for children 5 and up.

By Air

There are two small airlines that operate out of Sechelt and fly a scheduled service into the south terminal at Vancouver International Airport and also Nanaimo on Vancouver Island. **Coast Western Airlines,** 5878 Marine Way (© **604/885-4711**), offers flights at C$78 (US$52) one way and C$146 (US$96) return with a two-seat minimum. **Mid-Coast Airlines,** Sechelt Inlet Rd. (© **888/436-7776** or 604/740-8889), costs C$99 (US$65) one way and C$198 (US$131) return with a two-seat minimum. There are charter outfits, too: **Sechelt-Gibson Air,** top of Field Road, Wilson Creek (© **604/885-1062**); **Baxter Air,** at the Lighthouse Pub site, Porpoise Bay (© **800/661-5599**); **Goldwing Helicopters,** 2206 Field Rd., Wilson Creek (© **604/885-1062**); and **Airspan Helicopters,** 2076 Field Rd., Wilson Creek (© **604/885-7474**).

GIBSONS

This is a delightful seaside village that gives you the feeling that time has stood still. It's famous for a long-defunct CBC television series called *The Beachcombers,* and Molly's Reach, the restaurant that provided the main set for the series, still overlooks the harbor and serves food. You'll also find a great variety of restaurants and lots of funky shops and galleries. There are two sandy swimming beaches close to the action—one is at Armours Beach Park just off Marine Crescent, before you enter Gibsons Landing. The other is Georgia Beach (Georgia Drive) at Waterfront Park. When you enter Lower Gibsons, take Skyline Drive to the top of the bluff. Gibsons public indoor swimming pool is located on Gibsons Way (at Park Road).

WHERE TO EAT

Pack Ratt Louie's Grill ★★ WEST COAST It's worth a trip to the Sunshine Coast just to eat at this funky restaurant. The plates are heaped with reasonably priced food, everything from pasta and Szechwan dishes to pizzas and steak and burgers. It was also one of the most relaxing lunches we've had with the kids for a long time, mainly because the owners have put a lot of thought into what makes kids happy. It's not hard—some crayons, a menu, a small table heaped with toys, and a small library made up of kids' books from garage sales for older ones, and magazines in racks. There is also lots to look at. Some quite decent watercolors from local artists, old-fashioned school desks with healthy plants resting on top, a sewing machine and a large plastic rat at the door, a birdcage, and a pair of blue boots placed on the floor. Money was tight when the restaurant opened, so they made lights from aluminum flashing and whacked holes in them—it looks great. There is a trivia contest: if you can answer all 10 questions correctly you get a free entree. The kids' menu is a great deal at C$4 (US$2.65) and the drinks—pop or slushies—come in jars. There is an outdoor patio in the summer and real napkins on the tables. In fact, I'd walk over hot coals for the Bennie by the Sea (eggs benedict with a bunch of salmon and other seafood) heaped with fresh fruit, and the weekend brunch also has great French toast and omelets.

818 Gibsons Way, Gibsons (in Upper Gibsons). ✆ **604/886-1646**. Main courses C$10.95–$15.95 (US$7.25–$10.55), Sat and Sun brunch C$5.95–$8.95 (US$3.95–$5.90). AE, MC, V. Open Mon–Fri 11:30am–8pm, Sat–Sun 11am–8pm; stays open an hour or so later in the summer and when it's busy on weekends. Highchairs, boosters, kids' menu.

THINGS TO SEE & DO
Gibsons Lanes Here's an old-time eight-lane bowling alley with five-pin bowling, ideal for kids aged 4 and up. Has a snack bar.

724 Gibsons Way (below North Rd.), Gibsons. ✆ **604/886-2086**. C$16 (US$10.55) an hour per lane.

Maritime Museum You'll find lots of models of sailing ships, artifacts, and pictures of marine life. The museum is staffed by volunteers and tries to open Tuesdays, Thursdays, and Saturdays from 10am to 4pm, but it's best to call first.

Molly's Lane (by Molly's Reach Restaurant), Gibsons. ✆ **604/886-4114**. Admission by donation.

Sprockids This is a mountain bike park on a couple of acres of land, with courses for different abilities suitable for ages of about 8 and up. As you leave the Langdale Ferry terminal, go straight and where the road turns left into Gibsons, you turn right into the park. It's open all year around and there is a map at the entrance indicating the different trails.

ROBERTS CREEK
Travel about 14 kilometers (9 miles) from the ferry terminal down Highway 101 and take the Roberts Creek Road turnoff on your left. There's a pier that's both stroller and wheelchair accessible and there's a great beach for beach combing. Stop at the General Store for awesome Coast ice cream—they put a candy on top. If you are hungry, there is the **Gum Boot Garden Cafe,** 1057 Roberts Creek Rd. (✆ **604/885-4216**), which serves burritos and sandwiches with most meals well under C$10 (US$6.60). Nearby, there is a library, a post office, and a smattering of clothes shops and galleries.

THINGS TO SEE & DO
Chapman Creek Walk Disneyland this ain't, but it is a little like the Teddy Bear's picnic—if you go down to the woods today you're in for a big surprise. In this case it's gnomes. And my kids loved the gnomes' trail that leads to a gnome house built inside a large hollow tree. Kids can climb the stairs and play inside and then come out along the trail and search for the 17 chainsaw gnomes carved on the trees. (Hint: One is on the gnome house.) It's a fun and fairly easy walk for young children along the creek and over little bridges and rocky outcrops, but it's definitely not stroller friendly. Back at the park they can burn off energy safely on the swings and slide before heading back to the car.

Brookman Park This lovely spot is just past Roberts Creek and before Davis Bay. Go over the Chapman Creek Bridge and Brookman Park is immediately on your right. Park in the lot and follow the trail along the creek.

Chapman Creek Fish Hatchery The hatchery raises between 400,000 and 800,000 salmonids every year. If you don't know what these are, hands-on displays and presentations will tell you all about the different species of Pacific salmon, plus steelhead and cutthroat trout. Kids are given their own fishing rod and line and allowed to catch a rainbow trout to take home for dinner. It's a fundraiser for the hatchery and costs C$2.50 (US$1.65) per trout. From

September until about mid-December you can watch about a thousand or so migrating coho salmon return to Chapman Creek. One Saturday in July each year there is a "Kids' Catch a Fish Day"—for C$10 (US$6.60) kids get a book of tickets that allows them to catch and keep two trout, have their face painted, and get balloons.

4381 Parkway, Wilson Creek, VON 3A1. © 604/885-4136. Free. Open Mon–Fri 9am–4pm, Sat–Sun 10am–2pm.

DAVIS BAY

Davis Bay is about a 5-minute drive away from Roberts Creek, and when the tide is out, you will find a sandy beach. While we're not talking stretches of white Californian sand here, it's big enough to hold a sandcastle-building competition in July each year, and at low tide the rocks and tide pools offer up sea life. The dock is a great hangout for kids in the summer time, and they can jump off the dock or play volleyball on the nearby sand court. **Pier 17** is a great place to stop to grab an ice cream, some lunch from the Italian deli, or a coffee to take with you while you comb the beach, bake in the sun, or lounge after a swim. More like a market than a general store, you can eat inside or on the outside patio, buy water toys and organic produce, or simply lounge around with a magazine. Open Monday to Friday 5:30am to 11pm and weekends 7:30am to 11pm. On the same side of the road is the **Mosaic Market Tea Room,** 4780 Sunshine Coast Hwy. (Davis Bay), Sechelt (© 604/740-0047), where you will find about 25 vendors selling everything from antiques and cards to swimwear, kites, and Beanie Babies. You can have a cup of tea or coffee at the Tea Room or grab a homemade pie for lunch or just stop in for ice cream. On Tuesdays from noon to 3pm you can get your tea leaves read for C$10 (US$6.60). The Tea Room is open daily from 10am to 5:30pm.

WHERE TO STAY

Bella Beach Inn   Across the road from Davis Bay Beach, this motel is simple and clean and has drop-dead views of the ocean. All the units have either a balcony or ground-floor patio, the suites have a sofabed, and some rooms have fireplaces. The doubles have a double and a single bed and no kitchenette, so it's well worth upgrading to the suite if one is available. Kitchenettes come with fridge, hot plate, toaster, and tea kettle. Davis Bay is a great location, minutes from Sechelt and central to the ferry terminal, hikes, restaurants, and attractions.

4748 Sunshine Coast Hwy., Davis Bay, BC VON 3A2. © 800/665-1925 or 604/885-7191. Fax 604/885-3794. 32 units (11 suites). C$89–$99 (US$59–$65) double; C$99–$109 (US$65–$72) 1-bedroom suite; C$129–$139 (US$85–$92) 2-bedroom suite. MC, V. Free parking. **Amenities:** Restaurant (Japanese); non-smoking rooms. *In room:* TV, mini-fridge, coffeemaker, kitchenettes in suites, hairdryer.

SECHELT

Sechelt is the largest town on the Sunshine Coast and has lots of restaurants, shops, a beach, and a movie theater. Wander along the beach at Trail Bay and the kids will find lots of rocks to climb at Snickett Park, and there's a trail along the shore to the Sechelt Indian Band lands at the east end of town. **Porpoise Bay Provincial Park** on Sechelt Inlet Road is a great place to take your family. There is a good playground, nature hikes among second-growth Douglas fir, western red cedar, western hemlock, maple, and alder, and a sandy beach with a protected swimming area.

WHERE TO STAY

The Driftwood Inn   Five rooms have killer ocean views and either a balcony or ground-floor patio to enjoy them. It's a great location, right on the beach with no roads to cross, and close to trails, restaurants, shops, and attractions. The motel was built in 1981 and extensively renovated in 1994. The rooms are larger than normal and newly painted and pleasantly furnished. One of the doubles has two double beds and a bunk bed, and there are two suites with well-equipped kitchenettes.

5454 Trail Ave. (corner of Teredo St.), Box 829, Sechelt BC V0N 3A0. © **604/885-5811.** Fax 604/885-5836. www.travel.bc.ca/d/driftwood. 28 units (2 suites). C$89 (US$59) double; C$129 (US$85) double with view; C$139 (US$92) double with view, patio or balcony, and kitchenette. Kids under 17 stay free in parents' room. Cribs free, rollaways C$10 (US$6.60). AE, DC, MC, V. Free parking. Pets C$10 (US$6.60). **Amenities:** Restaurant (steak & seafood); babysitting; same-day laundry/dry cleaning; nonsmoking rooms. *In room:* TV, kitchenettes in some, coffeemaker.

WHERE TO EAT

Old Boot Eatery ITALIAN   This funky eatery has a tiled floor, lots of wood, and large airy windows on the street that give it that West Coast feel. It serves up great pasta and pizzas and has a small outdoor patio in the summer. The kids' menu has things like spaghetti and meat sauce, fettuccini Alfredo, and the signature Old Boot cheese and noodles, and dishes come with pop and ice cream. Crayons will keep the kids busy.

108A-5530 Wharf Street Plaza, Sechelt © **604/885-2727.** Main courses C$9–$19 (US$6–$12.50), kids' menu C$6 (US$4). AE, MC, V. Open Mon–Sat 11am–10pm. Highchairs, boosters, kids' menu.

THINGS TO SEE & DO

Raven's Cry Theatre   Check out first-run and foreign films and local theater productions including concerts and plays.

5555 Hwy. 101, Sechelt. © **604/886-6843.**

Sechelt's Rotary Chatelech Skateboard Park   This is one of the largest skateboard parks in Western Canada, where kids of about 10 and up tear around on skateboards and BMX bikes at breakneck speed. Turn right off Highway 101 at Shorncliffe Road, then left at Barnacle Street—you'll see the Anglican Church on the corner. Follow the street, which turns into Cowrie Street and then Pilot Way, up to the top of the hill.

PENDER HARBOUR

Pender Harbour is a huge area that includes Madeira Park, Garden Bay, and Irvines Landing, and by land it's a mass of winding roads that seem to go for miles past lakes and forests. If you are staying down here, water taxis may be the best and most interesting way of getting from point A to point B, or, in the summer, a scheduled passenger ferry connects Madeira Park to Garden Bay or Irvines Landing in about 10 minutes. If you are driving from one of these towns to another, give yourself about 20 minutes to navigate the winding country roads. Madeira Park has a small shopping area with a supermarket, a drug store, and a bakery that makes delicious lattes and things like shepherd's pie and also sells clothing. As the name suggests, the **Hamburger Stand** (© **604/883-9655**) sells hamburgers, hot dogs, or corn dogs. There are a few restaurants scattered around the area. In Garden Bay family restaurants are the **Sundowner Inn** and the **Garden Bay Restaurant,** and **Seiners Restaurants** is a family restaurant at Madeira Park, on Highway 101 just after the Madeira Park Road turnoff on the left.

The Pender Harbour indoor swimming pool is on Highway 101 behind the high school and about 1 kilometer (0.6 miles) past the Garden Bay Road turnoff.

WHERE TO STAY

Lowe's Resort   This ain't Club Med, but then again you're not paying those prices either. What you will find is a comfortable no-frills resort that makes a great springboard for touring the rest of the Sunshine Coast with your family. We stayed in a two-bedroom unit much like a mobile home. The walls were paper thin, but it had everything we needed, including a large kitchen with stove, fridge, microwave, toaster, dishes, cutlery, pots, and pans provided. There are several one- and two-bedroom cabins dotted around the site and some of the one-bedrooms have a water view. Pender Harbour is geared toward water activities and the resort has lots of grassy areas to picnic, a small sandy beach, and a campfire and barbecue area. If you tire of the water, you can rent adult-sized mountain bikes for C$6 (US$4) an hour (minimum of 2 hours).

12841 Lagoon Rd. (Box 153), Madeira Park, BC V0N 2H0. ℂ 877/883-2456 or 604/883-2474. www.lowes resort.bc.ca. 17 units. C$85–$95 1-, 2-, & 3- bedroom cottages, low-season discounts available. Extra charge C$10 ($6.60) per child over 11 years, C$5 (US$3.30) per child between 5 & 10, children under 5 free. Camp-sites C$15 (US$9.90) double, C$3 (US$2) extra person. Playpens and highchairs available free. MC, V. Free parking. **Amenities:** Boats, canoe & kayak rentals; tackle sales & rentals; mountain bike rentals; coin-op washers and dryers. *In room:* TV, full kitchen, coffeemaker, no phone.

 Boat, Canoe & Kayak Rentals

You don't need a license to rent power boats, but you do need to go over a safety check list before taking one out.

Bucccaneer Marine & Resort   Sans Souci Rd., Secret Cove ℂ **604/885-7888.** Buccaneer rents 17-foot, 60hp fiberglass craft for C$25 (US$16.50) an hour, or C$180 (US$119) a day. For people who need less speed, 14-foot aluminum fishing boats with 15hp rent for C$20 (US$13.20) an hour, or C$100 (US$66) a day. The limit is 6 adults or children.

Lowes Resort   12841 Lagoon Rd. (Box 153), Madeira Park, BC V0N 2H0. ℂ **877/883-2456** or 604/883-2474. www.lowesresort.bc.ca. Here you can rent anything from a 9-foot, 9hp boat for C$12 (US$8) an hour or C$60 (US$40) a day up to a 17-foot, 70hp boat for C$35 (US$23) an hour or C$170 (US$112) a day, plus canoes and kayaks for C$7 (US$4.60) an hour or C$30 (US$20) a day. Double kayaks are C$10 (US$6.60) an hour or C$45 (US$30) a day.

Pedals & Paddles at the Tillicum Bay Marina   4796 Naylor Rd. (turn off Sechelt Inlet Rd.), Sechelt. ℂ **877/885-6440.** This marina has lots of marine parks to paddle around and pebbly beaches to explore. Rent canoes and fiberglass kayaks—they say the latter are the safest and most popular for families. A double kayak has a central hatch that will fit a child to the age of about 7 or 8 and 2 adult paddlers; the cost is C$54 (US$36) for 4 hours or C$72 (US$48) for a full day. A double kayak costs C$32 (US$21) for 4 hours or C$46 (US$30) for a full day.

Sunshine Coast Resort   12695 Sunshine Coast Hwy., Madiera Park. ℂ **604/883-9177;** www.sunshinecoast-resort.com. Choose from 14-foot, 20hp boats for C$12 (US$7.90) an hour, C$75 (US$49.50) a day to 17-foot, 50hp boats at C$25 (US$16.50) an hour, C$150 (US$99) a day, or take out a canoe for C$5 (US$3.30) an hour, C$35 (US$23) a day.

THINGS TO SEE & DO

If you'd rather be on land than on the water, there are many trails and parks along the coast. This is one of our favorites.

Skookumchuck Trail   Keep heading along Highway 101 to Earls Cove, but turn off at the Egmont sign about 6 kilometers (4 miles) from the highway. Just before Egmont, you'll see the signs to Skookumchuck Trail. Park here and start your hike. We started hiking in from the car park down a residential road, past a house with a bakery and a sign on a tree that told you if it was closed or open, past the little village of Egmont and the water below. The walk takes about an hour, but would be much longer with our not-yet 3-year-old, and we decided that while he might make it in, it wouldn't be a pleasant trek back. Talking to others who have done the walk with families, it seems to be best for kids of about 5 and up, but I've been warned that the actual Narrows can be quite treacherous for little ones and family pets.

The idea is to time your hike so you arrive at one of the two fenced viewpoints when the tidal surge is at its strongest. Check tides before you leave at bigpacific.com or email the visitors center for copies of view tides at visitor info@dccnet.com. The center will also tell you that on a 3 meter (10 ft.) tide change, the rapids send some 200 billion gallons of water flowing through the Skookumchuck.

Tips Spike's Turf

If you're looking for sustenance before or after your hike, stop in at the **General Store**, 6781 Bathgate Rd., just a kilometer (0.6 miles) or so past the trail entrance. Built in 1948, there is a marina with boat rentals, a water taxi service, fax machine, laundromat, showers, tennis courts, and a sign that warns you that no dogs are allowed off the leash "except Spike."

KIDS' CALENDAR OF EVENTS ON THE SUNSHINE COAST

You can catch festivals of all types throughout the year, but of course most happen in the summer months.

January

Polar Bear Swim at Davis Bay Beach.

April

Sechelt Farmer's Market. Buy anything from local honey to hot sauces, jams and jellies, kites, natural herbal products, and, of course, fresh garden produce. Held at the Raven's Cry Theatre on Highway 101 just south of the stoplight in Sechelt from April to mid-October between 8:30am and 1pm.

Annual Quilt Show at Rockwood Lodge in Sechelt. © 604/885-8656.

May

Pender Harbour May Day Celebration. Crafts, music, and a basketball tournament. © 604/883-2561.

Go Fly a Kite. Takes place at the end of the month at Davis Bay Beach (weather permitting). © 604/885-1921.

June

Gibsons Landing Jazz Festival. As well as jazz, there is a craft fair, food booths, kids' events, and an after-hours street dance. Runs for 3 days from 11:30am to 7pm in Dougall Park in Lower Gibsons. ☎ 604/886-3384.

July

Canada Day Celebrations. In and around Gibsons every July 1. ☎ 604/886-2325.

Davis Bay Sandcastle Competition. From noon to 4pm. Register through the Sechelt Chamber of Commerce (☎ 877/663-2963) or sign up at the beach about an hour before the competition begins.

Sea Cavalcade. An annual 3-day community festival that includes a parade and fireworks. Held in Gibsons. ☎ 604/886-3059.

August

Festival of the Written Arts. Novelists, poets, playwrights, and journalists gather to share their latest work through readings and storytelling for 4 days. There are writers' workshops, receptions, and the annual salmon barbecue, and there is usually a least one event especially for children. Past guests include Michael Ondaatje, David Suzuki, Margaret Atwood, and Joni Mitchell. Rockwood Lodge, Sechelt. ☎ 800/565-9631 or 604/885-9631. www.sunshine.net/rockwood.

Lions Club Mid Summer Festival. Arts and crafts fair, games for kids, and food and beverage garden, held at Lions Park. ☎ 604/883-2286.

September

Iron Kids Triathlon. There are several different age groups for kids between 9 and 17, and the course is a 180-meter (600 ft.) swim, 9-kilometer (6 mile) bike ride, and 3.5-kilometer (2 mile) run. Held the first weekend of the month. Cost is C$20 ($13.20). Call ☎ 604/883-8857 or 604/885-4626 to sign up.

Pender Harbour Jazz Festival. Three-day event where musicians entertain in venues throughout the Pender area. On Sunday a family day, held at Lowes Resort in Madeira Park between 11am and 5pm. Tickets are C$15 (US$9.90) and kids under 16 are free. ☎ 877/883-2456 or 604/883-2456. www.sunshine.net/phjazzfest.

4 Parksville

35 kilometers (22 miles) NW of Nanaimo; 111 kilometers (69 miles) N of Victoria

Parksville is located on the east coast of Vancouver Island and is 35 kilometers (22 miles) from Nanaimo, or a 30-minute drive on Highway 19A. Places can't get much better than this for a family in the summer. We first went to Parksville a few years ago; now, every July we spend a week. There's the 19 kilometers (12 miles) of sandy beach, a great water park, and a playground in the downtown area, and for teens there's the **skate park** for skateboarders, BMX riders, and in-line skaters. There are loads of hiking and biking trails in **Rathtrevor Provincial Park** and nearby **Englishman River Falls Park,** and caves to explore at **Horne Lake Caves** Provincial Park. There are a several family restaurants, but if you are staying in accommodation with a kitchen, both Thrifty's and Quality Foods are excellent supermarkets with great prepared-food sections.

For more information, write to the **Oceanside Tourism Association,** Box 374, Qualicum Beach, BC V9K 1S9 (☎ 888/799-3222 or 250/752-2388; fax 250/752-2392; www.oceansidetourism.com). You can also get information from the

Parksville Chamber of Commerce, P.O. Box 99, Parksville, BC V9P 2G3 (© **250/248-3613;** fax 250/248-5210; www.chamber.parksville.bc.ca), on this area. For the Gulf Islands contact **Tourism Vancouver Island,** Suite 203, 335 Wesley St., Nanaimo BC V9R 2T5 (© **250/754-3500;** fax 250/754-3599; www.islands.bc.ca).

GETTING THERE
By Car & Ferry

There are two direct routes from Vancouver: the Mid-Island Express operates between Tsawwassen and Duke Point, about 11 kilometers (7 miles) south of Nanaimo. The 2-hour crossing runs six times daily between 5:30am and 11pm. The fares are the same as for the Tsawwassen-Swartz Bay in the Victoria section below, as are directions to get to Tsawwassen from Vancouver.

The Horseshoe Bay to Nanaimo ferry has eight daily sailings, and leaves Horseshoe Bay in West Vancouver, arriving 95 minutes later in Nanaimo. To reach Horseshoe Bay from Vancouver, take West Georgia Street over the Lions Gate Bridge, turn left at Marine Drive, then take the first right at Taylor Way and follow the signs to the Trans-Canada Highway and head west, and follow the signs to the ferry terminal.

For precise schedule information contact **BC Ferries** at © **888/223-3779** or 888/724-5223 (automated), or www.bcferries.com.

If you plan to drive from Victoria, the most direct route is to take Douglas Street, which turns into Highway 1 outside the downtown area. The distance is 111 kilometers (69 miles) and takes about 1½ hours.

By Train

Travelers on the Horseshoe Bay–Nanaimo ferry can board a train that winds down the Cowichan River Valley through Goldstream Provincial Park into Victoria. VIA Rail's **E&N Railiner** leaves daily from Nanaimo and the trip takes about 2½ hours. The Victoria **E&N Station,** 450 Pandora Ave. (near the Johnston Street Bridge) (© **800/561-8630** in Canada, **800/268-9503** for the hearing impaired; www.viarail.ca). The train also makes a scheduled stop in Parksville. The one-way fare from Nanaimo to Victoria is C$22.47 (US$14.83) for adults, C$11.77 (US$7.77) for children. From Nanaimo to Parksville the fare is C$14.98 (US$9.89) for adults, C$7.49 (US$4.95) for children. Seven-day advance-purchase discounts and other specials are available.

By Air

There are about 20 scheduled flights each day between Vancouver and the Nanaimo Airport, which is 15 kilometers (9 miles) south of downtown Nanaimo. As well, there are several daily scheduled harbor-to-harbor flights.

WestJet (© **800/538-5696**) has 6 scheduled flights per week into Comox, about 30 minutes north of Parksville. **Island Express** (© **866/273-8888**) provides a shuttle service to and from the airport.

By Bus

The **Nanaimo/Parksville Regional Busline** (© **250/954-1001,** www.rdn. bc.ca) runs buses between the two towns every 2 hours or about eight times a day. Fares are C$1.75 (US$1.15) for adults, C$1.50 (US$1) for children 5 and over. A day pass is C$4.50 (US$3) for adults and C$3.50 (US$2.30) for children 5 and over.

Fun Fact **The Marmot**

The Vancouver Island marmot, an endangered species, is more rare than the giant panda. Its primary habitat, just outside of Nanaimo, is protected by a special trust organization.

WHERE TO STAY

Oceans Trail Resort ⭐ We stayed here the first time we came to Parksville and it's a clean and comfortable resort with lots of grassy grounds, a great outdoor pool and Jacuzzi, tennis courts, and a pretty walk to Rathtrevor Beach just minutes away. The units are one-, two-, or three-bedrooms, all are nonsmoking, and they have a washer and dryer, fireplace, outdoor patio, and full kitchen with microwave and dishes, cutlery, pots, and pans provided. The resort has a supervised children's program that runs three afternoons for 3 hours in the summer for children aged 5 to 14 and costs C$5 (US$3.30) per child.

60-1035 East Island Highway, Parksville, BC V9P 2T5. © **888/248-6212** or 250/248-3636. Fax 250/248-3645. www.ocean-trails.com. 55 units. C$79–$139 (US$52–$92) 1-bedroom; C$99–$166 (US$65–$110) 2-bedroom; C$125–$199 (US$83–$131) 3-bedroom. Children 3–15 C$5 (US$3.30) extra, 16 & over C$10 (US$6.60) a night extra. Playpens C$5 (US$3.30). Rollaways C$10 (US$6.60). 7-night minimum stay in the high season (July 1–mid-Sept.). MC, V. Free parking. **Amenities:** Seasonal outdoor pool; Jacuzzi; basketball; volleyball; children's playground; video arcade; children's programs; babysitting. *In room:* TV, fax, dataport, full kitchen, fridge, coffeemaker, no phone.

Tigh na Mara Resort Hotel and Conference Centre ⭐⭐ There are three different styles of accommodation here, but what sold us on the place and keeps us coming back are the two-bedroom log cabins nestled in a forest setting and the terrific kids' programs. The hotel has some lovely ocean-view condominiums, but they are more suitable for couples than families. The lodge rooms are fairly big with a small kitchen and would accommodate a small family, but they are not nearly as fun or as private as the one- or two-bedroom cabins. These are a little on the dark side, but there's a patio and picnic area at the front and loads of room to ride bikes and kick a ball around out the front. They are also close to the pool and just a short walk to Rathtrevor Beach. Kids from about 5 to 12 will love the free children's program. There is something different each afternoon with activities and sports, treasure hunts, and beach combing. Twice a week they have a parents' night out, where for C$10 (US$6.60) a child, you can get away to eat on your own for 3 hours while the kids are fed and entertained. There is also a marshmallow roast and a Friday-night barbecue/dance geared to families. There are basketball and volleyball games scheduled for older kids, and each day's activities are posted outside the gift shop/office.

1095 East Island Highway, Parksville, BC V9P 1E5. © **800/663-7373** or 250/248-2072. www.tigh-na-mara. com. 162 units. C$79–$109 (US$52.15–$71.95) double in the lodge. 1-bedroom cottage C$119–$199 (US$78.55–$131.35), 2-bedroom C$139–$219 (US$91.75–$191.40), children 2–16 C$5 (US$3.30) a night, children under 2 free. Playpens C$2 (US$1.30), rollaways C$4 (US$2.65). AE, DC, MC, V. Cottages have a 1-week minimum stay in the summer. No pets July–Aug, other times of the year C$2 (US$1.30) a day. Free parking. **Amenities:** Restaurant (West Coast); indoor pool; Jacuzzi; sauna; exercise room; tennis court; table tennis; children's playgrounds; adults & children's bike rentals; extensive children's programs; babysitting; coin-op washers and dryers; nonsmoking rooms. *In room:* TV, kitchen, coffeemaker.

Travelodge Parksville Located across the road from Parksville's main beach, this motel was built in the mid-1990s and has an atrium-lobby entrance surrounded by tropical plants, but surprisingly few rooms with a view. Yet it is a great location, close to restaurants, the water park, and mini-golf, and it's unlikely you'd be spending too much time in the room anyway. There are six rooms that are larger than doubles, two with separate bedrooms, and they are, of course, at the higher end of the rate scale.

424 West Island Hwy., Parksville, BC, V9P 1K8 ℂ **800/661-3110** or 250/248-2232. Fax 250/248-3273. www.travelodgeparksville.com. 87 units. C$69–$189 (US$46–$125), rates include continental breakfast; children under 12 stay free in parents' room. Cribs & rollaways C$10 (US$6.60). AE, MC, V. Free parking. Four rooms accommodate pets C$10 (US$6.60) a day. **Amenities:** Indoor pool; Jacuzzi; babysitting; nonsmoking rooms. *In room:* A/C, TV, fax, dataport, coffeemaker, hairdryer.

WHERE TO EAT

Joey's Only Seafood Restaurant SEAFOOD   While the restaurant specializes in all types of seafood, it also serves chicken and ribs. It's very kid-friendly—staff hand out crayons and helium balloons to little ones—and has a kids' menu for C$4 (US$2.65) that includes pop and a choice of fish and chips, popcorn shrimp, and chicken drumsticks. Kids will also like the ocean murals, hanging nets, and blinking lights.

192 West Island Hwy., Parksville. ℂ **250/248-1036.** Reservations not accepted. Main courses C$5–$14 (US$3.30–$9.25). MC, V. Open Mon–Sat 11am–8pm, Sun noon–8pm, and later in the summer. Highchairs, boosters, kids' menu.

Lefty's Restaurant WEST COAST   Next to Thrifty's Foods in Parksville, Lefty's has toys for the kids and takes pride in the fact that it has no deep fryer. Instead of greasy chips, kids get oven-roasted potatoes served up with a salmon, veggie, or chicken burger, a bunwich, wraps, or Shanghai noodles for C$4.50 (US$3). The Qualicum location actually has a separate toy room, where you can shut the door if the kids get too noisy. And, of course, there are crayons. For adults there is everything from wraps to steaks and a good vegetarian selection.

101-280 East Island Hwy., Parksville. ℂ **250/954-3886.** Reservations recommended. Main courses C$6–$17.95 (US$3.95–$11.85). AE, MC, V. Open daily 8am–8pm and until about 10pm in the summer. Highchairs, boosters, kids' menu. Qualicum Beach: 710 Memorial St. ℂ **250/752-7530.**

Quality Foods   Yes, it's a supermarket, but it has a fine take-out section, especially its Chinese food, for which people actually line up some Friday nights. You can eat here on the landscaped patio, or pick up fresh produce to take back to your hotel. The store, which has its head office just up the road in Qualicum Beach, is painted in a Caribbean green color, with brass and oak that gives the store its West Coast look.

319A East Island Hwy., Parksville. ℂ **250/954-2262.** www.qualityfoods.com. Most prepared food items under C$8 (US$5). MC, V. Open daily 7am–10pm.

THINGS TO SEE & DO

Coombs   Just 12 kilometers (7 miles) west of Parksville on the Port Alberni Highway (Hwy. 4) is a little town that has an old western-style emporium and the amazing Old Country Market, open mid-March to October. You can grab a bit to eat here, get an ice cream, or pick up a wicker chair or perhaps some Mexican pottery. Don't forget to look for the live goats on the sod roof—always a photo opp for the kids. Nearby Butterfly World & Gardens (ℂ **250/248-7026;** www.natureworld.com), 1 kilometer (0.6 miles) west of Coombs on the Alberni Highway, has tropical gardens, a turtle pond, and a pond filled with koi.

Cathedral Grove   This is a dense, towering forest with an 800-year-old Douglas fir tree that managed to survive a fire 300 years ago. Located at the top end

of Cameron Lake in MacMillan Provincial Park 20 kilometers (12 miles) west
of Parksville on the Port Alberni Highway.

Lions Venture Playground and Spray Park   Here's a huge area good for
kids of all ages. Kids will definitely get wet, and mine loved the full-sized killer
whale. There's also the Parksville Community Beach—7.5 kilometers (5 miles)
of shoreline. The community park also houses an ice-skating rink, a skateboard
park, tennis courts, and a picnic area. And it's all in downtown Parksville.

Paradise Adventure Mini-Golf   375 West Island Hwy. ⓒ 250/248-6612;
www.golfvancouverisland.com. This is good for a half-day's entertainment. My
3-year-old couldn't hit the golf ball, but he had a blast wandering through the
course with a golf stick. There are two quite different 18-hole courses, and you
get a break on the price if you do both. There are large-scale scenes and figures,
beautiful flowers, night lighting, a gift shop, an ice-cream parlor, an amusement
center, and a games pavilion. In the summer it's open daily from 9:30am to 10pm.

Rathtrevor Beach   Our absolutely foremost reason for being here 5 kilometers (3 miles) of sandy beach. When the tide is out, over 1.5 kilometers
(1 mile) of beach stretches out into the Strait of Georgia. Just after lunch, families start coming with buckets and spades and serious digging devices to build
elaborate castles and moats and watch them wash away with the tide a few hours
later. The water is shallow and great for swimming or walking on and beach
combing in the morning, and there are miles of hiking/biking trails in the
Rathtrevor Provincial Park. And, naturally, it's free.

KIDS CALENDAR OF EVENTS AROUND PARKSVILLE

January
Polar Bear Swim. Parksville Public
Beach, January 1. ⓒ 250/752-
5014.

April
Brant Wildlife Festival. A 3-day
event that celebrates the return of
more than 20,000 mallard-sized
brant geese that stop over on their
way to breeding grounds in Alaska.
Art, photography, carving exhibits,
and nature walks. ⓒ 250/752-
9171.

May
Fire & Ice. Annual downtown ice-
carving competition at Qualicum
Beach. Street entertainment, a chili
cook-off, and a children's Jell-O
carving contest. ⓒ 250/752-9532.

Qualicum Beach Family Day.
Parade and lots of activities. ⓒ 250/
752-1942.

Hammerfest 8. Mountain biking
and downhill and cross-country

racing. Englishman River Falls.
ⓒ 250/248-4020; www.arrowsmith
mtbclub.com.

June
Coombs Rodeo. Western-style
activities and events, top bull riders,
junior barrel racing, barbecue dinner, and dances. Coombs Rodeo
Ground, 6 kilometers (4 miles) west
of Parksville. ⓒ 250/248-1009.

July
Parksville Canada Day. A parade,
giant birthday cake, entertainment,
and fireworks to celebrate Canada's
birthday July 1. ⓒ 250/248-3613.

August
Parksville Beach Festival. The
main event is the Sandcastle Competition, but there's also a kids'
festival and beach volleyball. At
the Waterfront Community Park.
ⓒ 250/248-3613.

Coombs Fall Fair. Country living and cooking competitions every year since 1913. © **250/752-9757.**

Kidfest. Kids' sandcastle competitions, clowns, storytellers, and entertainers. Parksville Beach. © **250/ 248-3252;** www.kidfest.parksville. bc.ca.

Just for the Heck of It No Reason at All Mid-Summer Nights Parade. Music throughout the day at the Old Country Market. Parade starts at 7pm at the Rodeo Grounds and finishes at the fair grounds. Don't miss the Coombs "chicken chucking champion" contest with prizes for throwing a rubber chicken the farthest. © **250/248-1072.**

December

Carol Ships Night. Carol ships sail the harbor, and there are sing-alongs, food, and drinks on land. At Deep Bay Marina. © **250/752-9623.**

Tips Tour the Coast

You can take a coastal circle tour of this area from Vancouver. If you want to visit Parksville, then continue on to the Sunshine Coast before returning to Vancouver, leave Parksville by Highway 19, and drive south to Comox. Then take a ferry to Powell River—see "The Sunshine Coast" earlier in this chapter. If you choose to take a circle tour, BC Ferries offers a 15% discount with its Sunshine Coast CirclePac and includes travel on the following routes: Horseshoe Bay–Langdale, Earls Cove–Saltery Bay, Powell River–Comox, and Vancouver Island–Mainland. For more information, contact **BC Ferries** at © **888/223-3779** or www.bcferries.com.

---

5 Victoria

We have done Victoria in a daytrip from Vancouver, but that was before we had kids. There's so much to see and do that it's worth adding at least one night to enjoy the capital of British Columbia. Plus, although the actual distance from Vancouver is only 100 kilometers (66 miles) and the ferry ride is under 2 hours, it tends to take about 4 hours to get from one city to the other, much of it sitting in the car.

Victoria is an easy city to find your way around. Get your bearings by heading down to the Inner Harbour and the waterfront, home to many of Victoria's attractions, and a place where you can listen to buskers, buy some local jewelry, or take a ferry ride. Look up and you can see the Fairmont Empress Hotel and the Parliament building. Ahead are the main arteries of Government and Douglas streets, two of the main business and shopping areas, and Wharf Street is to the north and is a continuation of the waterfront.

There are dozens of things to do here from afternoon tea to whale watching with lots of family-oriented attractions, some fine restaurants, and accommodations that range from inexpensive to luxurious. As well, Victoria boasts Canada's mildest climate with average annual rainfall at 66.5 centimeters (26.2 in.) (compared to over 127 cm/50 in. in New York) and it's always a kick to see the horses and carriages roaming the downtown streets.

For more information, contact **Tourism Victoria,** 812 Wharf St. (at the Inner Harbour), Victoria, BC V8W 1T3 (© **250/953-2033;** fax 250/382-6539; www.tourismvictoria.com), or call © **800/663-3883** for accommodation reservations. **Tourism Vancouver Island** (www.islands.bc.ca) is also a great place to get free maps and travel brochures ahead of time and has accommodations information; **Vancouver Island Abound** (www.vancouverislandabound.com) is a vacation planner for the island with outdoors and sports information including scuba diving, whale watching, kayaking, and caving.

GETTING THERE
By Car & Ferry

The most direct route to Victoria from Vancouver is the **Tsawwassen-Swartz Bay** ferry, which operates daily between 7am and 9pm. The ferries run every 2 hours in the winter and every hour in the summer. It's best to call BC Ferries (© **888/223-3779** or 888/724-5223), automated for precise schedule information or look online at www.bcferries.com. The actual crossing takes 95 minutes, but you should schedule an extra 2 to 3 hours for travel to and from both ferry terminals, including waiting time at the docks. If you are traveling in the peak periods, it's often worth the C$15 (US$9.90) each way to reserve a spot. The drive from Vancouver to Tsawwassen is about 19 kilometers (12 miles). Take Granville Street from downtown Vancouver to 70th Avenue. Turn left and then right again on the Oak Street Bridge. You will now be on Highway 99, which you take until the George Massey Tunnel. Follow the signs to the Tsawwassen ferry terminal on Highway 17. If you prefer to travel by public transit, **TransLink** has regular bus service to both terminals. From Swartz Bay on the other side, there's regular bus service to Victoria.

If you are arriving with your car at Swartz Bay ferry terminal, you have two choices to get to Victoria. The most direct route is Highway 17, a four-lane highway that is 32 kilometers (52 miles) north of Victoria. A quieter alternative is Highway 17A (West Saanich Road), which you can reach by turning west on Wain Road, and which also takes you by Brentwood Bay, **Butchart Gardens** and the **Victoria Butterfly Gardens.**

BC Ferries offer on-board facilities such as restaurants, snack bars, gift shops, inside and outside seating, a video arcade, and kids' play area. The one-way fare with tax included is C$9.50 (US$6.25) for adults in the peak season, and C$8 (US$5.30) in the low season; C$4.75 (US$3.15) children 5 to 11 in the peak season, and C$4 (US$2.65) in the low season; and C$33.50 (US$22.10) per car during the peak season on weekends, and C$31.50 (US$20.80) during the peak season on weekdays. In the low season the fare is C$25.50 (US$16.85) on the weekends and C$24 (US$15.85) during weekdays. Children under 5 are free.

Three ferry services offer daily, year-round connections between Port Angeles, Bellingham, or Seattle, Washington, and Victoria. **Black Ball Transport** (© **250/386-2202** in Victoria, or 360/457-4491 in Port Angeles; www.north olympic.com/coho) operates four daily sailings during the peak summer months (mid-June through September) and between one and three in the off-season between Port Angeles and Victoria. One-way fares are C$45 (US$29.75) for a car and driver, C$11.75 (US$7.75) adults, and C$5.90 (US$3.90) per child. The crossing takes 1½ hours.

Clipper Navigation, 1000A Wharf St., Victoria (© **250/382-8100** in Victoria, 206/443-2560 in Seattle; www.victoriaclipper.com), operates the *Victoria Clipper,* a high-speed catamaran that runs between Seattle's Pier 69 to

Victoria's Inner Harbour. This is a passenger-only service; sailing time is approximately 3 hours with daily sailings. Round-trip adult fares are C$150 to $189.40 (US$99 to $125), children C$74 to $94.70 (US$49.50 to $62.50), and one child is free when booked 7 days in advance.

From June through October, **Victoria San Juan Cruises'** MV *Victoria Star* (℃ **800/443-4552** in North America, or 360/738-8099; www.whales.com) departs the Fairhaven Terminal in Bellingham, Washington, at 9am and arrives in Victoria's Inner Harbour at noon. It departs Victoria at 5pm, arriving in Bellingham at 8pm. Round-trip fares are C$112.10 to $134.85 (US$74 to $89) for adult and C$59.85 to $67.40 (US$39.50 to $44.50) for children 6 to 17. Children 5 and under are free. The fare includes a choice of salmon or prime rib dinner on the return Victoria–Bellingham run. No meal is included with the trip from Bellingham to Victoria, but there is a snack bar with coffee service onboard.

Washington State Ferries (℃ **250/381-1551** or 250/656-1831; www.wsdot.wa.gov/ferries) operates two sailings a day in summer and one in winter between Anacortes, Washington, and Sidney, BC (27km/17 miles) northeast of Victoria).

By Air

The major airlines are **Air Canada/Air BC Connector** (℃ **888/247-2262,** 800/661-3936, 800/663-3721, 604/688-5515, or 250/360-9074; www.aircanada.ca) and **Horizon Air** (℃ **800/547-9308;** www.horizonairlines.com) and offer direct connections from Seattle, Vancouver, Portland, Calgary, Edmonton, Saskatoon, Winnipeg, and Toronto.

Provincial commuter airlines, including floatplanes that land in Victoria's Inner Harbour and helicopters, service the city as well. They include **Harbour Air Sea Planes** (℃ **604/688-1277** or 250/385-2203; www.harbour-air.com); **Pacific Coastal** (℃ **800/663-2872;** www.pacific-coastal.com), **Kenmore Air** (℃ **800/ 543-9595** or 206/486-1257; www.kenmoreair.com/index.html); **North Vancouver Air** (℃ **800/228-6608** or 604/278-1608; www.northvanair.com/index.htm); **West Coast Air** (℃ **800/347-2222** or 604/688-9115; www.westcoastair.com); **WestJet Airlines** (℃ **800/538-5696;** www.westjet.com), and **Helijet Airways** (℃ **800/665-4354,** 250/382-6222, or 604/273-1414; www.helijet.com).

By Bus

Pacific Coach Lines (℃ **800/661-1725,** 604/662-8074, or 250/385-4411; www.pacificcoach.com) operates 16 trips a day in the summer months, eight in winter between Vancouver and Victoria. The 4-hour trip from the Vancouver Bus Terminal (Pacific Central Station, 1150 Terminal Ave.) to the Victoria Depot (710 Douglas St.) includes passage on the Tsawwassen-Swartz Bay ferry and costs C$28 (US$18.50) one way for adults and C$14 (US$9.25) one way for children 5 to 11. Return fare is C$54 (US$35.65) adults, C$27 (US$17.80) children 5 to 11. Children under 5 are free. **Airporter Service** (℃ **250/386-2526**) meets all flights at Victoria International Airport and delivers to hotels and bed-and-breakfasts.

WHERE TO STAY

Best Western Carlton Plaza ⚓ At the end of 2000, this hotel decided it was going to go after the family market, and so far, it's paying off. It has a special check-in for kids, complete with a stepladder at the top of which they receive a bag that includes toys and things such as popcorn, a cup, and even a small

Victoria

HOTELS
Best Western Carlton Plaza **1**
Hotel Grand Pacific **2**
Royal Scot Suite Hotel **3**

DINING
Cheesecake Cafe **4**
Millos **5**
Santiago's Café **6**

TO SEE & DO
Crystal Gardens **7**
Pacific Undersea Gardens **8**
Royal British Columbia
Museum **9**
Royal London Wax Museum **10**
Victoria Bug Zoo **11**
Victoria Butterfly Gardens **12**

disposable camera. About half an hour after check-in, room service brings up complimentary milk and cookies for the kids. The hotel offers a year-round family package that includes a really large suite with two double beds and a pullout sofa. Some of the suites have a separate bedroom and all have a full kitchen with a stove, fridge, and microwave, and dishes, cutlery, pots, and pans are available free. There is no pool, but the hotel will give you free swimming passes to the nearby YMCA. Built in 1912, the hotel is close to Chinatown and Market Square and an easy walk to all the attractions, restaurants, and shopping in downtown Victoria. The restaurant and fitness areas were built in June 2000 and many of the rooms and the lobby were renovated in 2001.

642 Johnson St., Victoria, BC V8W 1M6. © 800/663-7241 or 250/388-5343. Fax 250/388-5343. www.best westerncarlton.com. 103 units (47 suites). May 1–Sept 30 C$159 (US$105) double, family suite package C$179 (US$118). Oct 1–Apr 30 C$89 (US$59) double, family suite package C$99 (US$65). Children under 18 stay free in parents' room. Cribs & rollaways free. AE, DC, DISC, MC, V. Free valet parking. Pets C$10 (US$6.60) per day. **Amenities:** Restaurant (pancake), kids' menu; exercise room; salon; babysitting; coin-op washers and dryers, same-day laundry/dry cleaning; nonsmoking rooms. *In room:* A/C, TV w/ pay movies, fax, dataport, coffeemaker, kitchenettes in suites, hairdryer, iron.

Hotel Grand Pacific *(F* This is a lovely hotel, built in 1991, which just got better for families with its latest renovation. Originally the hotel's entrance was on Quebec Street, close to the Parliament building, but in 1998 the hotel bought the Quality Inn in front, demolished it, and added a new wing complete with ponds and fountains, and larger rooms. Every room has a balcony and a stunning view of the harbor or the mountains. The renovation also took the hotel from 145 to 308 rooms. The elevator in the older section is glass and gives you a great panoramic view of the harbor and the downtown area on the way to your room. The double rooms are standard size and have an extra sink outside the bathroom with a hairdryer. Suites have tubs with whirlpool jets. Local phone calls are free, and kids under 5 eat free at the breakfast buffet. Kids will love the pool area, which has a 7.5 meter (25 ft.) lap pool under a huge airy atrium and a smaller toddlers' pool, and lots of pool equipment. *Note:* Adult-only times in the pool are 5 to 7pm weekdays and 10:30 to 11:30am weekends. There is a courtesy shuttle to downtown Victoria, local calls are free, and microwave, mini fridges, and kettles are available at no charge.

463 Belleville St. (next to the Parliament building), Victoria, BC V8V 1X3. © 800/663-7550 or 250/386-0450. Fax 250/380-4475. www.hotelgrandpacific.com. 308 units. May 1–Sept 30 C$199–$259 (US$131–$171) double, Oct 1–Apr 30 C$99–$179 (US$65–$118) double. May 1–Sept 30 suites start at C$309 (US$204), Oct 1–Apr 30 suites start at C$229 (US$151). Children under 17 stay free in parents' room. Playpens free. Rollaways C$30 (US$20). AE, DC, DISC, MC, V. Free parking. **Amenities:** Restaurant (West Coast), kids' menu; bar; indoor ozonated lap pool and separate toddlers pool with pool equipment; full spa with Jacuzzi, extensive exercise room with separate gym with fitness and Aquafit classes, massage therapist, 2 squash/racquet ball courts; concierge; salon; babysitting; 24-hour room service, same-day laundry/dry cleaning; nonsmoking rooms. *In room:* A/C, TV w/ pay movies & Nintendo, fax, dataport, coffeemaker, hairdryer, iron, safe.

Royal Scot Suite Hotel *(F(F* Originally an apartment building built in 1970, this hotel has huge rooms, which makes it the perfect family hotel. There are studio suites, which are quite large, with a divider separating the bedroom from the living area, or there are one- or two-bedroom suites available. Most rooms have a balcony. The suites have large living rooms with pullout sofabeds and some have swivel rocker chairs. Full kitchens in most of the rooms have a fridge, stove, and microwave, and dishes, cutlery, pots, and pans on hand, and a separate dining area. Our kids particularly liked having a television in the living

room and in each bedroom, and there are books on the shelves and the plants (although plastic) give it a more homey feel. Local calls are free and there is a courtesy shuttle to downtown Victoria, although it's only a few minutes' walk. The hotel is located steps from the Parliament building and the waterfront and in easy walking distance to dozens of restaurants, attractions, and shopping.

425 Quebec St. (near the Parliament building), Victoria, BC V8V 1W7. © **800/663-7515** or 250/388-5463. Fax 250/388-5452; www.royalscot.com 176 units. C$165–$230 (US$109–$152) studio suites; C$189–$379 1-bedroom; C$285–$395 (US$188–$260) 2-bedroom. Weekly & monthly rates available Oct 1–May 31. Children under 16 stay free in parents' room. Cribs free, rollaways C$20 (US$13.20). AE, DC, MC, V. Free parking. **Amenities:** Restaurant; indoor pool; Jacuzzi; sauna; exercise room; game room with video arcade and free billiards table; limited room service; babysitting; coin-op washers and dryers; same-day laundry/dry cleaning; nonsmoking rooms. *In room:* TV and VCR, kitchens in suites, coffeemaker, hairdryer, iron.

Fun Fact **Victoria According to Kipling**

"To realize Victoria you must take all that the eye admires in Bournemouth, Torquay, the Isle of Wight, the happy valley at Hong Kong, the Doon, Sorrento and Camp's Bay—add reminiscences of the Thousand Islands and arrange the whole around the Bay of Naples with some Himalayas for the background."

—Rudyard Kipling

WHERE TO EAT

Cheesecake Cafe *⊀* WEST COAST   Located on the second floor of a heritage building in the heart of downtown Victoria, this restaurant has a lovely woodsy, West Coast feel with lots of light flooding in from the floor-to-ceiling windows and booth-style seating. The service is attentive and it's a great place to bring the family, starting with the crayons and the extensive kids' menu. There are also some great appetizers—my kids opted for the potstickers, potato skins, and calamari from the main menu. As the name suggests, there is a huge display of mouth-watering cheesecakes—Amaretto, rocky road, banana chocolate—and, yes, they are as good as they look, so take one to go. The restaurant also has a huge menu with everything from pizza and pasta to fajitas and steaks. Another nice touch is the help-yourself baskets of chocolate chip cookies that dot the restaurant. The weekend brunch serves up French toast, quiches, waffles, and eggs in hollandaise sauce.

38-910 Government St., Victoria. © **250/382-2253.** Reservations recommended. Main courses C$8–$14 (US$5.25–$9.25). Kids' menu C$4 (US$2.65). Brunch menu C$6–C$9 (US$3.95–$5.95). AE, MC, V. Open Mon–Thurs 11am–11pm, Fri–Sat 10am–10pm, Sun brunch 10am–2:30pm. Highchairs, boosters, kids' menu.

Millos GREEK   You can't miss the blue and white windmill on this huge restaurant. It's noisy and upbeat, the service is friendly and fast, the food is good—all the ingredients for a good family meal. If you arrive between 4 and 6:30pm you are rewarded with the early bird special for C$9.95 (US$6.55), which will be something like generous servings of salmon or lemon chicken with rice and vegetables. The kids ordered chicken souvlaki, dolmades (grape leaves stuffed with ground beef), and spanakopita (spinach and feta cheese)—a combination of the kids' and the appetizer menus. On Friday and Saturday nights during the winter, and daily in the summer, there is Greek dancing and belly dancing and kids are welcome. The inside of the restaurant has lots of natural light, plants, blue or white tablecloths, and a definite Mediterranean feel. Other menu items include moussaka, roast lamb, rack of lamb, and calamari.

716 Burdett St. (behind the Fairmont Empress Hotel), Victoria. ✆ **250/382-4422**. Reservations recommended on weekends. Main courses C$12.95–$21.95 (US$8.55–$14.50), kids' menu C$6.95–$8.95 (US$4.60–$5.90). AE, MC, V. Open Mon–Sat 11am–11pm, Sun 4–11pm. Highchairs, boosters, kids' menu.

Santiago's Café SOUTH AMERICAN   We literally stumbled over this tiny place, which is tucked around the corner from the waterfront near the ferry terminal. What we first noticed was tables full of both adults and children madly scribbling on the paper tablecloths with the crayons provided, and then folding them up to take home with them. There is a kids' menu that the staff is happy to recite, with dishes like pizzas and plain cheese nachos and burgers. The burritos are excellent and there is a good tapas menu. We also enjoyed the unobtrusive Spanish music.

660 Oswego St., Victoria. ✆ **250/388-7376**. www.santiagos.com. Breakfast C$5.95–$7.95 (US$3.95–$5.25). Main courses C$8.95–$10.95 (US$5.90–$7.25). AE, MC, V. Open Fri–Sat 8am–11pm and Sun–Thurs 9:30am–11pm. Highchairs, boosters, kids' menu.

Tips   **Stroller Rentals in Victoria**

Budget Rent a Car rents strollers for toddlers for C$6 (US$4) an hour. 727 Courtney St. ✆ **250/953-5300**.

Harbour Rentals rents strollers for C$5 (US$3.30) an hour. 811 Wharf St. ✆ **250/995-1661**.

Sports Rent rents three-wheel running strollers for C$5 (US$3.30) an hour, C$12 (US$8) a day. Requires a C$60 (US$40) deposit. 611 Discovery St. ✆ **250/385-7368**.

THINGS TO SEE & DO

Crystal Gardens   Located just behind the Fairmont Empress Hotel, these gardens were a big hit with all three of my kids, and I noticed older ones enjoying it thoroughly also. Pink (actually they are orange) flamingos wander around and interact with you, and there are large koi in the pond, a large bridge to cross, lots of tropical plants, exotic birds, and a nocturnal bat display, where you can view the critters flying around. There is also a butterfly section you can walk through, although there was not much happening here in March, and you can see the world's smallest monkeys—they look a bit like 10-centimeter (4 in.) high jumping rats. If you go near closing time, the animals are getting hungry and are quite alert.

Douglas St. (across from the Royal BC Museum, behind the Fairmont Empress Hotel, Victoria. ✆ **250/381-1213**. www.bcpcc.com/crystal. MC, V. Open daily 10am–4:30pm. C$8 (US$5.30) adults, C$4 (US$2.65) children 5–16. Children 4 and under free.

Pacific Undersea Gardens   Located on a boat on the waterfront, this treat has been around for years. Kids will like the tour down the stairs into a dark room where lit-up fish tanks line the perimeter of the walls. Depending on the season, there are up to 9 and 16 20-minute live shows each day. The audience sits in a theater and watches the diver through large windows where a stage would normally be. The diver talks to the audience and points out various sea life—the giant Pacific octopus is pretty impressive—and staff have trained fish to flock at the sound of a dinner bell. Including the show, a visit here is probably good for about 45 minutes to an hour.

490 Belleville St. (at the Inner Harbour), Victoria. ✆ 250/387-5717. C$7.50 (US$4.95) adults, C$3.50 (US$2.30) children 5–11, C$5 (US$3.30) children 12–17, children under 5 free. MC, V. Open daily 10am–5pm winter, 10am–7pm summer. Closed Tues and Wed Nov–Mar.

⌒ Fun Fact

More than 20,000 gray whales travel along the west coast of Vancouver Island. February through April are the best viewing times for northbound grays, although some whales take up residence there until October.

Royal British Columbia Museum   This is a world-class museum. Unfortunately it's hard for little ones—mine are all under 10 and seem to have the attention span of fleas—to appreciate. We traveled through the exhibits at breakneck speed, with the highlight being the 30-minute deep-sea tour complete with film, deep-sea elevator ride, and a mock-up of a submarine. The natural history gallery was a hit, but the fabulous First Peoples' Gallery failed to hold their interest. There's not a lot to keep little ones entertained, although they should enjoy walking through the historic township. The IMAX theater is suitable for kids from about 5 and up.

675 Belleville St. (next to the Parliament building), Victoria. ✆ 250/387-3701. www.royalbbc museum.bc.ca. IMAX ✆ 250/953-IMAX. Museum only C$9 (US$6) adults, C$6 (US$4) children 6–18; IMAX only C$9.50 (US$6.25) adults, C$6.50 (US$4.30) children 6–18; combo C$16.50 (US$10.90) adults, C$12.25 (US$8.10) children 6–18. C$24 (US$15.85) for a family of 2 adults and children up to 18. Open daily 9am–5pm. IMAX open daily 10am–8pm.

Royal London Wax Museum   There's nothing particularly Canadian about this attraction, except a film and scene of the Inuit at the end. But if you are into the royal family, and want to get a look at them up close, this is the place to do it. There is also a bunch of former (and current) American presidents and a few Canadian prime ministers. Little ones will like the downstairs exhibits with Disney characters Snow White and the Seven Dwarfs, and older kids will love the Chamber of Horrors, which is about as scary as a *Goose Bumps* episode. There is also a bunch of American actors: Gary Cooper, Clint Eastwood, and Christopher Reeves as Superman. The Penny Lane Sweet Shop, through which you must exit, has lots of sours and pear drops, sherbet lemons, and other British-type sweet fare and was a definite hit.

470 Belleville St. (on the waterfront), Victoria. ✆ 250/388-4461. www.waxworld.com. C$8 (US$5.30) adults, C$6.50 (US$4.30) children 13–19, C$3.50 (US$2.30) children 6–12. Children 5 and under free. AE, DC, MC, V. Open daily 9:30am–5pm.

Victoria Bug Zoo   If your kids are really into the crawly things it's possible to arrange a sleepover in this building, which has glass boxes and boxes of bugs. You can hold a Giant African millipede, a White Eye Assassin bug, or a praying mantis, if you wish, or take home your own live tarantulas for C$60 to $100 (US$40 to $66). My favorite was the Green Leaf Mantis, which bites the head off her mate shortly after mating. The guides who hand out the bugs and explain about their habits make this a fun educational experience. On the way out, pick up the *Eat a Bug Cookbook: 33 Ways to Cook Grasshoppers, Ants, Bugs, Spiders, and Centipedes.*

1107 Wharf St. (along the waterfront), Victoria. ✆ 250/384-BUGS. www.bugzoo.bc.ca C$6 (US$3.95) adults, C$4 (US$2.65) children 3–16, children under 3 free. Open Mon–Sat 9:30am–5:30pm, Sun 11am–5:30pm. Open until 9pm in summer.

Victoria Butterfly Gardens   If your kids are very young or just into butter-flies, this is worth a stop on the way to or from the Swartz Bay ferry. Unfortu-nately, the novelty wore off for my older ones after about 10 minutes. It's built like a hot house, so of course it's hot, but it's quite neat to see dozens of differ-ent colored butterflies fluttering around, and the Giant Owl Butterfly was a par-ticular hit with my 9- and 6-year-olds. There is a 15-minute film that children most likely won't enjoy and tours on the half-hour that include a bit of a show with the parrots. There's also a waterfall and pond with koi.

1461 Benvenuto Ave. (West Saanich Rd. at Keating Cross Rd., near the entrance to the Butchart Gardens, Brentwood Bay). *C* 250/652-3822. www.butterflygardens.com. C$8 adults (US$5.30), C$4.50 (US$2.95) children 5–12, children under 5 free. MC, V. Open Mar–Oct daily 9:30am–4:30pm.

KIDS CALENDAR OF EVENTS IN VICTORIA

January
Polar Bear Swim. New Year's Day at Elk Lake.

April
TerrifVic Jazz Party. A 5-day jazz festival. For information call *C* 250/953-2011.

May
Harbour Festival. Musical enter-tainment, arts, and heritage events.

Victoria Day Parade. Marching bands and a floats parade starts at 9am from the Mayfair Mall on Douglas Street in downtown Victo-ria. Held the Saturday of Victoria Day weekend. *C* 250/382-3111.

Luxton Pro Rodeo. Cowboys and a bunch of events including a pet-ting farm. The parade starts at 10am on the Saturday, and the rodeo opens at noon. For informa-tion call *C* 250/478-2759.

June
Folkfest. Music, dance, food from around the world, and dozens of free performances. Ships Point parking lot, 900 Wharf St. *C* 250/388-4728. www.icavictoria.org/folkfest.

July
Canada Day celebrations. Events around the city and fireworks at the Inner Harbour. July 1.

The Great Canadian Family Pic-nic. Entertainment and the huge Canada Day cake at Beacon Hill Park. July 1. *C* 250/920-4607.

Rootsfest. The largest world-beat festival on the island, with a family area and a field of foods where kids 12 and under eat free when accom-panied by an adult. *C* 250/386-3655. www.rootsfest.com.

August
Dragon Boat Festival. Boat racing and multicultural entertainment in Victoria's Inner Harbour plus a Dragonland for kids. *C* 250/472-2628. www.victoriadragonboat.com

Latin Caribbean Music Festival. Live music at Market Square and other downtown venues, including 3 night dances and free afternoon shows noon to 5:30pm. *C* 250/361-9433. www.vircs.bc.ca.

December
ChristmasTime at the Butchart Gardens. Nightly illuminations, festive entertainment, and cuisine. 800 Benvenuto Ave., Brentwood Bay. *C* 250/652-4422. www.butch artgardens.bc.ca.

Santa Claus Parade and Lighted Sail Past. Fireworks, festive events, and a lighted boat parade in Sid-ney-by-the-Sea.

Index

See also Accommodations and Restaurant indexes, below.

ACCOMMODATIONS

I♦I

VANCOUVER, BRITISH COLUMBIA, CANADA

YOUR SPECTACULAR BY NATURE EXPERIENCE BEGINS WITH TOURISM VANCOUVER

Whether you're planning your trip or just beginning your visit, contact us first to make your vacation in *Spectacular by Nature* Vancouver a truly enjoyable experience.

Visit our online Kids Guide to Vancouver at **tourismvancouver.com**, or see us at any one of our three Visitor Info Centres.

DOWNTOWN LOCATION
At Burrard Street and Cordova Street

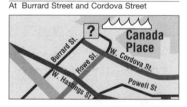

PEACE ARCH VISITOR INFO CENTRE
On Hwy 99 at the Canadian Border Crossing

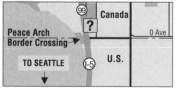

VANCOUVER INTERNATIONAL AIRPORT
At the Domestic and International Terminals

Canada for the whole family!

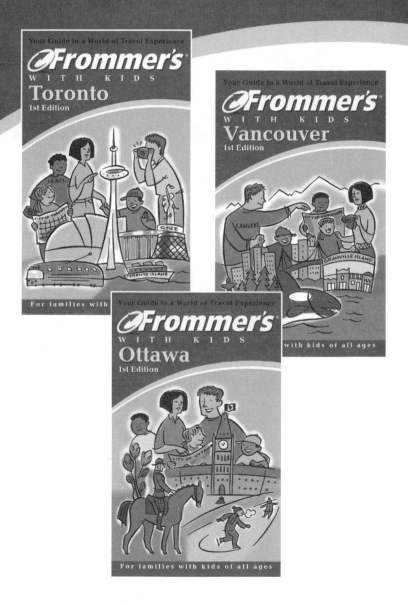

FROMMER'S® COMPLETE TRAVEL GUIDES

Alaska
Amsterdam
Argentina & Chile
Arizona
Atlanta
Australia
Austria
Bahamas
Barcelona, Madrid & Seville
Beijing
Belgium, Holland &
  Luxembourg
Bermuda
Boston
British Columbia & the
  Canadian Rockies
Budapest & the Best of Hungary
California
Canada
Cancún, Cozumel & the
  Yucatán
Cape Cod, Nantucket &
  Martha's Vineyard
Caribbean
Caribbean Cruises & Ports
  of Call
Caribbean Ports of Call
Carolinas & Georgia
Chicago
China
Colorado
Costa Rica
Denmark
Denver, Boulder & Colorado
  Springs
England
Europe

European Cruises & Ports of Call
Florida
France
Germany
Greece
Greek Islands
Hawaii
Hong Kong
Honolulu, Waikiki & Oahu
Ireland
Israel
Italy
Jamaica
Japan
Las Vegas
London
Los Angeles
Maryland & Delaware
Maui
Mexico
Montana & Wyoming
Montréal & Québec City
Munich & the Bavarian Alps
Nashville & Memphis
Nepal
New England
New Mexico
New Orleans
New York City
New Zealand
Nova Scotia, New Brunswick &
  Prince Edward Island
Oregon
Paris
Philadelphia & the Amish
  Country
Portugal

Prague & the Best of the Czech
  Republic
Provence & the Riviera
Puerto Rico
Rome
San Antonio & Austin
San Diego
San Francisco
Santa Fe, Taos & Albuquerque
Scandinavia
Scotland
Seattle & Portland
Shanghai
Singapore & Malaysia
South Africa
Southeast Asia
South Florida
South Pacific
Spain
Sweden
Switzerland
Texas
Thailand
Tokyo
Toronto
Tuscany & Umbria
USA
Utah
Vancouver & Victoria
Vermont, New Hampshire
  & Maine
Vienna & the Danube Valley
Virgin Islands
Virginia
Walt Disney World & Orlando
Washington, D.C.
Washington State

FROMMER'S® DOLLAR-A-DAY GUIDES

Australia from $50 a Day
California from $70 a Day
Caribbean from $60 a Day
England from $70 a Day
Europe from $70 a Day

Florida from $70 a Day
Hawaii from $70 a Day
Ireland from $60 a Day
Italy from $70 a Day
London from $85 a Day

New York from $80 a Day
Paris from $80 a Day
San Francisco from $60 a Day
Washington, D.C.,
  from $70 a Day

FROMMER'S® PORTABLE GUIDES

Acapulco, Ixtapa &
  Zihuatanejo
Alaska Cruises & Ports
  of Call
Amsterdam
Australia's Great Barrier Reef
Bahamas
Baja & Los Cabos
Berlin
Boston
California Wine Country
Charleston & Savannah
Chicago

Dublin
Hawaii: The Big Island
Hong Kong
Houston
Las Vegas
London
Los Angeles
Maine Coast
Maui
Miami
New Orleans
New York City
Paris

Phoenix & Scottsdale
Portland
Puerto Rico
Puerto Vallarta, Manzanillo &
  Guadalajara
San Diego
San Francisco
Seattle
Sydney
Tampa & St. Petersburg
Vancouver
Venice
Washington, D.C.

FROMMER'S® NATIONAL PARK GUIDES

Family Vacations in the
  National Parks
Grand Canyon

National Parks of the American
  West
Rocky Mountain
Yellowstone & Grand Teton

Yosemite & Sequoia/
  Kings Canyon
Zion & Bryce Canyon

FROMMER'S® MEMORABLE WALKS

Chicago	New York	San Francisco
London	Paris	Washington, D.C.

FROMMER'S® GREAT OUTDOOR GUIDES

Arizona & New Mexico	Northern California	Southern New England
New England	Southern California & Baja	Vermont & New Hampshire

FROMMER'S® BORN TO SHOP GUIDES

Born to Shop: France	Born to Shop: Italy	Born to Shop: New York
Born to Shop: Hong Kong,	Born to Shop: London	Born to Shop: Paris
Shanghai & Beijing		

FROMMER'S® IRREVERENT GUIDES

Amsterdam	Los Angeles	Seattle & Portland
Boston	Manhattan	Vancouver
Chicago	New Orleans	Walt Disney World
Las Vegas	Paris	Washington, D.C.
London	San Francisco	

FROMMER'S® BEST-LOVED DRIVING TOURS

America	France	New England
Britain	Germany	Scotland
California	Ireland	Spain
Florida	Italy	Western Europe

THE UNOFFICIAL GUIDES®

Bed & Breakfasts in California	Golf Vacations in the	New Orleans
Bed & Breakfasts in	Eastern U.S.	New York City
New England	The Great Smoky &	Paris
Bed & Breakfasts in the North-	Blue Ridge Mountains	San Francisco
west	Inside Disney	Skiing in the West
Bed & Breakfasts in Southeast	Hawaii	Southeast with Kids
Beyond Disney	Las Vegas	Walt Disney World
Branson, Missouri	London	Walt Disney World for
California with Kids	Mid-Atlantic with Kids	Grown-ups
Chicago	Mini Las Vegas	Walt Disney World for Kids
Cruises	Mini-Mickey	Washington, D.C.
Disneyland	New England with Kids	World's Best Diving Vacations
Florida with Kids		

SPECIAL-INTEREST TITLES

Frommer's Britain's Best Bed & Breakfasts and Country Inns	Hanging Out in Europe
Frommer's France's Best Bed & Breakfasts and Country Inns	Hanging Out in France
Frommer's Italy's Best Bed & Breakfasts and Country Inns	Hanging Out in Ireland
Frommer's Caribbean Hideaways	Hanging Out in Italy
Frommer's Adventure Guide to Australia & New Zealand	Hanging Out in Spain
Frommer's Adventure Guide to Central America	Israel Past & Present
Frommer's Adventure Guide to India & Pakistan	Frommer's The Moon
Frommer's Adventure Guide to South America	Frommer's New York City with Kids
Frommer's Adventure Guide to Southeast Asia	The New York Times' Guide to Unforgettable Weekends
Frommer's Adventure Guide to Southern Africa	Places Rated Almanac
Frommer's Gay & Lesbian Europe	Retirement Places Rated
Frommer's Exploring America by RV	Frommer's Road Atlas Britain
Hanging Out in England	Frommer's Road Atlas Europe
	Frommer's Washington, D.C., with Kids
	Frommer's What the Airlines Never Tell You